IFIP Advances in Information and Communication Technology

373

T0223919

IFIP – The International Federation for Information Processing

IFIP was founded in 1960 under the auspices of UNESCO, following the First World Computer Congress held in Paris the previous year. An umbrella organization for societies working in information processing, IFIP's aim is two-fold: to support information processing within ist member countries and to encourage technology transfer to developing nations. As ist mission statement clearly states,

> IFIP's mission is to be the leading, truly international, apolitical organization which encourages and assists in the development, exploitation and application of information technology for the benefit of all people.

IFIP is a non-profitmaking organization, run almost solely by 2500 volunteers. It operates through a number of technical committees, which organize events and publications. IFIP's events range from an international congress to local seminars, but the most important are:

- The IFIP World Computer Congress, held every second year;
- Open conferences;
- Working conferences.

The flagship event is the IFIP World Computer Congress, at which both invited and contributed papers are presented. Contributed papers are rigorously refereed and the rejection rate is high.

As with the Congress, participation in the open conferences is open to all and papers may be invited or submitted. Again, submitted papers are stringently refereed.

The working conferences are structured differently. They are usually run by a working group and attendance is small and by invitation only. Their purpose is to create an atmosphere conducive to innovation and development. Refereeing is less rigorous and papers are subjected to extensive group discussion.

Publications arising from IFIP events vary. The papers presented at the IFIP World Computer Congress and at open conferences are published as conference proceedings, while the results of the working conferences are often published as collections of selected and edited papers.

Any national society whose primary activity is in information may apply to become a full member of IFIP, although full membership is restricted to one society per country. Full members are entitled to vote at the annual General Assembly, National societies preferring a less committed involvement may apply for associate or corresponding membership. Associate members enjoy the same benefits as full members, but without voting rights. Corresponding members are not represented in IFIP bodies. Affiliated membership is open to non-national societies, and individual and honorary membership schemes are also offered.

José L. Ayala   David Atienza Alonso
Ricardo Reis (Eds.)

VLSI-SoC:
Forward-Looking Trends
in IC and Systems Design

18th IFIP WG 10.5/IEEE International Conference
on Very Large Scale Integration, VLSI-SoC 2010
Madrid, Spain, September 27-29, 2010
Revised Selected Papers

 Springer

Volume Editors

José L. Ayala
Complutense University of Madrid, Computer Science Faculty
28040 Madrid, Spain
E-mail: jayala@fdi.ucm.es

David Atienza Alonso
École Polytechnique Fédérale de Lausanne (EPFL)
Institute of EE, Embedded Systems Laboratory
ELG 131, Station 11, 1015 Lausanne, Switzerland
E-mail: david.atienza@epfl.ch

Ricardo Reis
Universidade Federal do Rio Grande do Sul, Instituto de Informática
Av. Bento Gonçalves, 9500, Campus do Vale
Bloco IV, CP 15064, 91501-970 Porto Alegre, Brazil
E-mail: reis@inf.ufrgs.br

ISSN 1868-4238   e-ISSN 1868-422X
ISBN 978-3-642-44175-2   ISBN 978-3-642-28566-0 (eBook)
DOI 10.1007/978-3-642-28566-0
Springer Heidelberg Dordrecht London New York

CR Subject Classification (1998): B.7-8, C.0, F.2, J.2-3, C.2.1

Typesetting: Camera-ready by author, data conversion by Scientific Publishing Services, Chennai, India

Printed on acid-free paper

Springer is part of Springer Science+Business Media (www.springer.com)

Preface

This book contains extended and revised versions of the best papers that were presented during the 18th edition of the IFIP/IEEE WG10.5 International Conference on Very Large Scale Integration, a global System-on-a-Chip Design and CAD conference. The 18th conference was held at the Complutense University, Madrid, Spain (September 27–29, 2010). Previous conferences have taken place in Edinburgh, Trondheim, Vancouver, Munich, Grenoble, Tokyo, Gramado, Lisbon, Montpellier, Darmstadt, Perth, Nice, Atlanta, Rhodes and Florianópolis.

The purpose of this conference sponsored by IFIP TC 10 Working Group 10.5, the IEEE Council on Electronic Design Automation (CEDA), and by IEEE Circuits and Systems Society, with the In-Cooperation of ACM SIGDA, is to provide a forum to exchange ideas and show industrial and academic research results in the field of microelectronics design. The current trend toward increasing chip integration and technology process advancements brings about stimulating new challenges both at the physical and system-design levels, as well in the test of these systems. VLSI-SOC conferences aim to address these exciting new issues.

The 2010 edition of VLSI-SoC maintained the traditional structure, which has been successful at the previous VLSI-SOC conferences. The quality of submissions (175 papers from 22 countries) made the selection process difficult, but finally 52 papers for oral presentation and 17 posters were accepted for presentation in VLSI-SoC 2010. Out of the 52 full papers presented at the conference, 14 regular papers were chosen by a selection committee to have an extended and revised version included in this book. The chapters of this book have authors from Belgium, China, Egypt, France, Singapore, Spain, Switzerland, Taiwan and the USA. The Technical Program Committee was composed of 109 members.

VLSI-SoC 2010 was the culmination of many dedicated volunteers: paper authors, reviewers, session chairs, invited speakers and various committee chairs, especially the local arrangements organizers. We thank them all for their contribution.

This book is intended for the VLSI community, mainly those who did not have the chance to take part in the VLSI-SOC 2010 conference. The papers were selected to cover a wide variety of excellence in VLSI technology and the advanced research they describe. We hope you will enjoy reading this book and find it useful in your professional life and for the development of the VLSI community as a whole.

December 2011

José L. Ayala
David Atienza
Ricardo Reis

Organization

The IFIP/IEEE International Conference on Very Large Scale Integration-System-on-Chip (VLSI-SoC) 2010 took place during September 27–29, 2010, in the Complutense University, Madrid, Spain. VLSI-SoC 2010 was the 18th in a series of international conferences, sponsored by IFIP TC 10 Working Group 10.5 (VLSI), IEEE CEDA and ACM SIGDA. The conference was organized by:

General Chair

David Atienza   EPFL, Switzerland

Program Chairs

José L. Ayala   Complutense University, Spain
Rajesh Gupta   UCSD, USA
Andrea Acquaviva   Politecnico di Torino, Italy

Special Session Chairs

Luca Benini   University of Bologna, Italy
Ayse K. Coskun   Boston University, USA

Local Arrangements Chair

Katzalin Olcoz   Complutense University, Spain

Publicity Chair

Praveen Raghavan   IMEC, Belgium

Publication Chairs

Jose I. Hidalgo   Complutense University, Spain
Ricardo Reis   UFRGS, Brazil

Finance Chair

Fernando Rincón   UCLM, Spain

PhD Forum Chairs

Matthew Guthaus   UCSC, USA
Andreas Burg   ETHZ, Switzerland

Institutional Relations Chairs

Roman Hermida   Complutense University, Spain
Francisco Tirado   Complutense University, Spain

Steering Committee

Manfred Glesner   TU Darmstadt, Germany
Salvador Mir   TIMA, France
Ricardo Reis   UFRGS, Brazil
Michel Robert   LIRMM, France
Luis Miguel Silveira   INESC ID, Portugal

Table of Contents

A 1-V CMOS Ultralow-Power Receiver Front End for the IEEE 802.15.4 Standard Using Tuned Passive Mixer Output Pole

Aaron V.T. Do[1], Chirn Chye Boon[2], Manthena Vamshi Krishna[2],
Anh Manh Do[2], and Kiat Seng Yeo[2]

[1] Marvell Asia Pte. Ltd., Singapore 534158
doaaron@marvell.com
[2] Nanyang Technological University, Singapore 639798
{eccboon,mkvamshi,emado,eksyeo}@ntu.edu.sg

Abstract. A simple method to tune the output pole of a passive mixer is proposed which leads to up to 33 dB improvement in an IEEE 802.15.4 standard compatible receiver's IF section IIP_3. This method is used in the design of an ultra-low power receiver front-end which consumes just 2.2 mW from a 1-V supply while achieving a SSB NF of approximately 9 dB. The energy-aware architecture allows for a 70 % reduction in the nominal power consumption (down to 0.7 mW) under strong signal conditions while improving the receiver's IIP_3 and not affecting the receiver's input matching. The receiver is designed in a 0.18-μm RFCMOS technology.

Keywords: RF Front End, CMOS RF Integrated Circuits, Low Power, System on Chip.

1   Introduction

The demand for low power, low data-rate, short-range communications for applications such as wireless sensor networks (WSN) for home and factory automation, and wireless personal area networks (WPAN) devices such as wireless mice and keyboards, has led to significant research in the field of low power RF CMOS IC design [1]-[9]. In 2003, the IEEE introduced the IEEE 802.15.4 standard [10] in order to accommodate such applications. The standard features relaxed noise and linearity requirements making ultra-low power design possible.

Typically, low-IF and direct-conversion receiver architectures are used in such applications where the receiver front-end would commonly be configured as shown in Fig. 1. The architecture consists of an off-chip band-select filter, an LNA, IQ mixers, and channel-select filters. In direct-conversion systems, low-pass channel filters are used [5], while complex band-pass channel filters are used in low-IF systems [1], [6]. In the 2.4 GHz Industrial, Scientific and Medical (ISM) Band, the receiver designs which consume the lowest power are presented in [2], and [3], and use 1.4 mW and 0.75 mW respectively. However, both designs involve significant tradeoffs which do

J.L. Ayala, D. Atienza, and R. Reis (Eds.): VLSI-SoC 2010, IFIP AICT 373, pp. 1–21, 2012.

not necessarily permit their use for the IEEE 802.15.4 standard [7] (neither work was designed to be compatible with the IEEE 802.15.4 standard). For instance, in [2], the IIP_3 is only -37 dBm which is insufficient to meet the standard's requirements. Furthermore, the NF was tested at an IF of 10 MHz and the authors did not discuss the possibility of lowering the IF. In [3], no input matching is used [11], which can lead to interface problems with external components, and no LNA is used, which can result in unwanted transmission of the local oscillator (LO) signal. Among works specifically designed to meet the IEEE 802.15.4 standard, the lowest power consumption is used in [4], at 4.05 mW.

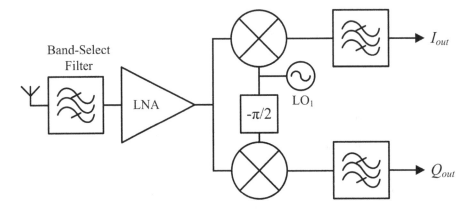

Fig. 1. A typical front-end for a low-IF or direct-conversion receiver

In this work, we present a passive mixer architecture which when used, allows for an ultra-low power IF section. This architecture was originally presented in [12] (simulated results only), and has been used to design a receiver front-end which consumes just 2.2 mW from a 1-V supply. We also build upon our previous research on energy-aware design [7], designing the receiver's power consumption to be controllable down to 0.7 mW. The proposed energy-aware design technique also makes the receiver's input matching virtually independent of the LNA power consumption. For the remainder of this paper, the front-end refers to the part of the receiver up to the channel filtering, and the IF section refers to the IF channel filter, where it is understood that there is no IF in a direct-conversion system, and the signal is directly translated to baseband.

2   Passive Mixer Architectures

For short-range, low-data-rate communications, CMOS based designs generally favor the use of passive down-conversion mixers as opposed to active mixers. On the positive side, passive mixers do not consume power, and offer very low flicker noise and high linearity. However, passive mixers essentially present a resistance in series with the signal path which can be noisy, and may also require a higher LO drive than their active counterparts. Active mixers work on the principle of current-commutation and offer the advantages of high output impedance, and better port to port isolation. Unfortunately, they tend to degrade linearity, and add considerable flicker noise. The disadvantages of active mixing as applied to short-range, low-data-rate systems outweigh the benefits.

To get an idea of how well different receivers perform using active and passive mixers, we can look at their overall sensitivity. The sensitivity can be broken down into two types, noise figure (NF) limited sensitivity, and third-order intercept (IIP$_3$) limited sensitivity. Since the overall performance of a receiver can be broken down into several nearly independent performance parameters (NF, IIP$_3$, phase noise, DC-offset, etc), other limiting factors on sensitivity are possible. Here we will only look at the NF, and the IIP$_3$ as they generally are the more dominant parameters which limit overall sensitivity [1]-[7]. *NF* limited sensitivity is easily calculated as,

$$Sen_{NF} = NF + 10log(kT\Delta f) + SNR_{req} \qquad (1)$$

while IIP$_3$ limited sensitivity is calculated as,

$$Sen_{IIP3} = -3 + 3P_{blk} + SNR_{req} - 2IIP_3 \qquad (2)$$

where *k* is Boltzmann's constant, T is the temperature in Kelvin (normally taken as 290 K), Δf is the bandwidth (2 MHz in this case), SNR$_{req}$ is the required SNR, and P$_{blk}$ is the power of the interfering signals. The addition of -3 in (2) accounts for the fact that IIP$_3$ should be measured with the desired signal 3 dB above the sensitivity level. The IEEE 802.15.4 standard specifies +0 dBc and +30 dBc interferers at the adjacent and alternate channels while the input signal is 3 dB above the sensitivity level (-85 dBm). Therefore, for the calculation of Sen$_{IIP3}$, P$_{blk}$ is set to -52 dBm. Based on [13], we estimate the required SNR to be approximately 14 dB. Based on (1) and (2), the required NF and IIP$_3$ can be calculated as 12 dB and -30 dBm respectively. Table 1 compares the sensitivities of several recently published low-power designs. As this work primarily deals with lowering the IF section power consumption, we also include the required IF section power consumption in Table 1.

Table 1. Overall Sensitivity Versus Mixer Type for Recent low-Power Front Ends

Reference	[1]	[2]	[3]	[4]	[5]	[6]	[7][B]
Sen$_{NF}$ (dBm)	-91.3	-92	-91.9	-91	-89.7	-87	-90.7
Sen$_{IIP3}$ (dBm)	-110	-68	-127	-118	-126	-112	-88
Mixer Type[A]	PC	A	PV	PV	PC	A	PC
Tech. (nm)	180	180	130	90	180	180	180
Power (mW)	10	1.4	0.75	4.05	6.3	10.8	5.4
IF Power (mW)	5.76[C]	0.5	0.75	1.15	4.5	-	0.36

[A] A: Active, PV: Passive Voltage-mode, PC: Passive Current-mode
[B] Second gain mode
[C] Estimated only.

From Table 1, for the designs using active mixers, the IIP$_3$ limited sensitivity in [2] is poor, while [6] consumes the most power and achieves the poorest Sen$_{NF}$. Although these findings are not conclusive, a trend is observable. It is well understood that the overall NF of the system is limited by the NF of the first LNA. This leads to rather high LNA power consumption in order to keep the NF low. However, the average front-end in Table 1 allocates 48 % of the power consumption to the IF section which indicates that the IF section still takes a significant portion of the overall power consumption. This work explores a mixer architecture which allows for an ultra-low power IF section.

2.1   Current-Mode and Voltage-Mode Passive Mixers

In Table 1, we have identified two classes of passive mixers. For passive mixers where the input impedance of the IF section is small compared to the passive mixer core's output impedance, we term the passive mixer a current-mode passive mixer. For passive mixers where the input impedance of the IF section is large compared to the passive mixer core's output impedance, we term the passive mixer a voltage-mode passive mixer. A basic diagram of current-mode and voltage-mode passive mixers is shown in Fig. 2. The passive mixer core is represented by a variable resistor whose resistance is controlled by a local oscillator (LO) voltage. The current-mode passive mixer core is normally followed by a transimpedance amplifier (TIA) [14], which can easily be modified into a channel-select filter (CSF) [1], [15]. In Fig. 2, the TIA is modified to form a simple low-pass filter.

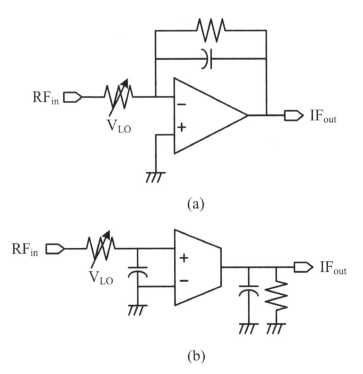

(a)

(b)

Fig. 2. A simplified illustration of connection between (a) a current-mode passive mixer and an op-amp based filter, and (b) a voltage-mode passive mixer and a g_m-C based filter

2.2   IF Section Pre-filtering

Both the current-mode and the voltage-mode passive mixers offer the possibility of pre-filtering the signal before the IF section. What we mean by this is that a single stage of filtering is realized before the signal is passed through any active components in the IF section. For the voltage-mode passive mixer in Fig. 2 (b), this is obvious as the mixer core's variable resistance forms an RC pole with the input capacitance of the IF section. This RC low-pass filter precedes any active amplification (in the IF section).

For the current-mode passive mixer this is also true. We illustrate this in Fig. 3. Assume the op-amp has a frequency-dependent gain as shown in Fig. 3 on the left y-axes. In Fig. 3 (a), we show the case where the TIA is formed by removing the capacitor in Fig. 2 (a). In Fig. 3 (b), we show the case where the TIA has been turned into a CSF using the circuit shown in Fig. 2 (a). Assuming the input to the overall filter is some represented by some broadband signal, the outputs to the op-amps would appear as they do in Fig. 3. The output in Fig. 3 (b) roughly corresponds to a broadband signal that has been filtered by a first order filter with a 1-MHz corner frequency while that in Fig. 3 (a) corresponds to a broadband signal that has been amplified. By extension, the inputs to the op-amps (not the inputs to the overall filters) must by equal to the outputs after subtracting the op-amp gain. The op-amp inputs are also shown in Fig. 3 and three discrete tones, A, B, and C are also shown. Clearly, the op-amp input level is reduced above the corner frequency for the op-amp based CSF. The reduced out-of-band input level leads to better out-of-band IIP$_3$.

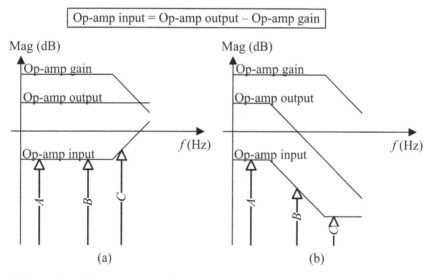

Fig. 3. Illustration of the pre-filtering effect of an op-amp based CSF. (a) The case with an op-amp based TIA, and (b) the case with an op-amp based CS.

The effect of this pre-filtering on the IF section (when compared to the case without pre-filtering) for both voltage- and current-mode passive mixers is a tremendous reduction in the required IF section IIP$_3$. We can estimate the required IIP$_3$ in dBm of the IF section as,

$$IIP_{3,IF} = \frac{1}{2}[2P_{blk1} + P_{blk2} - (P_{sen} - 3) + SNR_{req}] + G_{RF} \qquad (3)$$

where P_{blk1} and P_{blk2} are the power of the two interfering tones, P_{sen} is the required sensitivity level, and G_{RF} is the gain of the RF section. The addition of 3 comes from the requirement of the desired signal being 3 dB above the sensitivity level [10]. The derivation of (3) is rather straightforward, and is found by calculating the input level which causes the 3rd-order intermodulation component to exceed the allowable noise floor. The channel interference profile which the receiver must be able to tolerate is rather simple [6] and is shown in Fig. 4 (a) at the IF (after down-conversion) for a direct-conversion system. Based on the interference profile, we can estimate the required IF section IIP_3 under two worst-case scenarios.

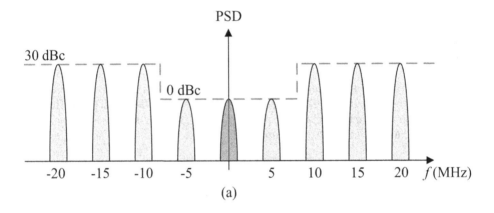

(a)

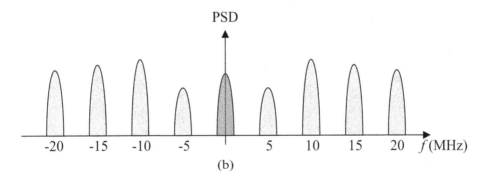

(b)

Fig. 4. Illustration of the effect of a single pole low-pass filter on IEEE 802.15.4 standard interference (a) before and (b) after filtering. The striped signals are interferers while the shaded signal is the desired signal.

The first scenario is when two blockers, in the adjacent and alternate channels respectively, intermodulate to create in-band distortion. Hence P_{blk1} is equal to -82 dBm, and P_{blk2} is equal to -52 dBm. If the gain of the RF section is 30 dB, then the required IF section IIP_3 in the first case is equal to -30 dBm. The second scenario involves two interferers in the alternate channel and at 20-MHz offset respectively. Both P_{blk1} and P_{blk2} are equal to -52 dBm. For the same RF section gain, the required IIP_3 of the IF section is 0 dBm. The overall receiver IIP_3 requirement is easily calculated by simply subtracting G_{RF} (30 dB) from the above results.

At a zero IF, the IEEE 802.15.4 standard signal bandwidth is 1 MHz [1]. The effect of a 1-MHz pre-IF section filter on the IEEE 802.15.4 standard interferers is shown in Fig. 4 for a direct conversion system. The adjacent channel is filtered by $20\log(5MHz/1MHz) = 14$ dB, while the alternate channel is filtered by $20\log(10MHz/1MHz) = 20$ dB. For the first scenario mentioned above, the effect on the required IF section IIP_3 is equal therefore equal to a reduction of 14 dB + ½ * 20 dB = 24 dB. For the second scenario, the required IF section IIP_3 is reduced by 20 dB + ½ * 13 dB = 33 dB. This is evident from (3). With such a reduction in IF section required IIP_3, one has the option of either increasing the LNA/Mixer gain, reducing the IF section IIP_3, or doing some combination of both. Both alternatives can lead to very low IF section power consumption.

2.3 Voltage-Mode versus Current-Mode Passive Mixers

We have illustrated how both voltage-mode and current-mode passive mixers offer the advantage of effectively pre-filtering the signal before active amplification. In this application, power consumption is critical. The filtering ability of op-amp based CSFs is determined by the unity-gain bandwidth (UGB) of the loop-gain of the feedback system. As the loop-gain falls below unity, the overall gain of the feedback system deviates from its ideal closed-loop gain, and the feed-forward path tends to dominate the transfer function [16]. As the filter only behaves correctly up to the UGB of the loop gain, it is desirable to have a high UGB op-amp. The UGB of an op-amp is limited by its power consumption under a given load condition. This is because for stability purposes, the UGB is generally limited by the non-dominant pole frequency. For instance, in a simple Miller compensated op-amp, for a 45 degree phase margin, the UGB is equal to the non-dominant pole frequency, and the non-dominant pole frequency is approximately equal to g_{m2}/C_L, where g_{m2} is the transconductance of the second stage, and C_L is the load capacitance. Increasing g_{m2} requires increasing the power consumption.

A major advantage of op-amp based active-RC filters is their excellent linearity resulting from their use of feedback. It can be shown that the IIP_3 and IIP_2 of a feedback system improves with the loop gain as [17], [18],

$$V_{IIP3,after} = V_{IIP3,before}(1 + LG)^{1.5} ,\qquad(4)$$

$$V_{IIP2,after} = V_{IIP2,before}(1 + LG)^{3} ,\qquad(5)$$

where LG is the loop gain, $V_{IIPn,before}$ is the IIP_n in volts before closing the feedback loop, and $V_{IIPn,after}$ is the IIP_n in volts after closing the feedback loop.

G_m-C type filters can generally be designed to operate at higher frequencies than their active-RC counterparts. The simplest possible transconductor in CMOS technology is a single MOSFET, and for differential circuits, a transconductor can take the form of a differential pair. Such a simple design inevitably achieves good noise performance due to the low component count (fewer noise generators). This naturally relaxes the power consumption requirements of the transconductor. Compared to an op-amp based active-RC filter, however, a G_m-C filter using simple differential pair suffers from significantly poorer linearity. Therefore, in most G_m-C filters, some form of transconductor linearization is needed [19].

3   The Proposed Architecture

In this work, rather than trying to linearize the transconductors, we use the idea of pre-filtering the signal using the passive-mixer's output pole. As this RC pole forms a first-order low-pass filter, the mixer favors a direct-conversion receiver architecture. A third-order Butterworth response provides sufficient filtering of the interference for the IEEE 802.15.4 standard [1], and since the real pole is formed at the passive mixer output, only a second-order active filter is necessary to form the desired response.

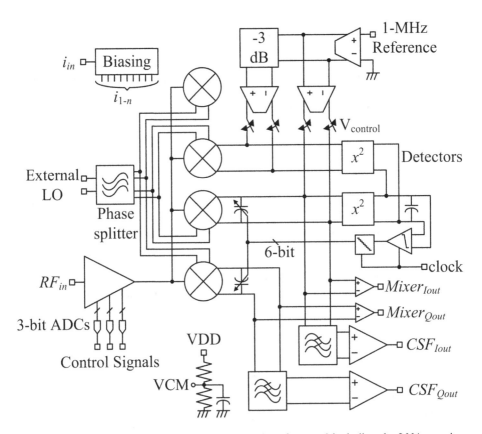

Fig. 5. A complete schematic of the proposed receiver front-end including the LNA, passive mixers, CSF, output buffers, LO phase splitter, and passive mixer tuning circuitry

The benefits of using the proposed mixer architecture can be summarized as follows: low-power G_m-C filters can be used, transconductor linearization is unnecessary, and only two active filter stages are necessary (as opposed to three in the current-mode passive mixer implementation). Unfortunately, the real pole formed by the switch resistance and the output capacitance of the voltage-mode passive mixer is generally not used for filtering because of the considerable variation in the switch resistance. The switch resistance can vary due to uncertainty in the LO voltage (V_{LO}), the switch threshold voltage, the switch size, and even the output impedance of the previous stage (the LNA output resistance affects the passive mixer output resistance [7]). Therefore, in order to ensure that the CSF behaves properly, the output pole of the voltage-mode passive mixer must be tuned. The proposed receiver architecture including the passive mixer tuning circuit is shown in Fig. 5. The tuning technique will be discussed in the section describing the passive mixer.

3.1   The Low-Noise Amplifier

The low-noise amplifier was implemented as a single-ended, single stage common-source amplifier. The schematic is shown in Fig. 6. The core of the amplifier is a simple common-source cascode configuration which offers good reverse isolation, and high output impedance. The transconductance of the core is controllable via V_{C1} to V_{C3} in 6 dB steps, and this also controls the power consumption of the LNA in the same proportion. The input and output frequency selective networks were made tunable (using digitally controlled capacitor banks) in order to avoid any frequency offset which may result from inadequate passive device modeling. The quality factor of the input and output frequency selective networks are 1.77 and 6.01 respectively. These networks were only tuned once before performing all of the main measurements and were not re-tuned for different power states.

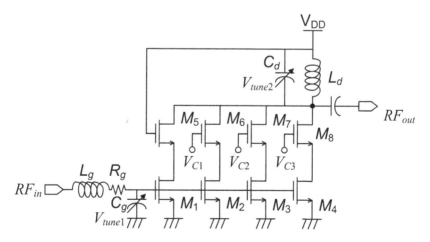

Fig. 6. Schematic of the proposed LNA. V_{C1} to V_{C3} control the gain/power consumption state of the amplifier, while V_{tune1} and V_{tune2} tune its frequency response.

Transistors M_1-M_4 are biased in the weak-inversion region [20], which has been shown to offer improved performance in the low GHz frequency range as compared to strong-inversion biasing. One way of accessing a transistor's overall performance is by looking at its maximum unilateral transducer gain, G_{TUmax} [21]. However, in practice, the quality factor of on-chip inductors limits the amount of voltage gain that can be achieved in a step-up matching network, and this is not reflected in the G_{TUmax} of a transistor. In order to correct for this, we have simulated G_{TUmax} for a transistor in a 0.18-μm RFCMOS process design kit (PDK) with 500-ohm shunt resistors added to the gate and drain nodes of the transistor (Fig. 7). The device drain current was set to 1 mA while the device width was swept. The threshold voltage was 0.48 V. From Fig. 7, G_{TUmax} is higher in the strong-inversion region at very high frequencies, but at very low frequencies, G_{TUmax} is optimum in the weak-inversion region. In this case, at 2.4 GHz, a gate-overdrive voltage of 35 mV appears to be optimum.

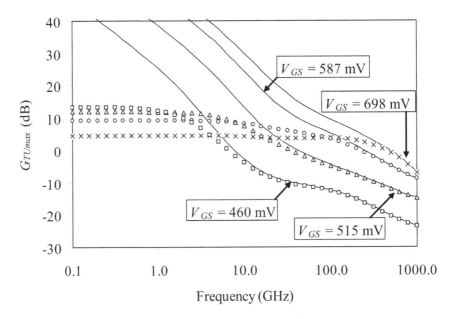

Fig. 7. Simulated transistor G_{TUmax} with (scatter plots) and without (solid line) 500-ohm resistors added in shunt to the gate and drain terminals. G_{TUmax} is higher in the strong-inversion region at very high frequencies, but higher in the weak-inversion region at very low frequencies. The drain current was fixed to 1 mA for all cases while the device width was swept.

In practice, it is difficult to power match a device directly to 50 ohm at 2.4 GHz due to the low quality factor of on-chip passive elements. Designers normally opt to create a virtual input resistance to match to, and inductive degeneration is a popular choice due to its ability to provide nearly simultaneous noise and impedance matching [22], while improving the linearity due to the use of feedback. However, it should be remembered that this impedance matching does not power match the device, and hence does not maximize the power output of the device. In cases where impedance matching is necessary, but a very low *NF* is not critical, impedance matching can be achieved by simply directly adding a resistor in series with the gate [20] and resonating out the gate-source capacitance as is done in Fig. 6. In our case, inductive degeneration is not a viable option since the LNA power control would affect the input resistance differently at different power levels. In our design, the input impedance is virtually independent of the power state since M_1-M_4 remain connected to the input node and in the on-state for all four power states.

Fig. 8 shows the measured S-parameters of the LNA for all power states. The input impedance of the mixer was simulated to be 2 kΩ, and this is chosen as the termination resistance of the LNA output port for measurement. The voltage gain of the LNA is found by adding 16 dB to S_{21} to account for the step up in impedance from the 50-Ω input to the 2-kΩ output. From the figure, the input reflection coefficient is nearly independent of the power state, while the S_{21} shows a 6 dB gain step. The S-parameters were measured by using a 50-Ω vector network analyzer (VNA) and then mathematically converting the output port to 2 kΩ [23]. When probing the LNA output, the mixer was turned off to prevent it from loading the LNA. The measured LNA NF is shown in Fig. 9. At the highest gain/power state, the measured NF is 4.8 dB at the center frequency. This is acceptable given the overall required NF of 12 dB. It is of note that for the proposed matching scheme, the minimum achievable NF is more than 3 dB.

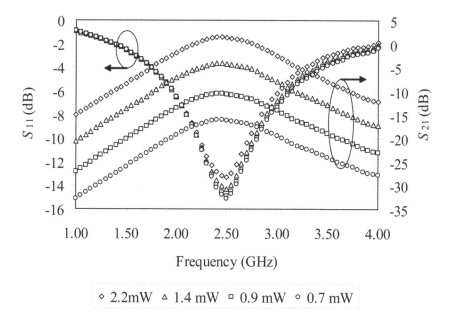

◇ 2.2 mW △ 1.4 mW □ 0.9 mW ○ 0.7 mW

Fig. 8. Measured S-parameters of the LNA for all four receiver power states. The input port is terminated in 50 Ω while the output port is terminated in 2 kΩ. For the voltage gain, 16 dB should be added to S_{21}.

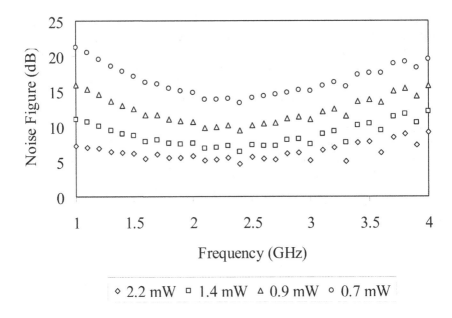

Fig. 9. Measured *NF* of the proposed LNA for all four receiver power states

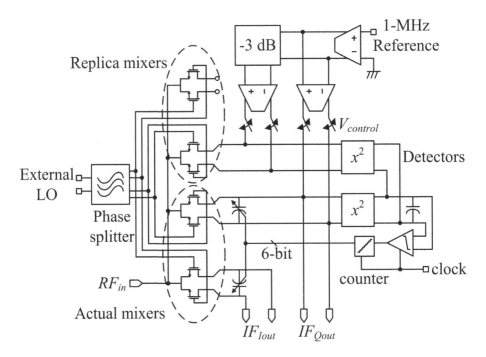

Fig. 10. Complete schematic of the proposed tuned-output-pole passive mixer

3.2   The Passive Mixer

The passive mixer consists of a switching core, replica passive mixers, and a tuning loop. These are shown in Fig. 10. The core switches act as variable resistors in series with the signal path, and hence were sized according to a tradeoff between noise performance, and capacitive loading to the LNA and frequency synthesizer. In this work, the 2.4 GHz LO signal is provided by a signal generator external to the chip, and split into quadrature signals using an on-chip RC poly-phase filter. The simulated LO amplitude is 300 mV for each switch. The IQ mixer core in the signal path is differentially loaded by tunable capacitors at each output, with a unit capacitance of 100 fF and 6-bit control.

The mixers also perform the single-ended to differential conversion operation. This allowed the use of a single-ended LNA thereby saving half of the LNA power consumption. The justification for this strategy is the relaxed IIP_2 requirements of the IEEE 802.15.4 standard. The main concern is unwanted DC-offset related to the self-mixing of either LO signals or strong interfering signals. Self mixing of LO signals results in a static DC offset which can be filtered before introducing any high gain stages to the signal. We can estimate the required IIP_2 based on self mixing of interfering signals as,

$$IIP_{2,req}(dBm) \geq 2P_{blk} - (P_{sen} + 3) + SNR_{req} \qquad (6)$$

Given alternate channel interferers equal to -52 dBm, the required IIP_2 is $2(-52) - (-82) + 14 = -8$ dBm. The achieved IIP_2 of the down-converter can be estimated as P_{LO}/G_{leak} where G_{leak} is the ratio of the differential RF signal at the gates of the switching stages to the single-ended RF signal at the source of the switching stages (note that G_{leak} does not include common-mode leakage) and P_{LO} is the LO power. G_{leak} is effectively a single-ended to differential leakage gain. In [24], it is shown that the IIP_2 of active mixers has similar dependency, while IIP_2 on the order of +40 dBm is typical.

To understand the operation of the tuning loop, we must first state that IF_{Iout} and IF_{Qout} are loaded by capacitive impedances. The replica passive mixer cores in Fig. 10 have no explicit capacitive loading and therefore, at the desired tuning frequency (1 MHz), present an impedance which is 3-dB higher than the impedance presented by the actual mixer core. We can inject 1-MHz signals into the mixer output nodes without affecting the impedances at the mixer nodes by using high output impedance transconductance amplifiers. On the replica mixer side, the 1-MHz reference signals are pre-attenuated by 3-dB to account for the 3-dB higher mixer output impedance. The resulting voltages which develop at the actual mixer output and the replica mixer output are then compared and used to tune the load capacitance of the actual mixer.

For the comparison loop, the two 1-MHz signals are first squared using Gilbert-Cell based multipliers. The outputs of the multipliers include even order harmonics which are filtered using a low-pass filter. The level of the harmonics determines the corner frequency of the loop filter and hence the maximum rate at which the comparator and counter can be clocked. As the Gilbert-Cells output a current-mode signal, the replica signal is easily subtracted from the desired signal before filtering. The resulting differential signal is input to a comparator to extract its sign. The output of the comparator drives a counter which is used to either increase or decrease the actual mixer's load capacitance. The comparison loop was designed simply to illustrate the principle of the proposed mixer. In theory, the loop could be significantly sped up by using a successive approximation architecture, or by attempting to cancel off the even-order harmonics. Fig. 11 shows the voltage on the loop filter node. When it reaches its steady state, the 6-bit control signal oscillates around the desired value by 1 least-significant-bit (LSB).

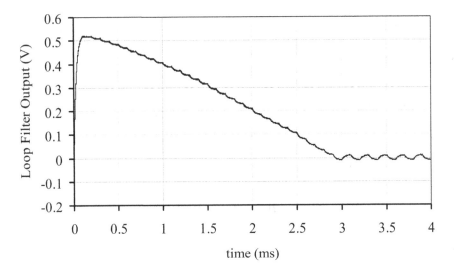

Fig. 11. The loop filter voltage versus time upon initiation of the tuning sequence

3.3   The G$_m$-C Filters

As previously mentioned, the first pole of the third-order Butterworth filters were provided by the output pole of the IQ passive mixer. Therefore, the active G$_m$-C filters are of second-order. A schematic of the filters is shown in Fig. 12. Each transconductor consists of a simple differential pair, and selected amplifiers include common-mode feedback (CMFB). It is easy to show that the DC gain of the filter is equal to g_{m1}/g_{m2} while the corner frequency is equal to $C^{-1}\sqrt{(g_{m2}g_{m3})}$ and the Q is equal to $\sqrt{(g_{m3}/g_{m2})}$. With four variables and three equations, we have one degree of freedom. This was used to select g_{m1} to provide the desired overall noise performance of the receiver system.

The transconductors used PMOS differential pairs to minimize the effects of flicker noise. Given a bandwidth of 1 MHz, a 100 kHz flicker noise corner frequency is sufficiently low as to have a negligible effect on the overall noise performance. Note that due to the 1/f nature of flicker noise, the intergrated flicker noise over any frequency decade is equal. If the flicker noise corner frequency is 100 kHz, then the flicker noise contribution from 100 kHz to 1 MHz is insignificant compared to the thermal noise contribution. This implies the same for the flicker noise contribution between 10 kHz and 100 kHz. Any flicker noise below that frequency can be removed by some form of high-pass filtering which is a standard feature of several IEEE 802.15.4 compatible receivers, and is mainly used to remove DC offset [1], [5].

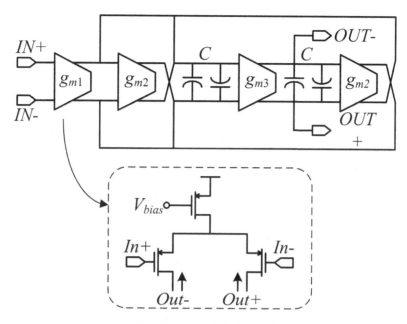

Fig. 12. Schematic of the G_m-C filters

Given only a 1-V power supply, the common-mode voltage of the IF section was selected to be 0.3 V. Gain compression in the receiver is dealt with by varying the gain of the LNA, and it should be noted that the IEEE 802.15.4 standard does not specify any large blocking signals which could otherwise desensitize the receiver. Nevertheless, any blocker sufficiently removed from the desired channel would be suppressed by the passive filtering at the mixer output pole.

4   Measurement Results

The design in Fig. 5 was implemented in a 0.18-μm RFCMOS process with 1 poly layer and 6 metal layers. The aluminum top metal is 2.52 μm thick allowing for sufficiently high-Q (around 8) on-chip inductors. The process also features metal-insulator-metal (MIM) capacitors. A micrograph of the proposed receiver is shown in Fig. 13. The chip was characterized using on-wafer probing. A 10-pin probe was used at the bottom part of the chip to provide the biasing, control signals and the clock signals. The LO was provided at the top of the chip via a ground-signal-signal-ground (GSSG) probe. At the low-frequency outputs, buffers were used to drive the 50-Ω instrumentation. The entire chip measures 1.5 mm by 1.5 mm, but less than half of that is used for the receiver design. Simple flash ADCs were used to convert the off-chip analog control signals into on-chip digital ones. These were used to control the receiver's gain-state, to initiate the calibration sequence, and to provide one-time tuning of the frequency selective networks. These ADCs are only for measurement purposes and in more complete works [1], a serial-peripheral interface (SPI) is commonly used.

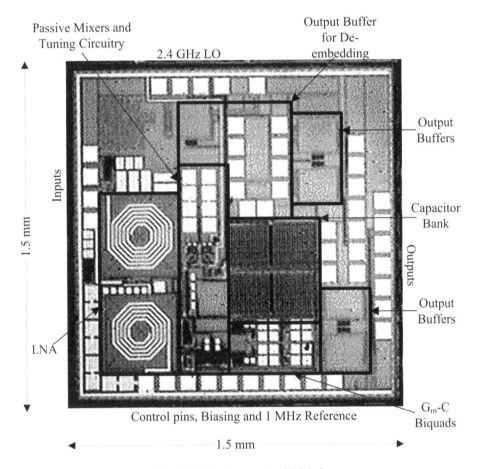

Fig. 13. Chip micrograph with labels

4.1   Measured Performance

Measured performance of the LNA was presented in Section III. The performance of the calibration loop is shown in Fig. 14. As mentioned in Section III.B, after a fixed amount of time (no more than 6.4 ms), the loop settles to its final state. For these measurements, the calibration sequence was manually initiated and stopped. From Fig. 14, before calibration, the passive mixer output pole frequency was around 500 kHz, while after calibration the pole frequency was 900 kHz. The 10 % error in the calibrated frequency may have been due to a mismatch in the resistor sizes in the 3-dB attenuator (see Fig. 10), or possibly due to a somewhat noisy power supply. This requires further investigation, however the basic principle of the calibration loop is verified.

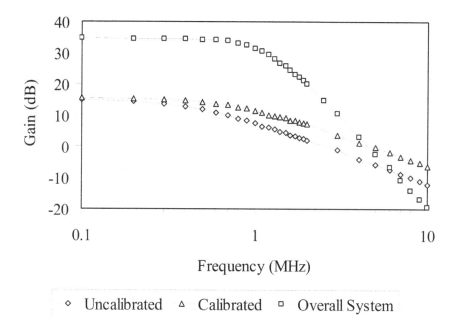

Fig. 14. Measured calibration loop performance

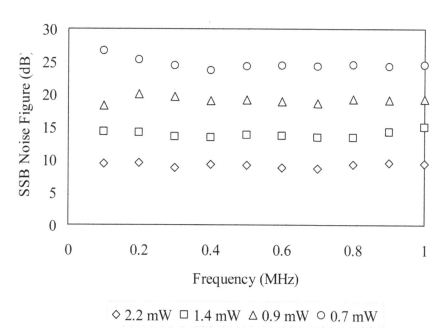

Fig. 15. Measured *NF* of the receiver

The overall single sideband (SSB) NF of the receiver is shown in Fig. 15. The NF was measured using the gain method. In this method, the total output noise, N_{out}, and the conversion gain, G_{conv}, are measured, allowing the overall NF to be calculated using the following formula,

$$NF = N_{out} - [10\log(kT\Delta f) + G_{conv}] \tag{7}$$

When compared to other works, the DSB NF should be estimated from the SSB NF. NF is calculated as the ratio of the total input referred noise to the source noise. Defining LNA_{NF}, SSB_{NF}, and DSB_{NF} as the LNA NF, the receiver SSB NF, and the receiver DSB NF, and N_S, LNA_{IRN}, and $MixCSF_{IRN}$, as the source noise, the LNA input-referred-noise, and the Mixer plus CSF input-referred-noise (the RF input) respectively, we can approximate DSB_{NF} using the following formulae.

$$LNA_{NF} = N_S^{-1}(N_S + LNA_{IRN}) \tag{8}$$

$$SSB_{NF} = N_S^{-1}[2(N_S + LNA_{IRN}) + MixCSF_{IRN}] \tag{9}$$

$$DSB_{NF} = N_S^{-1}[N_S + LNA_{IRN} + MixCSF_{IRN}] = SSB_{NF} - LNA_{NF} \tag{10}$$

Therefore, for comparison purposes, the DSB NF is 6.3 dB at the highest power state.

The overall receiver IIP_3 was measured using a two-tone test with the first tone at 5.0 MHz offset from the LO and the second tone 10.5 MHz offset from the LO to create a third-order intermodulation product at 0.5 MHz. The overall IIP_3 versus power state is shown in Fig. 16. In the worst case, the IIP_3 is -17 dBm which is well within specifications even for the more stringent interferer powers (Section 2.2).

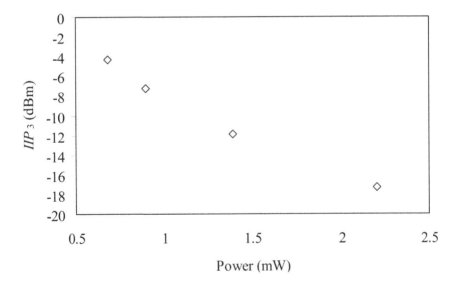

Fig. 16. Measured IIP_3 of the overall receiver

4.2   Comparison

The proposed receiver uses a combination of a tuned passive mixer output pole, and energy-aware control to achieve low power consumption without sacrificing performance. Table 2 summarizes the receiver's performance and compares it with several recent works. Using the proposed method, the IF power consumption was just 0.45 mW and the total power consumption was 2.2 mW in the highest power state.

Table 2. Comparison with Recent Literature

Reference	This Work				[1]	[2]	[3]	[4]
Band (GHz)			2.4					
Process (nm)[A]			180				130	90
IF (MHz)			0		2.0	10.0	-	6.0
Voltage (V)			1.0		1.8	1.2	0.4	1.35
Power (mW)	2.2	1.4	0.9	0.7	10	1.4	0.75	5.4
NF (dB)	5.6	10.4	15.6	21.2	5.7	5.0	5.1	6.0
IIP_3 (dBm)	-17	-12	-7	-4	-16	-37	-7.5	-12

[A] CMOS only

The table of comparison deserves some discussion before drawing any final conclusions. Firstly, the design in [1] was a very complete design including a full transceiver and supply regulation with a wide supply voltage compatibility range. Considering all of the auxiliary circuitry such as biasing circuits, it is difficult to gauge the performance in relation to the power consumption of the full design. We have mentioned the low power performance of [2], and [3] in the introduction, and have also discussed their short-comings.

Overall, the NF achieved in this work is comparable to state-of-the art designs, while still offering impedance matching at the input (impedance matching is not used in [3] and [4]). The power consumption is controllable from 2.2 mW down to 0.7 mW. This is comparable with the state-of-the-art for this application, and further improvement may not be meaningful given the power consumption requirements of other blocks such as the frequency synthesizer; to our knowledge, the lowest power 2.4-GHz frequency synthesizer for IEEE 802.15.4 standard applications uses 2.4 mW [25]. The IIP_3 in the proposed design is also well within specifications, despite the use of an un-linearized IF section, and is comparable with recent literature.

Acknowledgments. The authors would like to acknowledge MediaTek Inc, Singapore for sponsoring this work. The authors would also like to acknowledge the help of W. M. Lim, and T. S. Wong, Nanyang Technological University, Singapore, in the on-wafer measurement. Finally we would like to acknowledge members of the Designer's Guide Community for many useful discussions.

References

1. Kluge, W., Poegel, F., Roller, H., Lange, M., Ferchland, T., Dathe, L., Eggert, D.: A Fully Integrated 2.4-GHz IEEE 802.15.4-Compliant Transceiver for ZigBeeTM Applications. IEEE Journal of Solid-State Circuits 41(12), 2767–2775 (2006)
2. Perumana, B.G., Mukhopadhyay, R., Chakraborty, S., Lee, C.-H., Laskar, J.: A low-power fully monolithic subthreshold CMOS receiver with integrated LO generation for 2.4 GHz wireless PAN applications. IEEE J. Solid-State Circuits 43(10), 2229–2238 (2008)
3. Cook, B.W., Berny, A., Molnar, A., Lanzisera, S., Pister, K.S.J.: Low-Power 2.4-GHz Transceiver With Passive RX Front-End and 400-mV Supply. IEEE Journal of Solid-State Circuits 41(12), 2757–2766 (2006)
4. Camus, M., Butaye, B., Garcia, L., Sié, M., Pellat, B., Parra, T.: A 5.4 mW/0.07 mm2 2.4 GHz Front end Receiver in 90 nm CMOS for IEEE 802.15.4 WPAN Standard. IEEE Journal of Solid-State Circuits 43(6), 1372–1383 (2008)
5. Nguyen, T.-K., Oh, N.-J., Hoang, V.-H., Lee, S.-G.: A Low-Power CMOS Direct Conversion Receiver With 3-dB NF and 30-kHz Flicker Noise Corner for 915-MHz Band IEEE 802.15.4 ZigBee standard. IEEE Transactions on Microwave Theory and Techniques 54(2), 735–741 (2006)
6. Nam, I., Choi, K., Lee, J., Cha, H.-K., Seo, B.-I., Kwon, K., Lee, K.: A 2.4-GHz Low-Power Low-IF Receiver and Direct-Conversion Transmitter in 0.18-μm CMOS for IEEE 802.15.4 WPAN Applications. IEEE Transactions on Microwave Theory and Techniques 55(4), 682–689 (2007)
7. Do, A.V., Boon, C.C., Do, M.A., Yeo, K.S., Cabuk, A.: An Energy-Aware CMOS Receiver Front End for Low Power 2.4-GHz Applications. IEEE Transactions on Circuits and Systems – I: Regular Papers 57(10), 2675–2684 (2010)
8. Boon, C.C., Do, M.A., Yeo, K.S., Ma, J.G.: Fully Integrated CMOS Fractional-N Frequency Divider for Wide-Band Mobile Applications with Spurs Reduction. IEEE Transaction on Circuits and Systems- I 52(6), 1042–1048 (2005)
9. Meaamar, A., Boon, C.C., Yeo, K.-S., Do, M.A.: A Wideband Low Power Low-Noise Amplifier in CMOS Technology. IEEE Transactions on Circuits and Systems I: Regular Papers 57(4), 773–782 (2010)
10. IEEE 802.15.4 Standard For Local and Metropolitan Area Networks (2003)
11. Cook, B.W.: Low Energy RF Transceiver Design, PhD Thesis, University of California at Berkeley, May 16 (2007)
12. Do, A.V., Boon, C.C., Do, M.A., Yeo, K.S., Cabuk, A.: A 1-V CMOS Ultralow-Power Receiver Front End for the IEEE 802.15.4 Standard Using Tuned Passive Mixer Output Pole. Accepted for Presentation at the IFIP/IEEE International Conference on Very Large Scale Integration, September 27-29 (2010)
13. Gorday, P.: "802.15.4 Multipath", Internet (July 2004), https://mentor.ieee.org/802.15/file/04/ 15-04-0337-00-004b-802-15-4-multipath.ppt (October 2009)
14. Nguyen, T.-K., Krizhanovskii, V., Lee, J., Oh, N.-J., Han, S.-K., Lee, S.-G., Kim, N.-S., Pyo, C.-S.: A Low-Power RF Direct-Conversion Receiver/Transmitter for 2.4-GHz-Band IEEE 802.15.4 Standard in 0.18-μm CMOS Technology. IEEE Transactions on Microwave Theory and Techniques 54(12), 4062–4071 (2006)
15. Crols, J., Steyaert, M.S.J.: Low-IF Topologies for High-Performance Analog Front Ends of Fully Integrated Receivers. IEEE Transactions on Circuits and Systems-II: Analog and Digital Signal Processing 45(3), 269–282 (1998)

16. Middlebrook, R.D.: The general feedback theorem: a final solution for feedback systems. IEEE Microwave Magazine 7(2), 50–63 (2006)
17. Sansen, W.: Distortion in Elementary Transistor Circuits. IEEE Transactions on Circuits and Systems – II: Analog and Digital Signal Processing 46(3), 315–325 (1999)
18. Abidi, A.A.: General Relations Between IP2, IP3, and Offsets in Differential Circuits and the Effects of Feedback. IEEE Transactions on Microwave Theory and Techniques 51(5), 1610–1612 (2003)
19. Johns, D.A., Martin, K.: Continuous-Time Filters. In: Analog Integrated Circuit Design, ch. 15, Section 15.2-15.5, pp. 584–620. John Wiley and Sons (1997)
20. Do, A.V., Boon, C.C., Do, M.A., Yeo, K.S., Cabuk, A.: A Subthreshold Low-Noise Amplifier Optimized for Ultra-Low-Power Applications in the ISM Band. IEEE Trans. on Microwave Theory and Tech. 56(2), 286–292 (2008)
21. Ludwig, R., Bretchko, P.: RF Transistor Amplifier Designs. In: RF Circuit Design, ch.9, Section 9.2-9,4, pp. 465–502. Prentice Hall PTR, Upper Saddle River (2000)
22. Lee, T.H.: LNA Design. In: The Design of CMOS Radio-Frequency Integrated Circuits, 2nd edn., ch.12, pp. 365–380. Cambridge University Press, Cambridge (2004)
23. Kurokawa, K.: Power Waves and the Scattering Matrix. IEEE Transactions on Microwave Theory and Techniques 13(2) (March 1965)
24. Johns, D.A., Martin, K.: Continuous-Time Filters. In: Analog Integrated Circuit Design, 111 River Street, Hoboken, NJ 07030, ch.15, pp. 574–647. John Wiley and Sons, Inc. (1997)
25. Bernier, C., Hameau, F., Billiot, G., de Foucauld, E., Robinet, S., Durupt, J., Dehmas, F., Mercier, E., Vincent, P., Ouvry, L., Lattard, D., Gary, M., Bour, C., Prouvee, J., Dumas, S.: An ultra low power 130nm CMOS direct conversion transceiver for IEEE802.15.4. In: IEEE Radio Frequency Integrated Circuits Symposium, pp. 273–276 (April & June 2008)

Self-Timed Rings: A Promising Solution for Generating High-Speed High-Resolution Low-Phase Noise Clocks

Oussama Elissati[1,2], Sébastien Rieubon[2], Eslam Yahya[1,3], and Laurent Fesquet[1]

[1] TIMA Laboratory, Grenoble, France
{Oussama.Elissati,Eslam.Yahya,Laurent.Fesquet}@imag.fr
[2] ST-Ericsson, Grenoble, France
Sebastien.Rieubon@stericsson.com
[3] Benha Faculty of Engineering, Banha, Egypt

Abstract. A high-speed multi-phase oscillator based on self-timed ring is proposed. Self-timed rings (STR) are promising approach for designing high-speed serial links and clock generators. Indeed, the architecture of STR allows us to achieve high frequencies with multiphase outputs and their oscillation frequency is not only depending on the number of stages but also on the initial state of the ring. Moreover, this architecture allows us 3 dB phase noise reduction when, while keeping the same frequency, when the stage number is doubled. In this chapter, we propose a method to design STR able to generate high-speed multi-phase outputs and we suggest a design flow for designing low-phase noise self-timed ring oscillators. A test chip has been designed and fabricated in STMicroelectonics CMOS65nm technology to verify the theoretical claims and validate the simulation results.

Keywords: ring oscillators, self–timed rings, asynchronous logic, low-phase noise, multi-phase oscillators.

1   Introduction

Oscillators are essential building blocks in many applications. They are basic blocks in almost all designs: they are part of PLLs, clock recovery systems and frequency synthesizers. The design of low phase-noise multi-phase clock circuitry is crucial especially when a large number of phases is required. There are plenty of works covering the design of multiphase clocks [2-4] [18-21]. High frequency oscillators can be implemented using ring structures, relaxation circuits or LC circuits. Ring architectures can easily provide multiple clocks with a small die size.

Multiphase clock generation have two important features: the frequency and the resolution. We mean by resolution the lowest time interval between two phases of the multiphase oscillator output. High frequencies with a high resolution are often required in multiphase clocks. The inverter ring oscillators are usually used to produce such a clock generator. The main problem we face with inverter rings for implementing multiphase clocks is the exponential frequency drop with respect to the number of phases. In inverter ring oscillators, the frequency is only determined by the

J.L. Ayala, D. Atienza, and R. Reis (Eds.): VLSI-SoC 2010, IFIP AICT 373, pp. 22–42, 2012.

number of stages and the stage delay. Moreover, their resolution is limited to the stage delay and the only way to obtain more output phases is to add more stages, which decrease the maximum frequency and do not improve the resolution. Consequently, inverter-ring oscillators cannot be used in applications requiring high resolution or high-speed multiphase clocks.

For example, an important application that cannot use ring oscillators is precision waveform timing generation for single-chip testers [1]. When testing digital integrated circuits, the delay resolution which is required to have accurate measurements is often smaller than the gate delay of the device under test. This fine resolution can only be obtained with ring oscillators by using a higher speed integrated circuit technology for the tester than for the device under test. The main problem with inverter rings is the frequency drop when a large number of phases is required. It exists many architectural techniques which have been proposed to increase the maximum frequency of ring oscillators with multiphase outputs. Some of these techniques include the use of sub-feedback loops, output-interpolation methods [2], skewed delay schemes [3], multiple-feedback loops [4] and coupled oscillators [5]. However, these techniques require careful calibration to achieve high precision, their resolution is limited and the extra hardware increases the phase noise.

With the advanced nanometric technologies, it is required to deal with the process variability, the stability and the phase noise. Today many studies are oriented to Self-Timed Ring (STR) oscillators which present well-suited characteristics for managing process variability and offering an appropriate structure to limit the phase noise. Therefore self-timed rings are considered as promising solution for generating clocks. S. Fairbanks and S. Moore in [6] introduced the idea of the use of self-timed rings to generate high-resolution timing signals. Their robustness against process variability in comparison to inverter rings is proven in [7]. Moreover, self-timed rings can easily be configured to change their frequency by just controlling their initialization at reset time. At the opposite, inverter rings are not programmable. A Fully programmable/stoppable oscillator based on self-timed rings is also presented in [8].

This paper proposes a methodology to generate high-speed multi-phase clocks based on Self-timed rings. The oscillation frequency in STR does not only depend on the number of stages, but also on the initialization. We explain how this configurability can be used to reduce the phase noise by simply doubling the number of stages without changing the oscillation frequency. The article is structured as follows. Section 2 provides the background, definitions and principles of Self-timed Rings. Section 3 present the different CMOS implementations of Muller's C-element with is the main component of the self-timed rings. Section 4 explains the design rules to have high-speed multiphase oscillators. Section 5 shows how to reduce by -3dB the phase noise in STR by simply doubling the stage number while maintaining approximately the same frequency and the same resolution. Section 6 shows how this kind of oscillators can be used to generate à quadrature output signals. In section 7, we show how we can extend the frequency range thanks to the configurability. Section 8 proposes a design flow for implementing low-phase noise multiphase oscillators. Finally, Section 9 states the conclusions and future works.

2   Self-Timed Rings

2.1   Architecture

The C-element is the basic element in asynchronous circuit design, introduced by D. E. Muller. C-elements set their output to the input values if their inputs are equal and hold their output otherwise. Figure 1 shows a possible CMOS implementation where the initialization circuit is omitted. C-element implementations are detailed in section 3.

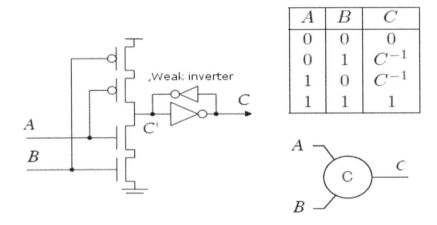

A	B	C
0	0	0
0	1	C^{-1}
1	0	C^{-1}
1	1	1

Fig. 1. Muller's C-element

Each stage of STR is composed of a C-element and an inverter connected to the input B. The input which is connected to the previous stage is marked F (Forward) and the input which is connected to the following stage is marked R (Reverse), C denotes the output of the stage, as shown in Figure 2.

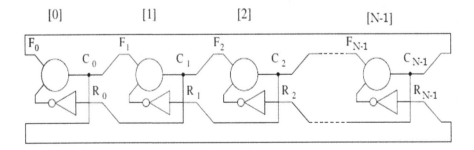

Fig. 2. A self-timed ring

2.2   Tokens and Bubbles

This subsection introduces the notions of Tokens "T" and Bubbles "B" which are very important to understand the behavior of the STR. $Stage_i$ contains a token if its output C_i is not equal to the output C_{i+1} of $stage_{i+1}$. On the other hand, $Stage_i$ contains a bubble if its output C_i is equal to the output C_{i+1} of $stage_{i+1}$.

$$C_i = C_{i+1} \Rightarrow Stage_i = \{Bubble\}$$

$$C_i \neq C_{i+1} \Rightarrow Stage_i = \{Token\}$$

The number of tokens and bubbles will be respectively denoted N_T and N_B. For keeping the ring oscillating, N_T must be an even number; this can be interpreted as an analogy when designing an inverter ring with a odd number of stages. Each stage of the STR contains either a token or a bubble. Notice that $N_T + N_B = N$, where N is the number of the ring stages.

2.3   Propagation Rules

If a token is present in $stage_i$, it will propagate to $stage_{i+1}$, if and only if $stage_{i+1}$ contains a bubble. The Bubble of $stage_{i+1}$ will move backward to $stage_i$. This implies a transition on $stage_{i+1}$ output. For example, hereafter the token/bubble movements in a five stage STR which contains 4 token and one bubble. The stage outputs are given between the parentheses.

Example: TTBTT (01001)➔ TBTTT (01101)➔ BTTTT (00101)➔ TTTTB (10101)➔ TTTBT (10100) ➔ TTBTT (01001)

Self-timed rings produce two different modes of oscillation: "Evenly spaced" or "Burst" modes. In the evenly spaced mode, the events inside the ring are equally spaced in time. In the burst mode, the events are non-uniformly spaced in time. In our application, we only target the evenly spaced mode.

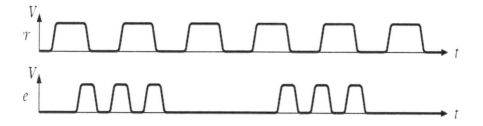

Fig. 3. Modes of Operation in Self-Timed Rings (Evenly spaced and burst mode)

2.4   Configurability

The oscillation frequency in STR depends on the initialization (number of tokens and bubbles). The oscillation frequency in a self-timed ring can be approximated according to the number of tokens and bubbles by the following formula [9]:

$$F_{OSC-STR} = \frac{1}{2.D.(R+1)} \tag{1}$$

$$(D,R) = \begin{cases} (D_{rr}, N_T/N_B) & \text{if} \quad D_{ff}/D_{rr} \le N_T/N_B \\ (D_{ff}, N_B/N_T) & \text{if} \quad D_{ff}/D_{rr} \ge N_T/N_B \end{cases}$$

where D_{ff} is the static forward propagation delay from input F to the output C and D_{rr} is the static reverse propagation delay from input R to the output C. The maximum frequency is achieved when $D_{ff}/D_{rr}=N_T/N_B$. This equality also ensures the evenly spaced propagation mode [7].The output number in STR is equal to the number of stages. The number of the different phases is determined by the number of stages in which the Token/Bubble combination allows us to have an irreducible ratio N_T/N_B. For instance, if we double the number of stages in the 5-stage example (4T and 1B; $N_T/N_B=4/1$), the ring will have ten phases (8T and 2B; $N_T/N_B=8/2=4/1$). However, only five of them are different phases. Each phase of the five "new" phase signals will be in phase with one of the five "original" phase signals. The resolution can be calculated by $T_{Ph}=T/N_{min}$. Where T is the oscillation period and N_{min} is the number of minimum stages to have an irreducible ratio N_T/N_B (which is 5 in the above example).

2.5   Modified Stage

In the STR architecture depicted in Figure 2, we have $D_{ff} > D_{rr}$. Therefore to achieve the maximum frequency with multiphase outputs, a higher number of bubbles than the number of tokens is required.

In order to have more flexibility in design and to improve the performance of the self-timed ring, we propose a modified ring stage. The modified stage is simply a C-element, without the R input inverter. We just interconnect the ring structure thank to the complementary outputs C' (which is natively available in a C-element structure but rarely used). Note that the complementary output is obtained from the internal structure of the C-Element (Figure 1) without any additional hardware. For each stage the output C is connected to the following stage input F and the complementary output C' is connected to the previous stage input R (Figure 4).

This modified self-timed ring (MSTR) stage allows us to improve the maximal speed by 30%. With such a modified structure, we can achieve a maximal frequency of 8.3 GHz in CMOS 65 nm. This modified structure of STR, in addition to the standard STR, offers more design flexibility to achieve high frequencies with a large number of multiphase outputs.

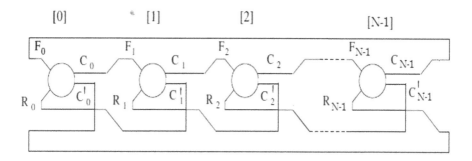

Fig. 4. Modified Self-Timed Rings

3   C-element Implementations

This section presents different implementations of the C-element. In addition to the dynamic implementation [17], there are different static implementations of the C-element in the literature such as the Weak-feedback by Martin [14], the Conventional by Sutherland [15] and Symmetric by Van Berkel [16].

The dynamic implementation [13] (Figure 5.a) is composed by an output inverter and the main stack of transistors of the C-element. These transistors called "switchers" contribute to the switching of the output.

For the static implementations, in addition to the "switchers" we have a mechanism for memorizing the output value; these transistors are called "keepers". The "keepers" are not active during the switching, they just provide a feedback to maintain the output state when the input values are different, so they are as small as possible to reduce their load and limit their current [17]

The weak feedback implementation of the C-element is shown in Figure 5.b; this implementation is composed by the same "switchers" of the dynamic one, in addition to a weak-reaction inverter (N4 and P4) to maintain the state of the output. This circuit suffers from a race problem at node C'.

In the conventional implementation (see Figure. 5.c), in addition to the weak-feedback inverter, we have four additional transistors (N5, N6, P5 and P6) to disconnect this weak-feedback inverter when the inputs are equal. N4, N5, N6, P4, P5 and P6 are sized at the minimal width allowed by the technology.

The C-element introduced by Van Berkel is illustrated in Figure 5.d. This implementation is slightly different from the previous ones. The transistors are split in two parts. The "keepers" are N4 and P4 and the splited transistors are also involved in the state holding.

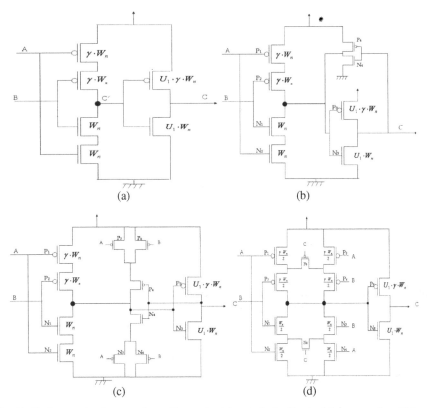

Fig. 5. C-element implementations: Dynamic (a), weak feedback (b), conventional(c) and Symmetric (d)

4   Designing High-Speed Multiphase Oscillators

In inverter-ring oscillators, the oscillation frequency and the number of phases depends on the number of inverters.

$$F_{OSC-INV} = \frac{1}{2.D_{inv}.N} \tag{2}$$

where D_{inv} is the inverter delay and N is number of stages. The number of different equidistant phases is equal to the number of stages N. Oscillation frequency is inversely related to the number of stages and the number of phases is directly related to the number of stages. This implies an inverse relation between the number of phases and the oscillation frequency. The more multiphase outputs the more the frequency drops. Some solutions have been proposed to increase speed but this improvement is really limited in the case of a large multiphase output number [2] [3] [4].

In STR oscillators, the oscillation frequency does not depend on the number of stages but depends on the ratio N_T/N_B. To achieve a high frequency with multiphase outputs, we have to choose N_T/N_B as near as possible to D_{ff}/D_{rr} with the condition that

N_T/N_B is irreducible. The oscillation frequency is related to the ratio N_T/N_B (not the number of stages) and the number of phases is related to the number of stages (with the condition N_T/N_B irreducible). This implies no direct relation between the number of phases and the oscillation frequency. This enables STR to increase/decrease their number of phases while maintaining a same oscillation frequency.

Table 1 presents the oscillation frequency and the number of equidistance phases produced for several rings based on modified stages with D_{rr}=21.3ps and D_{ff}=38.2ps (measurements in CMOS 65 nm technology from STMicroelectronics). We choose N_T/N_B as near as possible to D_{ff}/D_{rr}. This table shows that we achieve a high frequency and multiphase outputs at the same time. With larger rings, we have more possibilities to find N_T/N_B near to D_{ff}/D_{rr} which achieves the maximum frequency allowed by the ring. For example, 41-stage ring achieve an oscillation frequency of 7.19 GHz with 41 equidistant phase outputs and a 3.4 ps resolution.

Table 1. Frequency and number of phases for several configurations (Drr=21.3ps and Dff=38.2ps)

N	N_T	N_B	N_{Ph}	Frequency (GHz)
3	2	1	3	4.32
4	2	2	4	6.31
5	2	3	5	4.64
6	2	4	6	7.02
7	4	3	7	6.95
8	6	2	8	5.75
9	4	5	9	5.69
10	6	4	10	7.10
11	6	5	11	5.81
13	6	7	13	5.89
14	6	8	14	5.50
15	8	7	15	6.71
16	10	6	16	7.18
17	10	7	17	7.05
18	10	8	18	6.83
19	12	7	19	7.18
31	18	13	31	7.01
41	24	17	41	7.19

Figure 6 displays the oscillation frequency with respect to the number of phases produced by a conventional STR, a modified STR, a conventional inverter ring, Sun's[2] and Lee's solutions[3]. Note that the results of [2] and [3] have not been simulated but estimated according to the percentage improvement reported in the papers [2] and [3] compared to the conventional inverter ring. Only the conventional STR, the modified STR and the inverter ring have been implemented and simulated. In the work of Sun et al. [2], the topology is based on the use of interpolated inverter stage outputs for constructing fast sub-feedback loops in a long chain. The gain in speed with this topology is about 70% compared with conventional inverter ring. Lee's technique [3] uses inverters with negative delays; the speed was improved by 50% compared to a classical inverter ring.

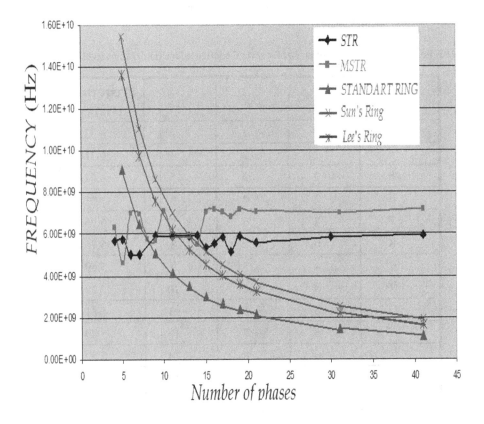

Fig. 6. Comparison between Inverter-Ring and STRs

As shown in the Figure 6, inverter rings can achieve higher frequencies when low numbers of phases are required. However, when a large number of phases is targeted, inverter rings loose their advantage. This comparison shows that using STR to generate high speed evenly-spaced multiphase clocks is the best choice if a large number of phases is required. Indeed, the frequency depends on the STR initial state and increasing the number of stages does not necessarily means decreasing the speed. The resolution of the STR is one of the most promising advantages because they are able to increase their phase number while keeping approximately the same oscillation frequency. This leads to a resolution enhancement for these multiphase oscillators. For instance, using 31 stages (as in Table 1) produces an output frequency of 7 GHz, 31 phases and a resolution of 4.6 ps. With 41 stages, we achieved slightly higher frequency with 41 evenly-spaced phases. Moreover, the resolution of the 41-stage STR is better (3.4 ps). This result is clearly not achievable with inverter rings; their resolution always remains determined by their stage delay.

Table 2 presents the performances of the three multi-phases oscillators. We designed these three oscillators by respecting the rules given in section III. The temporal parameters of the stages are D_{ff}=32.4ps d D_{rr}=42.4ps. To achieve the highest frequency with a maximum number of equidistant multiphase outputs (number of stages), we chose the Tokens/bubbles configuration with respect to $N_T/N_B \approx D_{ff}/D_{rr}$ and N_T/N_B irreducible.

The 9-stage STR ring oscillates with a higher frequency than the two others because its N_T/N_B ratio is the closest to D_{ff}/D_{rr}. This table shows that we can increase the resolution and reduce the phase noise by simply adding stages and maintaining the frequency. Compare to the 9-stage STR, the resolution of the 41-stage STR is improved by 4.5 times and the phase noise is reduced by 7.8dBc/Hz with a small change in the oscillation frequency. Notice that the oscillation frequency is totally independent of the ring size; the oscillation frequency of the 41-stage STR is higher than those of the 9-stage STR. Figure 7 shows the multiphase outputs generated by the 41 stage STR.

Table 2. Several Self-Timed Rings with $N_T/N_B \approx D_{ff}/D_{rr}$

Nb of stages	T/B	Frequ. (GHz)	Comsu. (mW)	Nb of phases	Resolution (ps)	PN at 1 MHz
9	4/5	6.41	1.94	9	17.3	-82.9
21	10/11	6.16	4.47	21	7.7	-87.6
41	20/21	6.02	8.62	41	4	-90.7

Table 2 shows that in addition to the improved resolution, the increase of the stage number also improves the phase noise. We improved the phase noise by 7.8dBc/Hz when we increase from 9 to 41 the stage number. At first glance this may appear absurd. How can we improve the phase noise by adding extra hardware? The explanations are given in the following section.

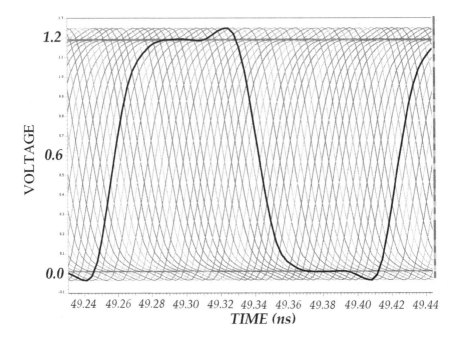

Fig. 7. 41 multiphase outputs generated by STR at 6.02 GHz

5   Phase Noise Analysis

The noise in the MOS transistors is usually splitted into two contributions: the thermal noise and the flicker noise. The thermal noise is responsible of the noise floor at high frequencies while the flicker noise is reflected by a noise rise at low frequencies. The up-conversion phenomenon of the amplitude noise into phase noise is complex and has different origins. However, beyond the offset frequency $f_0/2Q_{ch}$, HF thermal noise imposes a noise floor (see parameter definitions below).

The phase noise is given by the semi-empirical Leeson formula [11]

$$L(f_m) = 10 \times \log\left(\frac{1}{2}\left[1 + \left(\frac{f_0}{2Q_{ch}f_m}\right)^2\left(1 + \frac{f_c}{f_m}\right)\left(\frac{FkT_0}{P_s}\right)\right]\right) \tag{3}$$

where:

- Q_{ch} : Loaded Q-factor.
- f_0 : carrier frequency.
- f_m : Frequency offset.
- f_c : Corner frequency.

- F : Noise factor.
- k : Boltzmann's constant,.
- T_0 : Temperature (290K).
- P_s : Signal power.

The Figure Of Merit (FOM) is a parameter that allows oscillator comparison by standardizing the phase noise compared to the oscillation frequency and the power consumption. It is calculated using the following equation [12]:

$$FOM = L(f_m) - 20\log\left(\frac{f_0}{f_m}\right) + 10\log\left(\frac{P_s}{1mW}\right) \qquad (4)$$

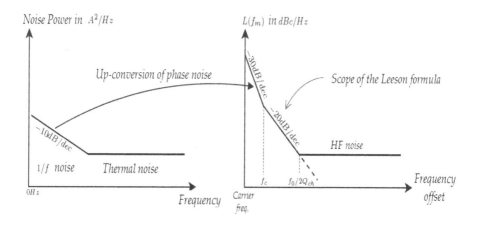

Fig. 8. Up-conversion of noise in oscillators

For two rings with different w_n (NMOS width), which oscillate at the same frequency and consume the same amount of power, the ring with a larger w_n will be better in term of phase noise. This is a result of the better characteristics of the falling and rising edges of the STR with larger w_n. This can be explained by the "Impulse Sensitivity Function" (ISF) introduced by Hajimiri [13] which represents the sensitivity to the signal disturbance. On one hand, when a pulse is injected during a transition, this results in a large phase shift. On the other hand, a pulse injection while the output is saturated has a minimal impact on the phase. Therefore the shorter the transition time, the less noise sensitive the signal.

Our experiments show that doubling the number of stages improves the phase noise by 3dB. According to Leeson's equation (3), there are two solutions to improve the phase noise: by improving the load factor Q or by increasing the signal power consumption Ps. The phase noise is inversely proportional to the oscillator power consumption. In other words, the phase noise can be reduced by 3dB by doubling the power consumption. The oscillators with the same ratio N_T/N_B have the same waveform output signal and so have the same load factor.

According to B. Razavi [10], the load factor Q is expressed by:

$$Q = \frac{\omega_0}{2}\sqrt{\left(\frac{dA}{d\omega}\right)^2 + \left(\frac{d\varphi}{d\omega}\right)^2} \qquad (5)$$

where A, φ and ω_0 is the amplitude, phase and the signal pulsation.

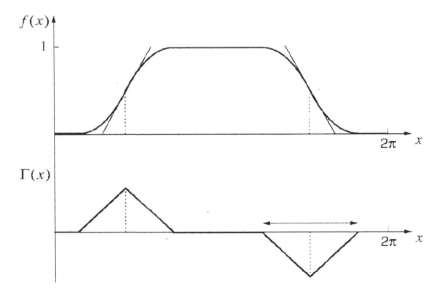

Fig. 9. Approximate waveform and ISF for ring oscillator

In inverter ring oscillators, the only way to increase the signal power is to increase the transistor width w_n and this implies a change in the oscillation frequency. On the contrary, we can increase the power consumption in STR while maintaining the same oscillation frequency; this is achievable by increasing the number of stages while maintaining the Token/Bubble ratio. This property is very attractive in STR oscillators because it allows us to have an additional degree of freedom during the design phase.

Another very important point is the symmetry between rising and falling edges; A.Hajimiri shows in [13] that the corner frequency f_C is related to the symmetry between the edges.

$$f_C = f_{1/f} \cdot \frac{\Gamma_{dc}^2}{\Gamma_{rms}^2} \tag{6}$$

where $f_{1/f}$ is a 1/f noise corner frequency, Γ_{dc}^2 and Γ_{rms}^2 are the DC and the RMS values of the ISF.

We can see from the Figure 9 and equation (6) that the more symmetrical the edges, the closest to zero f_c. Therefore the symmetry between edges tends to reduce the phase noise.

Moreover, we can improve the resolution of the ring and reducing the phase noise in the same time by adding stages and choosing N_T/N_B as near as possible to D_{ff}/D_{rr} with the condition N_T/N_B irreducible. With these rules, the maximal frequency remains the same, the resolution is improved and the phase noise is reduced. Table 3 presents the performances of STRs oscillators with the same Ratio N_T/N_B =2. These oscillators are oscillating at the same frequency. The phase noise is reduced by -3db when the number of stages is doubled which confirms our analysis. Of course, it is not possible to asymptotically create a zero phase noise ring having thousands of ring stages due to the noise floor imposed by the thermal noise (see Figure 8.).

Table 3. Self-Timed Rings with the same N_T/N_B ratio

N° of stages	T/B	Freq. (GHz)	Consum. (mW)	PN at 1M (dBc/Hz)	PN at 10M (dBc/Hz)
3	2T/1B	3.95	0.454	-82.97	-109.07
6	4T/2B	3.95	0.908	-85.98	-112.08
9	6T/3B	3.95	1.369	-87.74	-113.84
12	8T/4B	3.95	1.817	-88.99	-115.09
15	10T/5B	3.95	2.272	-89.96	-116.06
18	12T/6B	3.95	2.726	-90.75	-116.85
24	16T/8B	3.95	3.635	-92	-118.1

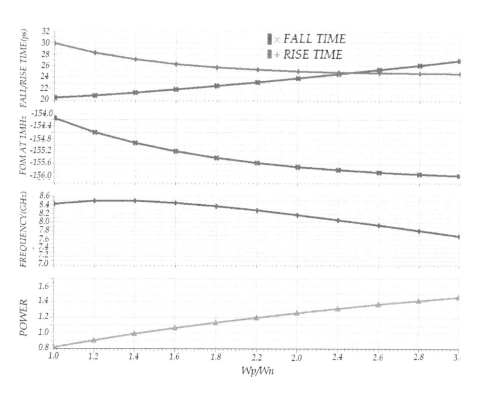

Fig. 10. FOM, frequency and power consumption vs. $\gamma = w_p / w_n$

Figure 10 shows the simulation results for a self-timed ring. The FOM, the frequency and the power consumption are plotted with respect to the $\gamma = w_p / w_n$ ratio (w_n and w_p are the NMOS and PMOS widths). We can see that the FOM is improved when the γ ratio increased and reaches excellent values when the edges are almost symmetric ($2 \leq \gamma \leq 3$). For high speed and low-power applications $1.2 \leq \gamma \leq 1.6$ would be a better compromise.

6   Quadrature Signal Generation

RF transmitter and receiver architectures use systematically frequency generators with quadrature output signals both in transmission and reception. The generation of signals in quadrature requires ring-based inverters with an even number of stages. However, it is unfortunately not possible with the standard structure of these oscillators. This requires the use of differential structures like CML "Current Mode Logic" [13] or feedback loops [2]. Many works deal with this subject [18-21].

Self-timed rings oscillators allow us to generate the quadrature output signals with a four stages oscillator initialized with two bubbles and two tokens. Indeed, it is the only configuration possible with this ring. We can also have quadrature output signals with multiple of four stages following the rules mentioned in section 3. Figure 11 shows the simulation results of a four stages self-timed ring. We notice a 90° phase shift between the four signals.

This oscillator has been designed using the conventional implementation of the C-element. The oscillation frequency is 5 GHz with a phase noise of -98dBc/Hz at 4 MHz offset and a consumption of 620μW. The phase noise is reduced 3dbc/Hz every time you double the number of stages. We get a figure of merit of -162dBc/Hz. Figure 12 shows the phase noise for this oscillator.

We conducted a comparison between the performance of this oscillator and the performances of published oscillators [18-21]. All these oscillators presented in the related articles are based on ring oscillators that generate quadrature phases designed in 0.18 microns technology in similar frequency ranges. Table 4 summarizes this comparison.

Table 4 shows that the self-timed ring oscillators are a serious alternative for the design of low-phase noise multiphase outputs oscillators. The FOM of our oscillator is -162dBc/Hz which is better than most of the cases presented in this table. The phase noise can be improved by duplicating the number of stages while remaining at the same value of the FOM.

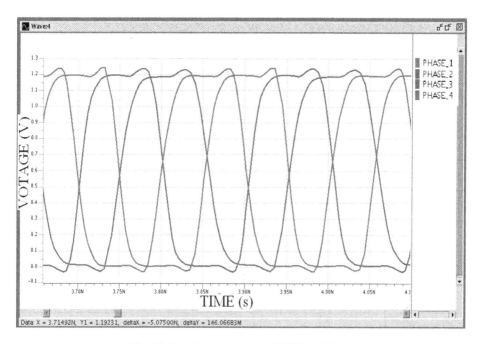

Fig. 11. Quadrature outputs of 2T/2B oscillator

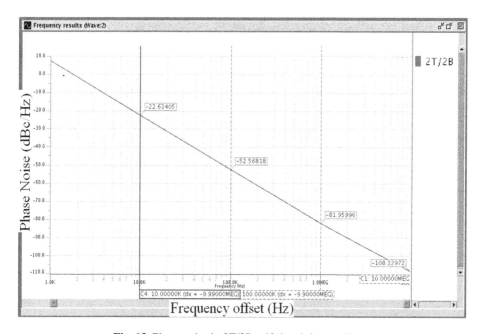

Fig. 12. Phase noise in 2T/2B self-timed ring oscillator

Table 4. Comparison with previous works

Ref.	Techno.	Freq. Max (GHz)	Conso. (mW)	Foff (MHz)	Phase noise (dBc/Hz)	FOM (dBc/Hz)
[18]	0.18μm	6.3	175	1	-101.4	-155.4
[19]	0.18μm	3.5	16	4	-106	-152.7
[20]	0.18μm	5.2	17	1	-90.1	-148.9
[21]	0.18μm	5.5	81	4	-116.06	-162.2
Our work (2T/2B) configuration	65 nm	5	0.62	4	-98	-162
Our work (8T/8B) configuration	65 nm	5	2.5	4	-104	-162

7   Frequency Range

Another important characteristic of self-timed rings, highly sought for the design of voltage controlled oscillator VCO, is the width of the frequency range [19]. Thanks to its configurability, we can design a VCO and coarsely tune its frequency by changing the tokens/bubbles configuration while the fine tuning is done with the classical voltage or current control techniques. For instance a 5-stage self-timed ring oscillator has two possible configurations: 2T/3B and 4T/1B. With 2T/3B configuration, the maximal frequency is reached. With 4T/1B configuration, the oscillation frequency is approximately divided by two. This oscillator produces five equidistant output signals with a 72° phase shift. We varied the supply voltage from 0.6V to 1.3V. The results are shown in Figure 13.

The frequency linearly varies with the supply voltage, which is preferable in voltage controlled oscillator (VCO) applications. In addition, the transition from one configuration to another one allows us to extend the frequency range.

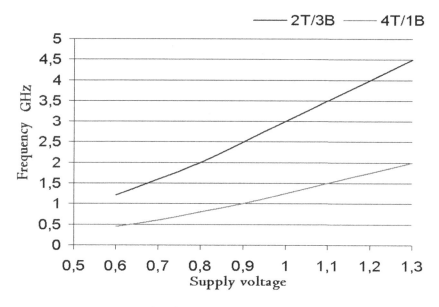

Fig. 13. Frequency Vs. Supply voltage

8   A Design Flow for the Self-Timed Ring Oscillators

Figure 14 presents a design flow for the self-timed rings oscillators. According to the specifications, thanks to the frequency calculation equation (1) and according to D_{ff} and D_{rr}, we can choose a preliminary architecture (number of stages, tokens and bubbles, stage implementation) which allows us to approach the targeted oscillation frequency and to reach the required number of phases. Moreover when we target multiphase oscillators, the tokens/bubbles ratio should be irreducible and as close as possible to the ratio D_{ff}/D_{rr}. In the case of quadrature outputs, a condition is added: the number of stages must be a multiple of four. w_n can be adjusted to achieve the targeted frequency before starting the phase noise optimization. If the phase noise requirement is not satisfied, we have two choices:

- The first solution consists in reducing the phase noise of 3 dB by doubling the number of stages and keeping constant the ratio N_T/N_B. The great advantage of this approach is that the oscillation frequency remains unchanged.

- The second solution increases the w_n of the transistors or optimizes the ratio w_p/w_n in terms of FOM. This implies a modification of the frequency. In this case, the architecture is changed by another one with a different ratio R.

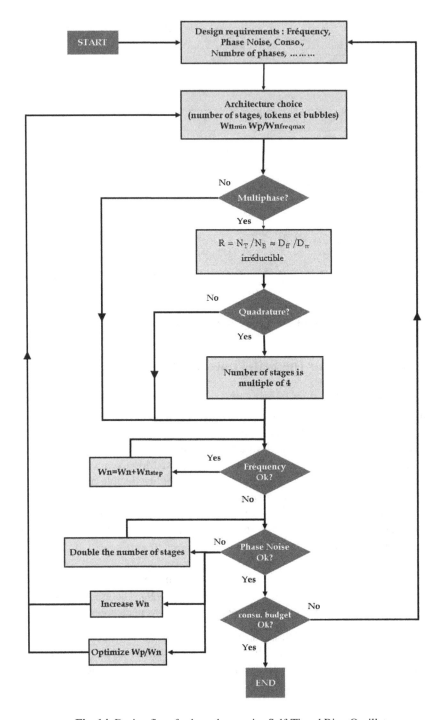

Fig. 14. Design flow for low phase noise Self-Timed Ring Oscillators

9   Conclusion

In this article, we presented a new oscillator topology based on self-timed rings for the generation of multiphase signals which are useful in many applications. Compared to inverter rings, one of the main advantages of the self-timed ring oscillators is their time resolution which is no more limited to the stage delay. Moreover, these oscillators are able oscillate at high frequency with a large number of multiphase outputs. A comparison with inverter ring oscillators clearly shows the advantages of our oscillators when a large number of phases is required. The self-timed ring oscillators are able to generate signals in phase quadrature which are especially useful in RF transmitters and receivers. A comparison with published studies shows the effectiveness of our method. In addition, we also demonstrated how to reduce the phase noise in self-timed rings oscillators by simply duplicating the number of stages. This feature provides to this type of oscillator an additional degree of freedom for designing s low-phase noise oscillator. In order to help the designers to implement such oscillators, a design flow dedicated to the self-timed ring oscillators is proposed. Finally, even if it is out the scope of this work which is focused on the self-timed ring design techniques, a test chip has been fabricated by STMicroelectronics in a CMOS 65 nm and the chip measurements confirm the relevance of our approach.

References

1. Gasbarro, J., Horowitz, M.: A Single-Chip, Functional Tester for VLSI Circuits. In: ISSCC 1990 Dig. Tech. Papers, pp. 84–85 (February 1990)
2. Sun, L., et al.: A 1.25-GHz 0.35-µm Monolithic CMOS PLL Based on a Multiphase Ring Oscillator. IEEE J. Solid-State Circuits, 910–916 (June 2001)
3. Lee, S.-J., Kim, B., Lee, K.: A novel high-speed ring oscillator for multiphase clock generation using negative skewed-delay scheme. IEEE J. Solid-State Circuits, 289–292 (February 1997)
4. Jeong, D.-Y., Chai, S.-H., Song, W.-C., Cho, G.-H.: CMOS current-controlled oscillators using multiple-feedback loop architectures. In: IEEE ISSCC 1997, Anag. Tech., pp. 491–493 (February 1997)
5. Maneatis, J.G., Horowitz, M.A.: Precise delay generation using coupled oscillators. IEEE Journal of Solid-State Circuits 28(12), 1273–1282
6. Fairbanks, S., Moore, S.: Analog micropipeline rings for high precision timing. In: ASYNC 2004, CRETE, Greece, pp. 41–50. IEEE (April 2004)
7. Hamon, J., Fesquet, L., Miscopein, B., Renaudin, M.: High-Level Time-Accurate Model for the Design of Self-Timed Ring Oscillators. In: ASYNC 2008, Newcastle, UK, pp. 29–38. IEEE (April 2008)
8. Yahya, E., Elissati, O., Zakaria, H., Fesquet, L., Renaudin, M.: Programmable/Stoppable Oscillator Based on Self-Timed Rings. In: 15th IEEE Symposium on ASYNC 2009, Chapel Hill, USA, May 17-20, pp. 3–12 (2009)
9. Elissati, O., Yahya, E., Fesquet, L., Rieubon, S.: Oscillation Period and Power Consumption in Configurable Self-Timed Ring Oscillators. In: IEEE NEWCAS-TIASA 2009, Toulouse, France, June 28-July 1, pp. 131–134 (2009)

10. Razavi, B.: A Study of Phase Noise in CMOS Oscillators. IEEE Journal of Solid-State Circuits 31(3) (March 1996)
11. Leeson, D.B.: A simple model of feedback oscillator noise spectrum. Proc. IEEE 54, 329–330 (1966)
12. Bunch, R.L.: A Fully Monolithic 2.5GHz LC Voltage Controlled Oscillator in 0.35mm CMOS Technology, Master of Science in Electrical Engineering, Virginia Polytechnic Institute and State University, pp. 1–7 & 53–72 (April 2001)
13. Hajimiri, A., Limotyrakis, S., Lee, T.H.: Jitter and phase noise in ring oscillators. IEEE Journal of Solid-State Circuits 34(6), 790–804 (1999)
14. Martin, A.J.: Formal progress transformations for VLSI circuit synthesis. In: Dijkstra, E.W. (ed.) Formal Development of Programs and Proofs, pp. 59–80. Addison-Wesley, Reading (1999)
15. Sutherland, I.E.: Micropipelines. Commun. ACM 32, 720–738 (1989)
16. van Berkel, K., Burgess, R., Kessels, J., Peeters, A., Roncken, M., Schalij, F.: A fully-asynchronous low-power error corrector for the DCC player. IEEE J. Solid-State Circuits 29, 1429–1439 (1994)
17. Shams, M., Ebergen, J.C., Elmasry, M.I.: Optimizing CMOS implementations of C-element. In: Proc. Int. Conf. Comput. Design (ICCD), pp. 700–705 (October 1997)
18. Uemura, J.P., Eken, Y.A.: The design of a 14 GHz I/Q ring oscillator in 0.18 μm CMOS. In: Proc. Int. Symp. Circuits Syst. (ISCAS 2004), vol. 4, pp. 133–136 (May 2004)
19. Grozing, M., Philip, B., Berroth, M.: CMOS ring oscillator with quadrature outputs and 100 MHz to 3.5 GHz tuning range. In: Proc. 29th Eur. Solid-State Circuits Conf. (ESSCIRC), pp. 697–682 (September 2003)
20. Tu, H., Yeh, J.-Y., Tsai, H.-C.: A 1.8 V 2.5–5.2 GHz CMOS dual-input two-stage ring VCO. In: Proc. IEEE Asia-Pasific Conf. Adv. Syst. Integ. Circuits, August 4-5, pp. 134–137 (2004)
21. Pokharel, R.K., Nizhnik, O., Tomar, A., Lingala, S., Kanaya, H., Yoshida, K.: Low Noise Wide Tuning Range Quadrature Ring Oscillator for Multi-Standard Transceiver. In: European Microwave Integrated Circuits Conference, EuMIC 2009, September 28-29, pp. 172–175 (2009)

Adaptive Logical Control of RF LNA Performances for Efficient Energy Consumption

Rafik Khereddine, Louay Abdallah, Emmanuel Simeu,
Salvador Mir, and Fabio Cenni

TIMA Laboratory
46 Av. Felix Viallet,
38031 Grenoble, France
{rafik.khereddine,louay.abdallah,
emmanuel.simeu,salvador.mir,
fabio.cenni}@imag.fr

Abstract. This work presents a new approach for controlling power consumption in RF devices. The approach is based on the definition of application-dependent performance modes for power hungry RF circuits and a logical control strategy that adjusts the power supply of each circuit to the mode required by the application. The control strategy uses embedded sensors, a recursive parameter identification approach and regression models for performance prediction, while demanding minimum embedded resources for computation. The control strategy is robust with respect to circuit parametric deviations due to the manufacturing process or ageing mechanisms. The strategy is illustrated for the case of an RF LNA using envelop detectors as embedded sensors. Simulation results of the control strategy at the transistor-level illustrate the energy savings that can be obtained for an example application.

Keywords: Control, parameter identification, ARX models, recursive least squares method, regression, RF transceivers.

1   Introduction

An efficient management of energy consumption is of paramount importance for battery-operated wireless devices. The autonomy and life span of these devices directly depends on procedures aimed at saving energy. The total power consumption is largely determined by the radio frequency (RF) front-end, in particular the power amplifier (PA) and the low noise amplifier (LNA) that are found, respectively, in the transmission and reception paths. Achieving high energy efficiency for these components, while maintaining a high degree of linearity, has been a major issue in low power wireless communications from a hardware design standpoint [1]. Energy savings can also be obtained using a software-based control. Most typically, energy hungry components are switched off during idle times.

J.L. Ayala, D. Atienza, and R. Reis (Eds.): VLSI-SoC 2010, IFIP AICT 373, pp. 43–68, 2012.
© IFIP International Federation for Information Processing 2012

In this work, we will study further energy savings that can be obtained by considering different performance modes for each RF circuit and controlling the required power supply. Each performance mode of a Circuit Under Control (CUC) has a different power consumption associated with it. The sequence and time duration of performance modes must be scheduled by the underlying application or by demand from the communication network. The implementation of such an approach is not straightforward. A major challenge is to guarantee the performance level during each CUC mode by just controlling the power supply during all the operational life of the device. In fact, for each CUC, parameter variability, ageing mechanisms and operation disturbances can make difficult to guarantee the required performance level while only power supply is controlled.

For this, we propose a closed loop logical control scheme to adjust the power consumption of an RF CUC according to the required performance mode. Since the CUC performances are not directly available for measurement, the controller must estimate them, regardless of the RF input and output signals of the CUC. The control algorithm compares the estimated performances with the target performances of the desired mode, and acts accordingly on the CUC power supply. The controller takes as input the signals coming from embedded sensors placed at the CUC input and output. These signals are used in a recursive real-time parameter identification algorithm to extract the coefficients of the input/output behavioural model. Regression functions stored in the controller map the behavioural model coefficients to CUC performances.

The rest of this work is organised as follows. Section 2 briefly reviews recent works on control, parameter identification and performance prediction for mixed-signal/RF integrated devices. Section 3 describes the models used by the controller for parameter identification and performance prediction. The on-line parameter identification procedure and the logical control strategy are described in Section 4. Section 5 describes a case-study RF LNA and the embedded sensors. An analytical study of the variation of LNA performances with the power supply is given and suitable performance modes for this circuit are identified. Section 6 presents simulation results at the transistor level of the logical control approach. Finally, some conclusions and directions for future work are given in Section 7.

2   Related Works

Integrated devices in nanometer technologies are highly susceptible to parametric deviations of the fabrication process, variations of the power supply, environmental disturbances and ageing effects. To address these problems, there is a rapidly growing interest on digitally-assisted analog design where digital logic is used to compensate for loss of mixed-signal/RF performance [2].

On-line parameter identification techniques have recently been considered for calibration and test of mixed-signal/RF circuits using recursive algorithms. For example, [3] uses a Sign-Data Least Mean Square (SD-LMS) algorithm for the calibration and test of a pipeline converter. The technique uses a reference ADC, which has high accuracy but low speed, in parallel with the pipeline ADC under test that operates at high speed but with less accuracy. The input analog signal is sampled and converted by both ADCs. A calibration block implements a recursive SD-LMS algorithm that takes as input the output of the pipeline ADC and the sign of the error committed between both ADCs. The output of the calibration block is a digital correction signal applied to the pipeline ADC in order to minimize the error.

The use of on-line parameter estimation of linear systems from binary data has partially been addressed in [4]. Nonlinear control for improving RF PA efficiency and linearity has been considered in [5]. The use of autoregressive models and parameter identification for analog test and diagnosis has been considered in [6,7].

A different paradigm for on-line test and tuning of RF systems has been introduced in [9,10]. The performances of the CUC are estimated using regression functions. These functions are obtained through Multi-variate Adaptive Regression Splines (MARS) and they are implemented in a Digital Signal Processor (DSP). The input for these functions is provided via embedded sensors that are placed in specific circuit nodes. The sensors extract characteristic device features that are used by the DSP in the regression-based performance prediction for testing [9] or tuning [10] purposes. In a recent work, [8] considers the tuning of RF performances using digital signatures. The Hamming distance between the reference signature and the actual signature is used to control the device, without the need of performance prediction from the observed responses. A set of possible operating levels is defined. At each iteration of the control algorithm, the device changes from one level of operation to another while minimizing the Hamming distance of the digital signature.

The novelty of our work stems from, firstly, a new procedure that uses both on-line recursive least mean square (LMS) parameter identification and regression functions for performance estimation and, secondly, the application of this procedure for efficient energy consumption in RF circuits for which different performance modes can be defined. Through signal converters for power supply control and sensor response measurement, we demonstrate a logical control algorithm that requires minimum digital resources for computation.

3   Model Building

The models required for the online logical control of a CUC must be computed at the design stage. These models include:

- a behavioural input/output model of the CUC, and
- a nonlinear model that links the set of parameters in the behavioural model to the performances of the CUC.

Figure 1 illustrates the procedure for the construction of these models. Monte Carlo simulation of N samples of the CUC (which includes the embedded sensors) is considered. For each sample i, the set of performances P_i are calculated by simulation. In addition, a transient simulation of the CUC is also carried with a persistently exciting input sequence $u(k)$ that covers the frequency range of the CUC. This is typically a Gaussian stimulus up converted to the CUC central frequency. The output sequence $y_i(k)$ is obtained via the embedded sensor, typically an envelop detector. For the set of N CUC samples, we obtain the set of performances $\mathbf{P} = \{P_1, \ldots, P_N\}$ and the set of output transient sequences $\mathbf{Y} = \{y_1(k), \ldots, y_N(k)\}$. For a given model structure with m parameters, an identification algorithm uses the input sequence $u(k)$ and the resulting set of output sequences $\mathbf{Y}$ to estimate the set of behavioural model parameters $\mathbf{\Theta} = \{\Theta_1, \ldots, \Theta_N\}$, where $\Theta_i = \{\theta_i^1, \ldots, \theta_i^m\}$ corresponds to the set of m behavioural parameters for the i-th sample. Finally, from the set of performances $\mathbf{P}$ and the set of behavioural model parameters $\mathbf{\Theta}$, nonlinear regression is used to compute a performance prediction model.

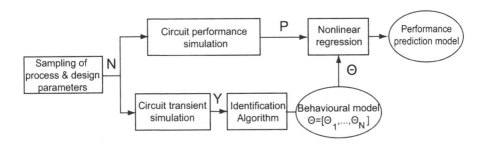

Fig. 1. Model building during the design phase

In Figure 1, the structure of the behavioural model for the identification algorithm is known a priori. In practice, the structure of this model may be obtained after several iterations until the most accurate prediction models are obtained.

3.1   Behavioural Input/Output Model

Behavioural modelling aims to find a mathematical relationship between the input/output transient sequences of the CUC. In this work we will use autoregressive models, so that the input/output relationship of the ith sample is expressed as

$$y_i(k) = f(\gamma_i(k), \Theta_i), \tag{1}$$
$$\gamma_i(k) = [y_i(k-1), \ldots, y_i(k-n_y), u(k-1), \ldots, u(k-n_u)]. \tag{2}$$

where $\gamma_i(k)$ defines first order regressors that consider the memory of the model. It contains n_u previous values of $u(k)$ and n_y previous values of $y_i(k)$. Θ_i is the parameter vector of the model. In most practical cases, the behavioural model is nonlinear with respect to the parameters. In this work, a priori knowledge of the CUC (e.g. an LNA) allows us to restrict the study to dynamic models that are linear with respect to the parameters and function $f(.)$ has a polynomial form.

To find the model structure, we apply the identification algorithm indicated in Figure 2. Some algorithm constants are fixed by the user according to his a priori knowledge of the CUC. These include the maximum memory allowed for the input sequence $u(k)$ and the output sequence $y(k)$, respectively, n_{u-max} and n_{y-max}. Also, since the model can be nonlinear with respect to the input, the maximum powers that can be applied for the input values $u(k-j)$ and output values $y(k-j)$ in the expression of the polynomial function $f(.)$, respectively, p_u and p_y, are also given as constants. The model structure of the ith CUC sample will now contain higher order regressors given by Equation 3:

$$\gamma_i(k) = [u(k-1), \ldots, u(k-n_{u-max}), \ldots, u(k-1)^{p_u}, \ldots, u(k-n_{u-max})^{p_u},$$
$$y_i(k-1), \ldots, y_i(k-n_{y-max})^{p_y}]. \tag{3}$$

The algorithm searches a model structure that contains regressors constructed from these variables. Each regressor has a weight w_j associated with it. These weights are used in the objective function to penalize or encourage the corresponding regressor. They are proportional to the memory and the exponential power of the variables in the regressor.

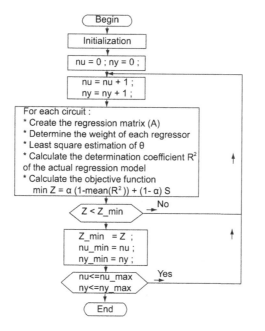

Fig. 2. Identification algorithm for deriving an input/output model structure

The identification algorithm is based on LMS estimation of the parameter vector Θ_i of the behavioural model, that is, the value of Θ_i that minimises the regression error ε_i in

$$Y_i = A_i\Theta_i + \varepsilon_i, \tag{4}$$

where

$$Y_i = \begin{pmatrix} y_i(k-1) \\ \vdots \\ y_i(k-n_{max}) \end{pmatrix} \tag{5}$$

is the output sequence of length n_{max} of the ith sample of the CUC, $n_{max} = max\{n_{u-max}, n_{y-max}\}$ and

$$A_i = \begin{pmatrix} \gamma_i^T(k) \\ \vdots \\ \gamma_i^T(n_{max}+1) \end{pmatrix} \tag{6}$$

is the regression matrix composed of vectors of the form of Equation 3, which are monomial terms of polynomial $f(.)$ in Equation 2.

The LMS estimation of Θ_i is given by

$$\hat{\Theta}_i = (A_i^T A_i)^{-1} A_i^T Y_i. \tag{7}$$

The quality of the regression is quantified by the determination coefficient R_i^2, given by

$$R_i^2 = 1 - \frac{\varepsilon_i^T \varepsilon_i}{\sum_k (y_i(k) - \overline{y_i})^2}. \tag{8}$$

Finally, a multi-objective cost function is used in the identification algorithm to select the most suitable model structure. This function is given by

$$Z = \alpha(1 - \frac{1}{m}\sum_{i=1}^{m} R_i^2) + (1-\alpha)S, \tag{9}$$

where α is a weighting factor for the two criteria of the objective function. S is a criterion used to penalize the complexity of the behavioural model structure as follows

$$S = \frac{\sum_{j \in selected-model} w_j}{\sum_{l \in full-model} w_l}, \tag{10}$$

where the numerator corresponds to the sum of the weighting factors of the regressors in the selected model, and the denominator to the sum of the weighting factors in a full model that contains all possible regressors.

3.2 Nonlinear Performance Prediction Model

Nonlinear regression is performed to obtain a relationship between each performance in the set $\mathbf{P}$ of CUC performances, and the set $\mathbf{\Theta}$ of estimated parameter vectors as shown in Figure 1. Simple functions are required in order to minimise the computation resources required on-chip. For this, we use a kind of Branch and Bound algorithm to explore a predefined space of regressors. These regressors use as variables the coefficients Θ of the model structure. The predefined space is limited to second order polynomial regressors. The steps of this algorithm for obtaining the regression functions for each performance are as follows:

- Circuit data $(\mathbf{P}, \Theta)$ are randomly separated into training and validation sets.
- The complete space of regressors is considered to form a reference regression matrix. Each column of this matrix corresponds to a regressor that is weighted according to its complexity given by the sum of the power of the involved variables. An initial value of predicted performances is obtained using the best correlated column of this matrix with the performance we want to predict.
- The algorithm keeps track of two subsets of columns: a subset of columns currently accepted in the model and a subset of columns in the reference matrix that have not yet been considered.
- In each iteration of the algorithm, the column of the reference matrix that is best correlated with the regression error obtained in the previous iteration is added to the model and LMS parameter estimation is performed.
- An objective cost function is calculated from the determination coefficient R^2 and the complexity of the model as in Equation (9).
- If a considerable improvement of the objective function is found, a new iteration is considered with the current model, otherwise we return to the previous model and another column is tried.
- The algorithm stops once there are no further columns to try (the space of regressors has been explored).

4   Adaptive Logical Control

The control of the CUC can be done either concurrently with the system normal operation, or during idle times using the same test sequence considered in the design phase (in this last case, the Gaussian-like persistently exciting input sequence will be generated by the controller, which can allow the extraction of a more precise behavioural model). As shown in Figure 3, the input/output sequences obtained via the embedded sensors are used by the controller to estimate the parameters of the CUC behavioural model from which the performances are predicted.

4.1   Recursive Parameter Identification

For online and offline estimation of the parameter vector Θ of the behavioural model, we use a recursive LMS algorithm that process data on the fly, thus saving memory resources, and which requires only additions and multiplications by a constant. The algorithm is initialized as

$$\Theta^{(0)} = 0, \ Q^{(0)} = \rho I, \tag{11}$$

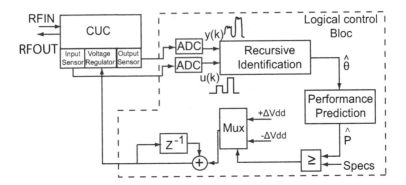

Fig. 3. Adaptive logical control strategy

where $Q^{(0)}$ is an initial variance-covariance matrix formed by multiplying the identity matrix (I) by a positive constant ρ (as discussed in Section 6). The classical recursive LMS algorithm is as follows

$$K^{(k)} = \frac{\lambda^{-1} Q^{(k-1)} \gamma'(k)}{1 + \lambda^{-1} \gamma'^T(k) Q^{(k-1)} \gamma'(k)}, 0 \ll \lambda \leq 1$$

$$\varepsilon^{(k)} = y^{(k)} - \gamma'^T(k) \hat{\Theta}^{(k-1)}$$

$$\hat{\Theta}^{(k)} = \hat{\Theta}^{(k-1)} + K^{(k)} \varepsilon^{(k)} \qquad (12)$$

$$Q^{(k)} = \lambda^{-1} Q^{(k-1)} - \lambda^{-1} K^{(k)} \gamma'^T(k) Q^{(k-1)},$$

where $\gamma'^T(k)$ is a subset of the structure given by Equation (3), according to the selected model structure. The recursive parameter estimation stops once convergence is reached ($\varepsilon^{(k)}$ is smaller than a given constant) or a pre-defined number of iterations is attained.

4.2 Logical Control Strategy

The logical control is not intended to be permanently on. It is activated when the application sets a new performance mode for the CUC which requires a different CUC power supply. The control follows an iterative algorithm that starts with the CUC power supply set at the maximum value. During each iteration, the behavioural parameters $\hat{\Theta}$ are estimated by the LMS recursive algorithm and used by the regression equations to predict the CUC performances $\hat{P}$. These are in turn compared with the specifications required by the new performance mode. If the specifications are met, the power supply of the CUC is reduced by a pre-defined value ΔVdd and a new iteration is considered. Otherwise, if the specifications are not met, the power supply is incremented by a value ΔVdd and the control stops.

5 Case Study

5.1 LNA: Low Noise Amplifier

Our CUC case-study is a Low Noise Amplifier (LNA) used in the 802.11g standard receivers that work in the 2.4 GHz ISM BAND. The LNA topology is presented in Fig. 4. This inductive degenerated cascade structure is compatible with narrow band applications and offers WiFi performances. The biasing stage of the circuit is formed by resistors R1, R2 and transistor M3. With the use of gate and source inductances, a real part of the input impedance can be generated without the need of actual resistances. Thus, inductors Lg and Ls provide appropriate input matching at 50 Ω. Using this topology we can match the circuit without adding noise which implies a lower noise figure of the LNA. The gain stage is composed by M1 and M2. M1 provides the high gain, whereas M2 isolates the input from the output, reducing the Miller capacitor and eliminating the dependency between the gate-drain capacitance and the drain inductance. Increasing the reverse isolation is important for: (1) lowering the effect of the Local oscillator leakage produced by the following mixer, and (2) minimizing the feedback from the output to the input. At the output of the circuit, the parallel Ld-Cd tank resonates at 2.4GHz and the resistor Rd controls the gain at this frequency. The LNA is designed using the 0.25 um BiCMOS7RF technology provided by ST Microelectonics. The principle performances of the LNA at 2.4 GHz are: Gain>12 dB, NF <1.6 dB and IIP3 >5.9 dBm.

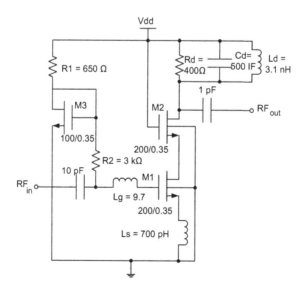

Fig. 4. LNA schematic

5.2 Envelope Detector

Different sensors that extract RF power and convert it into a low-frequency signal for BIST purposes are available in the litterature [11][12][13]. We have developed an envelope detector, with a very simple architecture, based on the following design constraints: (a) minimum silicon area overhead, (b) high input impedance in the frequency range of interest to avoid undesired loading of the CUC, (c) high dynamic range suitable for testing different on-chip CUCs, and (d) wide band of operation to monitor CUCs that work at different frequencies involved in the system. This circuit consists of two stages as shown in Fig.5.

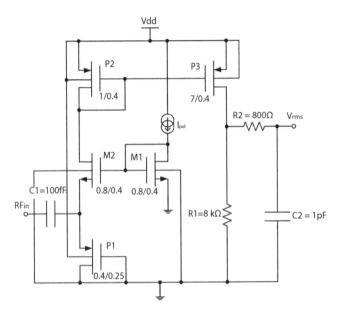

Fig. 5. CMOS envelope detector

The first stage is a rectifier that performs half-wave rectification on the current delivered at the source of the transistor M2. The half-wave rectifier works as follows. The operating point of the transistor M2 is controlled by the bias current Ipol which flows through the diode-connected transistor M1. The difference between the fixed gate voltage of M2 and its source voltage is very close to its threshold voltage, such that M2 is at the verge of conduction. When the current passing thought the source of M2 is positive, transistor M2 is off and the current passes entirely through transistor P1 to the ground. During the negative half-cycle, the source voltage of M2 decreases which activates M2. During this half-cycle, the current flowing through M2 is copied and amplified through the current mirror formed by transistors P2 and P3. It is important to note that the sensitivity of the detector is mainly controlled by Ipol. In particular, as this current is reduced, the rectifier is sensitive to smaller signal amplitudes and this characteristic is critical in an on-line monitoring scenario when the envelope detector is related to the input of the LNA. On the other hand, a main challenge exists between the high dynamic range of the envelope detector and its sensitivity. In the second stage, the amplified current is converted to voltage through Rout which is equivalent to the output resistor rds of the transistor P3 in parallel with the resistor R1. Finally, in the low pass filter R2-C2 a compromise exists between the time constant of the settling response and the ripple in the output voltage. The envelope detector has the following characteristics: an input impedance equal 1.5-11 kOhms in the band of operation 500 MHz -10 GHz, an input dynamic range of 35 dB and an area equal to 2170 μm^2, which corresponds to 0.543 % of the area of the LNA. Figure 6 plots the input-output characteristic of the envelope detector for the two edges of the frequency band. Furthermore, the study of the impact of the envelope detector on the LNA specifications is achieved by simulating the LNA performances with and without the envelope detector. The analysis shows just a low degradation thanks to the high impedance at the input of the envelope detector.

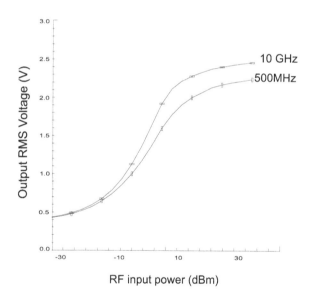

Fig. 6. Input-output characteristic of the envelope detector

5.3   Variation of Performances with the Power Supply Voltage

Input Matching and Input Reflection Parameter (S11). The input reflection parameter reflects the matching at the input of the LNA. This parameter is principally influenced by the input impedance. As the input impedance of the LNA gets closer to 50 Ω, S11 becomes more negative. From the small signal model shown in Figure 7, the input impedance of the LNA is calculated as

$$- Vin + \frac{Iin}{sCin} + \frac{Iin}{sCgs} + sLg\ Iin + sLs\ (Iin + gm_1\ Vgs) = 0 \qquad (13)$$

with s=jw, Cin is the input capacitor, Cgs is the gate to source voltage, Lg and Ls are respectively the gate and the source inductance and gm_1 is the transconductance of transistor M1 (notice that the transconductance of the overall cascode topology is equivalent to the transconductance of transistor M1).

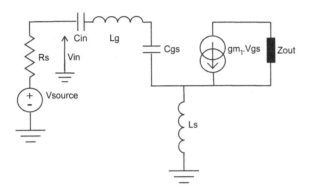

Fig. 7. Small signal model of the LNA

Since

$$Vgs = \frac{Iin}{sCgs} \qquad (14)$$

Equation (13) can be written as

$$- Vin + Iin(\frac{1}{sCin} + \frac{1}{sCgs} + sLg + sLs + \frac{gm_1\ Ls}{sCgs}) = 0. \qquad (15)$$

Since Cgs is very small compared to Cin

$$\frac{1}{sCin} + \frac{1}{sCgs} \approx \frac{1}{sCgs}, \qquad (16)$$

the input impedance of the circuit is approximately given by

$$Zin \approx \frac{Vin}{Iin} = \frac{gm_1\ Ls}{Cgs} + s(Ls + Lg) + \frac{1}{sCgs}. \qquad (17)$$

In order to accomplish the impedance-matched conditions at w_0 (equal to 2.4 GHz in our case), the LNA is designed such that the following condition is satisfied

$$w_0(Ls + Lg) = \frac{1}{w_0Cgs}. \qquad (18)$$

Thus, at 2.4 GHz the input impedance becomes

$$Zin = \frac{gm_1\ Ls}{Cgs} \qquad (19)$$

which is the real part that should be equal to 50Ω. From Equation (19) we can deduce that Zin is proportional to the transcanductance gm_1 as given by

$$gm_1 = 2\ Kn\ \frac{W}{L}\ (Vgs - Vt). \qquad (20)$$

The term Kn W/L is technology dependent. Vgs is controlled by the biasing stage of the circuit which is proportional to the power supply voltage, therefore gm_1 is directly proportional to the power supply voltage. At 3.3V the LNA is designed to be matched at 50Ω. Once the power supply voltage decreases, the input impedance will decrease and it will be far away from its initial value 50Ω which degrades the input reflection parameter S11, then S11 increases.

Gain (S21). The LNA is the first gain stage in a receiver system. It must amplify the very low amplitude signal from the antenna adding a minimum amount of noise. The gain of the LNA is of critical importance. We will derive next the relation between the power supply voltage and the gain. The small signal analysis shows that

$$Vout = -Zout\ gm_1\ Vgs = -Zout\ gm_1\ \frac{Iin}{sCgs} \qquad (21)$$

with

$$Zout = Cd//Ld//Rd//rds \qquad (22)$$

rds is the output impedance of the cascode stage given by

$$rds = rds_1.rds_2.gm_2 \qquad (23)$$

where rds_1 is the output impedance of the transisor M1, rds_2 is the output impedance of the transistor M2 and gm_2 is the transconductance of transistor M2. From Equations (17) and (21)

$$Vout = \frac{-Zout\ gm_1\ \frac{1}{sCgs}\ Vin}{Zin}. \qquad (24)$$

Also, from Figure 7 we can deduce that

$$-V_{source} + Rs.Iin + V_{in} = 0 \qquad (25)$$

and

$$V_{in} = \frac{V_{source}\ Zin}{Rs + Zin}. \qquad (26)$$

From Equations (24) and (26)

$$V_{out} = \frac{-Zout \, gm_1 \frac{1}{sCgs} \, Zin \, V_{source}}{(Rs + Zin) \, Zin} \tag{27}$$

and the gain of the LNA becomes

$$Gain = \frac{Vout}{Vin} = \frac{-Zout \, gm_1 \frac{1}{sCgs}}{Rs + \frac{gm_1 \, Ls}{Cgs} + s(Ls + Lg) + \frac{1}{sCgs}}. \tag{28}$$

At the resonant frequency and under impedance-matched conditions

$$w_0(Ls + Lg) = \frac{1}{sCgs} \tag{29}$$

$$\frac{gm_1 \, Ls}{Cgs} = Rs. \tag{30}$$

Finally, by substitution in Equation (28) we obtain

$$Gain = \frac{Vout}{Vin} = \frac{-Zout \, gm_1 \, W_0 \, (Lg + Ls)}{2 \, Rs}. \tag{31}$$

Hence we can see that the gain of the LNA is proportional to the tranconductance gm_1, which in turn is directly proportional to the power supply voltage. Thus, as the power supply voltage increases, the gain increases.

Noise Figure (NF). According to the Friis equation in a chain of n stages, the overall noise factor of the chain is expressed as

$$Ftotal = F1 + \left(\frac{F2 - 1}{G1}\right) + \left(\frac{F3 - 1}{G1G2}\right) + \dots + \left(\frac{Fn - 1}{G1G2....Gn}\right). \tag{32}$$

This formula allows us to highlight the importance of the noise factor (F1) and the gain (G1) of the first block of a chain. It mainly determines the entire system noise. In order to define the dependence between the noise figure and the power supply voltage, we consider the noise model shown in Figure 8. We will use this model to calculate the ratio of the total noise power at the output to the noise power at the output due only to the input source. This ratio represents the noise factor [14].

Neglecting the 1/f noise and the gate noise, the input noise will be generated by the source resistor

$$V_{nRs}^2(f) = 4.k.T.Rs \tag{33}$$

with k the Boltzman constant, and T the absolute temperature. So the output noise power due to the input noise is given by

$$V_o^2 = V_{nRs}^2(f). \, Gain^2. \tag{34}$$

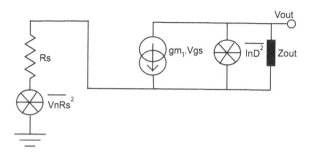

Fig. 8. Equivalent noise model ignoring gate noise

Additional output noise power comes from the thermal noise generated in the channel that can be expressed as

$$V_{nD}^2(f) = I_{nD}^2.Zout^2 \tag{35}$$

with

$$I_{nD}^2(f) = 4.k.T.\gamma.gm_1 \tag{36}$$

where γ is a function of the transistor parameters and is approximated to 2/3 when considering the thermal noise in the channel without the substrate effect.

As a result the noise factor of the LNA in our case study is

$$F = \frac{V_{nD}^2(f) + V_{nRs}^2(f).\ Gain^2}{V_{nRs}^2(f).\ Gain^2} = 1 + \frac{V_{nD}^2}{V_{nRs}^2(f).\ Gain^2} \tag{37}$$

and using the previous expressions

$$F = 1 + \frac{4.\gamma.Rs}{gm_1.W_0^2(Lg + Ls)^2}. \tag{38}$$

Finally, the noise figure is given by

$$NF = 10\ log(F) = 10\ log(1 + \frac{4.\gamma.Rs}{gm_1.W_0^2(Lg + Ls)^2}). \tag{39}$$

This Equations shows that the noise figure is inversely proportional to gm_1. Thus, as the power supply increases, NF decreases.

Non Linearity Effects (1dB Compression). We will derive next an expression for the 1dB compression point. Let $Vin(t)$ be the input signal of a system and $Vout(t)$ its output. The system behaviour can be modelled by

$$Vout(t) = \alpha_0 + \alpha_1\ Vin(t) + \alpha_2\ Vin^2(t) + \alpha_3\ Vin^3(t) + ... \tag{40}$$

For simplicity, we limit our study to the third harmonic. Considering an input signal Vin= Ain Cos $(w_0 t)$ and developing Equation 40, we see that the output amplitude of the signal at the fundamental frequency is a non linear function of the input amplitude

$$Aout = \alpha_1 \ Ain \ + \ \frac{3 \ \alpha_3 \ Ain^3}{4} \qquad (41)$$

where α_1 is the linear gain of the amplifier. Thus in order to calculate the 1-dB compression, we should calculate the input amplitude A_{1dB} for which the linear gain decreases of 1dB. For this, the gain equation (41) must be equal to the linear gain decrease of 1dB

$$20 \ log(Gv) + \frac{3 \ \alpha_3 \ A_{1dB}^2}{4} = 20 \ log \ Gv - 1dB. \qquad (42)$$

Therefore the 1dB compression point is

$$A_{1dB} = \sqrt{0.145 \ \frac{Gv}{\alpha_3}}. \qquad (43)$$

In order to show the dependence between the A_{1dB} and the power supply voltage, we assume the small input signal $Vin(t)$ around the bias (Vgs-Vt) so the output DC voltage is

$$Vout = Zout \ I_D = Zout \ \frac{Kn}{2}(Vgs - Vt)^2. \qquad (44)$$

For a submicron technology, the channel length is of the same order of magnitude as the depletion-layer widths (xdD, xdS) of the source and drain junctions. Thus, taking into account the short channel effects, the drain current is assumed to be equal to

$$I_D = \frac{Kn(Vgs - Vt)^2}{2[1 + \theta(Vgs - Vt)]}. \qquad (45)$$

Kn is a parameter dependent of the technology and θ is a factor that represents the velocity saturation and the mobility degradation. For an input small signal $Vin(t)$ around the bias voltage of the gate of the MOS (Vgs-Vt), the output Vout becomes

$$Vout = Zout \ I_D(t) = Zout \ \frac{Kn[Vin(t) + (Vgs - Vt)]^2}{2(1 + \theta[Vin(t) + (Vgs - Vt)])}. \qquad (46)$$

Since θ is very small comparing to 1,

$$\frac{1}{1 + \theta[Vin(t) + (Vgs - Vt)]} \approx 1 - \frac{\theta[Vin(t) + (Vgs - Vt)]}{2} \qquad (47)$$

and Equation (46) becomes

$$Vout = K[Vin(t) + (Vgs - Vt)]^2(1 - \frac{\theta[Vin(t) + (Vgs - Vt)]}{2}). \qquad (48)$$

with K = Kn Zout/2. Developing this Equation

$$Vout = K(Vg - Vt)^2 - \frac{K\Theta}{2}(Vgs - Vt)^3 + [2K(Vgs - Vt) - \frac{3K\Theta}{2}(Vgs$$

$$-Vt)^2]Vin(t) + [K - \frac{3K\theta(Vgs - Vt)}{2}]Vin^2(t) - \frac{K\theta}{2}Vin^3(t) \quad (49)$$

and by comparison to Equation (43), we deduce

$$\alpha_1 = 2K(Vgs - Vt) - \frac{3K\theta}{2}(Vgs - Vt)^2, \tag{50}$$

$$\alpha_3 = -\frac{K\theta}{2}. \tag{51}$$

Thus the 1dB compression is equal to

$$A_{IP1} = \sqrt{0.145\frac{2K(Vgs - Vt) - \frac{3K\theta}{2}(Vgs - Vt)^2}{\frac{K\theta}{2}}}. \tag{52}$$

Considering now that θ is very small compared to 1 (then $3(Vgs - Vt)^2$ can be ignored), (52) becomes

$$A_{IP1} = \sqrt{0.145\frac{4K(Vgs - Vt)}{\theta}}. \tag{53}$$

This Equation shows that A_{IP1} is proportional to the gate bias voltage (Vgs), therefore, when the power supply voltage decreases, A_{IP1} decreases.

Non Linearity Effects (IIP3). We will see next the effect of the power supply on the third order interception point. Considering Equation 40 for an input signal Vin = A cos(w_1t) + A cos(w_2t), we obtain

$$Vout = [\alpha_1 + \frac{9\alpha_3 A^2}{4}]Acos(w1(t)) + ...$$

$$+ \frac{3}{4}\alpha_3 A^3 cos(2w1 - w2) + \frac{3}{4}\alpha_3 A^3 cos(2w2 - w1). \tag{54}$$

Since α_1 is very large compared to $\frac{9\alpha_3 A^2}{4}$ [14], the input level for which the output components at w1 and w2 have the same amplitude as those at 2w1-w2 and 2w2-w1 is given by

$$\alpha_1 A_{IP3} = \frac{3\alpha_3 A^3}{4}. \tag{55}$$

Thus the input IP3 is:

$$A_{IP3} = \sqrt{\frac{4}{3}\frac{Gv}{\alpha_3}}. \tag{56}$$

Using now a similar development as for Equation 43 we obtain

$$A_{IP3} = \sqrt{\frac{16(Vgs - Vt)}{3\Theta}}. \tag{57}$$

As in the case of 1dB compression point, Equation (57) shows the proportionality between the power supply voltage and the third input intercept point.

Isolation Parameter (S12). As we mentioned above, the transistor M2 increases the isolation between the input and the output and as the isolation increases, S12 decreases. In this section we will show the dependency between the isolation and the power supply voltage. Using the Miller theory, the input-output impedance can be expressed as

$$Z = Z_{Miller}[1 - G(f)] \tag{58}$$

where Z is the impedance between the input and the output and G(f) is the gain at the defined frequency. At the resonant frequency the term 1-G(f) increases as the power supply increases. This increases the input-output impedance, improving the isolation, so S12 decreases.

Isolation Parameter (S22). S22 is the output port voltage reflection coefficient. The value of S22 decreases as the adaptation of output impedance approaches to 50 Ω. The output LNA impedance of the LNA is calculated by supposing a fictitious source voltage V_{fict} at the output that generated a fictitious current I_{fict} and then we calculate the output impedance as the ratio between V_{fict} and I_{fict}. Notice that when we calculate the output impedance, the input source voltage should be grounded and the current source should be opened in the small circuit analysis thus

$$Zout = Ld//Cd//Rd//rds1.rds2.gm2. \tag{59}$$

Since Rd is very small compared to rds1.rds2.gm2, we can deduce that, at the resonant frequency, the output impedance of the proposed architecture is mainly controlled by Rd which is independent from the power supply voltage.

5.4   LNA Performance Modes

The above analysis has been verified by simulation for the case-study LNA. Figure 9 shows transient-level simulations of the performance variation when the power supply is varied, for all performances except S22 (which does not vary significantly). These variations are in all cases monotonic.

For a typical application, gain and noise figure are the most important LNA performances to be controlled. S11 and S12 typically have maximum values that cannot be exceeded (e.g. $S11 < -10dB$ and $S12 < -40dB$). Similarly, IIP1 and IIP3 have minimum values that cannot be exceeded (e.g. $IIP1 > -20dBm$, $IIP3 > -10dBm$).

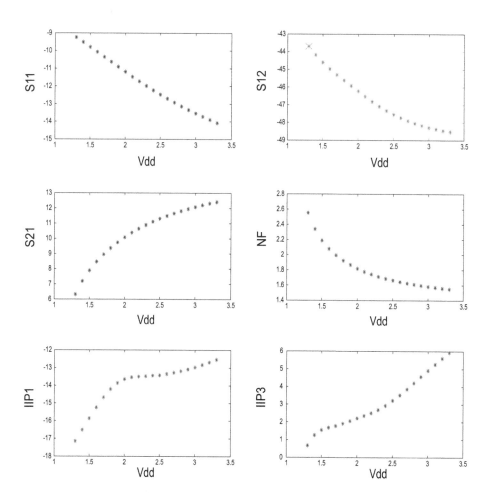

Fig. 9. LNA performances versus power supply

As an example, we define three different performances modes: a MAX mode of maximum power supply, a MIN mode of minimum power supply and an INT mode of intermediate power supply. In all modes, the above conditions for S11, S12, IIP1 and IIP3 must be respected. In MAX mode, $Gain > 11.5dB$ and $NF < 1.65dB$. In INT mode, $Gain > 10dB$ and $NF < 2dB$. Finally, in MIN mode, $Gain > 8dB$ and $NF < 2.2dB$.

The level of power supply required by each performance mode will be set by the controller. For later reference, Figure 10 shows the power consumption of the CUC as a function of the power supply voltage obtained by transistor-level simulation.

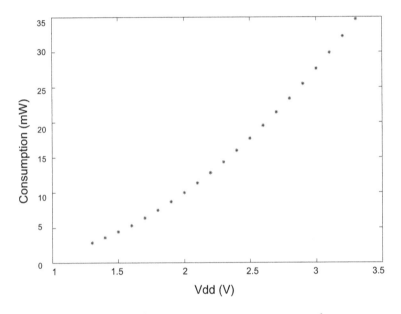

Fig. 10. LNA consumption versus power supply

6   Simulation Results

For building the behavioural and predictive models for the CUC of Figure 4, the CUC input stimulus is obtained by mixing a Gaussian signal with an average amplitude of 150 mV, sampled at 10 MHz, with a carrier signal at 2.4 GHz. As shown in Figure 11, 200 values of u(k) and y(k) are obtained for a simulation time of 10 us (the mixer and the ADC/DAC converters are considered ideal).

A Monte Carlo transistor-level simulation of the CUC, with N =1000, has been performed for three different levels of power supply: 3.3 V (maximum power supply voltage), 2.3 V and 1.3 V. For each level of power supply, the 200 values

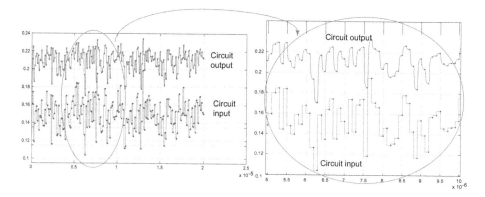

Fig. 11. Sampled input and ouput signal

of the input/output sequences of each circuit sample are used by the algorithm of Figure 2 to identify the model structure. In the three cases, the following model structure has been retained:

$$y(k) = \theta^0 + \theta^1 u(k) + \theta^2 u(k)^2 + \theta^3 u(k)^3. \tag{60}$$

This behavioural model gives a determination coefficient R^2 higher than 98% for all 3000 circuit samples. For example, the model identified for the 5-th circuit sample is given by

$$y_5(k) = -0.03 + 0.78 \ u(k) - 3.37 \ u(k)^2 + 6.76 \ u(k)^3. \tag{61}$$

Figure 12 compares the value predicted by the model and obtained by simulation of the circuit for 100 different time points. The predicted and the actual values are very close.

A prediction model is built using Branch and Bound algorithm for each performance. The prediction equations use only the parameters $\theta^0, \ldots, \theta^3$ of the behavioural model to predict the values of all CUC performances, as shown in Figure 13.

The simulation of the adaptive logical control strategy has been performed by considering the CUC at transistor-level and the controller modelled in Verilog A. The CUC is stimulated by the same stimulus described above. Initially, the CUC is set at the MAX mode, where the maximum power supply of 3.3 V is required. Next, we simulate the transition to a MIN mode, for which the performances are specified as indicated in Section 5.4.

Figure 14 shows the different iterations of the algorithm. Each iteration lasts 30 us, with the convergence time for the recursive parameter identification algorithm being somewhat smaller. This Figure also illustrates the convergence of the behavioural parameter θ^0, for different iterations. The choice of values for the variables in the recursive LMS algorithm is important, in particular θ^0, ρ and λ in Equations (11) and (12). The value of ρ must be as large as possible.

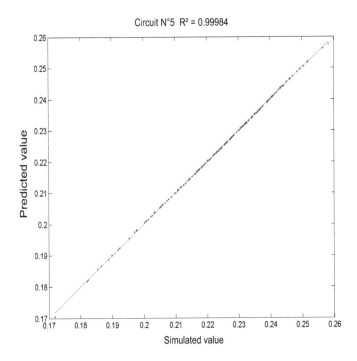

Fig. 12. Predicted and simulated output values of the CUC

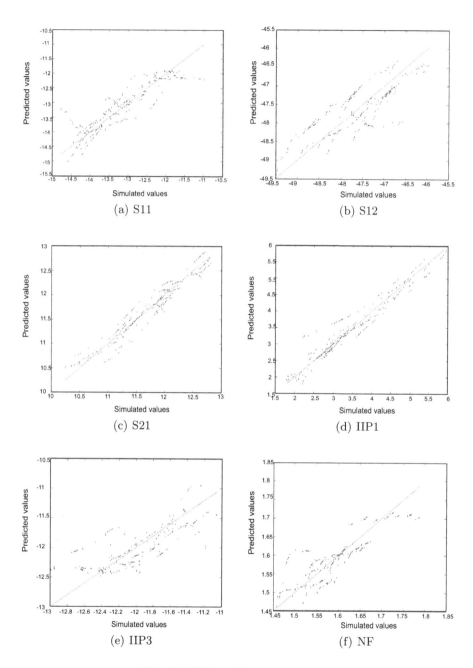

(a) S11

(b) S12

(c) S21

(d) IIP1

(e) IIP3

(f) NF

Fig. 13. LNA performances prediction

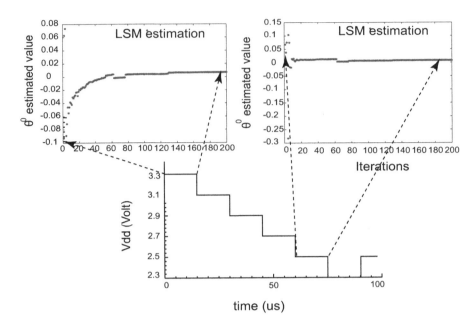

Fig. 14. Transistor-level simulation of the control strategy

Table 1. Performance prediction during logical control

Vdd (V)	Saved power(%)	Predicted/simulated values	NF ≤ 2.32	S11 ≤ −10	S12 ≤ −40	Gain ≥ 6.2	IIP1 ≥ −20	IIP3 ≥ −3
3.1V	-14	Prediction	1.70	-12.46	-43.65	10.41	-16.29	1.92
		Simulated value	1.57	-13.72	-48.37	12.20	-11.61	5.26
2.9V	-26	Prediction	1.74	-12.30	-43.23	10.06	-17.09	1.06
		Simulated value	1.59	-13.33	-48.17	11.95	-11.83	4.57
2.7V	-38	Prediction	1.99	-12.23	-42.99	8.97	-18.58	0.66
		Simulated value	1.62	-12.91	-47.90	11.65	-12.03	3.85
2.5V	-49	Prediction	2.25	-11.96	-42.88	7.86	-19.70	0.39
		Simulated value	1.66	-12.47	-47.54	11.31	-12.19	3.21
2.3V	-54	Prediction	2.39	-11.35	-42.90	7.16	-19.73	0.22
		Simulated value	1.71	-11.98	-47.08	10.89	-12.26	2.6902

The closer the value of λ to 1 the slower the convergence of the algorithm, but the variance of $\hat{\theta}$ after convergence is smaller, oscillating around the optimum value. If λ is closer to 0, the opposite behaviour is observed.

The circuit performances are estimated by the end of each iteration, once convergence has been achieved. Figure 14 shows that the control algorithm needs six iterations to reach a power supply voltage level of 2.3 V for which one of the specifications of the MIN mode is no longer respected. In the next iteration, the control stops with a power supply voltage level of 2.5 V, since the controller uses power supply voltage steps of 200 mV (this large value is used here to reduce simulation time). Table 1 illustrates the evolution of the performances predicted, and the reduction of power consumption at each level of power supply voltage (according to Figure 10). For example, the MIN mode with the power supply controlled at 2.5 V has a power consumption reduction of 54%.

7 Conclusion

This work has presented a new approach for reducing power consumption in RF devices based on adapting the power supply voltage by means of a logical control strategy. This strategy relies on embedded sensors, real-time parameter identification and performance prediction, and makes use of simple on-chip resources. Significant power savings have been demonstrated at the transistor-level for an RF LNA with different performance modes. The control algorithm can guarantee the required specifications for each performance mode, despite circuit parametric deviations due to the manufacturing process or ageing mechanisms. Current work is aimed at validating this approach in hardware.

Acknowledgements. This work has been carried out with partial support from the LSI Carnot Institute in Grenoble, France.

References

1. Sahu, B., Rincon-Mora, G.A.: A high-efficient linear RF power amplifier with a power-tracking dynamically adaptive buck-boost supply. IEEE Transactions on Microwave Theory and Techniques, 112–120 (January 2004)
2. Murmann, B.: A/D converter trends: power dissipation, scaling and digitally-assisted architectures. In: IEEE Custom Integrated Circuits Conference, pp. 105–112 (March 2008)
3. Chang, H.M., Chen, C.H., Lin, K.Y., Cheng, K.-T.: Calibration and testing time reduction techniques for a digitally-calibrated pipelined ADC. In: 27th IEEE VLSI Test Symposium, pp. 291–296 (May 2009)
4. Juillard, J., Colinet, E.: Initialization of the BIMBO self-test method using binary inputs and outputs. In: Proc. 46th IEEE International Conference on Decision and Control, New Orleans, USA, pp. 578–583 (December 2007)
5. Kenmington, P.B.: High Linearity RF Amplifier design. Artech House, Norwood (2000)
6. Khereddine, R., Simeu, E., Mir, S.: Parameter identification of RF transceiver blocks using regressive models. In: Programmable Devices and Embedded Systems (PDES 2009), Roznov, Czech Republic (February 2009)
7. Bernieri, A., D'Apuzzo, M., Sansone, L., Savastano, M.: A neural network approach for identification and fault diagnosis on dynamic systems. IEEE Transactions on Instrumentation and Measurement 43(6) (December 1994)
8. Devarakond, S., Natarajan, V., Banerjee, A., Choi, H., Sen, S., Chatterjee, A.: Digitally assisted concurrent built-in tuning of rf systems using hamming distance proportional signatures. In: European Test Symposium (2010)

9. Natarajan, V., Srinivasan, G., Chatterjee, A.: On-line error detection in wireless RF transmitters using real-time streaming data. In: 12th IEEE International On-line Testing Symposium (2006)

10. Senguttuvan, R., Natarajan, V., Chatterjee, A.: Built-in test enabled diagnosis and tuning of RF transmitter systems. In: IEEE International Mixed-Signals Sensors and Systems Test Workshop, pp. 80–86 (2007)

11. Abdallah, L., Stratigopoulos, H., Kelma, C., Mir, S.: Sensors for builtin alternate RF test. In: 15th IEEE European Test Symposium, pp. 49–54 (May 2010)

12. Valdes-Garcia, A., Venkatasubramanian, R., Silva-Martinez, J., Sanchez- Sinencio, E.: A broadband CMOS amplitude detector for on-chip RF measurements. IEEE Trans. on Instrumentation and Measurement 57(7), 1470–1477 (2008)

13. Hsieh, H.H., Lu, L.H.: Integrated CMOS power sensors for RF BIST applications. In: Proc. VLSI Test Symposium, pp. 234–239 (2006)

14. Lee, T.H.: The design of CMOS radio-frequency integrated circuits. Cambridge University Press (2004)

15. Khereddine, R.: Méthode de contrôle logique et de test des circuits AMS/RF, PhD thesis, Grenoble université (September 2011)

A 1.8-V 3.6-mW 2.4-GHz Fully Integrated CMOS Frequency Synthesizer for the IEEE 802.15.4

Manthena Vamshi Krishna[1], Xuan Jie[1], Anh Manh Do[1], Chirn Chye Boon[1], Kiat Seng Yeo[1], and Aaron V.T. Do[2]

[1] Nanyang Technological University, Singapore 639798
{mkvamshi,xiej0005,emado,eccboon,eksyeo}@ntu.edu.sg
[2] Marvell Asia Pte. Ltd., Singapore 534158
doaaron@marvell.com

Abstract. This paper presents a low power 2.4-GHz fully integrated 1 MHz resolution IEEE 802.15.4 frequency synthesizer designed using 0.18um CMOS technology. An integer-N fully programmable divider employs a novel True-single-phase-clock (TSPC) 47/48 prescaler and a 6 bit P and S counters to provide the 1 MHz output with nearly 45% duty cycle. The PLL uses a series quadrature voltage controlled oscillator (S-QVCO) to generate quadrature signals. The PLL consumes 3.6 mW of power at 1.8 V supply with the fully programmable divider consuming only 600 uW. The S-QVCO consumes 2.8 mW of power with a phase noise of -122dBc/Hz at 1 MHz offset.

Keywords: D flip-flop (DFF), Frequency synthesizer, Phase-locked loop (PLL), Voltage controlled oscillator (VCO), Dual-modulus prescaler.

1   Introduction

Most of the wireless communication standards prior to IEEE 802.15.4/Zigbee were tailored towards high data rate and multimedia friendly applications. The need for low data rate and low power wireless solutions with emphasis on sensor network applications resulted in the development of IEEE 802.15.4 standard. The recent development and advanced scaling CMOS technologies have made it more attractive to implement a single chip CMOS wireless transceiver featuring both high level of integration and low power consumption [1].

The higher power consumption in the frequency synthesizer is mainly due to the VCO and the first stage divider which is driven by the VCO. The 2.4 GHz synthesizer reported in [2] with a frequency resolution of 5 MHz consumes a power of 7.85 mW at 1.8 V power supply in 0.18 um CMOS technology. Here, the first stage divider is designed using current-mode logic (CML) [6] which consumes a large amount of power. The synthesizer reported in [3] consumes 2.4 mW at 1.2 V supply in 0.13 um CMOS technology. It uses a 16/17 dynamic logic prescaler as first stage divider which consumes only 176 uA at 2.5 GHz and the complete divider is designed with 5

J.L. Ayala, D. Atienza, and R. Reis (Eds.): VLSI-SoC 2010, IFIP AICT 373, pp. 69–99, 2012.

MHz resolution. Here, the VCO provides only differential phase signals. The frequency synthesizer reported in [4] proposes a new spur suppression technique, but consumes a power of 18 mW. Reference [5] provides a synthesizer for IEEE 802.15.4/Zigbee applications consumes a power of 15 mW in 0.18 um CMOS technology. For the popular transceiver's architecture shown in Fig.1 with direct up-conversion for the TX and low IF down-conversion, the synthesizer needs to generate LO outputs having both I-Q outputs. In this article, an integer-N, low power 2.4 GHz frequency synthesizer with quadrature signal generation is proposed. In this design, the fully programmable 1 MHz resolution divider is implemented using dynamic logic circuits.

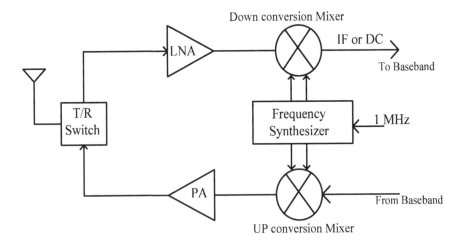

Fig. 1. Transceiver architecture

2   System Specification

2.1   Frequency Synthesis

The IEEE 802.15.4 standard has 16 channels, spaced at 5 MHz apart over the frequency range from 2405 MHz to 2480 MHz. The synthesizer needs to synthesize 16 channel selection frequencies with 40-ppm frequency accuracy. If direct conversion is used in both the transmitter and receiver, then the 16 channel selection frequencies would be from 2405 MHz to 2480 MHz in steps of 5 MHz. If a low IF architecture is used for the RX, then the local oscillator frequencies could be different from the channel frequencies for both the transmitter and receiver. In order to have more flexibility to accommodate channel selections for both kind of architecture, the resolution of the divider and reference frequency chosen is 1 MHz which gives a resolution of 1 MHz to the channel selection frequency. For example, if the IF frequency is chosen to be 2 MHz, the divider is programmed to have the local oscillator frequencies equal to 2403, 2408....2478 MHz or 2407, 2412....2482 MHz. For the IEEE 802.15.4 standard, the channel bandwidth is 2 MHz.

2.2   Phase Noise

According to [7], the required phase noise at a frequency offset determined by the frequency offset of P_{int} can be calculated by,

$$PN\left(dBc/Hz\right) = (P_{sig} - P_{int}) - SNR_{req} - 10\log\left(BW\right) \tag{1}$$

The system simulations in [8] shows that SNR_{out} should be at least 14 dB. Based on this value, from (1) the required phase noise at 5 MHz offset and 10 MHz offset would be -77dBc/Hz, and -107dBc/Hz respectively. Assuming a margin of 10 dB due to non-idealities of the system, the required phase noise at 5 MHz offset and 10 MHz offset is -87dBc/Hz and -117dBc/Hz respectively.

2.3   Spur Rejection

The IEEE 802.15.4 standard specifies the adjacent channel interference of +0 dB (relative to the carrier) at an offset of 5 MHz. The spur suppression requirement for the synthesizer can be calculated by [5]

$$PN\left(dBc/Hz\right) = (P_{sig} - P_{int}) - SNR_{req} - 10\log\left(BW\right) \tag{2}$$

For the IEEE 802.15.4 standard, the required spur suppression is -14 dBc at 5 MHz offset, and -44 dBc at 10 MHz offset.

2.4   Settling Time

The IEEE 802.15.4 supports a data rate of 250 Kbps with each symbol consisting of 4-bits and a symbol rate of 62.5 Ksymbols/sec. The maximum Tx-Rx turn-around time is 12 symbol periods, which is equivalent to 192 us. Thus the worst case settling time of the synthesizer is estimated to be 192 us.

The synthesizer is designed to meet all the above specifications with a supply voltage of 1.8 V and low power consumption with on-chip filter in RF CMOS 01.8um technology.

3   Architecture of the Implemented Frequency Synthesizer

The synthesizer is designed to generate quadrature differential output signals of 1 MHz resolution over the 2.4 GHz ISM band. The architecture of the frequency synthesizer is chosen to be a type-2, fourth order loop using a charge pump as shown in Fig.2. The synthesizer consists of a phase-frequency detector (PFD), a charge pump (CP), a series Q-VCO, a 3rd order loop filter and a fully programmable 1 MHz resolution divider.

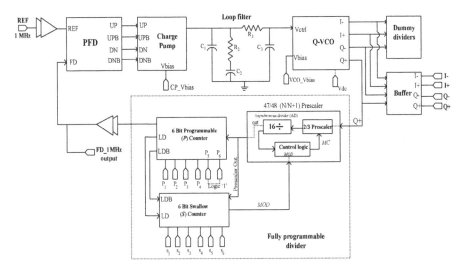

Fig. 2. System Level architecture of the implemented 2.4 GHz frequency synthesizer

Compared to lower order loop, the additional poles provide higher spurious filtering, thus reducing the spurs generated by the input reference without decreasing the loop bandwidth or increasing the settling time. Since the divider is based on dynamic logic circuits whose input is single-phase, only one of the outputs of the quad-phase VCO is applied to the divider while the remaining 3 outputs of the VCO are connected to the dummy divider loads. Based on the optimization of the loop parameters, the loop bandwidth is chosen to at 45 KHz as described in section 6.

4   Fully Programmable 1 MHz Resolution Divider

The fully programmable 1 MHz resolution divider used in this design is based on the pulse-swallow topology shown in Fig.3. The pulse-swallow frequency divider consists of a dual-modulus prescaler (DMP), a programmable (P) counter and a swallow (S) counter. The dual-modulus prescaler is based on both synchronous and asynchronous divider which scales the input frequency to a lower frequency to ease the complexity of asynchronous presettable modulo-P and modulo-S counters. In this technique, S input pulses are swallowed in the preceding arrangement such that the output period becomes longer by S reference periods.

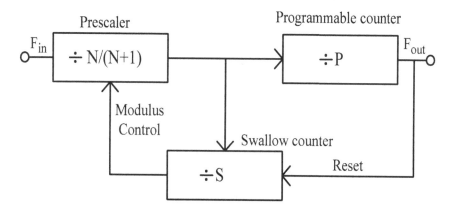

Fig. 3. Pulse-swallow frequency divider

In the initial state, the modulus control (*MC*) signal remains at logic '0' and allows the DMP to operate in the divide-by-(N+1) mode and the programmable P-counter and swallow S counter are loaded to their initial states. Since P>S, the S-counter reaches the final state earlier than P-counter and the end-of-count logic of the S-counter changes the *MC* to logic '1' allowing the DMP to switch to divide-by-N mode where the P-counter counts the remaining (P-S) input periods of 'N'. Thus the total division ratio is given by

$$F_{out} = ((N+1)S + N(P-S))F_{in} = (NP+S)F_{in} \qquad (3)$$

In this design, the fully programmable divider is constructed using a TSPC [9] 47/48 (N/N+1) dual-modulus prescaler, a 6-bit programmable P-counter and a 6-bit swallow S-counter.

4.1   A TSPC 47/48 Dual-Modulus Prescaler

The proposed 47/48 prescaler circuit as shown in Fig.4 is similar to the 32/33 prescaler reported in [10] except for an additional inverter which is added between the output of the NAND2 gate and the control signal (*MC*) input of the 2/3 prescaler. The 47/48 prescaler consists of 2/3 prescaler [10], four asynchronous divide-by-2 circuits and additional logic gates to control the division ratio between 47 and 48. When *MC*='0', the 2/3 prescaler of the 32/33 prescaler in [10] operates in divide-by-3 mode whereas the 2/3 prescaler in the proposed 47/48 prescaler operates in divide-by-2 mode. Thus the inverter swaps the operation modes of the 2/3 prescaler.

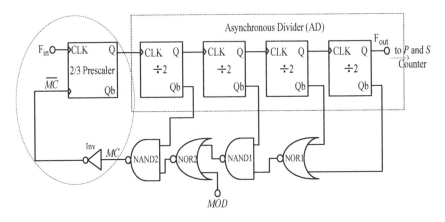

Fig. 4. Proposed TSPC 47/48 prescaler

Divide-by-48 operation (MOD='1'): When the control signal MOD is '1', the output of NOR2 in Fig.4 always remains at logic '0' and forces the output of NAND2 to logic '1' irrespective of data on Q_{b1}. Since MC is always equal to logic '1' ($\overline{MC}$ ='0'), the 2/3 prescaler remains in divide-by-3 mode. The equivalent circuit of inverter and the 2/3 prescaler is equal to divide-by-3 counter as shown in Fig.5. Thus the 47/48 prescaler operates in divide-by-48 mode when MOD='1'. Fig.6 shows the transient simulations of divide-by-48 mode of operation. If we denote the synchronous 2/3 prescaler as M/M+1 and the four asynchronous dividers whose division ratio equal to 16 by 'AD', the division ratio of the 47/48 prescaler in this mode (MOD='1') is given by

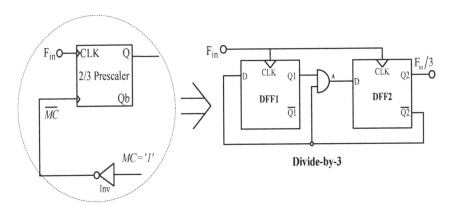

Fig. 5. Divide-by-48 mode of operation

$$F_{48} = (AD - \overline{MOD}) \times (M+1) + \overline{MOD} \times M = (16-0) \times (2+1) + 0 \times 2 = 48 \qquad (4)$$

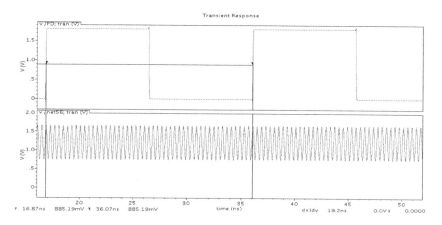

Fig. 6. Transient simulations of divide-by-48 mode of operation

Divide-by-47 operation (*MOD*='0'): The proposed 47/48 prescaler operates as divide-by-47 when *MOD*='0'. By using the combination of logic NOR and NAND gates, the asynchronous divide-by-16 counter is made to count an extra input clock. In the initial state, the 2/3 prescaler will be in divide-by-3 mode (*MC*='1') and the asynchronous divide-by16 starts counting the output pulses of 2/3 prescaler from "0000" to "1111". When the asynchronous counter value reaches "1110", the logic signal MC goes low (*MC*='0') and 2/3 prescaler operates in divide-by-2 mode, where the asynchronous counter counts an extra input clock pulse. During this operation, the 2/3 prescaler operates in the divide-by-3 mode for 45 input clock cycles and in the divide-2 mode for 2 input clock cycles. The division ratio of the 47/48 prescaler in this mode is given by

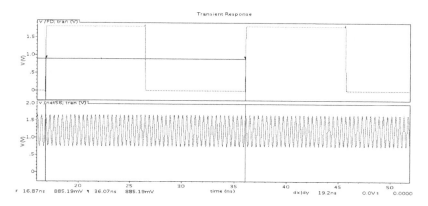

Fig. 7. Transient simulations of divide-by-47 mode of operation

The transient simulation of divide-by-47 mode of operation is shown in Fig.7. The Post layout simulation results shows that the proposed dual modulus 47/48 prescaler consumes a current of 269.3 uA and 262.8 uA during the divide-by-47 and divide-by-48 modes respectively and the maximum operating frequency is 4.8 GHz.

4.2   A Low Power TSPC 2/3 Prescaler [10]

Fig.8 shows the ultra-low power TSPC 2/3 prescaler reported in [10]. In this design, an extra PMOS transistor M_{1a} is connected between the power supply and DFF1 whose input is the controlled by the logic signal *MC*. As discussed in the section 3.6.1, during the divide-by-2 operation, one of the input logic signals MC. During the divide-by-2 operation, one of the inputs of second NOR gate is always zero since transistor M_{10} blocks the data at the input of DFF1 to propagate to the output node.

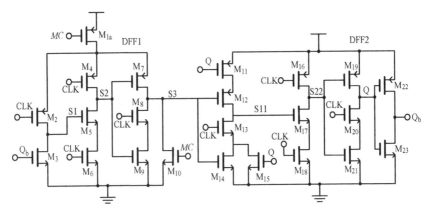

Fig. 8. Ultra-low power TSPC 2/3 prescaler [10]

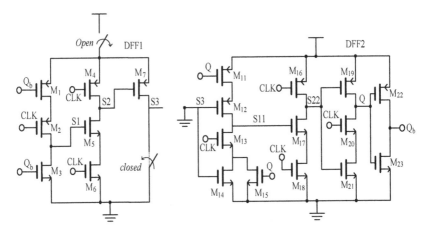

Fig. 9. Divide-by-2 operation of the ultra-low power TSPC 2/3 prescaler [10]

In this design, when the control logic signal *MC* is '1' during the divide-by-2 mode, the PMOS transistor M_{1a} is turned-off and DFF1 is disconnected from the power supply. Fig.9 shows the simplified schematic of the 2/3 prescaler in the divide-by-2 mode of operation. Even though M_{10} is always turned-on, the source of M_7 is at virtual ground and short-circuit power is completely avoided. Even if the output 'Q_b' switches continuously, the nodes S1 and S2 and S3 always remain at logic '0' and thus the switching activities are blocked in DFF1 resulting in zero switching power.

The ultra-low power 2/3 prescaler is fabricated using the chartered 1P6M 0.18 um CMOS process and the PMOS and NMOS transistor sizes are fixed to 3 um/0.18 um, 2 um/0.18 um respectively. On-wafer measurements are carried out using an 8 inch RF probe station. The input signal for the measurement is provided by the 83650B 10 MHZ-50 GHz HP signal generator and the output signals are captured by the Lecroy Wave master 8600A 6G oscilloscope.

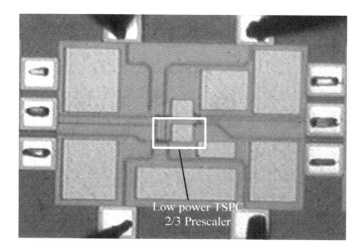

Fig. 10. Die photograph of the ultra-low power TSPC 2/3 prescaler

Fig.10 shows the die photograph of ultra-low power TSPC 2/3 prescaler fabricated in Global foundries 0.18um CMOS technology. The measured maximum operating frequency of 2/3 prescaler is 4.9 GHz. The power consumption of the 2/3 prescaler during the divide-by-2 and divide-by-3 modes is 0.6 mW, 0.922 mW respectively, when the input frequency is 4.8 GHz. Fig.11 shows the measured output waveforms of the 2/3 prescaler at 4.8 GHz during the divide-by-2 and divide-by-3 modes of operation.

4.3   Programmable P-Counter

The 6 bit programmable P-counter used in the design of fully programmable divider is shown in Fig. 12. It consists of proposed 6 asynchronous reloadable bit-cells [11], a NOR-embedded DFF [12] and an end-of-count (EOC) detector with reload circuit.

Here, bit P_6 and P_5 are always at logic '1' and bit P_4 at logic '0' to have a programmable values of 51 and 52. By choosing a fixed value of 51 and 52, the swallow S-counter is programmed in steps of one-bit to provide a division ratio from 2400 to 2484 with 1 MHz resolution.

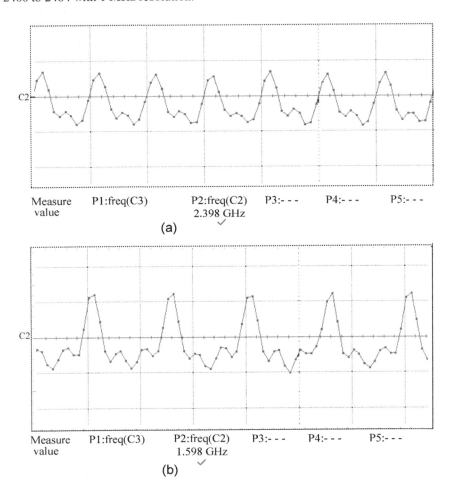

Fig. 11. Measured waveforms of the proposed prescaler at 4.8 GHz (a) divide-by-2 mode, (b) divide-by-3 mode

In this design, the state $Q_6Q_5Q_4Q_3Q_2Q_1$="000010" is detected by the EOC logic circuit. As soon as the state "0000010" is reached, the signals A and B go low after a delay introduced by the logic gates which is assumed to be less than half of the input clock cycle. However, the output of the embedded-NOR gate is latched to output only at the next rising edge of clock after the state "0000001" is reached. This output "LD" signal will initialize the P and S counters and the counting process continues. If the state "0000001" is chosen to detect, then it results in the undercounting due to the delays.

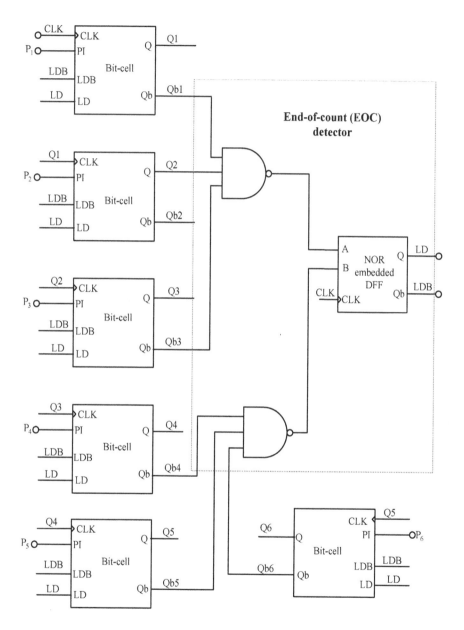

Fig. 12. A 6-bit Programmable P-counter with EOC logic circuit

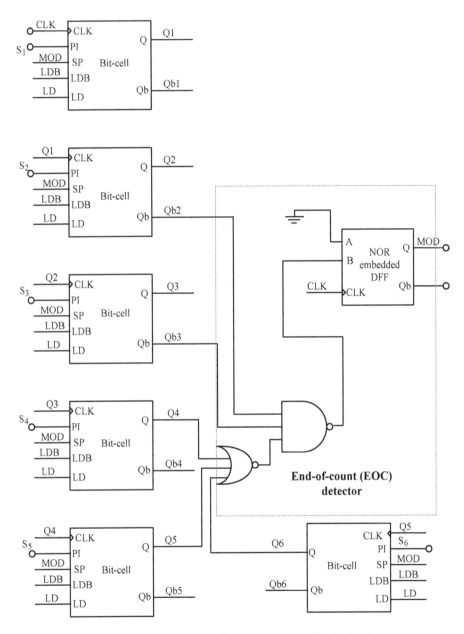

Fig. 13. A 6-bit Swallow S-counter with EOC logic circuit

4.4   Swallow S-Counter

The 6 bit swallow S-counter used in the fully programmable divider is shown in Fig. 13. It consists of proposed 6 asynchronous reloadable bit-cells, a NOR-embedded DFF [12] and an end-of-count (EOC) detector with reload circuit. Here the state $Q_6Q_5Q_4Q_3Q_2$="000000" is detected by the EOC logic circuit. The S-counter in this programmable divider can be programmed from 0-47 in steps of 1 for a fixed value of the P-counter.

Since the counter is asynchronous and based on the ring topology, the complementary output of the first DFF is fed as the clock signal to the input of next flip-flop. In the initial state, all the reloadable FF's are loaded by the programmable value set by pins S_1-S_6. In the S-counter all states from 0-47 are usable and adjustable in steps of 1 to obtain a resolution of 1MHz. Once the counter is triggered by the output of the prescaler, the S-counter starts down counting till the final state is reached, which is detected by the EOC logic circuit and the MOD signal goes high until the P-counter finishes its counting. Since the value of 'P' is always greater than value of 'S' in pulse-swallow divider, the S-counter remains idle for a period of (P-S)*N clock cycles.

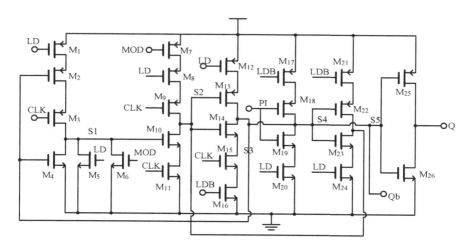

Fig. 14. Reloadable TSPC DFF for S-counter

The signal MOD goes high only when the outputs of all the reloadable DFF in the S-counter go low and remain in the same state until the LD signal from the P-counter goes high. The state where MOD remains at logic high indicate the S-counter has finished counting. The S-counter cannot use the EOC logic circuit of the P-counter since MOD has to remain high until the P-counter reaches the state "0000010" when the LD signal goes high for one clock cycle. Moreover in the S-counter, all zero state is detected by EOC circuit unlike in the P-counter.

Fig.14 shows the schematic of an improved reloadable TSPC DFF used in the design of 6-bit S-counter. This reload DFF is similar to the reloadable DFF used in the design of P-counter [11]. However, the reloadable DFF for the S-counter needs an extra logic function MOD to be incorporated. When MOD goes high, the S-counter remains idle for a period of N*(P-S) clock cycles and the reloadable DFF of the S-counter consumes some switching power. In the improved design, transistors M_6 and M_7 are added to reduce the switching activities in the reloadable DFF. When the state "0000" is reached, MOD goes high, M_6 is turned-on and M_7 is turned-off such that node S1 and S2 remain at logic '0' for the remaining N*(P-S) clock cycles until LD becomes high. During this period, since LD='0', the right hand side portion of the circuit is de-activated similar to the reloadable DFF reported in [11]. Thus there is no switching activity at any node during the idle state of the S-counter and switching power is saved for a period of N*(P-S) clock cycles.

Table 1. Operation of the Reloadable DFF of the S-counter

MOD	Load (LD)	Programmable Input (PI)	Output (Q)
1	X	X	1
0	0	0	CLK/2
0	0	1	CLK/2
0	1	0	0
0	1	1	1

In other conditions, the operation of the improved reloadable DFF for S-counter is similar to the operation of the reloadable DFF used for the P-counter described in previous section. Table 1 shows the operation of reloadable DFF used in the S-counter. In this design, the P-counter is programmable from 51 to 52 (P_1 and P_2 are only programmable) and the S-counter is programmable from 0 to 47 (S_1 to S_6) in steps of 1 to accommodate division ratios from 2400 to 2484. The frequency division (FD) performed by the programmable divider is given by,

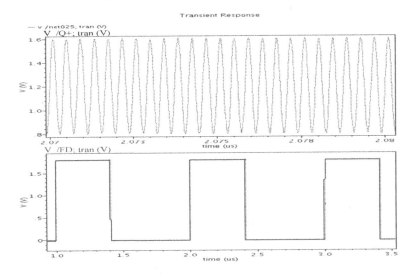

Fig. 15. Post layout results of the fully programmable divider with 2400 division ratio

$$FD = N \times S + ((N+1) \times (P-S)) = ((N+1) \times P) - S \qquad (5)$$

The fully programmable divider at 2.4 GHz consumes a power of 0.6 mW. Fig. 15 shows the post layout results of the fully programmable divider at 2.4 GHz with 1 MHz output signal of the divider having nearly 45% duty cycle. The P and S counter's programmable value for the division ratios between 2400-2484 is shown in Table 2.

Table 2. Programmable values of the programmable counters

Frequency division ratio	Prescaler (N/N+1)	Programmable-counter (P)	Swallow counter (S)
2400-2448	N=47	P=51	S=0-47
2449-2484	N=47	P=52	S=14-47

5   Quadrature Voltage-Controlled Oscillator (QVCO)

The VCO implemented in this design is a series quadrature VCO (S-QVCO) and its schematic is shown in Fig.16. The S-QVCO has been proven to eliminate the trade-off

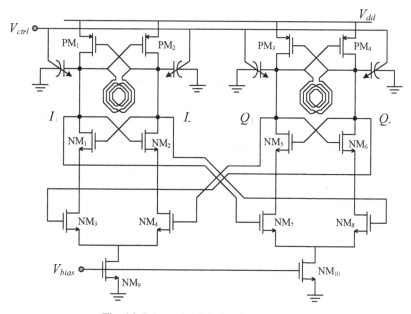

Fig. 16. Schematic of the implemented Q-VCO

between phase noise and I/Q mismatch [13]. Therefore, the design can be optimized for phase noise performance, while keeping I/Q mismatch low. Compare to the parallel QVCO, the coupling transistors NM_3-NM_4 and NM_7-NM_8 are in series with the switching transistors NM_1-NM_2 and NM_5-NM_6. Hence the tail current for the coupling transistor is removed and the S-QVCO consumes less power.

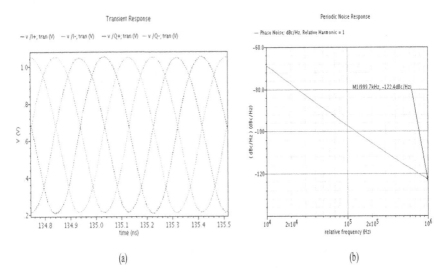

(a)   (b)

Fig. 17. a) Quadrature signals of S-QVCO **b)** Phase noise

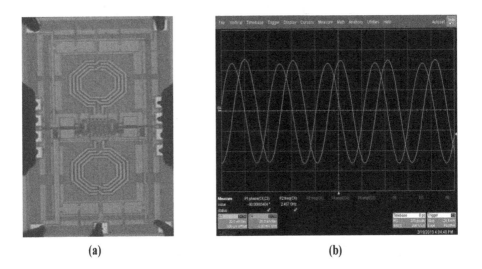

(a)   **(b)**

Fig. 18. a) die photograph of S-QVCO b) I/Q signal

The current –reuse technique is used to further reduce the current consumption of the S-QVCO by adding cross-coupled PMOS transistors on top of the cross-coupled NMOS transistors. Open-drain transistors are added to the output nodes of the S-QVCO to serve as the buffer to the testing equipment. The gain of the S-QVCO from post layout results is 280 MHz/V and Fig. 17 shows the quadrature output signals and phase noise of the S-QVCO. The S-QVCO has phase noise of -122.4dBc/Hz at 1 MHz. The 2/3 prescaler is directly driven by the S-QVCO and it requires input signal with smaller amplitude for low power consumption. Thus S-QVCO bias current can be reduced to provide smaller amplitude which in turn reduces the power consumption of S-QVCO.

The measured phase noise is -122dBc/Hz at 1 MHz offset as shown in Fig.19 and the output signal amplitude is around 300 mV. The total power consumption of the S-QVCO is 2.7 mW at 1.8 V power supply. A widely used figure of merit (FOM) for the VCO is defined as [14]

$$FOM = L\{f_{offset}\} - 20\log(\frac{f_o}{f_{offset}}) + 20\log(\frac{P_{DC}}{1mW}) \qquad (6)$$

Where $L\{f_{offset}\}$ is the measured phase-noise at offset frequency f_{offset} from the carrier frequency f_o. P_{DC} is VCO power consumption in mW. Table 3 summarizes the performance of the S-QVCO.

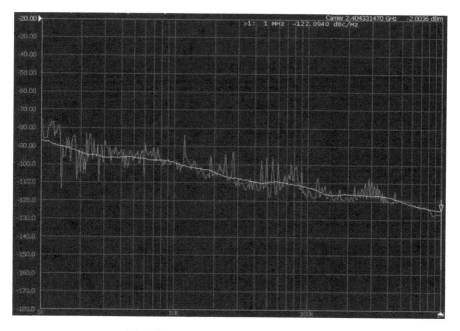

Fig. 19. Measured phase noise of the S-QVCO

Table 3. Performance of S-QVCO

Parameters	This Design
Power supply	1.8V
Technology	RF CMOS 0.18um
Frequency	2.2 -2.7 GHz
Tuning range	20.4%
VCO gain (KVCO)	414 MHz/V
Phase Noise	-122 dBc/Hz @ 1 MHz offset
Output amplitude	300 mV
I/Q phase difference	90.2°
Power consumption	2.88 mW
FOM	--177.4

6   Phase Frequency Detector (PFD) and Charge Pump (CP)

The PFD used in this design is a conventional NAND based circuit [15] as shown in Fig.20 which consists of two TSPC DFF registers, a AND gate. A certain amount of delay is introduced after the AND gate before resetting the DFF to keep the pulse width of UP and DN signals finite so as to eliminate the problem caused by dead zone. The half-transparent DFF reported in [12] is implemented as the DFF register in this design. The dead-zone removal pulse is of 11ns, which is sufficient to turn-on UP and DN switches of the charge pump during the locked condition.

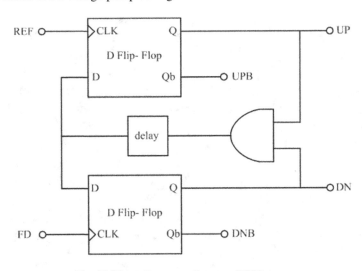

Fig. 20. Phase frequency detector (PFD)

The schematic of the charge pump used in the design of PLL synthesizer is shown in Fig.21. The charge pump circuit consists of two input differential pairs M_1-M_2 and M_3-M_4 which act as the switches, two current sources M_5 and M_6 supply stable current to the differential switches, a pump-up sub circuit formed by M_7 and M_{12} outputs the charge current I_{charge} and a pump-down sub-circuit formed by M_8, M_9, M_{10} and M_{11} which helps to discharge the current $I_{discharge}$.

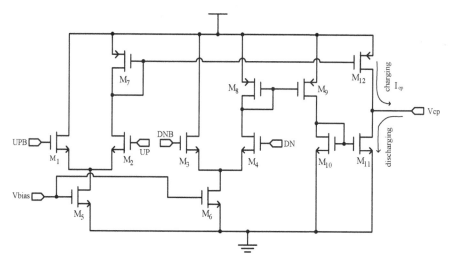

Fig. 21. Implemented Charge pump

Case-I: UP='1' and DN='0'. When the UP signal is high (UP='1') and the DN signal is low (DN='0'), M_4 is turned-off, M_2 is turned-on which switches on the pump-up sub-circuit. Hence the charging current I_{charge} flows through M_{12} charging up the loop filter. Since M_4 is turned-off, the pump-down sub-circuit is turned-off and no discharge current $I_{discharge}$ current flows in M_{11}.

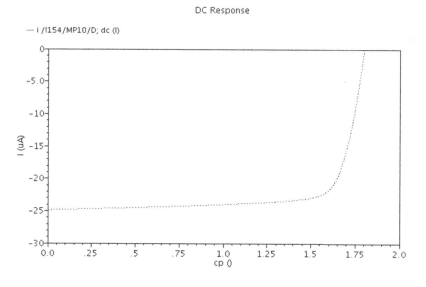

Fig. 22. Charging current from charge pump when UP is high and DN is low

Case-II: UP='0' and DN='1'. When the UP signal is low (UP='0') and the DN signal is high (DN='1'), M_2 is turned-off, M_4 is turned-on which switches on the pump-down sub-circuit. Hence the discharging current $I_{discharge}$ flows through M_{11} to the ground discharging the loop filter. Since M_2 is turned-off, the pump-up sub-circuit is turned-off and no charge current I_{charge} current flows in M_{12}. Fig.22 and Fig.23 shows the simulated DC simulations of UP and DN currents of the charge pump.

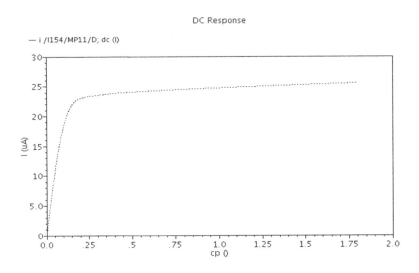

Fig. 23. Discharging current from charge pump when UP is low and DN is high

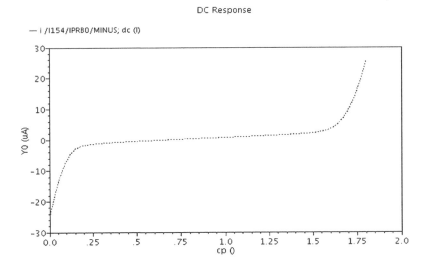

Fig. 24. Mismatch current from charge pump when UP and DN are high

Case-III: UP='1' and DN='1'. When both the UP and DN signals are driven high (UP='1' and DN='1'), both M_4 and M_2 are turned-on and switch on both the pump-up and pump-down sub-circuits allowing the currents to steer through M_{11} and M_{12}. If both charging (I_{charge}) and discharging ($I_{discharge}$) currents are equal, the charge stored on the loop filter remains same and doesn't affect the control voltage at the input of VCO. However, there exists a mismatch between charging and discharging current due to the mismatch of devices M_{11} and M_{12}, and a net current of (I_{charge} -$I_{discharge}$) leaks in to the loop filter and alters the control voltage.

In this design, both the differential switches M_1-M_2 and M_3-M_4 are implemented by NMOS transistors to avoid the switching mismatches. To have precise matching in the charging and discharging currents, the length of the output stage transistors are kept high to increase the output impedance. Here the charge pump current chosen is 25 uA. Fig.24 shows the mismatch between the UP and down currents and the average mismatch current is around 1.4 uA.

7   Loop Filter Design

The loop filter used in this design is 3rd order as shown in Fig. 25. The loop filter parameters are imposed by the system level performance specifications such as settling time, phase noise and spur suppression. Initially a 2nd order filter is designed and later a RC low-pass section is added to improve the spurs and reduce the ripples on control voltage. The reference frequency used in this design is 1 MHz. The 2nd order filter is assumed to be a critically damped system ($\xi = 1$) with a loop bandwidth (f_c) of 45 KHz to satisfy the Gardner's stability criterion [16]. For an optimal stability, for a passive second order filter, the relation between unity gain cross-over frequency (ω_c) and natural frequency (ω_n) is given by [17]

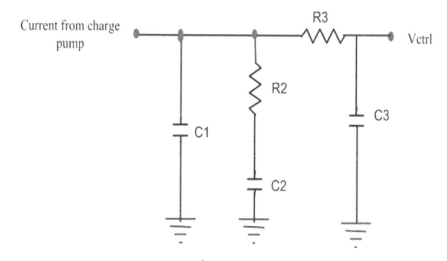

Fig. 25. 3rd order loop filter

$$\omega_c = 2\xi\omega_n \tag{7}$$

Since the damping factor is equal to unity, the natural frequency (f_n) is found to be 22.5 KHz. For a charge pump PLL with 2nd order loop filter and damping factor $\xi = 1$, the relation between zero frequency (f_{z1}) and cross-over frequency (f_c) is given by [5]

$$4 = \frac{(K_{vco}I_{cp}R_2) \times (C_2 R_2)}{2\pi N} = \frac{f_c}{f_{z1}} \tag{8}$$

Similarly, the relation between pole frequency (f_{p1}) and cross-over frequency (f_c) is given by

$$4 = \frac{(K_{vco}I_{cp}R_2) \times (C_2 R_2)}{2\pi N} = 2\pi f_c (16 \times C_1 R_2) = \frac{16 \times f_c}{f_{p1}} \Rightarrow f_{p1} = 4 f_c \tag{9}$$

Based on **(9)** and **(10)**, the zero frequency and pole frequency are 11.25 KHz and 180 KHz respectively. The phase margin is given as

$$\phi = \tan^{-1}(\frac{f_c}{f_{z1}}) - \tan^{-1}(\frac{f_{p1}}{f_c}) = \tan^{-1}(4) - \tan^{-1}(\frac{1}{4}) = 61.92^0 \tag{10}$$

With a charge pump current of 25 uA (I_{cp}), VCO gain (K_{vco}) of 414MHz/V and division ratio (N) of 2450, the values of R_2, C_2 and C_1 are calculated as,

$$C_2 = \frac{I_{cp} \times K_{vco}}{2\pi \times N \times (2\pi f_n)^2} = 207\, pF \tag{11}$$

$$R_2 = \frac{1}{2\pi \times f_{z1} \times C_2} = 78.5 k\Omega \tag{12}$$

$$C_1 = \frac{C_2}{16} = 12.9\, pF \tag{13}$$

The open loop PLL with a 2nd order loop filter is simulated in Matlab and Fig.26 shows the root locus plot of the open loop PLL. Fig.27 shows the simulated Bode diagram of the open loop PLL where the phase margin is around 62. Fig.28 shows the open loop gain and phase margin

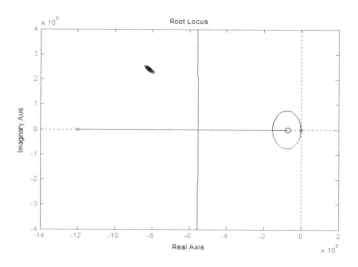

Fig. 26. Root locus of open loop PLL with 2nd order filter

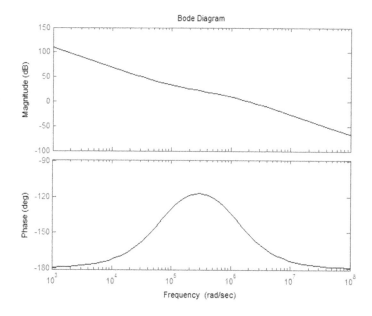

Fig. 27. Bode plot with 2nd order filter

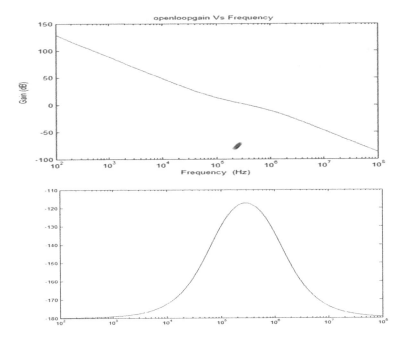

Fig. 28. Open loop response of PLL

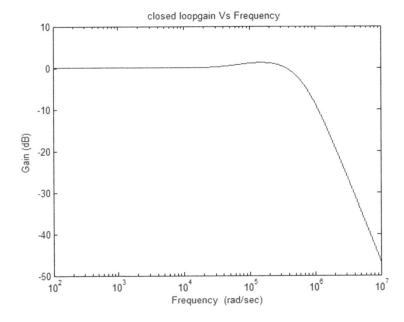

Fig. 29. Closed loop gain of PLL

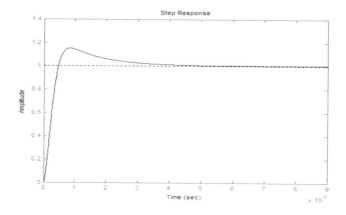

Fig. 30. Step response of the closed loop PLL

Fig. 29 and Fig.30 shows the closed loop gain and step response of the PLL. An additional RC low pass section is added to reduce the amount of reference spurs at the cost of reduced phase margin and increased settling time. The additional RC low pass section is added to the 2nd order filter such that the phase margin won't reduce to lesser value than 55 degrees. With additional RC section, damping factor reduces to slightly less than 1. The value of R_3 and C_3 are found to be 98.9 Kohms and 3.75 pF respectively. With frequency accuracy of 40 ppm, the calculated settling time is $48\,\mu$ s, which is nearly four times less than the required settling time for IEEE 802.15.4 standard (192 μ s).

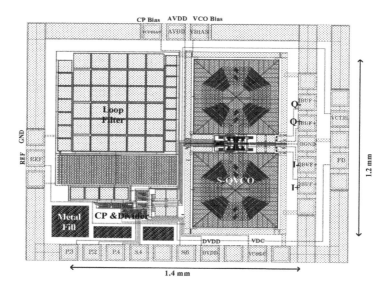

Fig. 31. Layout of 2.4 GHz frequency synthesizer with testing pads

The layout of the fully programmable 2.4 GHz synthesizer with on-chip 3rd order loop filter and testing pads is shown in Fig. 31. The synthesizer occupies an area of $1.4*1.2\ mm^2$ with testing pads and the core area is $0.95*0.9\ mm^2$. The simulations are performed using Cadence SPECTRE RF for a 0.18um CMOS process. The settling time for the synthesizer is around $58\ \mu$ s which is 4 times lesser than the value required by IEEE 802.15.4 standard.

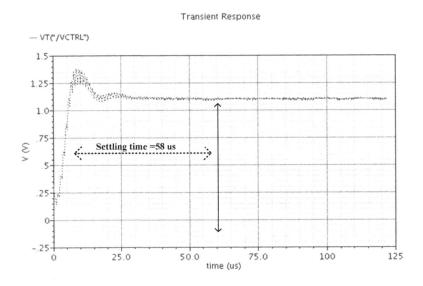

Fig. 32. Settling behavior of the implemented frequency synthesizer

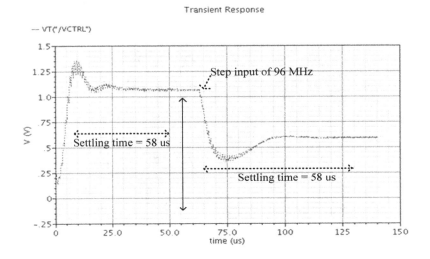

Fig. 33. Settling behavior of synthesizer with change of N from 2400 to 2496

Fig.32 shows the settling behavior of the synthesizer for fixed channel which shows the settling time is around 58 us. Fig.33 shows the settling behavior of the synthesizer when the division ratio is changed from 2400 to 2496. The implemented fully programmable 1 MHz resolution frequency synthesizer consumes 3.6 mW (2 mA) from a power supply of 1.8 V, which is significantly lesser than the synthesizers reported in literature implemented with dynamic logic dividers.

8   Measured Results

For silicon verification, the proposed fully programmable 2.4 GHz frequency synthesizer is fabricated using the chartered 1P6M 0.18 um CMOS process. Fig.34 shows the die photograph of the implemented 2.4 GHz frequency synthesizer. On-wafer measurements are carried out using an 8 inch RF probe station. The input signal for the measurement is provided by the Agilent 33120A arbitrary signal generator and the output signals are captured by the Lecroy Wave master 8600A 6G oscilloscope. The output spectrum and phase noise of the synthesizer is measured using the Agilent E4407B 9 kHz-26.5 GHz spectrum analyzer. Fig.35 shows the measured output spectrum of the PLL.

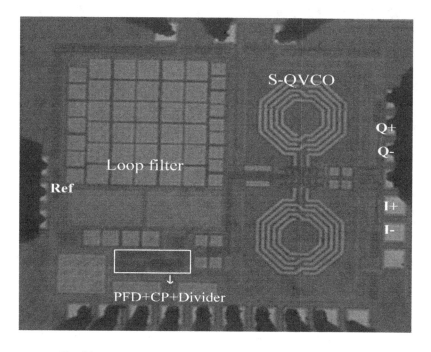

Fig. 34. Die photograph of 2.4 GHz PLL frequency synthesizer

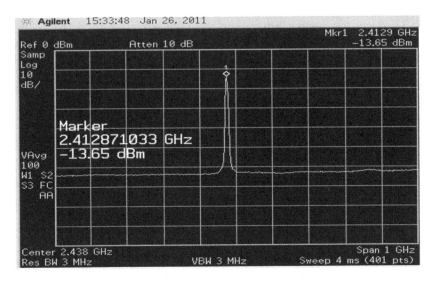

Fig. 35. Measured PLL output spectrum

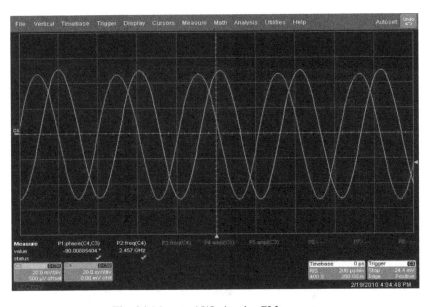

Fig. 36. Measured I/Q signal at PLL output

The VCO tuning range is from 2.369 GHz-2.692 GHz (323 MHz) and output amplitude is around 300 mV as shown in Fig.36. The power consumption of S-QVCO is 2.9 mW. The measured ripples on the control voltage is around 1 mV and power consumption of divider , charge pump other blocks is around 0.9 mW. Fig.37 shows the 1 MHz output from the fully programmable divider whose duty cycle is around

43%. The phase noise of the PLL is -111.4dBc/Hz at 1 MHz offset as shown in Fig.38. The performance of the implemented low power 2.4 GHz frequency synthesizer is analyzed in Table 4.

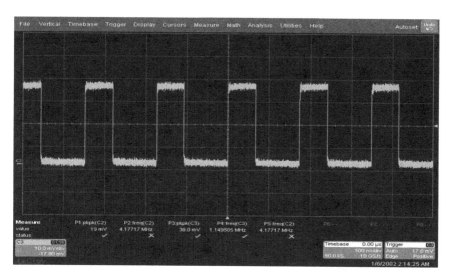

Fig. 37. Measured 1 MHz output of the divider

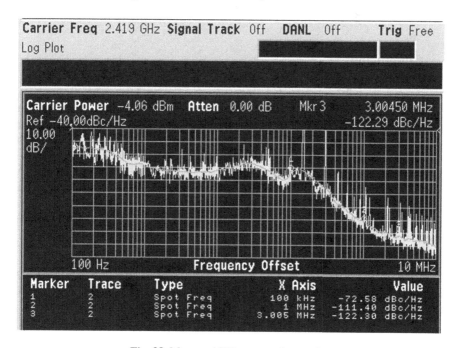

Fig. 38. Measured PLL output phase noise

Table 4. State of Art Synthesizer Comparison

Reference	[4]	[5]	[18]	[19]	This work
Process	0.25um	0.18um	0.18 um	0.2 um CMOS/SOI	0.18 um
Channel spacing	1 MHz	5 MHz	3 MHz	1 MHz	1 MHz
Frequency Range (GHz)	2.4-2.527	2.29-2.64	2.44-2.47	2.4	2.2-2.5
Loop filter	On- chip	On- chip	On- chip	Off- chip	On- chip
Phase noise (dBc/Hz)	-112 @1 MHz	-130 @10MHz	-112 @1 MHz	-104 @1MHz	-111.4 @1MHz
Settling time	60 us	55 us	500 us	600 us	35us
Power consumption	20 mW at 2.5V	15 mW at 3 V	8.2 mW at 1.8V	17 mW at 1 V	4.9mW at 1.8V

9   Conclusion

In this paper, a fully integrated 1 MHz resolution 2.4 GHz CMOS frequency synthesizer for IEEE 802.15.4 standard is designed using Global foundries 0.18 um CMOS technology is presented. A new 47/48 dual-modulus prescaler based on true-single phase clock is proposed along with the improved reloadable DFF for the swallow S-counter. The fully programmable divider only consumes 600 uW which is very compared to the fully programmable dividers reported in literature. The measured tuning range of the S-QVCO is 2.369 GHz-2.692 GHz and the output amplitude is 300 mV, which is sufficient to drive the divider. The phase noise of the PLL is -111.4dBc/Hz at 1 MHz offset and the total power consumption of the synthesizer is 3.8 mW.

Acknowledgments. The authors would also like to acknowledge the help of W. M. Lim, and T. S. Wong, Nanyang Technological University, Singapore, in the on-wafer measurement.

References

1. Aaron, V., Do, C.C., Boon, M.A., Do, K.S., Yeo, K.S., Cabuk, A.: An Energy-Aware CMOS Receiver Front End for Low-Power 2.4-GHz Applications. IEEE Tran. on Circuits and Systems-I: Regular papers (TCAS-I) 51(9), 1665–1674 (2010)
2. Debashis, M., Bhatacharyya, T.K.: Implementation of CMOS Low-Power Integer-N Frequency Synthesizer for SOC Design. Journal of Computers 3(4), 31–38 (2008)
3. Bernier, C., et al.: An ultra-low power 130nm CMOS direct conversion transceiver for IEEE 802.15.4. In: IEEE Radio Frequency Circuits Symposium, pp. 273–276 (June 2008)
4. Lee, T.C., Razavi, B.: A stabilization Technique for Phase-Locked Frequency Synthesizers. IEEE Journal of Solid-State Circuits 38, 888–894 (2003)
5. Srinivasan, R., et al.: A Low-Power Frequency Synthesizer with Quadrature Signal Generation for 2.4 GHz Zigbee Applications. In: IEEE ISCAS, pp. 429–432 (2007)
6. Nonis, R., et al.: A Design Methodology for MOS Current-Mode Logic Frequency Dividers. IEEE Trans. Circuits & Systems-I: Reg. Papers 54(2), 245–254 (2007)
7. Oh, N.-J., Lee, S.-G.: A CMOS 868/915 MHz Direct Conversion Zigbee Single-Chip Radio. IEEE Communications Magazine 43(12), 100–109 (2005)
8. Gorday, P.: 802.15.4 Multipath (July 2005)
9. Ji-ren, Y., Karlsson, I., Svensson, C.: A true single-phase clock dynamic CMOS circuit technique. IEEE J. Solid-State Circuits 24(2), 62–70 (1989)
10. Vamshi Krishna, M., et al.: Design and Analysis of Ultra Low Power True Single Phase Clock CMOS 2/3 Prescaler. IEEE Trans. Circuits & Systems-I: Reg. Papers 57(1), 72–82 (2010)
11. Yu, X.P., Do, M.A., Jia, L., Ma, J.G., Yeo, K.S.: Design of a low power wide-band high resolution programmable frequency divider. IEEE Trans. on Very Large Scale Integration Systems 13(9) (September 2005)
12. Yan, W.S.T.: A 2-V 900-MHz Monolithic CMOS Dual-Loop Frequency Synthesizer for GSM Receivers, Master Thesis, Department of EEE, HKUST (November 1999)
13. Andreani, P.: A low phase noise low phase error 1.8 GHz quadrature CMOS VCO. In: Proc. of IEEE ISSCC, pp. 290–291 (February 2006)
14. Fong, N., Plouchart, J., Zamdmer, N., Liu, D., Wagner, L., Plett, C., Tarr, N.: Design of wide-band CMOS VCO for multiband wireless LAN applications. IEEE J. Solid-State Circuits (JSSC) 38(8), 1333–1342 (2003)
15. Razavi, B.: Monolithic Phase-Locked Loops and Clock Recover Circuits. IEEE Press, NJ (1996)
16. Gardner, F.: Charge Pump Phase-Lock Loops. IEEE Trans. on Communications 28, 1849–1858 (1980)
17. Banerjee, D.: PLL Performance, Simulation, and Design, 4th edn. (2006)
18. Yamagishi, A., Ugajin, M., Tsukahara, T.: A 1-V 2.4-GHz PLL Synthesizer with a fully differential prescaler and a Low-off-Leakage charge pump. In: Microwave Symposium Digest, pp. 733–736 (June 2003)
19. Shin, S., Lee, K., Kang, S.-M.: Low Power 2.4GHz CMOS Frequency Synthesizer with Differentially Controlled MOS Varactors. In: IEEE ISCAS, pp. 553–556 (May 2006)

Design and Optimization of a Digital Baseband Receiver ASIC for GSM/EDGE

Christian Benkeser[1,2] and Qiuting Huang[1,2]

[1] Integrated Systems Laboratory
ETH Zurich
8092 Zurich, Switzerland
[2] Advanced Circuit Pursuit AG
8702 Zollikon, Switzerland
{benkeser,huang}@iis.ee.ethz.ch
http://www.iis.ee.ethz.ch
http://www.newacp.ch

Abstract. This paper addresses complexity issues at algorithmic and architectural level of digital baseband receiver ASIC design for the standards GSM/GPRS/EDGE, in order to reduce power consumption and die area as desired for cellular applications. To this end, the hardware implementation of a channel shortening pre-filter combined with a delayed decision-feedback sequence estimator (DFSE) for channel equalization is described. The digital receiver back-end including a flexible Viterbi decoder implementation is presented and hardware savings that can be achieved by using hard-decisions are discussed. Design trade-offs are highlighted to prove the efficiency of the implemented 2.5G multimode architecture. The ASIC in $0.13\,\mu$m CMOS technology occupies $1.0\,\text{mm}^2$ and dissipates only $1.3\,\text{mW}$ in fastest EDGE data transmission mode.

Keywords: Mobile communication, GSM, EDGE, baseband, pre-filter, Levinson, equalizer, DFSE, Viterbi decoder, low-power, ASIC, VLSI.

1   Introduction

Cellular wireless communications has changed our lives in the past 20 years. Today, with 3.5 billion subscribers [1] the far most important cellular communication system GSM is used by all sorts of people all around the world. Simple 2G data communication is possible with the standard extension GPRS, but good user experience during wireless web-browsing and other non-voice applications can only be achieved since 2.5G EDGE data-services have been introduced.

EDGE increases 2G peak data rates to 240 kbps, mainly due to a higher modulation order (8PSK) and stronger channel coding. The symbol rate of 270 kbps is identical with basic GSM, but 8PSK modulation improves the spectral efficiency, which comes at the cost of receiver complexity. Especially channel equalization and symbol demodulation is a challenging task in EDGE, and requires

J.L. Ayala, D. Atienza, and R. Reis (Eds.): VLSI-SoC 2010, IFIP AICT 373, pp. 100–127, 2012.

sophisticated low-complexity solutions to preserve the power-advantage and cost-advantage of 2G receivers. Although basic GSM can be implemented on advanced signal processors with tolerable power-levels today, EDGE requires efficient ASIC accelerators to reduce the power consumption to the required level in modern cellular phones.

In basic GSM with GMSK modulation typically the (optimum) Maximum-Likelihood Sequence-Estimator (MLSE) is used for channel equalization and demodulation. The complexity of an MLSE algorithm for 8PSK signals, however, would even exceed what can be implemented on ASICs. Therefore, in recent years a lot of work on channel equalization for EDGE has been performed. It has been shown that sub-optimum variants of the MLSE algorithm with acceptable computational complexity, like reduced-state sequence estimation [2] or decision-feedback sequence estimation [3], are suitable for channel equalization of 8PSK modulated EDGE signals (e.g., [4,5]). Turbo equalization has also been discussed [6] and proposed as a solution for EDGE [7]. However, all these explorations are simulation-based system analyses where implementation aspects and crucial design metrics like power consumption are not considered. Further, a practical multi-mode solution supporting GMSK as well as 8PSK modulation has not been treated so far.

This work describes the design of a low-power and low-cost digital baseband receiver for GSM/GPRS/EDGE with focus on the most challenging block, the channel equalization. The entire receiver chain has been mapped to dedicated hardware in order to achieve best design metrics. Hardware realizations for key components of the receiver ASIC realization have been optimized to provide the flexibility required for the specified modulation types and coding schemes. Costly hardware resources are shared to keep the silicon area low, and algorithmic/architectural optimizations have been applied to achieve very low power consumption.

1.1 Outline

The paper is organized as follows. In Section 2 the GSM baseband transmitter and channel model are introduced. In Section 3 the high-level architecture of the receiver ASIC realized in this work is presented. Section 4 describes the implemented channel equalizer solution in detail. In Section 5 the implemented channel decoder solution is explained together with an analysis of the impact of hard-/soft-decision equalizer outputs on receiver implementation complexity. Measurement results and key figures of the receiver ASIC implementation are presented in Section 6. The paper is concluded in Section 7.

2   System Overview

Fig. 1 shows the GSM/EDGE baseband transceiver system model used in this work. On the transmitter side the input data is first encoded with a convolutional

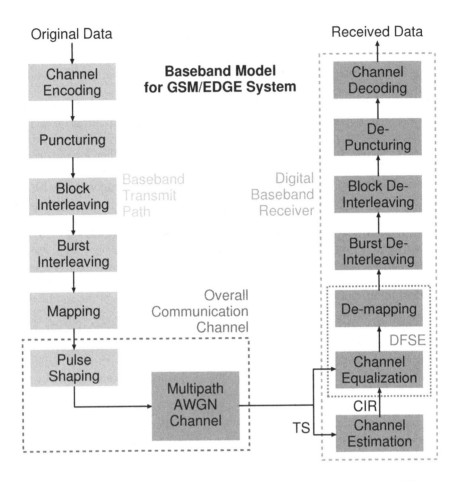

Fig. 1. System model of the GSM/EDGE baseband transceiver model

encoder (rate 1/2 for GSM/GPRS or rate 1/3 for the coding schemes specified for EDGE). Then, selected bits are removed in the puncturing unit to adjust the code rate as required for the specific transmission mode. After that, the order of bits is scrambled in the block interleaver to distribute *radio blocks* of up to 1184 bits across 4 or 8 bursts[1]. The resulting bits (information bits) are mapped in interleaved order on bursts with a length of 156.25 symbols (3 bits per symbol in 8PSK mode), which includes fixed tail bits for channel equalization, a fixed training sequence (TS) for channel estimation and a guard period[2] as shown in Fig. 2. Finally, in the symbol mapper and pulse shaping filter the bursts are GMSK or 8PSK modulated with a symbol period of $T_s = 3.69\,\mu s$ as

---

[1] Depending on the specific modulation and coding scheme the bits can be interleaved over 4 or 8 bursts [8].

[2] The guard period of 8.25 symbols ensures that subsequent bursts do not interfere with each other due to inter-symbol interference.

specified [9]. Typically the bursts are transmitted every 8 time slots as indicated in Fig. 2 according to the time division multiple access scheme defined for GSM, and the remaining 7 slots are reserved for other users. However, several slots can be reserved for data traffic of a single user in high-speed EDGE data transmission modes.

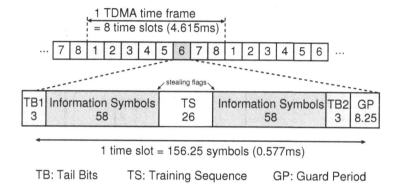

Fig. 2. Time division multiple access and the *normal burst* in GSM

The bursts are submitted through a multipath communication channel with additive white Gaussian noise (AWGN). The GSM test channel profiles [10] have a delay spread of up to $5\,T_s$, causing considerable inter symbol interference (ISI). Even more ISI is introduced by the system itself, because the GSM channel bandwidth of 200 kHz is significantly lower than the symbol rate. Therefore, an overall communication channel with a delay spread of up to $8\,T_s$ has to be considered when removing ISI in the receiver with the channel equalizer.

3   Digital Baseband Receiver

The complete receive chain shown in Fig. 1 has been implemented in our ASIC. As indicated in the corresponding simplified block-diagram (Fig. 3) two 2.5 kb RAMs allow the buffering of up to 2 GSM bursts, each comprising the in-phase and quadrature-phase component of 156 symbols. Each time a new GSM burst has been received the channel impulse response (CIR) is estimated with the training sequence by using the Least Squares technique [11]. The ISI of unknown data symbols adjacent to the training sequence causes estimation errors when considering all 26 symbols of TS. In our implementation only the central 16 symbols of TS are used to estimate the CIR. Since linear 8PSK modulation can be realized with simple FIR filtering in the transmitter, the CIR of the overall communication channel including the pulse shaping filter can be estimated at the receiver (cf., Fig. 1). In (non-linear) GMSK instead, the signal is modulated indirectly by filtering and accumulating the phase. Hence, the transmitter pulse shaping cannot simply be included in the estimated CIR.

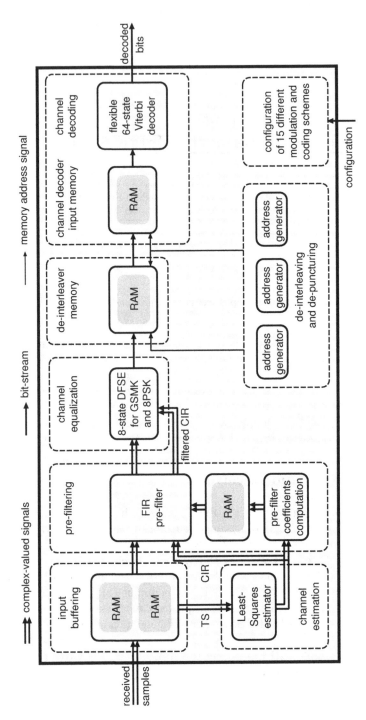

Fig. 3. GSM/EDGE receiver ASIC block diagram

Channel equalization and demodulation are performed in our receiver implementation with the combination of a minimum-phase FIR pre-filter and a Decision-Feedback Sequence Estimator (DFSE) which are explained in detail in Section 4. The pre-filter coefficients computed with the estimated CIR are buffered to be used to filter the CIR and the stream of received samples. These are fed into the DFSE for channel equalization and demodulation.

High-speed EDGE transmission modes require continuous burst reception, because more than one burst can be allocated to a specific user in each time frame. Therefore, the demodulation of each burst has to be finished in one burst period of $T_b = 577\,\mu s$. When a radio block (4 or 8 bursts) has been demodulated, the de-interleaver can begin to reorder the bits. Both, burst and block de-interleaving are performed by generating the specific RAM addresses for writing to and reading from the de-interleaver memory. The de-puncturing unit introduces zeros (no a-priori information on the demodulated symbol) into the data stream to provide data blocks to the channel decoder with the correct code rate. A flexible Viterbi decoder for trellises with up to 64 states has been implemented to support 15 specified coding schemes. The channel decoder processes all branches in parallel to keep the receiver latency low.

4   A Combined Pre-filter and DFSE Solution

In an MLSE, as can be used for optimum equalization in GSM, all possible symbol combinations of length L that could have been transmitted are generated as reference symbol sequences. These sequences are modulated and convolved with the CIR to emulate the effect of ISI. The resulting reference signals are compared with the received samples to generate branch metrics which are a measure for the likelihood that the specific symbol sequence has been transmitted, given the received signal. The branch metrics are used by the Viterbi algorithm in a trellis diagram to find the most probable transmitted symbols. Contrary to implementations of Viterbi decoders, the branch metric generation is the most challenging part in an MLSE. The computational complexity can be characterized with the number of trellis branches $B = M^L$ to be processed, where M denotes the modulation order (alphabet size) with $M = 1$ for GMSK and $M = 3$ for 8PSK. The length of the reference symbol sequences L defines the maximum tap delay (delay spread) in the channel profile that is considered in the equalization. The storage requirements are defined by the number of states in each trellis stage according to $S = M^{L-1}$. When considering the impact of 7 previously transmitted symbols, i.e. $L = 8$, as required for GSM (cf., Section 2), the MLSE trellis is large in the GMSK case, and even beyond what can be realized with any hardware platform when processing 8PSK signals.

Contrary to the MLSE algorithm, in the DFSE not all possible symbol combinations of the reference sequence are used for the comparison with the received samples. Decisions of the Viterbi algorithm on previous symbols, so-called per-survivor estimates, are taken as fixed assumptions to reduce the number of branch metrics to be computed. Only the permutations of the first D symbols are considered as separate state transitions in the trellis, which reduces the number of branches to be processed to $B = M^D$ and the required number of trellis states to $S = M^{D-1}$. Therefore, the taps of the CIR which correspond to these first D symbols have greatest impact on the equalizer performance. In channels with strong delayed taps and comparably weak main taps, correct symbol demodulation can be difficult or even impossible for the DFSE algorithm. Therefore, minimum-phase pre-filtering is required to transform such channels into channels better suited for the DFSE. Such a pre-filter concentrates the energy of the channel taps in the front, in order to maximize the impact of the first D symbols during equalization, thus improving the DFSE performance (cf., Fig. 4).

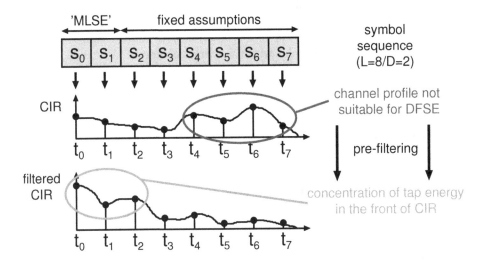

Fig. 4. The concept of pre-filtering required for the DFSE

Simulations have shown that, depending on the channel profile, varying D from 2 to 4 brings a maximum performance gain of 1.6 dB in terms of SNR required to achieve an uncoded DFSE bit error-rate (BER) of 10^{-3} with both GMSK and 8PSK modulated signals. The simulation results for the specified Hilly Terrain (HT) channel [10] profile for different DFSE configurations with pre-filtering are shown in Fig. 5. As can be seen increasing D from 2 to 4 improves the performance in this case by only 0.9 dB and 0.6 dB for GMSK and 8PSK modulated signals respectively. Almost optimum (MLSE) performance can be achieved with $D = 4$. Further increasing of D introduces additional complexity without a noticeable performance gain.

Instead, the impact of the pre-filter can be dramatic. The uncoded BER of demodulated 8PSK signals, impaired by the HT channel are shown in Fig. 6. Different filter orders p for the pre-filter in front of a DFSE with $D = 2$ have been simulated. As can be seen, without pre-filtering the symbol sequence cannot be

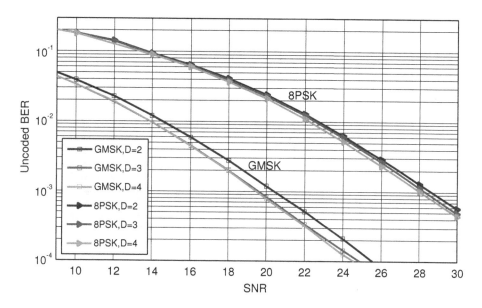

Fig. 5. Uncoded BER of GMSK and 8PSK modulated signals after pre-filtering with pre-filter order $p = 32$ and $D = \{2, 3, 4\}$. The specified Hilly Terrain (HT) channel profile (no vehicle speed) has been used for the simulations

equalized with a DFSE properly. A pre-filter order p of only 16 causes the curves to saturate at a BER$\geq 10^{-3}$, whereas the BER does not improve significantly with increasing the filter order beyond 32.

The most critical parts of our GSM/EDGE channel equalizer solution, i.e., the matrix inversion for the pre-filter coefficients computation and the DFSE realization, are described in detail in the following.

4.1 Pre-filter Implementation

A suitable pre-filter transforms the CIR to its minimum-phase equivalent, where the energy of the first filter taps is maximum compared to the impulse response of all other causal and stable filters with the same magnitude response [12, 13]. Such pre-filtering can be realized with a hardware-friendly FIR filter, however, the computation of the corresponding pre-filter coefficients is costly. Hence, a thorough complexity analysis of techniques for the generation of these filter coefficients is required.

In order to be able to make a fair comparison between algorithms, we have implemented the Linear Prediction (LP) method [14] and performed floating-point simulations for a filter order of $p = 32$ with our framework. Then, the MMSE-DFE [12] and cepstrum method [15] (recently proposed for GSM/EDGE in [16]) have been implemented, and the parameters have been optimized, such that these algorithms provide the same BER performance at certain SNR points

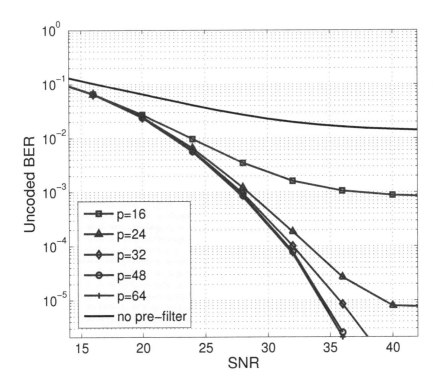

Fig. 6. Uncoded BER of 8PSK modulated signals after pre-filtering and channel equalization with DFSE ($D = 2$) with variable pre-filter order p. The specified Hilly Terrain (HT) channel profile (no vehicle speed) has been used for the simulations

as the simulations with the LP method. It has been shown, that the cepstrum (MMSE-DFE) method requires $p = 32$ and $p = 24$ ($p = 32$ and $p = 20$) at SNR points corresponding to an uncoded BER of 1% and 0.1% respectively.

In Fig. 7 the complexity of the different algorithms in terms of number of complex-valued multiplications and additions is compared[3]. The complexity has been evaluated at different BER operating points, because the MMSE-DFE method shows slightly better performance in low SNR regimes when compared to the LP and cepstrum approach. As can be seen, the computation of the pre-filter coefficients via LP is significantly less complex than using MMSE-DFE or the cepstrum method.

Consequently, in our digital baseband receiver ASIC we have implemented a pre-filter with filter coefficients computation based on LP, which will be depicted shortly in the following (a detailed description can be found in [14]). We denote the discrete time received baseband signal as follows:

---

[3] Real-valued multiplications/additions have been counted as 0.25/0.5 complex-valued operations here.

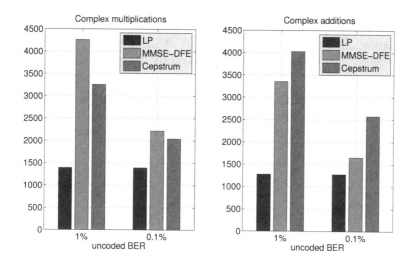

Fig. 7. Complexity comparison of different algorithms for channel shortening pre-filters

$$r[n] = \sum_{k=1}^{L} h[k] \cdot s[n-k] + w[n] \tag{1}$$

where $h[n]$ denotes the complex baseband response of the overall channel with delay spread L (cf., Section 3), $s[n]$ the GMSK or 8PSK modulated transmitted symbols, and $w[n]$ complex additive white Gaussian noise (AWGN). $H(z)$ denotes the transfer function that corresponds to the channel:

$$H(z) = \sum_{k=1}^{L} h[k] \cdot z^{-k}. \tag{2}$$

Ideally, a discrete-time pre-filter $A(z)$ transforms $H(z)$ to its minimum-phase equivalent $H_{min}(z)$ according to

$$H_{min}(z) = A(z) \cdot H(z), \tag{3}$$

with all-pass characteristic

$$|A(z)| = 1. \tag{4}$$

Due to (4) the transfer function $A(z)$ of the desired pre-filter can be written as a cascade of two filters according to

$$A(z) = \underbrace{H^*(1/z^*)}_{A_{MF}} \cdot \underbrace{\frac{1}{H_{min}^*(1/z^*)}}_{A_{WF}} \cdot \tag{5}$$

A_{MF} is a matched filter, matched to the channel $h[n]$, where the filter coefficients are simply the complex-conjugated and time-reversed impulse response taps. Unfortunately, obtaining the filter coefficients of the whitening[4] filter $A_{WF}(z)$ is a much more complex task that requires a costly matrix inversion.

Computation of Filter Coefficients with LP. A linear predictor is based on the assumption that samples of a sequence can be (approximately) written as a linear combination of past samples. The linear prediction filter $P(z)$ used to compute the filter coefficients of $A_{WF}(z)$ is defined as

$$\hat{h}[n] = \sum_{i=1}^{p} a_i \cdot h[n-i], \tag{6}$$

with the linear predictor coefficients a_i and the filter order p. The prediction-error can be computed according to

$$e[n] = h[n] - \hat{h}[n]. \tag{7}$$

The filter coefficients are obtained by minimizing the mean-squared prediction error which leads to the *normal equations* or *Yule-Walker equations* [17,18]:

$$\boldsymbol{\Phi}\boldsymbol{a} = \boldsymbol{\varphi}$$

with the filter coefficients vector

$$\boldsymbol{a} = \begin{bmatrix} a_1 \ a_2 \ \cdots \ a_p \end{bmatrix}^T$$

and the Toeplitz matrix

$$\boldsymbol{\Phi} = \begin{bmatrix} \varphi_0 & \varphi_{-1} & \cdots & \varphi_{-(p-1)} \\ \varphi_1 & \varphi_0 & \cdots & \varphi_{-(p-2)} \\ \vdots & & \ddots & \vdots \\ \varphi_{p-1} & \varphi_{p-2} & \cdots & \varphi_0 \end{bmatrix} \tag{8}$$

with

$$\boldsymbol{\varphi} = \begin{bmatrix} \varphi_1 \ \varphi_2 \ \cdots \ \varphi_p \end{bmatrix}^T$$

The coefficients φ_k are given by the autocorrelation function (ACF) of $h[n]$ according to

$$\varphi_k = h[k] * h^*[-k].$$

As can be seen in Fig. 8 the prediction-error filter $F(z)$ that corresponds to the linear predictor $P(z)$ is given by

---

[4] Details on the noise-whitening characteristic of this filter can be found in [17].

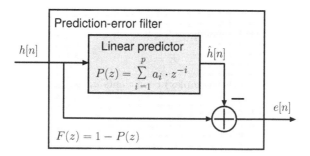

Fig. 8. Block diagram of prediction-error filter used for the pre-filter coefficients computation in the LP approach

$$F(z) = 1 - P(z) \tag{9}$$

The generation of the A_{WF} filter coefficients exploits the fact that such prediction-error filters are always minimum phase [17]. It has been shown in [14], that

$$A_{WF}(z) = F^*(1/z^*) \tag{10}$$

is valid for an infinite filter order $p \to \infty$ and that

$$A_{WF}(z) \approx F^*(1/z^*) \tag{11}$$

is a good approximation for high filter orders p.

4.2 Matrix Inversion

In a pre-filter implementation with LP the far most complex part is the inversion of the complex-valued $p \times p$ Toeplitz matrix (8) required to generate the pre-filter coefficients. In our digital baseband receiver ASIC a pre-filter with order $p = 32$ has been implemented to guarantee high DFSE performance, even when the received signals have been impaired by channels with strong delayed taps. The required inversion of a 32×32 matrix with an internal precision of 2×20 bits has been implemented in our design by excessively applying time-multiplexing and resource sharing to curtail silicon area. To this end, the recursive Levinson-Durbin (LD) algorithm shown in Alg. 1 is used. Its recursive nature is highly suitable for sequential implementations and the computational complexity is close to optimum matrix inversion algorithms for Toeplitz matrices [19].

To improve the efficiency of an implementation of the LD recursion, the algorithm has been modified as follows:

- Initialization of the (real) scaling factor E

$$E = \varphi_0 \tag{12}$$

- Recursive generation of the (complex) coefficients a_i by looping over $1 \leq i \leq p$

  - Computation of the unscaled a'

$$a' = - \left[\varphi_i + \sum_{j=i}^{i-1} a_j \cdot \varphi_{i-j} \right] \tag{13}$$

  - Scaling with E to generate the new a_i

$$a_i = \frac{a'}{E} \tag{14}$$

  - Updating a_j by looping over $1 \leq j \leq i-1$

$$a_j = a_j + a_i \cdot a_{i-j}^* \tag{15}$$

  - Generation of the new scaling factor

$$E = (1 - |a_i|^2)E \tag{16}$$

- The LP filter coefficients of P(z) are given by a_i with $1 \leq i \leq p$

Alg. 1. LD recursion for complex coefficients

- The initialization in equation (12) has been replaced with

$$E_{inv} = \frac{1}{\varphi_0}$$

- The scaling of a' in equation (14) has been replaced with

$$a_i = a' \cdot E_{inv}$$

- The generation of the new scaling factor in equation (16) has been replaced with

$$E_{inv} = \frac{E_{inv}}{(1 - |a_i|^2)}$$

Working with the inverse of the scaling factor $E_{inv} = 1/E$ can be exploited to process the algorithm more efficiently in hardware (cf., the block diagram of the LD algorithm implementation in our receiver ASIC in Fig. 9): the division of the complex-valued a' in (14) is replaced by a multiplication, and the multiplication in (16) is replaced with a real-valued division. Thus, one costly real-valued

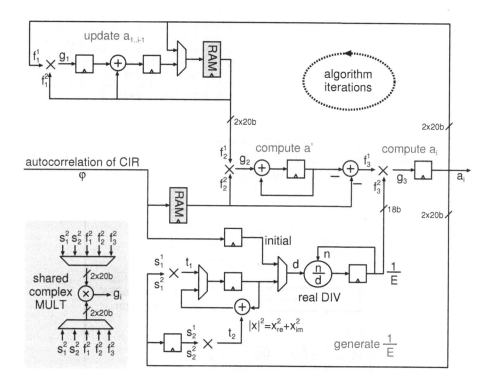

Fig. 9. Block diagram of the LD recursion implementation

division is saved in each iteration of the LD recursion. Further, the division now has to be performed for the generation of the new (inverse) scaling factor, and therefore can be performed mostly in parallel to updating a_j. It can be realized with a low-complexity sequential divider without stalling the LD recursion loop for many clock cycles. The sequential divider implementation in our design takes 9 clock cycles per division and requires only 1.7 k gate equivalents (kGE). It significantly reduces the logic depth of the costly divide operation such that timing closure of our receiver ASIC is not affected. In our design the matrix inversion of the complex-valued 32×32 matrix takes 2630 clock cycles.

Costly hardware resources like multipliers, register arrays and RAMs, used in the LD recursion implementation, are also shared with other units of the pre-filter block. As in the implementation of the LD recursion, the sequential data flow in the pre-filter coefficients computation allows time-multiplexing of costly hardware resources. Thus, the total pre-filter coefficients computation together with the actual FIR pre-filtering requires only 32 kGE and 2.5 kb memory. The total pre-filter coefficients computation takes less than 3000 clock cycles, and the FIR pre-filter of the received burst provides one filtered symbol per 16 clock cycles to the DFSE.

4.3   DFSE Design for GMSK and 8PSK

To support processing both GMSK and 8PSK modulated signals with little overhead, our implementation of the DFSE algorithm always operates on the same number of trellis states. In GMSK mode 8 states allow $D = 4$ symbols to be considered in building the trellis, such that near MLSE performance can be achieved. In 8PSK mode with $D = 2$ the high-order pre-filter allows for good performance without having to introduce additional trellis states as previously shown. The binary alphabet in GMSK requires only 2 branches per trellis state to be processed, whereas 8PSK has 8 branches in the trellis going to each trellis state, which leads to a 4x higher computational complexity.

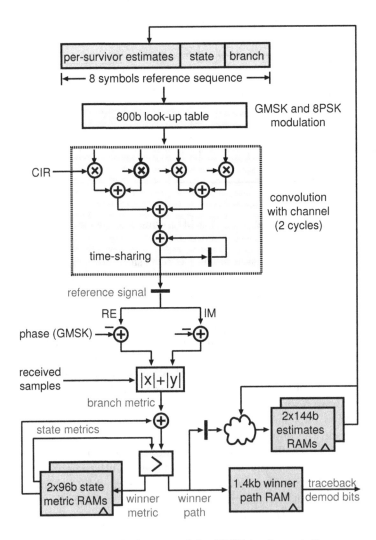

Fig. 10. Block diagram of the DFSE implementation

The symbols of the training sequence do not have to be demodulated since they are known at the receiver[5]. Therefore, computations can be saved by simply skipping the received symbols that correspond to the training sequence. Our DFSE implementation builds two separate sub-trellises per burst: one trellis for the first 58 information symbols, using TB1 and the first symbols of TS as tail bits, and one trellis for the second 58 information symbols, using the last symbols of TS and TB2 as tail bits (cf., Fig. 2). Consequently, tail bits for both sub-trellises are known in the DFSE, which enables reliable demodulation of the information symbols with 20% less symbols to be processed.

Fig. 10 shows the block-diagram of the implemented DFSE algorithm. To enable the equalization of all specified channel profiles, channel taps with a maximum delay of $L = 8$ symbol periods are considered in our DFSE implementation (cf., Section 2). Therefore, the reference symbol sequences have a length of 8 symbols, and the (pre-filtered) CIR fed into the DFSE block consists of 8 symbol-spaced taps.

To modulate the symbols each reference sequence (one for each trellis branch) is fed into a look-up table (LUT) to generate the corresponding constellation points. In GMSK mode all $2^L = 256$ possible constellation points which arise from ISI due to the pulse shaping filter have to be stored. In 8PSK mode, where the estimated CIR also comprises transmitter pulse shaping, only 2×8 different constellation points have to be stored[6]. With a precision of 6 bit and 8 bit for the GMSK and 8PSK constellation points respectively, the LUT can be reduced to only 0.8 kb by exploiting symmetries.

The vector product of the modulated reference symbol sequence with the pre-filtered CIR, both complex-valued and with a length of 8, is by far the most computation-intensive part in a DFSE implementation: 8 multiplications and 7 additions are required for each trellis branch, leading to high implementation complexity. To keep the silicon area low we have time-multiplexed the vector product implementation for 4 symbols with 4 channel taps, thus spending 2 clock cycles for the generation of each reference signal.

In GMSK mode, after the convolution with the channel a phase rotation of $\pi/2$ introduced in the transmitter modulator [9] is compensated for[7]. Finally, the trellis branch metrics typically are computed by building the Euclidean (ℓ^2-) distance

$$d_{\ell^2} = \sqrt{(x_I - y_I)^2 + (x_Q - y_Q)^2} \qquad (17)$$

---

[5] In our prototype ASIC implementation the training sequence code (TSC) #1 has been used. The specifications allow the base station to choose among 8 different TSCs with similar autocorrelation properties.

[6] 16 instead of 8 constellation points have to be considered, because a phase rotation of $3\pi/8$ between subsequent transmitted symbols is specified [9].

[7] The sign of the GMSK phase rotation depends on the symbol to be transmitted. However, it can be shown that due to differential encoding on the transmitter side, the received symbols can be de-rotated for the comparison in the Viterbi equalizer without having to consider previous symbols.

between the reference signal and the received sample. To avoid costly square operations in this time critical path in our implementation we generate the ℓ^1-distance

$$d_{\ell^1} = |x_I - y_I| + |x_Q - y_Q| \tag{18}$$

as an approximation. In terms of SNR the performance degradation with this sub-optimal solution is less than 0.5 dB in GMSK and within 1 dB in 8PSK mode [20].

Each branch metric is added to the state metric of the state from which the specific branch is originating. The smallest metric incident on each state is selected and stored in the state metric memory, which is double-buffered with 2 RAMs to avoid that the old state metrics are overwritten. The decision on the winner branch is stored in the *winner path* and the *estimates* RAMs (cf., Fig. 10). To avoid access problems two *estimates* RAM instantiations are required for the storage of the last $8 - D$ per-survivor estimates for each of the 8 trellis states. The *winner path* RAM stores all decisions in the trellis to find the most likely symbol sequence during final back-tracing.

The total DFSE implementation requires only 18 kGE and less than 2 kb memory. The demodulation of one GMSK burst takes 6228 clock cycles, and processing an 8PSK modulated burst requires 17360 cycles. When taking into account the time required to generate the pre-filter coefficients plus 128 cycles for the channel estimation, burst-wise operation of the fastest EDGE transmission modes is possible with a system clock frequency of only 40 MHz.

4.4   Complexity of Combined Pre-filter and DFSE

The pre-filter block is almost twice as complex in terms of silicon area as the DFSE, and occupies one third of the logic cells of the total digital receiver. As previously shown, proper pre-filtering is essential to achieve high DFSE performance, especially when reducing the number of trellis states with $D < 4$. Although, the significant complexity of the pre-filter block gives rise to the question, if a pre-filter with a lower order and a DFSE with more trellis states would achieve a similar performance at a reduced total equalizer implementation complexity.

Lowering the filter order p reduces the filter's ability to compute the optimum minimum-phase equivalent of the CIR. The lower the filter order the more energy will be (in average) in the delayed taps of the filtered CIR. Further, the all-pass characteristic of the pre-filter (cf., equation 4) deteriorates for small p. Such sub-optimum pre-filtering causes higher error rates after DFSE equalization and demodulation as shown in Fig. 6. Increasing the number of trellis states processed in the DFSE can (partially) compensate for this performance loss. But increasing the number of channel taps considered in building the trellis for example from $D = 2$ to $D = 3$ increases the number of branches to be processed by a factor of 8 in 8PSK modulation. Hence, the processing delay would increase by more than 120 k cycles with our architecture. On the other hand, with the highly sequential and resource-saving architecture of the proposed low-complexity pre-filter implementation, going down from a pre-filter order of 32 to for example[8] 16 would save less than 2 k cycles. Furthermore, the silicon area of the pre-filter cannot be reduced significantly when lowering the filter order, because hardware resources have already been extensively re-used in the proposed architecture. Concluding, the implementation of a pre-filter with a high filter order pays off because it allows for excellent BER performance at a significantly reduced implementation complexity of the DFSE equalizer.

5 Hard-Decision Receiver Back-End Realization

The TDMA-based architecture of GSM/EDGE foresees burst-wise processing in the receiver: to save power only the signal streams on time slots with data dedicated for the specific user are equalized and demodulated. However, after the de-mapping of the bursts, de-interleaving, de-puncturing and channel decoding is required on a radio block basis, because block-interleaving is performed over 4 or 8 bursts in the transmitter signal processing chain (cf., Section 2).

In GSM/GPRS radio blocks of up to 456 bits contain one radio link control (RLC) block of information bits and in specific transmission modes (CS2-4) a short sequence called uplink state flag (USF)[9]. The coding scheme used for the information bits can be determined on the receiver side by checking the de-modulated *stealing flag* bits on either side of the training sequence (cf., Fig. 2). In EDGE the radio blocks comprise the USF sequence, one or two (separately encoded) RLC blocks of information bits, and an RLC/MAC *header* part. To ensure strong header protection the header is encoded, interleaved and punc-tured independently from the information bits [21]. In EDGE the stealing flags indicate the coding used for the header, and the header itself provides control information, e.g. the modulation and coding scheme (MCS1-9) used for the cod-ing of the information bits and an RLC block identifier. This block identifier is used by the *incremental redundancy* (IR) management on higher layers to deter-mine if the received RLC blocks are a re-transmission of previously transmitted RLC blocks which have not been correctly decoded. IR uses different puncturing schemes for the re-transmission of RLC blocks, such that they can be combined with the previously received and stored blocks to increase the chance of correct decoding.

In the following de-mapping, block de-interleaving, de-puncturing and chan-nel decoding as implemented in our receiver ASIC are described, highlighting the enormous complexity reduction that can be achieved by generating hard-decisions (instead of soft-decisions) in the DFSE equalizer implementation.

---

[8] Simulations have shown that the performance degradation due to reducing the filter order from 32 to 16 cannot even be compensated for completely by increasing D to 4.

[9] The USF indicates to the user equipment (UE) in which time slot a radio block can be transmitted in the case that two UEs share the same physical channel.

5.1 De-mapping, De-interleaving and De-puncturing

The implemented DFSE equalizer demodulates the received data stream and generates hard-decisions for each transmitted information symbol. Due to the nature of the Viterbi algorithm [22] the DFSE provides the demodulated symbols d_k with $k = 0..115$ for each sub-trellis corresponding to 58 information symbols i in inverse order, more specifically

$$d_k = i_{58}^{sub1}, i_{57}^{sub1}, .., i_1^{sub1}, i_{58}^{sub2}, i_{57}^{sub2}, .., i_1^{sub2}. \tag{19}$$

The symbols are de-mapped to actual bits and written into the de-interleaver memory. Burst de-interleaving is a simple task and can be performed by applying the specific memory write addresses. When a radio block of 4 or 8 bursts has been buffered in the de-interleaver memory block de-interleaving can begin.

The rules for the generation of the interleaved bit order (as defined for block interleaving on the transmitter side) seem to be complex and not suitable for an integration in hardware. Modulo and integer divisions are used in the specifications to compute the interleaved addresses, e.g., for MCS-9 the standard specifies the interleaving according to

$$\Pi(k) = 306(k \bmod 4) + 3\left(44k \bmod 102 + \left\lfloor \frac{k}{4} \right\rfloor \bmod 2\right) + \left(k + 2 - \left\lfloor \frac{k}{408} \right\rfloor\right) \bmod 3 \tag{20}$$

with $k = 0..1223$, such that each encoded bit of a radio block that was not punctured is interleaved to the address $\Pi(k)$. Obtaining the de-interleaved address $\Pi^{-1}(k)$ for a specific bit position k is even more complex and difficult to realize. However, when generating the interleaved addresses in ascending order, i.e., $k = 0, 1, 2, ..$, complex modulo and division operations can be replaced by simple add-compare-select stages and counters (an example for such a simplified implementation is illustrated in Fig. 11 for a modulo and for a divide operation of (20)). Therefore, the de-interleaving can be performed most efficiently by applying the interleaved positions (generated in ascending order) as read addresses to the de-interleaver memory and writing the corresponding data items to the channel decoder input memory in natural order. With de-/puncturing the situation is similar: generating the bit positions which have to be punctured can be implemented efficiently with counters, whereas the inverse operation of determining if a specific address has been punctured is a complex task.

In order to minimize implementation complexity in our ASIC design, we apply the write addresses to the decoder input memory in natural (ascending) order and perform the de-puncturing and de-interleaving in a combined step:

 - Initialization of the de-interleaver counter to $q = 0$.
 - For all $k = 0, 1, 2, ..$ in ascending order check if the kth bit has been punctured in the transmitter.
    - If 'yes', write a zero (no a-priori information available for channel decoding) to the kth position of the channel decoder input memory.

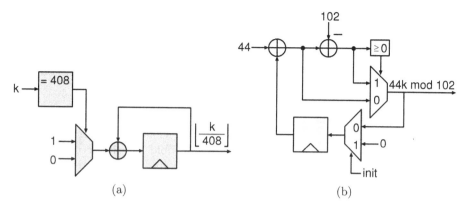

Fig. 11. Simplified implementation of integer division (a) and modulo operation (b) as required for interleaving

- If 'no', generate $\Pi(q)$ to read the corresponding data item from the de-interleaver memory: write +1 for a stored logic '0' and -1 for a stored logic '1' to the kth position of the decoder memory, and increment the de-interleaver counter q by one.

It may seem a waste of hardware resources that memory space is provided for the zeros corresponding to the punctured bits. The de-puncturing could also be performed when reading the bits from the channel decoder input memory into the channel decoder. However, the memory space for the punctured bits is required because the received radio block could be a re-transmission initiated by the IR management. In this case, the received information and the information of the previously received and stored blocks has to be combined and written into the channel decoder input memory to be used by the channel decoder. Therefore, the capacity of the channel decoder input memory is defined by the maximum (encoded) RLC block size before puncturing.

5.2   Flexible Hard-Decision Viterbi Decoder

Channel coding for the different transmission modes in GSM, GPRS and EDGE is all based on convolutional encoding. However, the coding schemes differ in code rate r, constraint length c, decoder block size B, and trellis termination with tail bits [8]:

- The convolutional code for basic GSM and GPRS transmission modes has a code rate of $r = 1/2$ and a constraint length of $c = 5$. Block sizes vary from less than 100 up to 338.
- The RLC blocks in the EDGE modes are encoded with a $r = 1/3$ convolutional code with $c = 7$. Block sizes vary from less than 200 up to 612.

- To reduce the coding overhead in the relatively short header sequences of the EDGE modes, the headers are encoded with *tail-biting codes* [23,24]. Here, no tail bits indicating the initial and final state of the convolutional encoder are transmitted. Instead, only the fact that the initial and final state of the tail-biting convolutional encoder are identical can be used by the decoder to find the most probable sequence.

In order to maximize the utilization of hardware resources, a single flexible Viterbi decoder solution is favorable over separate channel decoder implementations for the different requirements. Such a flexible Viterbi decoder has to support up to 64 trellis-states ($c = 7$) by taking into consideration up to 3 encoded input data items to compute the branch metrics ($r = 1/3$). Further, standard trellis-termination has to be supported as well as uninitialized trellis processing for the tail-biting codes. Finally, the channel decoder input memory has to be capable of storing up to $3 \cdot 612 = 1836$ data items.

We have implemented a fully-parallel 64-state sliding-window Viterbi decoder which supports the trellis structures required for GSM/GPRS and for EDGE. The data blocks are processed in windows of W=32 with an acquisition length of A=32 to reduce the memory requirements of the decoder (more details on Viterbi decoder design can be found, e.g., in [25]). In transmission modes that use convolutional codes with $c < 7$ only the required hardware resources are activated in order to save power. Although all trellis states that correspond to a bit to be decoded are processed in parallel, the complexity of the Viterbi decoder is comparably small. Since hard-decisions are demodulated in our receiver ASIC, the channel decoder inputs can be represented with only 2 bits which keeps the numeric range of the state metrics small[10]. The branch metric computation can be realized very efficiently when taking into consideration that

- the 2 bit inputs $i \in \{-1,0,1\}$
- the (ideal) encoder output corresponding to the trellis state $e \in \{-1,1\}$
- the resulting difference is $|i - e| \in \{0,1,2\}$.

As can be seen in the block diagram of our Viterbi decoder implementation in Fig. 12, calculating the distance between decoder inputs and state-specific encoder outputs can be realized with only two logic gates. Depending on the code rate r, two or three units to compute the distance are enabled in each of the 128 branch metric computation units (BMUs) for the generation of the branch metrics b. The complexity of the state metric recursions can be kept low as well because the metric increase in each trellis stage is limited to

$$\Delta m_{max} = c_{max} \cdot \max |i - e| = 6. \tag{21}$$

Therefore, in our implementation with W=32 the state metrics m can be realized with only 8 bit without the need for normalization circuits. The initialization of

---

[10] Hard-decisions in the original sense require only 1 bit. Another bit has to be spent to be able to represent the zero (no a-priori information) for the punctured bits.

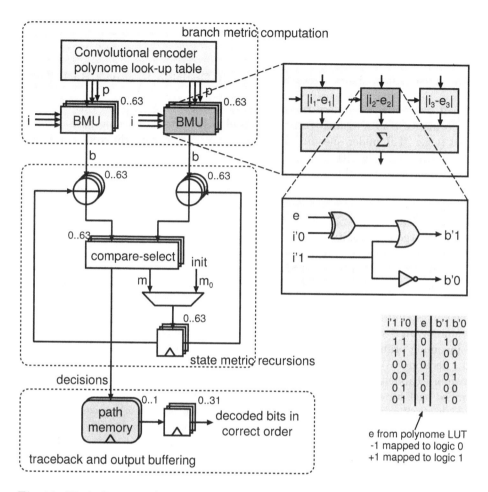

Fig. 12. Block diagram of the flexible 64-state parallel Viterbi decoder implemented in our design

the state metrics m_0 is configurable in our implementation to allow for uninitialized decoder runs in order to find the most probable start- and end-state of the trellis in tail-biting mode. Then, these are used in a second decoder run to decode the (header) bit sequence (details on decoding tail-biting codes can be found, e.g., in [26, 27]).

The trace-back provides the decoded bits in windows of W=32 according to the decisions stored in the path memory in inverse order, such that an output buffer for 32 bits is necessary to bring them into natural order. Our channel decoder implementation requires about 150 cycles to decode the header and 4000 cycles to decode the two RLC blocks in the fastest EDGE transmission mode MCS-9. With a target clock frequency of 40 MHz the decoder latency translates to only about 100 μs, which allows to compensate for potential delays between header and data block decoding[11].

5.3   Discussion: Hard-Decision vs. Soft-Decision Receiver Back-End

When designing a wireless receiver many decisions have to be taken where performance trades against complexity and cost. Often a specific performance goal (e.g., BER under specific conditions) can be met with different combinations of devices, algorithms and architectures. E.g., choosing a radio-frequency IC with a comparably high noise-figure could be (at least partially) compensated for in the digital baseband receiver by implementing the best-performing channel equalizer and decoder algorithms. To find the optimum implementation for a given application under specific constraints it is crucial to know the performance as well as the complexity increase of the different design options.

Using demodulated soft-decision values can improve the BER after channel decoding by 2-3 dB in terms of SNR (e.g., [28]). However, the generation of soft-decision outputs with a Viterbi equalizer is complex and significantly increases the required memory capacity. For each incoming branch to each trellis state the corresponding sum of the branch and state metric has to be stored. Hence, assuming an 8-state DFSE with a 58-stage trellis using 12 bit state metrics and 8 incoming branches (8PSK) to each trellis state (as implemented in our ASIC, cf., Section 4.3) the soft-output DFSE would require an additional 44.5 kb of memory capacity. To generate reliable soft-decisions several paths have to be traced back for each trellis stage [29] which is difficult to realize in hardware and which significantly increases the required number of memory accesses during back-tracing, leading to higher power consumption.

Storing soft-decisions instead of hard-decisions in the de-interleaver and channel decoder input memory requires a higher storage capacity, and processing soft-inputs in the Viterbi decoder increases the complexity of the BMU and state metric recursion units.

The implemented digital baseband receiver ASIC with hard-decision DFSE outputs contains RAMs to store 20 kb. With typical soft-decisions of 5 bit instead, 76 kb memory would be required which translates to an increase of the core size by a factor of more than 2, and to a chip where more than 2/3 of the silicon area are occupied only by memory.

Even more dramatic are the savings achieved by using hard-decision equalizer outputs when thinking of the memory required for the storage of previously received and not correctly decoded radio blocks for IR. According to the specifications, a multi-slot class 12 user equipment [12] has to store up to 24 radio blocks

---

[11] The header information has to be extracted and processed first (typically by higher layers) to obtain the coding scheme, puncturing pattern and RLC block identifier. When a re-transmission has occurred the previously received data block will be restored from an IR memory to combine it with the received data block in the channel decoder input memory.

[12] Such a MS is capable of receiving on 4 time slots per frame.

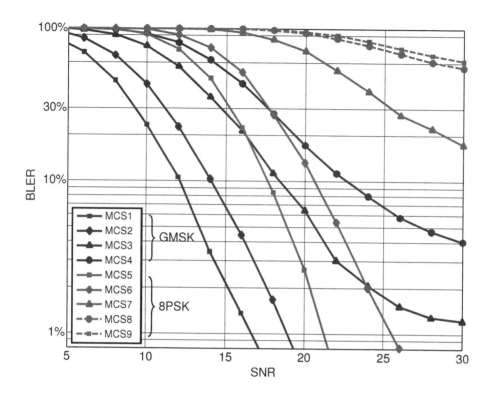

Fig. 13. Receiver block error-rates in various modulation and coding schemes (MCS) of EDGE for the specified Hilly Terrain (HT) test channel with a vehicle speed of 100 km/h

with the modulation and coding scheme MCS-9, which translates to about 150 kb using 5 bit soft-values. With hard-decisions only the puncturing pattern and the actual bits have to be stored, which saves as much as 120 kb memory.

6 Implementation Results

Functional tests and power measurements of fabricated chips (see Fig. 14) have been performed on a digital tester. The fixed-point simulation model of the implemented design has been verified and used to generate the block error-rates (BLERs) of the receiver as shown in Fig. 13 for the various modulation and coding schemes (MCS) of EDGE with the specified Hilly Terrain (HT) test channel with a vehicle speed of 100 km/h. It should be noted that the standard requires MCS1-6 to achieve a BLER of 10 % and MCS7 to achieve a BLER of 30 % at a certain receive power level. For MCS8-9 there are no specifications for these propagation conditions. Assuming the noise-figure of a state-of-the-art

RF transceiver IC[13] these BLERs can be achieved at the specified power levels. Other key characteristics are summarized in Table 1. The ASIC occupies $1.0\,mm^2$ in $0.13\,\mu m$ CMOS, comprising $97\,kGE$ and $20\,kb$ of memory. A measured maximum clock frequency of $172\,MHz$ allows the supply voltage to be lowered to $0.6\,V$ when operating at the target frequency of $40\,MHz$. During continuous burst reception the average power consumption is as low as $5.2\,mW$ in the fastest EDGE transmission mode MCS9, and only $1.3\,mW$ when lowering the supply voltage to $0.6\,V$.

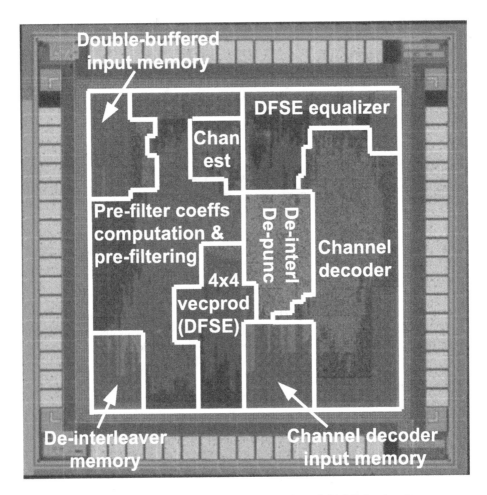

Fig. 14. EDGE receiver ASIC micrograph with highlighted units

---

[13] E.g., *IRIS305* from ACP AG, a single-chip RF transceiver supporting both TD-SCDMA/HSPA (3G) and GSM/GPRS/EDGE (2.5G) standards.

Table 1. Key characteristics of the receiver ASIC implementation

Technology	**0.13 μm CMOS**
Supply Voltage V_{DD}	**1.2 V-0.6 V**
Core Size	**1.0 mm^2**
Gate Count	**97 kGE**
Total Memory	**20.3 kb**
Max. System Clock Frequency	**172 MHz**
Leakage current @ V_{DD}=1.2 V (0.6 V)	**0.49 mA (0.15 mA)**
Average power measured during continuous burst reception @ target frequency f=40 MHz, V_{DD}=1.2 V (0.6 V)	
GSM CS1 (GMSK)	**2.4 mW (0.6 mW)**
EDGE MCS9 (8PSK)	**5.2 mW (1.3 mW)**

7 Conclusion

EDGE enables 2G data services all over the world with data rates suitable for many cellular applications. The introduction of 8PSK modulation improves the bandwidth utilization, but significantly increases equalizer complexity. Latest 65 nm signal processors provide the computational power required to perform the digital baseband signal processing for EDGE. However, power and silicon area of such implementations exceed what is desirable for a low-power, low-cost 2.5G solution required in modern cellular phones.

In this work a combined architecture for GSM/GPRS/EDGE has been presented. We have shown how the digital baseband can be mapped efficiently to dedicated hardware by using suitable algorithms and architectures to share hardware resources with little overhead. A certain amount of flexibility can support the specified transmission modes with different modulation and coding schemes. Our approach to reduce complexity in the most crucial block, the channel equalizer, is to maximize the effort in the pre-processing FIR filtering, in order to be able to reduce DFSE complexity. Using hard-decisions at the equalizer output is the key to curtail memory requirements in the back-end of a digital baseband receiver for EDGE.

With 1.0 mm^2 and only 1.3 mW average power consumption our ASIC implementation shows that cost-effective multi-mode digital baseband receiver accelerators for GSM/EDGE can be realized at ultra low-power.

Acknowledgments. The authors would like to thank Andreas Burg, Andreas Bubenhofer, Johannes Widmer, Stefan Zwicky, Harald Kröll, and Christoph Roth for their support. This project was funded by CTI (No. 11370.1), Switzerland in collaboration with Advanced Circuit Pursuit AG.

References

1. GSM Association, Market Data (August 2009), http://www.gsmworld.com
2. Eyuboglu, M., Qureshi, S.: Reduced-state sequence estimation with set partitioning and decision feedback. IEEE Transactions on Communications 36, 13–20 (1988)
3. Duel-Hallen, A., Heegard, C.: Delayed decision-feedback sequence estimation. IEEE Transactions on Communications 37, 428–436 (1989)
4. Olivier, J., et al.: Efficient equalization and symbol detection for 8-PSK EDGE cellular system. IEEE Transactions on Vehicular Technology 52, 525–529 (2003)
5. Gerstacker, W., Schober, R.: Equalization concepts for EDGE. IEEE Transactions on Wireless Communications 1, 190–199 (2002)
6. Szczecinski, L., Soto, I.: Is turbo equalization useful in EDGE systems? In: Vehicular Technology Conference, vol. 1, pp. 80–84 (2002)
7. Laot, C., Le Bidan, R., Leroux, D.: Low-complexity MMSE turbo equalization: a possible solution for EDGE. IEEE Transactions on Wireless Communications 4, 965–974 (2005)
8. 3GPP Organizational Partners, Sophia Antipolis Valbonne, France, 3rd Generation Partnership Project; Technical Specification Group GSM/EDGE Radio Access Network; Channel Coding (June 2009)
9. 3GPP Organizational Partners, Sophia Antipolis Valbonne, France, 3rd Generation Partnership Project; Technical Specification Group GSM/EDGE Radio Access Network; Modulation (December 2008)
10. 3GPP Organizational Partners, Sophia Antipolis Valbonne, France, 3rd Generation Partnership Project; Technical Specification Group GSM/EDGE Radio Access Network; Radio transmission and reception (June 2009)
11. Proakis, J.: Digital Communications, 4th edn. McGraw-Hill Higher Education, New York (2001)
12. Schmidt, M., Fettweis, G.: Fractionally-spaced prefiltering for reduced state equalization. In: Global Telecommunications Conference, GLOBECOM 1999, vol. 5, pp. 2291–2295 (1999)
13. Smith III, J.O.: Introduction to Digital Filters: with Audio Applications. W3K Publishing (2004)
14. Gerstacker, W., et al.: On prefilter computation for reduced-state equalization. IEEE Transactions on Wireless Communications 1 (October 2002)
15. Oppenheim, A.V., Schafer, R.W.: Digital Signal Processing, 1st edn. Prentice-Hall, Inc., Englewood Cliffs (1989)
16. Detert, T.: Prefiltered low complexity tree detection for frequency selective fading channels. In: IEEE 65th Vehicular Technology Conference, VTC 2007 Spring, pp. 2364–2368 (April 2007)
17. Chu, W.C.: Speech coding algorithms: foundation and evolution of standardized coders. John Wiley & Sons, Inc., Hoboken (2003)
18. Makhoul, J.: Linear prediction: A tutorial review. Proceedings of the IEEE, 561–580 (April 1975)
19. Golub, G., Van Loan, C.: Matrix computations. Johns Hopkins University Press (1996)
20. Benkeser, C.: Power Efficiency and the Mapping of Communication Algorithms into VLSI. PhD thesis, ETH Zürich, Switzerland, Series in Microelectronics, vol. 209. Hartung-Gorre Verlag Konstanz (2010)
21. Seurre, E., Savelli, P., Pietri, P.-J.: EDGE for Mobile Internet. Artech House, Norwood (2003)

22. Viterbi, A.: Error bounds for convolutional codes and an asymptotically optimum decoding algorithm. IEEE Transactions on Information Theory 13, 260–269 (1967)
23. Ma, H., Wolf, J.: On tail biting convolutional codes. IEEE Transactions on Communications 34, 104–111 (1986)
24. Biglieri, E.: Coding for wireless channels. Springer, New York (2005)
25. Truong, T., Shih, M.-T., Reed, I., Satorius, E.: A VLSI design for a trace-back Viterbi decoder. IEEE Transactions on Communications 40, 616–624 (1992)
26. Cox, R., Sundberg, C.: An efficient adaptive circular Viterbi algorithm for decoding generalized tailbiting convolutional codes. IEEE Transactions on Vehicular Technology 43, 57–68 (1994)
27. Anderson, J., Hladik, S.: An optimal circular Viterbi decoder for the bounded distance criterion. IEEE Transactions on Communications 50, 1736–1742 (2002)
28. Clark, G., Cain, J.: Error-correction coding for digital communications. Plenum Press, New York (1981)
29. Hagenauer, J., Hoeher, P.: A Viterbi algorithm with soft-decision outputs and its applications. In: Global Telecommunications Conference, 1989, and Exhibition. Communications Technology for the 1990s and Beyond. GLOBECOM 1989, IEEE, vol. 3, pp. 1680–1686 (November 1989)

VLSI Implementation of Hard- and Soft-Output Sphere Decoding for Wide-Band MIMO Systems

Christoph Studer[1], Markus Wenk[2], and Andreas Burg[3]

[1] Dept. of Electrical and Computer Engineering, Rice University,
Houston, TX 77005, USA
studer@rice.edu
[2] Dept. of Information Technology and Electrical Engineering, ETH Zurich,
8092 Zurich, Switzerland
mawenk@iis.ee.ethz.ch
[3] School of Engineering, EPF Lausanne,
1015 Lausanne, Switzerland
andreas.burg@epfl.ch

Abstract. Multiple-input multiple-output (MIMO) technology in combination with orthogonal frequency-division multiplexing (OFDM) is the key to meet the demands for data rate and link reliability of modern wide-band wireless communication systems, such as IEEE 802.11n or 3GPP-LTE. The full potential of such systems can, however, only be achieved by high-performance data-detection algorithms, which typically exhibit prohibitive computational complexity. Hard-output sphere decoding (SD) and soft-output single tree-search (STS) SD are promising means for realizing high-performance MIMO detection and have been demonstrated to enable efficient implementations in practical systems. In this chapter, we consider the design and optimization of register transfer-level implementations of hard-output SD and soft-output STS-SD with minimum area-delay product, which are well-suited for wide-band MIMO systems. We explain in detail the design, implementation, and optimization of VLSI architectures and present corresponding implementation results for 130 nm CMOS technology. The reported implementations significantly outperform the area-delay product of previously reported hard-output SD and soft-output STS-SD implementations.

Keywords: VLSI implementation, MIMO-OFDM communication systems, sphere decoding (SD), single tree-search (STS) SD algorithm.

1 Introduction

The evolution of data rate and quality-of-service in modern wide-band wireless communication systems is fueled by novel physical-layer technologies providing high spectral efficiency and excellent link reliability. Multiple-input multiple-output (MIMO) technology [1, 2], which employs multiple antennas at both ends of the wireless link, in combination with spatial multiplexing, orthogonal frequency-division multiplexing (OFDM), and channel coding is believed to

J.L. Ayala, D. Atienza, and R. Reis (Eds.): VLSI-SoC 2010, IFIP AICT 373, pp. 128–154, 2012.

be the key for reliable, high-speed, and bandwidth-efficient data transmission. Therefore, MIMO-OFDM technology is incorporated in many modern wide-band wireless communication standards, such as IEEE 802.11n [3] or 3GPP-LTE [4].

In such systems, data detection, i.e., the separation of the multiplexed data streams, is (besides channel decoding) typically among the main implementation challenges in terms of computational complexity and power consumption. Therefore, corresponding *efficient VLSI implementations* are the key to enable high-performance, low-power, and low-cost user equipment. The performance of MIMO technology critically depends on the employed data-detection algorithm and corresponding high-performance methods usually entail very high complexity. In particular, a straightforward implementation of hard-output maximum-likelihood (ML) detection and soft-output a-posteriori probability (APP) detection—both providing excellent error-rate performance—requires to exhaustively test all possible transmit symbols, which results in prohibitive complexity, even for moderate data rates and in deep submicron technologies.

The sphere-decoding (SD) algorithm [5–11] is known to be a promising means for efficient hard-output ML and soft-output APP detection. The key idea of SD is to transform MIMO detection into a tree-search problem, which can then be solved efficiently through a branch-and-bound procedure. The drawback of this approach lies in the fact that the decoding effort—measured in terms of the *number of nodes* to be examined during the tree search—depends on the instantaneous channel and noise realization. In the worst-case, the number of visited nodes, which typically corresponds to the number of clock cycles required for detection in VLSI [11, 12], is equivalent to that of an exhaustive search [13]. Since on-chip storage and higher-layer requirements limit the processing latency that may be inferred to support the processing of received data, the worst-case complexity of SD renders its application in real-world systems extremely challenging. This challenge can be mastered by limiting the maximum decoding effort by means of *early termination* of the decoding process [11, 14, 15]. This approach, however, leads to a trade-off between the maximum decoding effort and the performance of the MIMO detector. Therefore, a universally applicable VLSI architecture for SD-based MIMO detection suitable for wide-band MIMO wireless communication systems must provide a robust solution allowing for the smooth adjustment of this trade-off while minimizing the required silicon area for a given minimum performance requirement.

1.1 Contributions

In this chapter, we describe an SD-based detector architecture for wide-band MIMO communication systems and detail corresponding design and implementation trade-offs of hard- and soft-output SD. To this end, we first review the hard-output SD algorithm and the soft-output single tree-search (STS) SD algorithm. Then, a VLSI architecture suitable for efficient data detection in wide-band MIMO systems is presented and we argue that the optimization target for the parallelly-operating SD cores corresponds to minimizing the area-delay product, which differs fundamentally from minimizing the area or maximizing the throughput, as it would be the case for narrow-band systems. To arrive at SD architectures that minimize the area-delay product, we start with the VLSI implementations for hard-output SD [12] and soft-output STS-SD [11] and propose a variety of optimizations, which improve (i.e., lower) the area-delay product of the detectors. In particular, we propose a low-complexity approximation to the Schnorr-Euchner (SE) enumeration scheme and employ pipeline interleaving, which enables us to achieve the desired design goals. We finally present implementation results for 130 nm CMOS technology and perform a comparison to previously reported implementations of SD.

1.2   Outline of the Chapter

The remainder of this chapter is organized as follows. In Section 2, the MIMO system model is introduced and the employed hard-output and soft-output STS-SD algorithms are reviewed. In Section 3, we develop a receiver architecture suitable for wide-band MIMO systems and analyze the optimization goals for the SD-core implementations. The VLSI architectures for hard-output SD and soft-output STS-SD along with corresponding optimization techniques are detailed in Section 4 and Section 5, respectively. VLSI-implementation results are presented in Section 6 and we conclude in Section 7.

1.3   Notation

Matrices are set in boldface capital letters, column-vectors in boldface lowercase letters. The superscripts T and H stand for transposition and conjugate transposition, respectively. The real and imaginary part of a complex-valued number x are denoted by $\Re(x)$ and $\Im(x)$, respectively. The ℓ_2-norm (or Euclidean norm) of a vector $\mathbf{x}$ is designated by $\|\mathbf{x}\|$, the ℓ_∞-norm of $\mathbf{x}$ is $\|\mathbf{x}\|_\infty = \max_i |x_i|$, and the $\ell_{\widetilde{\infty}}$-norm is defined as $\|\mathbf{x}\|_{\widetilde{\infty}} = \max\{\|\Re(\mathbf{x})\|_\infty, \|\Im(\mathbf{x})\|_\infty\}$. The binary complement of $x \in \{0,1\}$ is denoted by $\overline{x}$. Probability and expectation are referred to as $\Pr[\cdot]$ and $\mathsf{E}[\cdot]$, respectively.

2   MIMO System Model and Sphere Decoding

In this section, we introduce the wide-band MIMO system model and summarize the hard-output and soft-output SD algorithms investigated in the remainder of the chapter.

2.1   Wide-Band MIMO System Model

We consider a coded wide-band MIMO system employing spatial multiplexing with M_T transmit and $M_R \geq M_T$ receive antennas (see Fig. 1) and orthogonal frequency-division multiplexing (OFDM). The information bits $\mathbf{b}$ are encoded (e.g., using a convolutional code) and interleaved (denoted by $\prod$ in Fig. 1). The resulting coded bit-stream $\mathbf{x}$ is mapped (using Gray labeling) to a sequence of transmit vectors $\mathbf{s}[k] \in \mathcal{O}^{M_T}$, where $\mathcal{O}$ corresponds to the scalar complex

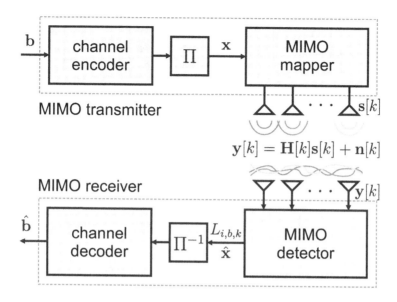

Fig. 1. Coded wide-band MIMO communication system

constitution of size 2^Q and $k = 1, \ldots, T$ designates the OFDM-tone index; the maximum number of OFDM carriers corresponds to T. Each transmit vector $\mathbf{s}[k]$ is associated with $M_T Q$ binary values $x_{i,b,k} \in \{0,1\}$, $i = 1, \ldots, M_T$, $b = 1, \ldots, Q$ corresponding to the bth bit of the ith entry (i.e., spatial stream) of $\mathbf{s}[k]$. The baseband input-output relation of the wireless MIMO channel for each OFDM tone is given by

$$\mathbf{y}[k] = \mathbf{H}[k]\mathbf{s}[k] + \mathbf{n}[k] \tag{1}$$

where $\mathbf{H}[k]$ stands for the $M_R \times M_T$ complex-valued channel matrix on OFDM tone k, $\mathbf{y}[k]$ is the M_R-dimensional received vector, and $\mathbf{n}[k]$ is M_R-dimensional i.i.d. zero-mean complex Gaussian distributed noise with variance N_0 per entry. We assume $\mathsf{E}[\mathbf{s}[k]\mathbf{s}[k]^H] = \frac{1}{M_T}\mathbf{I}_{M_T}$ in the following.

In the receiver, a hard-output MIMO detector computes estimates $\hat{\mathbf{s}}[k]$ for the transmit vector, which are then used to generate binary-valued estimates $\hat{\mathbf{x}}$ for the coded bit-stream $\mathbf{x}$. If a soft-output MIMO detector is used, reliability information in the form of log-likelihood ratios (LLRs) $L_{i,b,k}$ for each coded bit $x_{i,b,k}$ is generated instead. For both detection schemes we assume coherent detection, i.e., the channel matrices $\mathbf{H}[k]$, $k = 1, \ldots, T$, and the noise variance N_0 are perfectly known by the receiver. Finally, the MIMO receiver generates estimates for the information bits $\hat{\mathbf{b}}$ using the channel decoder, which operates either on the basis of the de-interleaved (denoted by $\prod^{-1}$ in Fig. 1) bit stream $\hat{\mathbf{x}}$ for hard-output MIMO detectors or on the de-interleaved sequence of LLRs $L_{i,b,k}$ generated by the soft-output MIMO detector. Since the MIMO detector can treat the OFDM tones independently of each other, the tone index k is omitted in the remainder of the chapter.

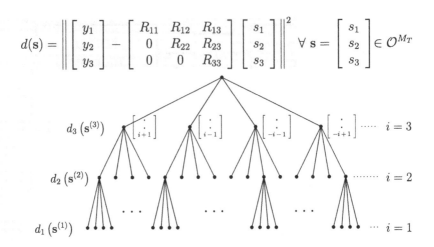

$$d(\mathbf{s}) = \left\| \begin{bmatrix} y_1 \\ y_2 \\ y_3 \end{bmatrix} - \begin{bmatrix} R_{11} & R_{12} & R_{13} \\ 0 & R_{22} & R_{23} \\ 0 & 0 & R_{33} \end{bmatrix} \begin{bmatrix} s_1 \\ s_2 \\ s_3 \end{bmatrix} \right\|^2 \quad \forall\, \mathbf{s} = \begin{bmatrix} s_1 \\ s_2 \\ s_3 \end{bmatrix} \in \mathcal{O}^{M_T}$$

Fig. 2. MIMO detection reformulated as a tree-search problem for $M_T = 3$ spatial streams and QPSK modulation

2.2   ML Detection Using the Sphere-Decoding Algorithm

Hard-output MIMO detection using the ML-detection rule maximizes the probability of detecting the correct transmitted vector $\mathbf{s}$. The ML rule for the input-output relation (1) corresponds to [1,2]

$$\hat{\mathbf{s}} = \arg\min_{\mathbf{s} \in \mathcal{O}^{M_T}} \|\mathbf{y} - \mathbf{H}\mathbf{s}\|^2 \tag{2}$$

and a straightforward evaluation of (2) requires an exhaustive search over all transmit-vectors $\mathbf{s} \in \mathcal{O}^{M_T}$. Since $|\mathcal{O}^{M_T}| = 2^{M_T Q}$, this approach leads—even for a small number of transmit-antennas—to a prohibitive computational complexity. To alleviate this complexity issue, a variety of low-complexity algorithms have been proposed in the literature (see, e.g., [1,2] and the references therein). Unfortunately, most of the existing low-complexity MIMO detection schemes sacrifice error-rate performance for complexity, which is not desirable for high-performance transceiver implementations. We next summarize the hard-output SD algorithm, which is able to provide ML performance at low (average) computational complexity.

Sphere-Decoding Algorithm. The SD algorithm [5–9] starts with the QR decomposition (QRD) of the channel matrix $\mathbf{H} = \mathbf{Q}\mathbf{R}$, where the $M_R \times M_T$ matrix $\mathbf{Q}$ satisfies $\mathbf{Q}^H \mathbf{Q} = \mathbf{I}_{M_T}$, and the $M_T \times M_T$ matrix $\mathbf{R}$ is upper-triangular. The QRD enables us to rewrite the ML-detection problem (2) as follows:

$$\hat{\mathbf{s}} = \arg\min_{\mathbf{s} \in \mathcal{O}^{M_T}} \|\hat{\mathbf{y}} - \mathbf{R}\mathbf{s}\|^2 \tag{3}$$

with $\hat{\mathbf{y}} = \mathbf{Q}^H \mathbf{y}$. Thanks to the upper-triangular structure of $\mathbf{R}$, the minimization in (3) can be transformed into a tree-search problem where the nodes of the tree on level i are associated with a partial symbol vector $\mathbf{s}^{(i)} = [\, s_i \; \cdots \; s_{M_T} \,]^T$ and with a corresponding partial Euclidean distance (PED) $d_i(\mathbf{s}^{(i)})$. Fig. 2 illustrates the corresponding tree for a MIMO system with $M_T = M_R = 3$ using QPSK modulation. It is important to realize that when starting from the root of the tree (at level $i = M_T + 1$ with $d_{M_T+1} = 0$), the PEDs can efficiently be computed in a recursive manner as follows:

$$d_i(\mathbf{s}^{(i)}) = d_{i+1}(\mathbf{s}^{(i+1)}) + |b_{i+1} - R_{i,i} s_i|^2 \qquad (4)$$

with the definition

$$b_{i+1} = \hat{y}_i - \sum_{k=i+1}^{M_T} R_{i,k} s_k \qquad (5)$$

when proceeding from a parent node on level $i + 1$ to one of its children on level i. Each path from the root down to a leaf corresponds to a symbol vector $\mathbf{s} \in \mathcal{O}^{M_T}$. Since the dependence of the PED d_i on the symbol vector $\mathbf{s}$ is only through $\mathbf{s}^{(i)}$, we have transformed ML detection into a tree-search problem. The ML solution (3) corresponds to the path through the tree starting by the root and leading to the leaf associated with the smallest PED.

The basic ideas underlying the SD algorithm, as described in [9,12], are briefly summarized as follows: The search in the tree is constrained to nodes which lie within a *radius* r around $\tilde{\mathbf{y}}$ (and hence, nodes from the tree are pruned for which $d_i(\mathbf{s}^{(i)})$ is larger than r) and tree traversal is performed depth-first, visiting the children of a given node in ascending order of their PEDs. The method using this enumeration scheme is also known as the Schnorr-Euchner (SE) SD algorithm [6]. In the following, we refer to the condition $d_i(\mathbf{s}^{(i)}) < r$ as the *sphere constraint* (SC). We additionally employ *radius reduction*, which amounts to starting the algorithm with $r = \infty$ and updating the radius according to $r \leftarrow d_1(\mathbf{s}^{(1)})$ whenever a leaf $\mathbf{s} = \mathbf{s}^{(1)}$ has been reached. This technique avoids the problem of choosing a suitable initial radius and still leads to efficient pruning of the tree. At the same time, it guarantees that the algorithm terminates only when the ML solution has been found.

In the remainder of the chapter, the computational complexity of SD is characterized by the *number of visited nodes* (including the root node but excluding the leaves), which was shown in [11,12] to be closely related to the throughput of corresponding VLSI implementations.

Channel-Matrix Preprocessing. A common approach to reduce the complexity of SD without compromising performance is to adapt the detection order of the spatial streams to the instantaneous channel realization by performing a QR-decomposition on $\mathbf{HP}$ (rather than $\mathbf{H}$), where $\mathbf{P}$ is a suitably chosen $M_T \times M_T$ permutation matrix. More efficient pruning of the tree is obtained if sorting is performed such that "stronger streams" (in terms of effective SNR) correspond to levels closer to the root, i.e., if $\mathbf{P}$ is chosen such that the main diagonal entries of $\mathbf{R}$ in $\mathbf{HP} = \mathbf{QR}$ are sorted in ascending order. An effective way to accomplish this goal was proposed in [16] and will be referred to as sorted QRD (SQRD) in the following.

An additional preprocessing method which further lowers the computational complexity, while slightly reducing the error-rate performance of SD is known as *regularization*, e.g., [11]. The main idea of regularization is to realize that poorly conditioned channel realizations $\mathbf{H}$ typically lead to high search complexity due to the low effective SNR on one or more of the effective spatial streams. An efficient way to counter ill-conditioned channel matrices is to operate on a *regularized* version of the channel matrix by computing the (sorted) QR-decomposition of

$$\begin{bmatrix} \mathbf{H} \\ \alpha \mathbf{I}_{M_T} \end{bmatrix} \mathbf{P} = \mathbf{QR} \tag{6}$$

where α is a suitably chosen regularization parameter, $\mathbf{Q}$ is a $(M_R + M_T) \times M_T$ matrix satisfying $\mathbf{QQ}^H = \mathbf{I}_{M_T}$, and $\mathbf{R}$ is of dimension $M_T \times M_T$. By partitioning $\mathbf{Q}$ according to $\mathbf{Q} = [\mathbf{Q}_1^T \ \mathbf{Q}_2^T]^T$, where $\mathbf{Q}_1$ is of dimension $M_R \times M_T$ and $\mathbf{Q}_2$ is of dimension $M_T \times M_T$, the ML rule in (3) can be approximated as

$$\hat{\mathbf{s}} \approx \arg \min_{\tilde{\mathbf{s}} \in \mathcal{O}^{M_T}} \|\tilde{\mathbf{y}} - \mathbf{R}\tilde{\mathbf{s}}\|^2 \tag{7}$$

where $\tilde{\mathbf{y}} = \mathbf{Q}_1^H \mathbf{y}$ and $\tilde{\mathbf{s}} = \mathbf{Ps}$. Setting the regularization parameter $\alpha = \sqrt{N_o M_T}$ corresponds to MMSE regularization [17], which was shown in [11] to result in a good performance/complexity trade-off for hard- and soft-output SD algorithms.

2.3   Soft-Output Single Tree-Search Sphere Decoding

In coded MIMO systems, the computation of reliability information (i.e., soft-outputs) in the form of LLRs $L_{i,b}$ for each transmitted bit $x_{i,b}$ improves (often significantly) the error-rate performance compared to hard-output detection, which only computes binary-valued estimates for $x_{i,b}$.

Computation of the Max-Log LLRs. Soft-output MIMO detection amounts to computing LLR-values $L_{i,b}$ for each transmitted bit $x_{i,b}$ according to [10,11]

$$L_{i,b} = \log \left(\frac{\Pr[x_{i,b} = 1 \mid \mathbf{y}]}{\Pr[x_{i,b} = 0 \mid \mathbf{y}]} \right). \tag{8}$$

Straightforward computation of (8) results in prohibitive computational complexity. In order to reduce the complexity of LLR computation, we employ the *max-log approximation* [10,11]

$$L_{i,b} \approx \min_{\mathbf{s} \in \mathcal{X}_{i,b}^{(0)}} \|\hat{\mathbf{y}} - \mathbf{Rs}\|^2 - \min_{\mathbf{s} \in \mathcal{X}_{i,b}^{(1)}} \|\hat{\mathbf{y}} - \mathbf{Rs}\|^2 \tag{9}$$

where $\mathcal{X}_{i,b}^{(0)}$ and $\mathcal{X}_{i,b}^{(1)}$ are the sets of symbol vectors that have the bth bit in the label of the jth scalar symbol equal to 0 and 1, respectively. We emphasize that the LLRs in (9) are *normalized* with respect to the noise variance N_o in order to get rid of the factor $1/N_0$ on the right hand side (RHS) of (9). This normalization simplifies the exposition and does *not* degrade the error rate performance with max-log-based channel decoders (see [11] for the details).

For each transmitted bit $x_{i,b}$, one of the two minima in (9) is given by the metric $\lambda^{\mathrm{ML}} = \|\hat{\mathbf{y}} - \mathbf{R}\mathbf{s}^{\mathrm{ML}}\|^2$ associated with the ML solution $\mathbf{s}^{\mathrm{ML}} = \hat{\mathbf{s}}$ of the MIMO detection problem in (3). The other minimum in (9) can be written as

$$\lambda_{i,b}^{\overline{\mathrm{ML}}} = \min_{\mathbf{s} \in \mathcal{X}_{i,b}^{\overline{\mathrm{ML}}}} \|\hat{\mathbf{y}} - \mathbf{R}\mathbf{s}\|^2 \tag{10}$$

where $\mathcal{X}_{i,b}^{\overline{\mathrm{ML}}}$ corresponds to the subset of $\mathcal{O}^{M_\mathrm{T}}$ for which the (i, b)th bit is equal to the *counter-hypothesis* $\overline{x_{i,b}^{\mathrm{ML}}}$, denoting the binary complement of the bth bit in the label of the ith entry of $\mathbf{s}^{\mathrm{ML}}$. With (3) and (10) the max-log LLRs (9) can be re-written as

$$L_{i,b} \approx \begin{cases} \lambda^{\mathrm{ML}} - \lambda_{i,b}^{\overline{\mathrm{ML}}} , & x_{i,b}^{\mathrm{ML}} = 0 \\ \lambda_{i,b}^{\overline{\mathrm{ML}}} - \lambda^{\mathrm{ML}} , & x_{i,b}^{\mathrm{ML}} = 1 . \end{cases} \tag{11}$$

From (11), it is obvious that soft-output MIMO detection breaks down to efficiently identifying $\mathbf{s}^{\mathrm{ML}}$, λ^{ML}, and $\lambda_{i,b}^{\overline{\mathrm{ML}}}$ for $i = 1, \ldots, M_\mathrm{T}$ and $b = 1, \ldots, Q$.

Single Tree-Search Sphere Decoding. Computation of the max-log LLRs in (11) requires the metrics $\lambda_{i,b}^{\overline{\mathrm{ML}}}$, which, for given i, b, is accomplished by traversing only those parts of the tree that have leaves in $\mathcal{X}_{i,b}^{\overline{\mathrm{ML}}}$. Since this computation has to be carried out for every bit, it is immediately obvious that soft-output MIMO detection results in significantly higher computational complexity compared to hard-output ML detection using the SD algorithm. The soft-output STS-SD algorithm proposed in [11] is key in keeping the complexity increase (compared to hard-output SD) at a minimum and is summarized next.

The main idea of the soft-output STS-SD algorithm is to ensure that every node in the tree is visited at most once, which can be accomplished by searching for the ML solution and all counter-hypotheses *concurrently*. To this end, the algorithm searches the subtree originating from a given node only if the result can lead to an update of at least λ^{ML} or one of the $\lambda_{i,b}^{\overline{\mathrm{ML}}}$. In the ensuing discussion, the bit-label vector of the current ML hypothesis and the corresponding metric are denoted by $\mathbf{x}^{\mathrm{ML}}$ and λ^{ML}, respectively. The soft-output STS-SD algorithm consists of two main tasks, namely *list administration* and *tree pruning*:

List Administration: The algorithm is initialized with $\lambda^{\mathrm{ML}} = \lambda_{i,b}^{\overline{\mathrm{ML}}} = \infty$, $\forall i, b$. Whenever a leaf with corresponding bit-label $\mathbf{x}$ has been reached, the algorithm distinguishes between two cases:

1) If a new ML hypothesis is found, i.e., if $d(\mathbf{x}) < \lambda^{\text{ML}}$, then all $\lambda_{i,b}^{\overline{\text{ML}}}$ for which $x_{i,b} = \overline{x_{i,b}^{\text{ML}}}$ are set to λ^{ML} followed by the updates $\lambda^{\text{ML}} \leftarrow d(\mathbf{x})$ and $\mathbf{x}^{\text{ML}} \leftarrow \mathbf{x}$; this ensures that for each bit in the ML hypothesis that is changed in the process of the update, the metric of the *former* ML hypothesis becomes the metric of the *new* counter-hypothesis, followed by an update of the ML hypothesis.

2) In the case $d(\mathbf{x}) \geq \lambda^{\text{ML}}$, only the counter-hypotheses need to be checked. Here, the decoder updates $\lambda_{i,b}^{\overline{\text{ML}}} \leftarrow d(\mathbf{x})$ for all i and b satisfying $x_{i,b} = \overline{x_{i,b}^{\text{ML}}}$ and $d(\mathbf{x}) < \lambda_{i,b}^{\overline{\text{ML}}}$.

Tree Pruning: The second key aspect of STS-SD is the following tree-pruning criterion: Consider a given node $\mathbf{s}^{(j)}$ (on level j) and the corresponding label $\mathbf{x}^{(j)}$ consisting of the bits $x_{i,b}$ ($i = j, \ldots, M_T$, $b = 1, \ldots, Q$). Assume that the subtree originating from the node under consideration and corresponding to the bits $x_{i,b}$ ($i = 1, \ldots, j-1$, $b = 1, \ldots, Q$) has not been expanded yet. The pruning criterion for $\mathbf{s}^{(j)}$ along with its subtree is compiled from two conditions. First, the bits in the partial bit-label $\mathbf{x}^{(j)}$ associated to $\mathbf{s}^{(j)}$ are compared with the corresponding bits in the label of the current ML hypothesis $\mathbf{x}^{\text{ML}}$. All metrics $\lambda_{i,b}^{\overline{\text{ML}}}$ with $x_{i,b} = \overline{x_{i,b}^{\text{ML}}}$ found in this comparison may be affected when searching the subtree of $\mathbf{s}^{(j)}$. Second, the metrics $\lambda_{i,b}^{\overline{\text{ML}}}$ ($i = 1, \ldots, j-1$, $b = 1, \ldots, Q$) corresponding to the counter-hypotheses in the subtree of $\mathbf{s}^{(j)}$ may be affected as well. In summary, the metrics which may be affected during the search in the subtree emanating from the node $\mathbf{s}^{(j)}$ are given by the set

$$\mathcal{A}(\mathbf{x}^{(j)}) = \left\{ \lambda_{i,b}^{\overline{\text{ML}}} \,\middle|\, (i \geq j, b = 1, \ldots, Q) \wedge (x_{i,b} = \overline{x_{i,b}^{\text{ML}}}) \right\}$$
$$\cup \left\{ \lambda_{i,b}^{\overline{\text{ML}}} \,\middle|\, i < j, b = 1, \ldots, Q \right\}.$$

The node $\mathbf{x}^{(j)}$ along with its subtree is pruned if its PED satisfies

$$d(\mathbf{x}^{(j)}) > \max_{a \in \mathcal{A}(\mathbf{x}^{(j)})} a. \tag{12}$$

The STS-SD pruning criterion ensures that a given node and the entire subtree originating from that node are explored only if this could lead to an update of either λ^{ML} or of at least one of the $\lambda_{i,b}^{\overline{\text{ML}}}$, which enables significant complexity savings compared to other tree-search based soft-output MIMO detection algorithms, e.g., [10, 18].

LLR Clipping. In practical systems, it is often desirable to tune the performance and complexity of the detection algorithm at run-time. LLR clipping [19] offers a convenient way to adjust this trade-off with the STS-SD algorithm. The key idea is to bound the dynamic range of the max-log LLRs so that

$$|L_{i,b}| \leq L_{\max} \quad \forall i, b \tag{13}$$

and to incorporate the clipping constraint (13) into the STS-SD algorithm. In particular, LLR clipping can be built into the algorithm by simply applying the update [11]

$$\lambda_{i,b}^{\overline{\mathrm{ML}}} \leftarrow \min\left\{\lambda_{i,b}^{\overline{\mathrm{ML}}}, \lambda^{\mathrm{ML}} + L_{\max}\right\} \tag{14}$$

to all counter-hypotheses, after carrying out the steps in Case 1) of the list administration procedure described above. The remaining steps of the STS-SD algorithm are not affected. For $L_{\max} = \infty$, STS-SD obviously delivers the exact max-log LLRs, whereas for $L_{\max} = 0$, we obtain hard-output SD performance as the decoder's output is $\mathbf{x}^{\mathrm{ML}}$, λ^{ML}, and $L_{i,b} = 0$ for all i and b. As shown in [11], the LLR-clipping parameter $L_{\max}$ can indeed be used to gracefully adjust the performance and complexity of the soft-output STS-SD algorithm.

3   Wide-Band MIMO Receiver Architecture

We next show that for wide-band MIMO wireless communication systems, such as IEEE 802.11n or 3GPP-LTE, a single SD core turns out to be insufficient to simultaneously support the high bandwidth and the (error-rate) performance requirements, even when implementing the receiver in deep submicron CMOS technologies. We therefore present an architecture consisting of multiple SD-cores, which is able to meet the throughput and performance requirements of modern wide-band MIMO systems.

3.1   Run-Time Constraints

The computational complexity (required to find the ML solution or the LLR values) of the algorithms discussed above depends on the transmitted signals $\mathbf{s}$, the instantaneous realizations of the (random) channel matrix $\mathbf{H}$, and the noise vector $\mathbf{n}$. Consequently, the throughput of SD-based algorithms is variable and, in particular, random, which constitutes a significant problem in many practical application scenarios. Furthermore, the worst-case complexity of SD-based algorithms is equivalent to that of an exhaustive search [13]. Consequently, to meet the practically important requirement of a fixed throughput, the algorithm's run-time must be constrained. This, in turn, leads to a constraint on the maximum detection effort or, equivalently, to a constraint on the maximum number of nodes that the SD is allowed to visit, which will clearly prevent the detector from achieving ML performance or to be able to deliver the exact max-log LLRs in (9). It is therefore of paramount importance to find a way of imposing run-time constraints while keeping the resulting performance degradation at a minimum. Moreover, it is highly desirable in practice to have a smooth performance degradation as the run-time constraint becomes more stringent. Early-termination methods allowing for a smooth performance degradation suitable for narrow-band systems have been proposed in [11, 14]. The approach and architecture described next enables an efficient way to incorporate run-time constraints for wide-band MIMO wireless communication systems.

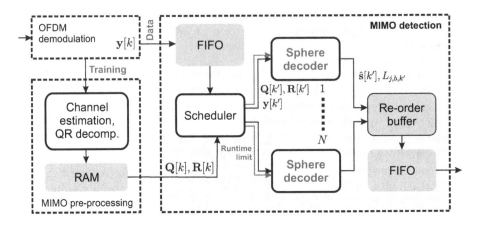

Fig. 3. High-level system architecture of a SD-based MIMO-OFDM receiver

3.2   Receiver Architecture for Wide-Band MIMO Systems

The high-level architecture of a wide-band MIMO receiver based on SD is illustrated in Fig. 3. The data flow starts with the OFDM demodulation. During a training phase, received training symbols are delivered to a MIMO preprocessing unit, which estimates the channel matrices $\mathbf{H}[k]$ for all OFDM tones and performs necessary pre-computations on $\mathbf{H}[k]$ (i.e., the sorted and regularized QRD). During the data phase, the demodulation unit and the MIMO preprocessing unit forward the received vectors $\mathbf{y}[k]$ and the results of the preprocessing unit to the MIMO detector at a constant arrival rate, which is essentially given by the communication bandwidth of the system. In the MIMO-detection block, the information required to decode a symbol is first queued in a FIFO buffer. A scheduler reads the entries of the FIFO buffer and forwards them to the next available SD core together with a runtime constraint (i.e., an upper limit on the number of nodes that are allowed to be examined by the SD). When the FIFO fills up, the runtime constraints are reduced to ensure that no data is lost. Note that this reduction of the maximum runtime degrades the quality of the detection.[1] The outputs from the N instantiated SD cores are collected and re-ordered since the variable runtime may cause decoded symbols to arrive out-of-order. The reordered symbol estimates (either hard- or soft-outputs) are finally forwarded to the interleaver and the channel decoder.

3.3   Implications on SD-Core Optimization

With the above described architecture, the average decoding effort, i.e., the number of visited nodes that can be allocated for decoding of each symbol is determined by

---

[1] The particularities of the employed scheduling mechanism and the associated performance trade-offs can be found in [11].

$$\Phi \propto \frac{N}{T_c B} \quad [\text{nodes}]$$

where B denotes the bandwidth of the system (i.e., the arrival-rate of the symbols to be decoded), T_c is the clock period of each SD core (assuming that one node in the tree is checked in each clock cycle), and N denotes the number of SD instances. At the system-level, the performance/complexity trade-off can now be adjusted by the choice of N, i.e., instantiating more SD cores improves the error-rate performance but clearly comes at the cost of increased silicon area. In particular, the resulting area of the presented architecture corresponds to $A_{\text{tot}} = N A_{\text{SD}}$, where A_{SD} denotes the silicon area of a single SD core.[2] For a large number of SD cores, the overall silicon area for a guaranteed number of visited nodes $\bar{\Phi}$ that can be used for decoding received symbols, is given by

$$A_{\text{tot}} \propto \bar{\Phi} B \rho_{\text{SD}} \quad \text{with} \quad \rho_{\text{SD}} = T_c A_{\text{SD}}. \tag{15}$$

Consequently, it follows from (15) that *whenever* multiple SD cores are necessary to meet the performance and throughput requirements of a wide-band MIMO system, the focus for the optimization of the SD core shifts from minimizing the area or maximizing the throughput (as it is typically the case for narrow-band systems) to minimizing the corresponding *area-delay (AT-)product* ρ_{SD}. In the next two sections, we describe architectures for hard-output SD and soft-output STS-SD, which are optimized for minimum AT-product.

4   VLSI Architecture of Hard-Output SD

The hard-output SD architecture described next is based on the architecture template presented in [12]. We first summarize this architecture and then describe additional techniques that substantially improve (i.e., reduce) the associated AT-product.

4.1   High-Level Architecture

Fig. 4 shows the high-level block diagram of the proposed SD architecture. The design is comprised of a metric computation unit (MCU), a metric enumeration unit (MEU), an SC check unit, a level-select multiplexer, and a cache.

Metric Computation Unit: The MCU is responsible for the forward-iteration of the depth-first tree-traversal. In the implementation [12], this forward iteration includes the *sequential* evaluation of (5) and the computation of the PED in (4). In the present circuit (cf. Fig. 5) a slicer-unit performs a decision on the nearest constellation point and the MCU computes b_i (instead of b_{i+1}) in parallel to the

---

[2] We neglect the area overhead in the FIFOs and re-order buffers.

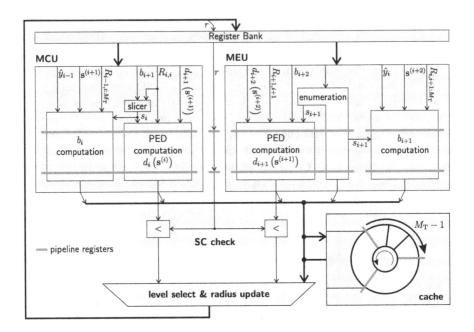

Fig. 4. High-level architecture of the hard-output SD unit. The shaded registers and the ring buffer (in the cache) are only required in when pipeline interleaving is used.

PED of level $i + 1$. The result b_i is then used in the next iteration (provided that the SC is met); this approach was shown to reduce the critical path of the SD-core without increasing the circuit area [20, 21].

Metric Enumeration Unit: The MEU operates in parallel to the MCU. While the MCU processes a node on layer i, the MEU selects the next-best constellation point on layer $i + 1$ according to the used enumeration scheme and computes its PED. Hence, once the SD algorithm needs to move upward in the tree (i.e., is performing backtracking), the MCU can directly start the next forward iteration as all required intermediate results have already been computed beforehand by the MEU. The register transfer-level (RTL) architecture of the MEU (cf. Fig. 5) is similar to the one of the MCU. However, the slicer-unit that determines the closest CP is replaced by an enumeration unit, which is used to determine the CP that is considered next on layer $i + 1$.

Remaining Units: The cache is used to store intermediate results for each level computed by the MEU and the MCU. The SC check is carried out immediately after the computation of the new PEDs. MEU, MCU, level cache, and the result of the SC check decide on which layer the SD algorithm proceeds next. If a valid leaf is found, i.e., whose metric fulfills the SC, the radius r is updated. In this case, an additional clock cycle is necessary, as the PEDs in the level cache need to be checked against the new radius.

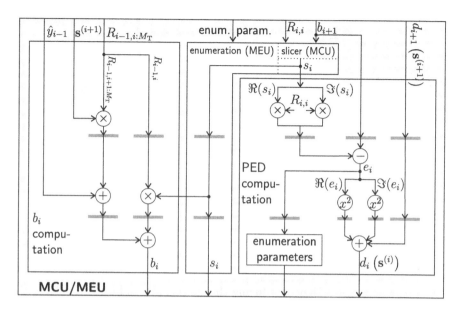

Fig. 5. RTL block diagram of the MCU and MEU. The shaded registers are only required when pipeline interleaving is applied.

4.2   Schnorr-Euchner Enumeration

The enumeration strategy (which is implemented by the *enumeration unit* in the MEU) defines the order in which the children of a node are examined. Radius reduction (cf. Section 2.2) is most efficient in combination with the SE enumeration [6,9], which visits the children of a node in ascending order of their PEDs. An important advantage of this enumeration strategy is that leaves that are more likely to lead to the ML solution (or corresponding counter-hypotheses for the STS-SD) are found early, which expedites the pruning of the tree. Moreover, enumeration of the children of a node can terminate as soon as a child violates the SC or, in the case of the STS-SD fulfills the corresponding pruning criterion.

For each visited node, SE enumeration comprises two types of operations: The first operation is to initialize the enumeration of the children by identifying the child associated with the smallest PED. This task can easily be accomplished by comparing b_{i+1} in (5) to a number of decision boundaries, i.e., by performing a slicing operation in the MCU shown in Fig. 4. The second type of operation is to enumerate the remaining children in ascending order of their PEDs, which is a non-trivial task for complex-valued constellations.[3] Unfortunately, the enumeration process has a significant impact on the complexity and on the critical path

---

[3] Note that for *real-valued* CPs, SE enumeration of the remaining child-nodes is immediately given by a zig-zag enumeration around the closest CP [9].

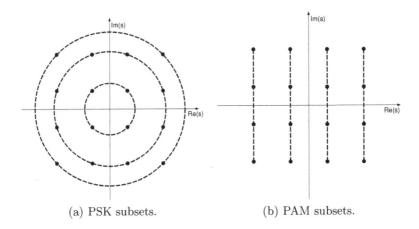

(a) PSK subsets.   (b) PAM subsets.

Fig. 6. The 16-QAM alphabet divided into one-dimensional subsets

of SD implementations. Hence, reducing the complexity and critical path of the enumeration unit is *essential* to minimize the AT-product ρ_{SD} of corresponding efficient SD implementations.

Exhaustive Enumeration. This method is a straightforward (but rather inefficient) solution to perform SE enumeration [12]. The idea is to first compute the PEDs of *all* children of a given node. During enumeration, a min-search (limited to the subset of children that have not yet been visited) identifies the next child. The main drawbacks of this solution are i) the area requirement to compute the PEDs of all children of a node, ii) the memory needed to store all PEDs in the cache, and iii) the fact that a min-search is costly in terms of area and timing, especially for higher order constellations. Hence, this approach is not suited for the efficient implementation of SD in hardware.

Subset Enumeration. More elaborate solutions for SE enumeration were presented in [10,12,22]. The main idea of these approaches is to divide the complex-valued (i.e., two-dimensional) constellation into one-dimensional subsets, which only require to compute and store one PED per subset. The SE enumeration then chooses the child with the smallest PED among the preferred children in these subsets, which leads to a complexity reduction in the min-search stage and reduces the memory requirements in the cache.

Fig. 6 illustrates two subset enumeration schemes. For phase-shift keying (PSK) subsets proposed in [10] and [12], the constellation is decomposed into several concentric circles (see Fig. 6(a)). The second method shown in Fig. 6(b) was proposed in [22] and employs pulse-amplitude modulation (PAM) subsets (i.e., stripes). Both methods suffer from the fact that the number of required subsets becomes large when targeting higher modulation orders (e.g., 64-QAM requires eight PAM subsets), which contributes considerably to the resulting circuit area and timing of the entire architecture (as sorting across all subsets is required). In order to further reduce the complexity of SE enumeration, one needs to resort to *approximate* SE enumeration schemes such as the ones described next.

4.3   Approximate Schnorr-Euchner Enumeration Schemes

The goal of considering approximations to SE enumeration is to perform the candidate enumeration without the need for computing, caching, and comparing PEDs of multiple children of the same node. Such methods yield significant reduction in terms of circuit area and critical path delay at the cost of a (often negligible) reduction in terms of error-rate performance and are, therefore, well-suited to reduce the AT-product of corresponding SD implementations. The basic idea of most of these approaches [23, 24] is to store predefined enumeration sequences in one or multiple look-up tables (LUTs). A fixed sequence is chosen based upon several geometric rules that analyze the position of the received point b_{i+1} in the complex plane relative to the closest CP. The accuracy of these techniques (i.e., how closely they follow the Schnorr-Euchner enumeration sequence) can be adjusted by the number and complexity of the associated selection criteria together with the number of predefined LUTs.

Search-Sequence Determination. This approach applies a few rules to the distance between the received point b_{i+1} and the closest CP denoted as a_i [23]. The number of rules applied to determine the position of b_{i+1} relative to the closest CP defines for how many nodes the resulting search sequence corresponds to the SE enumeration. For instance, the following first rule $\Re(a_i) \geq \Im(a_i)$ can determine the order of the first three nodes to be equal to the first three nodes of SE enumeration. Adding a second rule $1 - \Re(a_i) \geq 2\Im(a_i)$ allows to determine the SE enumeration order for the first four nodes. Each additional rule brings the search sequence closer to SE enumeration. However, in practice, a few rules or even only the first rule combined with enumeration of the remaining siblings according to a predefined order stored in look-up tables (LUTs) [24] often suffices to keep the performance loss negligible compared to SE enumeration.

Ordered $\ell_{\widetilde{\infty}}$-Norm Enumeration. The approach implemented here is inspired by the $\ell_{\widetilde{\infty}}$-norm SD algorithm [12, 25]. Here, however, the $\ell_{\widetilde{\infty}}$-norm is only used for enumeration purposes, whereas the SD algorithm in [12, 25] also uses it for distance computations. The enumeration scheme initially proposed in [21] can be implemented efficiently without requiring LUTs and therefore, scales well to higher-order constellations (i.e., constellations including and beyond 64-QAM). The starting point for the enumeration is trivially determined by the closest CP (in terms of Euclidean distance). However, the subsequent CPs are enumerated according to their distance from b_{i+1} in terms of the $\ell_{\widetilde{\infty}}$-norm:

$$d_{\widetilde{\infty}} = |b_{i+1} - R_{i,i}s_i|_{\widetilde{\infty}} = \max\{|\Re(b_{i+1} - R_{i,i}s_i)|, |\Im(b_{i+1} - R_{i,i}s_i)|\}.$$

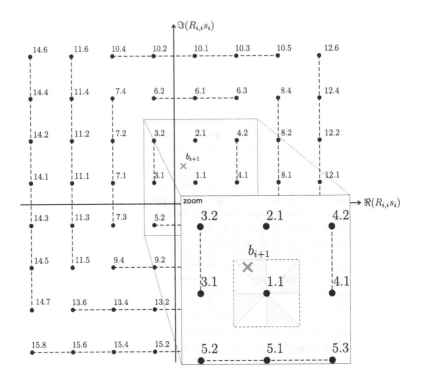

Fig. 7. Principle of ordered $\ell_{\widetilde{\infty}}$-norm enumeration for 64-QAM modulation

To this end, the area around the closest CP is first subdivided into eight sectors as illustrated in the lower right corner of Fig. 7. The sector containing b_{i+1} is identified with simple geometric rules to define the second CP in the enumeration and the direction for the ordered $\ell_{\widetilde{\infty}}$-norm enumeration. CPs with identical $\ell_{\widetilde{\infty}}$-norm form one-dimensional subsets. All nodes within the same subset are processed before the algorithm selects the next subset. In the example provided in Fig. 7, the processing order of the one-dimensional subsets is illustrated by the leading number attached to each CP. Within each subset, zig-zag enumeration is applied around the CP closest to b_{i+1}, which is illustrated by the corresponding trailing number in Fig. 7. The members of each subset are returned in SE order and subsets are enumerated in order of increasing $\ell_{\widetilde{\infty}}$-norm.

Implementation: The above-described enumeration scheme can be split into two basic tasks: i) Tracking of the position, size, and orientation of the linear subsets and ii) zig-zag enumeration within the subsets and checking for the boundaries of the finite-size modulation alphabet. Both tasks can be implemented using simple combinational logic, comparators, and only three counters. Hence, the circuit complexity of ordered $\ell_{\widetilde{\infty}}$-norm enumeration is very low.

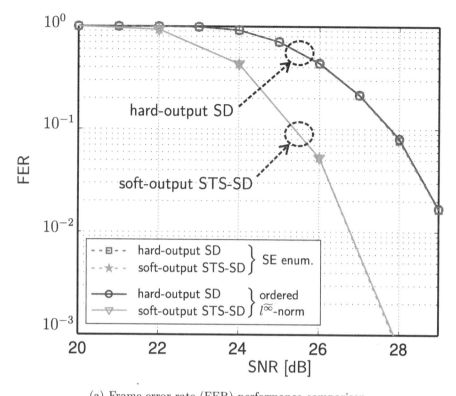

(a) Frame error-rate (FER) performance comparison.

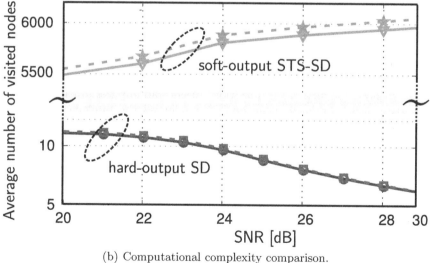

(b) Computational complexity comparison.

Fig. 8. FER performance and computational complexity (in average number of visited nodes) for ordered $\ell_{\widetilde{\infty}}$-norm and SE enumeration ($M_T = M_R = 4$ using 64-QAM)

Impact on Performance and Complexity: Besides a reduction in terms of hardware complexity, the ordered $\ell_{\widetilde{\infty}}$-norm enumeration has an impact on the computational complexity (i.e., number of visited nodes) and on the (error-rate) performance of hard- and soft-output SD. The reason for this impact lies in the fact that the approximation does not guarantee that the children of a node are always enumerated strictly in ascending order of their PEDs (i.e., only the first three CPs always correspond to the first three CPs obtained by SE enumeration). In order to characterize the impact on performance and complexity, numerical simulations are carried out in order to verify that the loss in error-rate and increase in computational complexity is negligible. Corresponding simulation results[4] for hard- and soft-output SD are shown in Fig. 8. It can be observed that the loss in terms of the coded frame-error rate (FER) performance is negligible (see Fig. 8(a)) for both detection methods and the number of visited nodes with $\ell_{\widetilde{\infty}}$-norm enumeration is slightly smaller (i.e., approximately 5%) compared to that achieved by exact SE enumeration (see Fig. 8(b)). Hence, ordered $\ell_{\widetilde{\infty}}$-norm enumeration is well-suited for high-performance implementations of hard-output SD and soft-output STS-SD.

4.4 Pipeline Interleaving

Due to the first-order feedback path present in SD-architectures, pipelining cannot be applied in a straightforward way. Nevertheless, symbol-wise pipeline interleaving can be used to shorten the critical path and hence, to improve the AT-product of the SD-core implementation. The main idea of this approach applied to SD is to detect multiple (and independent) symbol-vectors in parallel within the same SD-unit [21, 27, 28].

Fig. 4 and Fig. 5 illustrate the location of the pipeline registers (in light grey boxes) in the VLSI architecture for three pipeline stages. The locations of the pipeline registers were chosen manually in order to balance the path delays between each pipeline stage. Furthermore, automated retiming was used during synthesis for further optimization. Besides adding the pipeline registers in the data-path, the level cache in Fig. 4 required the implementation of a ring-buffer, in which each set of entries is associated with one of the symbols in the pipeline and corresponds to one instance of the original level cache. Note that the number of pipeline stages affects the throughput and silicon area of the detector. A corresponding investigation of the resulting area/throughput trade-off is provided in Section 6.

---

[4] We consider coded (rate 2/3 convolutional code, constraint length 7, generator polynomials [133_o 171_o], and random interleaving across space and frequency) MIMO-OFDM transmission with $M_R = M_T = 4$, 64-QAM (Gray mapping), 64 OFDM tones. One frame consists of 1536 coded bits. A TGn type C [26] channel model is used. We assume perfect channel state information at the receiver and employ minimum mean-square error sorted QR decomposition (MMSE-SQRD) [17] for SD-preprocessing. The SNR is per receive antenna.

5 VLSI Architecture of Soft-Output STS-SD

The high-level block diagram of the soft-output STS-SD implementation is shown in Fig. 9. Compared to the architecture for hard-output SD described in Section 4, modifications are necessary in the MCU and two additional units are required, one for list administration and one for the implementation of the STS-SD pruning criterion [11]. We next describe the specifics of these changes.

5.1 Architectural Changes in the MCU

From a high-level perspective, there is one fundamental difference between tree-traversal for hard-output SD and for the soft-output STS-SD algorithm: When the node currently examined by the MCU is on the level just above the leaves (i.e., on level $i = 2$), the hard-output SD algorithm considers only one child, namely the one associated with the smallest PED. The STS-SD algorithm, however, has to compute the PEDs of all children that do not qualify for pruning according to the criterion (12) since these children may lead to updates of the metrics $\lambda_{i,b}^{\overline{ML}}$. To perform this *leaf enumeration* procedure, STS-SD must revisit the current node at level $i = 2$, which requires additional clock cycles and a leaf enumeration unit shown in Fig. 9. This unit does, however, not require an additional arithmetic unit for the PED computation as it can reuse the PED computation unit in the MCU (see Fig. 9).

The computational complexity involved in this leaf-enumeration approach can be reduced significantly, by taking advantage of the Gray mapping of the information bits for the constellation symbols [21]. The leaf nodes of interest to the computation of max-log LLR values, are obtained by flipping every bit of the leaf that is closest to b_2. Furthermore, by considering the distance differences between the constellation symbols, it can be shown that no costly squaring operations are necessary. The data path able to carry out these computations merely encompasses a shifter, an adder and a multiplication.

5.2 List Administration and Tree Pruning

In addition to the modifications in the MCU described above, the soft-output STS-ST algorithm requires two additional units [11]:

List-Administration Unit (LAU). The LAU is responsible for maintaining and updating the list containing $\mathbf{x}^{ML}$, λ^{ML}, and the $\lambda_{i,b}^{\overline{ML}}$. The corresponding unit is active during the leaf-enumeration process described above. Since the update rules implemented by the LAU require only a small number of logic operations, the silicon area of this unit is small and is dominated by the storage space (λ cache) required for the metrics λ^{ML} and $\lambda_{i,b}^{\overline{ML}}$. This cache needs to provide storage for all the metrics of all symbols being processed in parallel by pipeline interleaving.

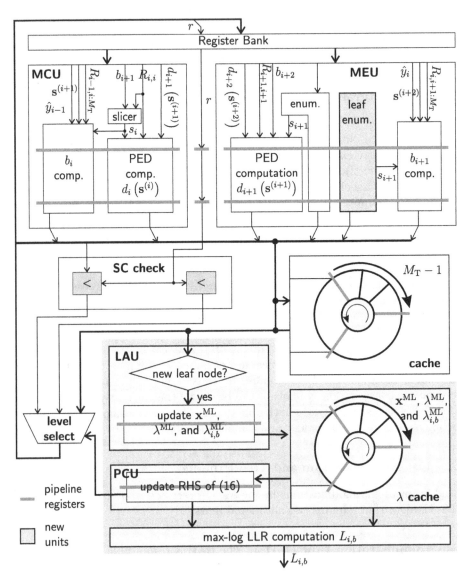

Fig. 9. Block diagram of the proposed VLSI architecture for the soft-output STS-SD. Additional required units (compared to hard-output SD) are highlighted.

Pruning Criterion Unit (PCU). The PCU is responsible for computing the RHS of (12). From an implementation perspective, the reference metric on level j depending on the partial label $\mathbf{x}^{(j)}$ constitutes a major problem. More specifically, this dependence causes the criterion for pruning the child of a parent node on level $j + 1$ to depend on the partial label $\mathbf{x}^{(j)}$ of that child. This, in turn, implies that enumeration of the children on level j in ascending order of their PEDs according to the SE criterion cannot be applied, which results in the need for exhaustive-search enumeration (see Section 4.2). As mentioned above, exhaustive enumeration is ill-suited for the efficient implementation in VLSI (cf. [12]). A modification of the pruning criterion in (12) proposed in [11] solves this problem. To this end, define

$$\mathcal{B}\left(\mathbf{x}^{(j+1)}\right) = \left\{ \lambda_{i,b}^{\overline{\mathrm{ML}}} \,\middle|\, (i > j, b = 1, \ldots, Q) \wedge (x_{i,b} = \overline{x_{i,b}^{\mathrm{ML}}}) \right\}$$
$$\cup \left\{ \lambda_{i,b}^{\overline{\mathrm{ML}}} \,\middle|\, i \leq j, b = 1, \ldots, Q \right\}$$

and prune the node $\mathbf{x}^{(j)}$ (corresponding to the partial symbol vector $\mathbf{s}^{(j)}$) along with its subtree if $d\left(\mathbf{x}^{(j)}\right)$ satisfies

$$d\left(\mathbf{x}^{(j)}\right) > \max_{b \in \mathcal{B}\left(\mathbf{x}^{(j+1)}\right)} b. \tag{16}$$

Note that compared to (12), the RHS of the modified pruning criterion (16) depends on the partial label $\mathbf{x}^{(j+1)}$ rather than on $\mathbf{x}^{(j)}$. Consequently, the enumeration of the children of a node on level $j + 1$ can be carried out using SE enumeration or an approximation thereof (see Section 4.2 and Section 4.3).

The approach described above entails a slight increase in terms of complexity compared to the original pruning criterion for the STS-SD algorithm in (12). Nevertheless, the corresponding complexity increase is significantly smaller than what would be incurred if (12) would be applied directly. A corresponding detailed discussion can be found in [11].

6 Implementation Results and Comparison

In the following, we present implementation results for hard-output SD and soft-output STS-SD in a 130 nm CMOS technology. Furthermore, a comparison to existing hard- and soft-output SD implementations demonstrates the performance advantage of the AT-product-optimized VLSI architectures detailed in this chapter.

6.1 Implementation Results for Hard-Output SD

The AT-diagram in Fig. 10 shows the synthesis results of hard-output SD with ordered $\ell_{\widetilde{\infty}}$-norm enumeration and pipeline interleaving with different number of pipeline stages.[5] The proposed architectures have been implemented with support for multiple modulation schemes (BPSK, QPSK, 16-QAM, and 64-QAM) and for up to four spatial streams (configurable at runtime).

Fig. 10 shows that the architecture with three pipeline stages achieves the best AT-product. Nevertheless, the architectures with more than three pipeline stages come close to the one achieving the optimal AT product, whereas the architectures with fewer pipeline stages are clearly outperformed in terms of the AT-product. As a comparison, implementation results of previously reported hard-output SD implementations are also included in Fig. 10 (the results are also summarized in Tbl. 1). It can be seen that the proposed hard-output SD implementation without pipelining already outperforms all existing designs without pipelining by a least 23% in terms of area and by at least 28% in terms of clock frequency[6]. Furthermore, the AT-product (in [kGE/MHz]) of the proposed architecture with pipeline interleaving is more than 2× better than that of the pipelined implementation in [27].

6.2   Implementation Results for Soft-Output STS-SD

Ordered $\ell_{\widetilde{\infty}}$-norm enumeration and pipeline interleaving can also be applied to the soft-output STS-SD architecture described in Section 4. Corresponding implementation results for soft-output STS-SD are shown in Tbl. 2 and are compared to existing soft-output SD implementations [11,24]. The AT-optimized implementation is superior in terms of area and clock frequency compared to the soft-output detector described in [24]. Note that the original implementation of soft-output STS-SD in [11] only supports 16-QAM modulation, which is the main reason for the smaller area in the unpipelined case. For hard-output SD, pipeline interleaving with three pipeline stages appears to be optimal in terms of the AT-product. As the additional units required for soft-output STS-SD do not influence the critical path, STS-SD was also implemented with three pipeline stages. Tbl. 2 shows that pipeline interleaving also improves the AT-product for soft-output SD implementations and yields a gain of more than 30% compared to the unpipelined design.

6.3   The Case for Multiple SD-Cores

In Section 2, we argued that a single SD core is insufficient to meet the bandwidth and error-rate performance requirements of modern wireless communication standards such as IEEE 802.11n, where a throughput of 600 Mb/s is required. From Tbl. 1, we observe that a single instance of hard-output SD meets the throughput requirement when early-termination and block-processing according to [11,14] are applied. For soft-output STS-SD, however, the number of visited nodes is significantly increased: From seven for hard-output SD to a

---

[5] The results were obtained by synthesizing the RTL description in VHDL with different timing constraints.

[6] The clock frequencies of all designs are normalized to 130 nm CMOS technology.

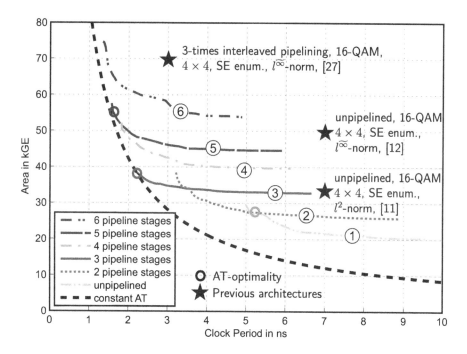

Fig. 10. AT-diagram of hard-output SD with different number of pipeline stages. The optimal synthesis results (in terms of the area/delay trade-off) are highlighted by circles and implementation results of previous architectures are indicated by stars. All designs are scaled to 130 nm CMOS technology.

least 100 for soft-output STS-SD [11]. To illustrate the necessity for multiple soft-output STS-SD cores, we assume LLR clipping is used to adjust the average complexity to $D_{avg} = 100$ for 64-QAM modulation which typically results only in a negligible error rate performance degradation. In this case, the throughput of one STS-SD core is 92 Mb/s and therefore, in order to meet the throughput requirement of IEEE 802.11n, seven AT-optimized soft-output STS-SD cores are required.

7   Summary and Conclusion

In order to meet the throughput and latency requirements of modern wide-band wireless communication systems, such as IEEE 802.11n or 3GPP-LTE, using the sphere decoding (SD) algorithm, multiple parallel detection cores are necessary. Therefore, the main optimization goal for each SD core is to minimize the area-delay product, which represents the hardware-efficiency. Ordered ℓ^∞-norm enumeration and pipeline interleaving are two key techniques that are both suitable to achieve this goal. The approximate enumeration strategy significantly reduces circuit area and the critical path-delay and corresponding simulations

Table 1. Implementation results and comparison of hard-output SD

	[12]	[11]	[27]	This work		
CMOS tech.	250 nm	250 nm	130 nm	130 nm		
Antennas	4×4	4×4	4×4	1×1 to 4×4		
Modulation	16-QAM	16-QAM	16-QAM	BPSK to 64-QAM		
Norm	$\ell_{\widetilde{\infty}}$	ℓ_2	ℓ_∞	ℓ_2		
Enumeration	SE	SE	SE	ordered $\ell_{\widetilde{\infty}}$-norm		
Pipeline stages	no	no	3×	no	3×	5×
Area[a] [kGE]	50	34.4	70	27.1	38.4	55.3
Freq. [MHz]	137[b]	140[b]	333	196	455	625
[kGE/MHz]	0.37	0.25	0.21	0.14	0.08	0.09
Throughput for $D_{\mathrm{avg}} = 7$[c] [Mb/s]						
	470	480	1141	672	1560	2143

Table 2. Implementation results and comparison of soft-output algorithms

	[24]	[11]	This work	
CMOS Technology	130 nm	250 nm	130 nm	
Modulation	64-QAM	16-QAM	BPSK to 64-QAM	
Algorithm	MBF-FD	STS-SD	STS-SD	
Enumeration	tabular	SE	ordered $\ell_{\widetilde{\infty}}$-norm	
Pipeline stages	no	no	no	3×
Area[a] [kGE]	350	56.8	70.4	97.1
Max. frequency [MHz]	198	137[b]	183	383
AT-product [kGE/MHz]	1.77	0.41	0.38	0.25

[a]One GE corresponds to the area of a two-input drive-one NAND gate.

[b]Scaled from 250 nm to a 130 nm CMOS technology by multiplying with 250/130.

[c]D_{avg} denotes the average number of nodes used for block processing [11, 14].

show, that the performance loss is negligible. With pipeline interleaving, the critical path of each SD core can significantly be reduced, which additionally improves the AT-product. A design-space exploration with different number of pipeline stages reveals that an architecture with three pipeline stages (for hard-output and soft-output SD) is the most efficient in terms of the AT-product and should, therefore, be preferred for implementation.

Acknowledgments. The authors would like to thank L. Bruderer, H. Friederich, and P. Luethi for their contributions during the design and implementation of the SD architectures. Furthermore, the authors gratefully acknowledge the support from H. Bölcskei, N. Felber, H. Kaeslin, and W. Fichtner. This work was partially supported by the STREP project MASCOT (IST-026905) within the Sixth Framework of the European Commission and by the Swiss National Science Foundation (SNSF) Grants PP002-119052 and PA00P2-134155.

References

1. Paulraj, A., Nabar, R., Gore, D.: Introduction to Space-Time Wireless Communications. Cambridge Univ. Press (2003)
2. Bölcskei, H., Gesbert, D., Papadias, C., van der Veen, A.J. (eds.): Space-Time Wireless Systems: From Array Processing to MIMO Communications. Cambridge Univ. Press (2006)
3. IEEE Draft Standard; Part 11: Wireless LAN Medium Access Control (MAC) and Physical Layer (PHY) specifications; Amendment 4: Enhancements for Higher Throughput, P802.11n/D3.0 (September 2007)
4. 3rd Generation Partnership Project; Technical Specification Group Radio Access Network; Evolved Universal Terrestrial Radio Access (E-UTRA); Multiplexing and channel coding (Release 9), 3GPP Organizational Partners TS 36.212, Rev. 8.3.0 (May 2008)
5. Fincke, U., Pohst, M.: Improved methods for calculating vectors of short length in a lattice, including a complexity analysis. Math. Computation 44(170), 463–471 (1985)
6. Schnorr, C.P., Euchner, M.: Lattice basis reduction: Improved practical algorithms and solving subset sum problems. Math. Programming 66(2), 181–191 (1994)
7. Viterbo, E., Biglieri, E.: A universal decoding algorithm for lattice codes. Colloq. GRETSI 14, 611–614 (1993)
8. Viterbo, E., Boutros, J.: A universal lattice code decoder for fading channels. IEEE Transactions on Information Theory 45(5), 1639–1642 (1999)
9. Agrell, E., Eriksson, T., Vardy, A., Zeger, K.: Closest point search in lattices. IEEE Trans. Inf. Theory 48(8), 2201–2214 (2002)
10. Hochwald, B.M., ten Brink, S.: Achieving near-capacity on a multiple-antenna channel. IEEE Trans. Commun. 51(3), 389–399 (2003)
11. Studer, C., Burg, A., Bölcskei, H.: Soft-output sphere decoding: Algorithms and VLSI implementation. IEEE J. Sel. Areas Commun. 26(2), 290–300 (2008)
12. Burg, A., Borgmann, M., Wenk, M., Zellweger, M., Fichtner, W., Bölcskei, H.: VLSI implementation of MIMO detection using the sphere decoding algorithm. IEEE J. Solid-State Circuits 40(7), 1566–1577 (2005)
13. Studer, C., Seethaler, D., Bölcskei, H.: Finite lattice-size effects in MIMO detection. In: Proc. of 42th Asilomar Conf. on Signals, Systems and Computers, Pacific Grove, CA, USA (October 2008)
14. Burg, A., Borgmann, M., Wenk, M., Studer, C., Bölcskei, H.: Advanced receiver algorithms for MIMO wireless communications. In: Proc. of DATE, pp. 593–598 (March 2006)
15. Studer, C.: Iterative MIMO decoding: Algorithms and VLSI implementation aspects. Ph.D. dissertation, ETH Zürich, Switzerland, Series in Microelectronics, vol. 202. Hartung-Gorre Verlag Konstanz (2009)
16. Wübben, D., Böhnke, R., Rinas, J., Kühn, V., Kammeyer, K.-D.: Efficient algorithm for decoding layered space-time codes. IEE Electronics Letters 37(22), 1348–1350 (2001)

17. Wübben, D., Böhnke, R., Kühn, V., Kammeyer, K.-D.: MMSE extension of V-BLAST based on sorted QR decomposition. In: Proc. IEEE 58th VTC, pp. 508–512 (October 2003)
18. Wang, R., Giannakis, G.B.: Approaching MIMO channel capacity with reduced-complexity soft sphere decoding. In: Proc. of IEEE Wireless Communications and Networking Conf (WCNC), vol. 3, pp. 1620–1625 (March 2004)
19. Yee, M.S.: Max-Log-Map sphere decoder. In: Proc. IEEE ICASSP 2005, vol. 3, pp. 1013–1016 (March 2005)
20. Witte, E.M., Borlenghi, F., Ascheid, G., Leupers, R., Meyr, H.: A scalable VLSI architecture for soft-input soft-output depth-first sphere decoding (2009), http://arxiv.org/abs/0910.3427
21. Wenk, M., Bruderer, L., Burg, A., Studer, C.: Area- and throughput-optimized VLSI architecture of sphere decoding. In: Proc. of IEEE/IFIP Int. Conf. on VLSI and System-on-Chip (VLSI-SoC), Madrid, Spain (September 2010)
22. Hess, C., Wenk, M., Burg, A., Luethi, P., Studer, C., Felber, N., Fichtner, W.: Reduced-complexity MIMO detector with close-to ML error rate performance. In: Proc. 17th ACM Great Lakes Symposium on VLSI, pp. 200–203 (2007)
23. Mennenga, B., Fettweis, G.: Search sequence determination for tree search based detection algorithms. In: IEEE Sarnoff Symposium, pp. 1–6 (April 2009)
24. Chun-Hao, L., To-Ping, W., Tzi-Dar, C.: A 74.8 mW soft-output detector IC for 8× 8 spatial-multiplexing MIMO communications. IEEE J. Solid-State Circuits 45(2), 411–421 (2010)
25. Seethaler, D., Bölcskei, H.: Performance and complexity analysis of infinity-norm sphere-decoding. IEEE Trans. Inf. Theory 56(3), 1085–1105 (2010)
26. Erceg, V., et al.: TGn channel models. IEEE 802.11-03/940r4 (May 2004)
27. Burg, A., Wenk, M., Fichtner, W.: VLSI implementation of pipelined sphere decoding with early termination. In: Proc. EUSIPCO (September 2006)
28. Lee, J., Park, S.-C., Park, S.: A pipelined VLSI architecture for a list sphere decoder. In: Proc. IEEE Int. Symp. on Circuits and Systems (ISCAS 2006), pp. 397–400 (September 2006)

Joint Optimization of Low-Power DCT Architecture and Efficient Quantization Technique for Embedded Image Compression

Maher Jridi and Ayman Alfalou

L@bISen Laboratory, Equipe Vision
ISEN-Brest CS 42807 Brest, France
maher.jridi@isen.fr
http://www.isen.fr/brest

Abstract. The Discrete Cosine Transform (DCT)-based image compression is widely used in today's communication systems. Significant research devoted to this domain has demonstrated that the optical compression methods can offer a higher speed but suffer from bad image quality and a growing complexity. To meet the challenges of higher image quality and high speed processing, in this chapter, we present a joint system for DCT-based image compression by combining a VLSI architecture of the DCT algorithm and an efficient quantization technique. Our approach is, firstly, based on a new granularity method in order to take advantage of the adjacent pixel correlation of the input blocks and to improve the visual quality of the reconstructed image. Second, a new architecture based on the Canonical Signed Digit and a novel Common Subexpression Elimination technique is proposed to replace the constant multipliers. Finally, a reconfigurable quantization method is presented to effectively save the computational complexity. Experimental results obtained with a prototype based on FPGA implementation and comparisons with existing works corroborate the validity of the proposed optimizations in terms of power reduction, speed increase, silicon area saving and PSNR improvement.

Keywords: Embedded Image and video compression, Digital hardware implementation, VLSI, Granularity analysis, Multiplierless DCT, Canonical Signed Digit.

1 Introduction

Today, the needs for new processing, transmissions and communications tools have increased significantly to support the extraordinary development of modern telecommunications systems. For fast multimedia communication systems it becomes urgent to compress the target images. At source, as the image is in optical form, many researchers and groups have proposed and validated new optical compression methods [1]. The use of optics is also motivated by the very fast computing time with which the optic allows to process an image. In addition, it is possible to combine the optical compression step with the encryption step

J.L. Ayala, D. Atienza, and R. Reis (Eds.): VLSI-SoC 2010, IFIP AICT 373, pp. 155–181, 2012.
© IFIP International Federation for Information Processing 2012

needed to keep the intellectual and/or private property for a target image [2]. One possibility to achieve these optical methods consists in the processing in the frequency domain [1]. To obtain this frequency domain a transformation of the image plane is needed; one of these used transformations is the Discrete Cosine Transform DCT.

We have implemented optically and validated some image compression methods based on the DCT algorithm [3]. But this solution suffers from bad reconstructed image quality and higher material complexity due to the use of Spatial Light Modulator (SLM), optical components. After this optical implementation of an adapted JPEG model, we are interested in the implementation of a simultaneous compression and encryption system [3] and [4].

With all these optical set-ups implementing several architectures, we have concluded that an all optical implementation is not easily possible to replace all the potential of digital processing. In addition, for complex applications, an all optical processing is not enough to have a reliable system. Therefore, an optical processing should be only a part of the system.

On the other hand, reconfigurable hardware, such us FPGAs, are considered as an attractive solution for signal and image processing implementation due to their high-speed I/Os, embedded memories and to their capability to efficiently implement highly parallelized architecture. In 2011, FPGAs under industrialization (Xilinx Series 7) use the 28 nm technology, 2 million logic cells with clock speeds of up to 600 MHz. The new trends on the manufacturing process consists in using Intellectual Properties (IP). And, the goal behind this is to reduce dramatically the Time To Market. However, the dedicated architecture of IP hard cores constitutes a limitation for the implementation of image coding algorithms such as JPEG, MPEG and H26x. In fact, these standards only normalize the algorithm and the decoding format. The method of encoding is left free to competition, as long as the image produced is decoded by a standard decoder [5]. Consequently, flexibility and adaptive computing capabilities are needed to enhance the encoding efficiency and to meet the real-time requirement. It becomes contradictory to design flexible and computational intensive systems with fixed architecture of IP hard cores without an increase in consumed power and silicon area. According to this point of view, we are interested in this chapter on the gate level description of an optimized digital realization of an image compression scheme.

Indeed, one of the most popular image compression scheme is the JPEG coding system largely used in World-Wide-Web and in digital cameras. More recent video encoders such as H.263 [6] and MPEG-4 Part 2 [7] use the same JPEG structure for compression with additional algorithms such as Motion Estimator (ME). This means that the proposed architectures in this chapter may be easily adapted for video encoding.

A simplified block diagram of the JPEG encoder is presented in Fig.1. The first operation consists in dividing the input image into several 8x8 pixel blocks. Then, the 2D-DCT algorithm is applied to decorrelate each block of input pixels. The calculated DCT coefficients are quantized to represent them in a

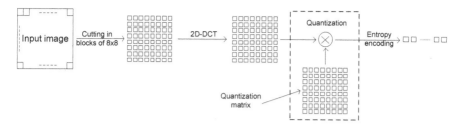

Fig. 1. Simplified block diagram of the JPEG encoder

reduced range of values using a quantization matrix. Finally, the JPEG standard arranges the quantized components in a zigzag order and then employs the Run-Length Encoding (RLE) algorithm that groups similar frequencies together and then uses Huffman coding or arithmetic coding as entropy encoders. Since the DCT algorithm and quantization process are computation-intensive, several improvements are proposed in literature for computing them efficiently. Significant research work has been devoted to the problems of DCT and quantization complexity. These works (analyzed in section II) can be classified into three parts. The first part is the earliest and concerns the reduction of the number of required arithmetic operators of the DCT algorithm [8–14]. The second research thematic is related to the complexity reduction of the constant multipliers used in the DCT. Typically, ROM-based design [15], Distributed Arithmetic (DA) architecture [16–21], the New Distributed Arithmetic (NEDA) [22], the LUT-based design [23] and CORDIC-based design [24, 25] are the most interesting improvements for the multiplierless DCT. Finally, the third part is about the joint optimization of the DCT and the quantization for scalable and reconfigurable image and video encoder [27–30].

In this chapter, we propose three contributions.

1. First, we present an efficient granularity of input pixels to take advantage of the adjacent pixel correlation and to reduce the word length of the multiplier input and consequently the roundoff error. However, we have to underline that the proposed granularity needs a small changes in standard decoders to reorder the generated code stream.
2. Then, we propose a novel architecture of the DCT based on the Canonical Signed Digit (CSD) encoding based on our recent work of [31]. In fact, the use of subtractor with adders and shift operators allows an efficient implementation [32, 33]. Hartley in [34] identify common elements in CSD constant coefficients of FIR filter and share required resources. The latter is named Common Subexpression Elimination (CSE). The use of this technique, with the same manner as in FIR filter, is studied in this paper but the results are not satisfying. To overcome this problem we propose to identify multiple subexpression occurrences in intermediate signals (but not in constant coefficients as in [34]) in order to compute DCT outputs. Since the calculation

of multiple identical subexpression needs to be implemented only once, the resources necessary for these operations can be shared. The total number of required adders and subtractors can be reduced.

3. Finally, we introduce a simple reconfigurable scheme of image compression based on the joint optimization between the DCT computation and the quantization process. We demonstrate by computing some specific DCT coefficients that the visual quality of reconstructed images is very close to the quality obtained with encoder standard which use matrix multiplications. A tradeoffs between image visual quality, power, silicon area and computing time is made.

This paper is organized as follows: an overview of fundamental design issues is given in section 2. Analysis of granularity of input pixel is presented in Section 3. DCT optimization based on CSD and subexpression sharing is described in section 4. Then, a joint optimization of quantization and DCT algorithm is proposed in section 5 along with experimental results before the conclusion.

2   DCT Optimization Techniques

2.1   Choice of the Algorithm

In this section the DCT algorithm is reviewed. Given an input sequence $x(n)$, $n \in [0, N-1]$, the N-point DCT is defined as:

$$X(n) = \sqrt{\frac{2}{N}} C(n) \sum_{k=0}^{N-1} x(k) \cos \frac{(2k+1)n\pi}{2N} \tag{1}$$

where $C(0) = 1/\sqrt{2}$ and $C(n) = 1$ if $n \neq 0$.

As stated in the introduction, DCT optimization has focused first on reducing the number of required arithmetic operators. In literature, many fast DCT algorithms are reported. All of them use the symmetry of the cosine function to reduce the number of multipliers. In [35] a summary of these algorithms was presented. Table 1 sums up these results.

In [14], the authors have showed that the theoretical lower limit of 8-point DCT algorithm is 11 multiplications. Since the number of multiplications of Loeffler's algorithm [13] reaches the theoretical limit, our work is based on this algorithm.

Table 1. Complexity of different DCT algorithms

Reference	Chen [8]	Lee [9]	Vitterli [10]	Suehiro [11]	Hou [12]	Loeffler [13]
Multipliers	16	12	12	12	12	11
Adders	26	29	29	29	29	29

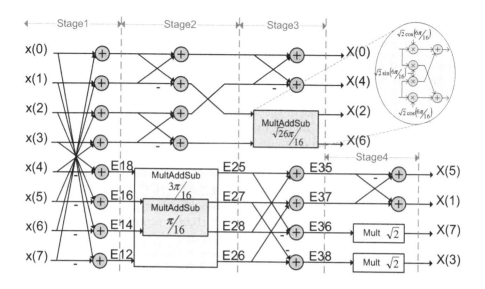

Fig. 2. Loeffler architecture of 8-point DCT algorithm

Loeffler in [13] has proposed to compute DCT by using four stages as shown in Fig. 2. The first stage is performed by 4 adders and 4 subtractors while the second one is composed of 2 adders, 2 subtractors and 2 MultAddSub (Multiplier, Adder and subtractor) blocks. Each MultAddSub block uses 4 multiplications and can be reduced to 3 multiplications by constant arrangements. The fourth stage uses 2 Mult blocks to compute the multiplication by $\sqrt{2}$.

2.2 Multiplierless DCT Architecture

The multipliers are used in DCT to solve the equation of inner product detailed in (2):

$$Y = \sum_{k=0}^{N-1} x(k).c(k) \tag{2}$$

where $c(k)$ are fixed coefficients and equal to $cos\frac{(2k+1)\pi}{2N}$ and $x(k)$ are the input image pixels.

One possible implementation of the inner product consists in using embedded multipliers of the FPGA. However, embedded multipliers are not designed for constant multipliers. Consequently, they are not power efficient and consume a large silicon area. Moreover, the obtained design is not portable to all FPGA families and ASICs since we use specified IP hard cores. Many multiplierless architectures have, therefore, been introduced for efficient computation of the inner product in DSP applications. The ROM-based design [15], the Distributed

Arithmetic (DA) [16, 18], the LUT-based computing [23], the New Distributed Arithmetic (NEDA) [22] and the CORDIC [24] are the most popular architectures.

ROM-Based Multiplier. The ROM-based multiplier computing is close to human-like computing. This solution is presented in [15] to design a special-purpose VLSI processors of 8x8 2-D DCT/IDCT chip that can be used for high rate image and video coding. In the case of DCT, the coefficient matrix is constant; hence the authors of [15] precomputed all the multiplier outputs and store them in a ROM rather than compute these values on line. As the dynamic range of input pixels is 2^8 for gray scale images, the number of stored values in the ROM is equal to $N.2^8$. Each value is encoded using 16 bits. For example, for an 8-point inner product, the ROM size is about $8 * 2^8 * 16$ bits which is equivalent to 32.768 kbits. To obtain 8-point DCT, 8 8-point inner products are required and consequently, the ROM size becomes exorbitant especially for image compression.

Distributed Arithmetic (DA). Authors of [18] use the recursive DCT algorithm and their design requires less area than conventional algorithms. The design of [18] consider the same inner product in (2) and rewrite the variable $x(k)$ as follows:

$$x(k) = \sum_{b=0}^{B-1} x_b(k) . 2^b \qquad x_b(k) = \{0, 1\} \qquad (3)$$

where $x_b(k)$ is the bth bit of $x(k)$ and B is the resolution of the input vector. Finally, the inner product can be rewritten as follows:

$$Y = \sum_{k=0}^{N-1} c(k) \sum_{b=0}^{B-1} x_b(k) . 2^b \qquad (4)$$

The equation (4) can be rearranged as follows:

$$Y = \sum_{b=0}^{B-1} \left[\sum_{k=0}^{N-1} c(k) . x_b(k) \right] . 2^b \qquad (5)$$

Equation (5) defines distributed arithmetic computation. In fact, the bracketed term in (5) may have only 2^N possible values since $x_b(k)$ may take on values of 0 and 1 only. Since $c(k)$ are fixed coefficient values, we can compute the bracketed term in (5) by storing 2^N possible combinations in a ROM. Input data can be used to address the ROM. Now, for the computation of the inner product, we can use an accumulator with a shift operator as mentioned in the Fig. 3. The result of the inner product is available after N clock cycles. By precomputing all the possible values and storing these values in a ROM, the DA method speeds

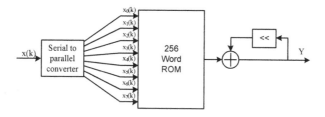

Fig. 3. Distributed Arithmetic principle

up the multiply process. Unfortunately, the size of ROM grows exponentially when the number of inputs and internal precision increase. This is inherent to the DA mechanism where a great amount of redundancy is introduced into the ROM to accommodate all possible combinations of bit patterns exhibited by the input signal.

New Distributed Arithmetic (NEDA). The New Distributed Arithmetic (NEDA) is based on the optimization of DA architecture. The bits of the constant DCT coefficients are distributed to perform the DCT operation with just addition operations. The NEDA architecture is without ROMs and multipliers. This results in a low power, high throughput architecture for the DCT. Nevertheless, the implementation of NEDA has two main disadvantages, [22]:

- the parallel data input leads to higher scanning rate which will severely limit the operating frequency of the architecture;
- the assumption of serial data input leads to lower hardware utilization.

LUT-Based Multiplier. A recent work on LUT-based multiplier computing [23] employs three optimization techniques for inner-product calculation used in many DSP applications such as FIR filters, convolutions and sinusoidal transforms. The first technique is the Odd-Multiple Storage (OMS) scheme which consists on storing only the odd multiple of the constant, the even multiples could be derived from the stored words. The second technique is the Anti-symmetric Product Coding (APC) scheme which involves only half the number of product words are to be saved. The last technique is the Input Coding (IC) scheme where the input word x is decomposed into certain number of segments or sub-words $x = (x_1, x_2, ..., x_T)$ and fed to separate LUTs.

Obtained performances with the LUT-based multiplier are at least similar to DA approach for the same throughput.

CORDIC. COordinate Rotation DIgital Computer (CORDIC) is a very interesting technique for phase to sine amplitude conversion. This algorithm proposed in [24] utilizes dynamic transformation rather than static ROM addressing. The CORDIC method can be employed in two different modes: the rotation mode and the vectoring mode. In the rotation mode, the algorithm basic idea consists in decomposing rotation operation into successive basic rotations. Each basic rotation can be realized by shifting and adding arithmetic operations to compute the sine and cosine functions. A detailed architecture of the CORDIC algorithm applied to digital synthesizer can be found in [26].

C.-C. Sun et al. in [25] presented an efficient Loeffler DCT architecture based on the CORDIC algorithm. However, the use of dynamic computation of cosine function in iterative way is time consuming (long latency), power consuming and requires a complicated compensation method.

To implement the constant multiplication a new solution is proposed in section IV. Comparison results with NEDA and CORDIC are provided.

2.3   Joint Optimization

One way of optimizing DCT computation consists in computing DCT coefficients jointly with other algorithms used in the compression scheme. Many work about the DCT joint optimization adapt the implementation of the DCT to the compression standards and reduce the material requirement and the power consumption. Some of them use the statistic behavior of DCT input signals to yield with the DCT coefficients and the others simplify the DCT architecture by introducing the quantization operation, the motion estimation and compensation algorithms or also the entropy encoding algorithm.

Xanthopoulos and Chandraksan in [27] exploited the signal correlation to design a DCT core. They used an MSB rejection module to reduce the number of arithmetic operations. Their chip allows the user to program statically the maximum desired precision due to quantization.

Huang and Lee in [29] proposed an efficient video transcoder architecture. To design the motion estimation and compensation, they used the DCT statistical properties.

Yang and Wang investigated in [5] the joint optimization of the Huffman tables, quantization and DCT. They tried to find the performance limit of the JPEG encoder by presenting an iterative algorithm to find the optimal DCT coefficients for a given Huffman tables and quantization step sizes.

A prediction algorithm is developed in [30] by Hsu and Cheng to reduce the computation complexity of the DCT and the quantization process of the H264 standard. They built a mathematical model based on the offset of the DCT algorithm to develop a prediction algorithm to save the computational complexity of the video encoder components.

3   Granularity Analysis

3.1   Principle

The most common way to implement the 2D-DCT algorithm is the row/column decomposition. The row/column approach consists of two 1D-DCTs algorithm and one transposed memory to realize a 2D-DCT chip. All the realizations of

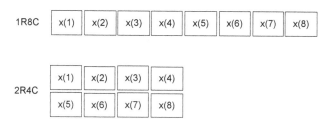

Fig. 4. Granularities distribution

1D-DCT use 8 pixels which constitute a good compromise between the consumed material resources and the operating frequency. In this section we are interested to the 1D-DCT optimization which may be used in our dedicated image compression scheme based on 1D-DCT or 2D-DCT algorithms. This means that the proposed design of 1D-DCT can be easily extended for 2D algorithm.

For a given 8x8 pixel block, the 8 input pixels for the DCT are always taken in the same row and on 8 consecutive columns. We give the name of 1R8C for this configuration. Therefore, we propose to study a non-standard-compliant granularity using 2 consecutive rows and 4 consecutive columns to form the 8 input pixels. We give the name of 2R4C for this proposed granularity. These granularities are presented in Fig. 4.

The advantage of the second granularity compared to the first one relies on the fact that the input pixels have a strong dependency since the image used are often natural and highly structured images. Thus, the pixels of 2R4C granularity are, in general, more correlated than those of 1R8C granularity. This remark is very interesting in the case of signals at the output of subtractors in the first stage of the 1D-DCT algorithm in Fig. 2. In fact, in the case of 2R4C, signals E12, E14 and E16 use more correlated inputs and consequently the dynamic ranges of these signal are reduced. Hence, two solutions are possible. The first one consists in encoding these signals with fewer bits and consequently the multiplier requirements of the stage 2 of the 1D-DCT are reduced. The second solution consists in keeping constant the length of these signals in order to minimize the roundoff error of arithmetic operators in the following stages (the signal truncating is done in the last stage). This second solution is adopted in this paper in order to obtain a high image quality. For the multiplier requirements, a solution will be given in the section 4.

3.2 Verification

To verify the advantage of the proposed granularity compared to the 1R8C, we define for a given row of 8 pixels (in the case of 1R8C), $dx_k(j)$ as the difference between the intensities of two pixels spaced by $k-1$ pixels as:

$$dx_k(j) = |x(j) - x(j+k)| \tag{6}$$

Table 2. Intensity distributions of th first stage subtraction outputs

Signal	Expression	1R8C	2R4C
E12	$x(1) - x(8)$	dx_7	$dx_3 + dy$
E14	$x(2) - x(7)$	dx_5	$dx_1 + dy$
E16	$x(3) - x(6)$	dx_3	$dx_1 + dy$
E18	$x(4) - x(5)$	dx_1	$dx_3 + dy$

where $k \in [1, 7]$ and j is the pixel index, $j \in [1, 8 - k]$. For example, if $k = 7$, $j = 1$ and $dx_7(1)$ calculates the absolute difference between the intensities of the first and the eighth pixel. For the 2R4C granularity, we define the same $dx_k(j)$ where $k \in [1, 3]$ and $j \in [1, 4 - k]$. Furthermore, we define $dy(i)$ as the absolute difference between two adjacent vertical pixels as:

$$dy(i) = |x(i) - x(i + 4)| \tag{7}$$

with $i \in [1, 4]$.

Without loss of generality, we assume that absolute difference between two adjacent vertical pixels do not depend on the position of the pixels in the block. Consequently, we suppose that $dy(i)$, for $i \in [1, 4]$, have the same distribution in terms of standard deviation and dynamic range. Hereafter, we use dy for the absolute difference between two adjacent vertical pixels. In the same manner, we use dx_k for the absolute difference between the intensities of two pixels spaced by $k - 1$ pixels. Table 2 uses dy and dx_k to determine the intensity distribution of the DCT first stage subtraction outputs using 1R8C and 2R4C granularities. For E12, E14 and E16 signals, the dynamic range of the absolute difference of pixel intensity is reduced in the case of 2R4C.

3.3 Validation

To show the advantage of the 2R4C granularity, a statistical study is performed. The Table 3 shows the standard deviations of intermediate signals E12, E14, E16, E18 using six 256x256 standard gray scaled images. We can notice for the first five images that the granularity 2R4C is more interesting than 1R8C since the standard deviation is smaller for the E12, E14, E16 signals. Moreover, the dynamic range of these signals is smaller in the case of 2R4C. This has a great impact on the visual quality of the reconstructed image. In fact, all arithmetic operators have a fixed-point arithmetic because it is not possible to keep an infinite resolution of operators. Consequently, a roundoff noise due to arithmetic rounding operation is created. It is obvious that, for a fixed point operation, the magnitude of the roundoff noise is proportional to the input dynamic range. Consequently, the 2R4C granularity is more interesting than 1R8C one in terms of reconstructed image quality.

Table 3. Standard deviations of intermediate signals

Image	E12		E14		E16		E18	
	2R4C	1R8C	2R4C	1R8C	2R4C	1R8C	2R4C	1R8C
Lena	33.46	46.67	21.73	40.81	19.02	32.30	31.89	19.88
Barbara	28.02	53.22	16.80	50.26	15.36	40.27	26.55	21.84
Mandrill	40.81	44.75	37.31	43.37	38.46	40.50	40.89	32.26
Peppers	46.88	65.38	28.91	51.68	27.74	39.26	46.11	19.24
Finger-point	85.83	95.23	67.7804	107.18	75.22	112.43	86.55	59.86
Horizontal texture	8.48	0.18	8.48	0.17	8.47	0.15	8.47	0.11

To emphasize this effect, two compression and decompression models are proposed using the 1R8C and the 2R4C granularities to form 8 input pixels for the 1D-DCT. For these two configurations, a 1D-DCT fixed point (FxP) Loeffler algorithm is used. To reconstruct the images, 1D-Inverse DCT (1D-IDCT) floating point (FlP) function of Matlab tool is employed. In these models the quantization step is bypassed in order to evaluate the difference between the granularities for any given bit rate. A synoptic diagram of these models is shown in Fig. 5 and used to compare the two configurations.

The Peak Signal to Noise Ratio (PSNR) is used as criteria to compare the visual quality of the reconstructed images compared with original images. The evaluation of the PSNR is illustrated in Fig. 6. According to these results, for a given DCT output length, an effective gain of PSNR is achieved with the proposed granularity. For a DCT output length of 10 bits, the 2R4C granularity presents about 7 dB and 4 dB more than the 1R8C granularity respectively for Lena and Mandrill 256x256 gray scale images.

According to these results, for a given DCT output length, an effective gain of PSNR is achieved with the proposed granularity. For a DCT output length of 10 bits, the 2R4C granularity presents about 7 dB and 4 dB more than the 1R8C granularity respectively for Lena and Mandrill 256x256 gray scale images.

3.4   Critical Analysis

As stated before, the proposed 2R4C granularity presents more correlation between input pixels and consequently the intermediate signals E12, E14 and E16 have a smaller standard deviation and dynamic range. Conversely, signal E18 presents a different behavior. Despite this, we still have gain in PSNR because signal E18 contributes equally with E12, E14 and E16 to compute the DCT outputs.

On the other side, there is a second critical point needing more details. In fact, we can see in Table 3 that the image called horizontal texture presents a smaller standard deviation in the case of 1R8C. Hence, for these kind of images the 1R8C

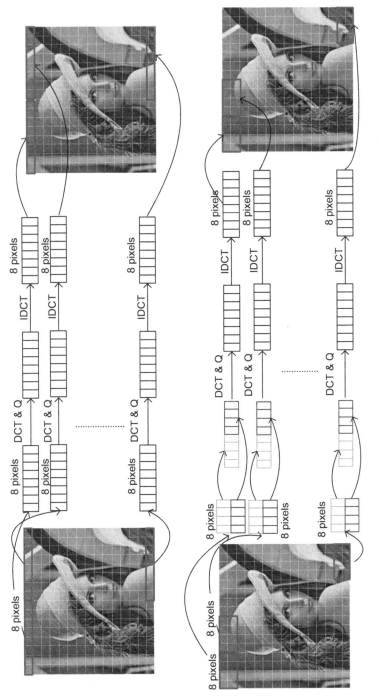

Fig. 5. Synoptic diagram of the compression model based on 1D-DCT and 1D-IDCT

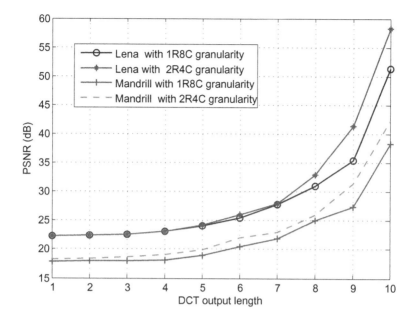

Fig. 6. Simulation results of the compression models

is better. But, we have to notice that for this image the standard deviation of 2R4C granularity is small compared to other standard images. Consequently, the size of arithmetic operators in stage 2 of 1D-DCT in Fig. 2 stills small.

4 A New Power-Efficient DCT

In this section a new multiplierless and romless low-power DCT based in the CSD encoding is presented.

4.1 Principle

The CSD representation was first introduced by Avizienis in [32] as a signed representation. This data representation was created originally to eliminate the carry propagation chains in arithmetic operations. The CSD representation is a unique signed data representation containing the fewest number of nonzero bits. Consequently, for constant multipliers, the number of additions and subtractions will be minimum.

In fact, for a constant coefficient c, the CSD representation is expressed as follows:

$$c = \sum_{i=0}^{N-1} c_i.2^i \qquad c_i = \{-1, 0, 1\} \tag{8}$$

CSD numbers have essentially two properties:

Table 4. Cosine coefficients representation of 8-point DCT

Real value	Decimal	Natural binary	Partial products	CSD	Partial products
$cos\frac{3\pi}{16}$	106	01101010	4	+0-0+0+0	4
$sin\frac{3\pi}{16}$	71	01000111	4	0+00+00-	3
$cos\frac{\pi}{16}$	126	01111110	6	+00000-0	2
$sin\frac{\pi}{16}$	25	00011001	3	00+0-00+	3
$cos\frac{6\pi}{16}$	49	00110001	3	0+0-000+	3
$sin\frac{6\pi}{16}$	118	01110110	5	+000-0-0	3
$\sqrt{2}$	181	10110101	5	+0-0-0+0+	5
Total Partial products		30		23	

- No 2 consecutive bits in a CSD number are nonzero;
- The CSD representation of a number contains the minimum possible number of nonzero bits, thus the name canonic.

Examples of conversion between natural binary representation and CSD representation are given in Tables 4 and 5 where the converted values are the constants used in 8-point and 16-point DCT Loeffler algorithm respectively. Symbols 1,-1 are respectively represented by +,-. For high order DCT such as 16-point DCT, the CSD representation of cosine coefficients is mentioned in Table 5. In the line 4 of Table 4, $128 * cos (\pi/16) \approx 126$ contains 6 partial products since its binary representation is 01111110. In CSD convention, 126 is represented by +00000-0 which is $+2^7 - 2^1$. An extended study of CSD encoding applied to 16-point DCT algorithm is made. The number of partial products is 71 for binary representation and 52 for CSD representation (26% saving). Finally, a generalized statistical study about the average of nonzero elements in N-bit CSD numbers is presented in [32] and prove that this number tends asymptotically to N/3 + 1/9. Hence, on average, CSD numbers contain about 33% fewer nonzero bits than two complement numbers. Therefore, for constant multipliers, the numbers of partial products are reduced and consequently the speed and power could be enhanced.

4.2 New CSE Technique for DCT Algorithm

To enhance the use of adders, subtractors and shift operators we propose to employ the Common Subexpression Elimination (CSE) technique. CSE was introduced in [34] and applied to digital filters. For FIR filters, this technique uses bit pattern occurrence in filter coefficients. Identification of occurrences permits to create subexpression and after that economize hardware resources. Bit pattern occurrence can be detected between two or more different filter coefficients or in the same filter coefficient. Since several constant coefficients multiply only

Table 5. Cosine coefficients representation of 16-point DCT

Real value	Decimal	Natural binary	Partial products	CSD	Partial products
$\cos\frac{-15\pi}{32}$	13	00001101	3	000+0-0+	3
$\sin\frac{-15\pi}{32}$	-127	01111111	7	+000000-	2
$\cos\frac{3\pi}{32}$	122	01111010	5	+000-0+0	3
$\sin\frac{3\pi}{32}$	37	00100101	3	00+00+0+	3
$\cos\frac{-11\pi}{32}$	60	00111100	4	0+000-00	2
$\sin\frac{-11\pi}{32}$	-113	01110001	4	+00-000+	3
$\cos\frac{7\pi}{32}$	99	01100011	4	+0-00+0-	4
$\sin\frac{7\pi}{32}$	81	01010001	3	0+0+000+	3
$\cos\frac{10\pi}{32}$	71	01000111	4	0+00+00-	3
$\sin\frac{10\pi}{32}$	106	01101010	4	+0-0+0+0	4
$\cos\frac{14\pi}{32}$	25	00011001	3	00+0-00+	3
$\sin\frac{14\pi}{32}$	126	01111110	6	+00000-0	2
$\cos\frac{12\pi}{32}$	49	00110001	3	0+0-000+	3
$\sin\frac{12\pi}{32}$	118	01110110	5	+000-0-0	3
$\cos\frac{-12\pi}{32}$	49	00110001	3	0+0-000+	3
$\sin\frac{-12\pi}{32}$	-118	01110110	5	+000-0-0	3
$\sqrt{2}$	181	10110101	5	+0-0-0+0+	5
Total Partial products			71		52

one output data (signal to be filtered), CSE of filter coefficients implies less computation and less power consumption.

Contrary to FIR filters, constant coefficients of DCT in Table 4 multiply 8 different input data since the DCT consists in transforming 8 points in the input to 8 points in the output. From this observation, we can not exploit the redundancy between different constants. Moreover, for bit patterns in the same constant, Table 4 shows that only the constant $\sqrt{2}$ presents one common subexpression which is +0- repeated once with an opposite sign. Consequently, we cannot use the CSE technique in the same manner as in the FIR filters.

In order to take advantage of CSE technique, we adapt the CSE for DCT optimization. Proceeding towards this goal, we do not consider occurrences in CSD coefficients but we consider the interaction of these codes. On the other hand, according to our compression method (detailed in the subsection 5.1) we will use only some DCT outputs (1 to 8 among 8). Hence, it is necessary to compute specific outputs separately. To emphasize the CSE effect, we take the example of $X(2)$ and $X(4)$ calculation. In fact, the computation of $X(8)$ and $X(6)$ may be determined from $X(2)$ and $X(4)$ respectively by using the same computation techniques detailed in this subsection. The computations of $X(3)$

and $X\,(7)$ require multiplication but we can apply only the CSD encoding rather that the binary encoding. And, the computation of $X\,(1)$ and $X\,(5)$ coefficients do not need multiplications.

$X\,(2)$ Calculation. According to Fig. 2, we can express $X\,(2)$ as follows:

$$X(2) = (E35 + E37) \tag{9}$$

And, E35 is expressed by

$$
\begin{aligned}
E35 &= (E25 + E28) \\
&= (E18 * cos\,(3\pi/16) + E12 * sin\,(3\pi/16)) \\
&+ (E14 * cos\,(\pi/16) - E16 * sin\,(\pi/16))
\end{aligned} \tag{10}
$$

Using CSD encoding of Table 4, (10) is equivalent to:

$$
\begin{aligned}
E35 &= E18\left(2^7 - 2^5 + 2^3 + 2^1\right) + E12\left(2^6 + 2^3 - 2^0\right) \\
&- E16\left(2^5 - 2^3 + 2^0\right) + E14\left(2^7 - 2^1\right)
\end{aligned} \tag{11}
$$

After rearrangement (11) is equivalent to:

$$
\begin{aligned}
E35 &= 2^7(E18 + E14) + 2^6 E12 - 2^5(E16 + E18) \\
&+ 2^3(E12 + E16 + E18) + 2^1(E18 - E14) - 2^0(E12 + E16)
\end{aligned} \tag{12}
$$

In the same way, we can determine E37:

$$
\begin{aligned}
E37 &= (E26 + E27) \\
&= (E18 * cos\,(3\pi/16) - E12 * sin\,(3\pi/16)) \\
&+ (E16 * cos\,(\pi/16) + E14 * sin\,(\pi/16))
\end{aligned} \tag{13}
$$

After CSD encoding (13) gives

$$
\begin{aligned}
E37 &= 2^7(E12 + E16) - 2^6 E18 + 2^5(E14 - E12) \\
&+ 2^3(E12 - E14 - E18) + 2^1(E12 - E16) + 2^0(E14 + E18)
\end{aligned} \tag{14}
$$

Equations (12) and (14) give:

$$
\begin{aligned}
X(2) &= 2^7(\overbrace{(E16 + E18)}^{CS1} + E12 + E14) + 2^6(E12 - E18) \\
&- 2^5(\overbrace{(E12 - E14)}^{CS2} + \overbrace{(E16 + E18)}^{CS1}) + 2^3(\overbrace{(E12 - E14)}^{CS2} + E12 + E16) \\
&+ 2^1(\overbrace{(E18 - E16)}^{CS3} + \overbrace{(E12 - E14)}^{CS2}) + 2^0(\overbrace{(E14 - E12)}^{CS2} + \overbrace{(E18 - E16)}^{CS3})
\end{aligned} \tag{15}
$$

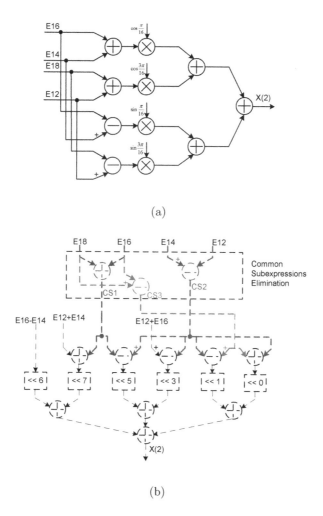

(a)

(b)

Fig. 7. X(2) calculation (a): Conventional method, (b): Shared subexpression using CSD encoding [31]

where CS1, CS2 and CS3 denote 3 common subexpressions. In fact, the identification of common subexpressions can give an important hardware and power consumption reductions. For example, CS2 appears 4 times in X(2). This subexpression is implemented only once and resources needed to compute CS2 are shared. An illustration of resources sharing is given in Fig. 7.

Symbols $<< n$ denote right shift operators by n positions. It is important to notice that non-overbraced terms in (15) are a potential common subexpressions with other DCT coefficients such us X(4), X(6) and X(8).

According to this analysis, $X(2)$ is computed by using 11 adders and 4 embedded multipliers or 23 adders and subtractors if the CSD encoding is applied to the constant cosine values. The proposed contribution enables to compute $X(2)$

Table 6. Macro Statistics of X(2) calculation

	Multiplier	CSD	CSD&CSE
Adders/Subtractors	11	23	16
Registers	125	188	119
MULT18X18SIOs	4	0	0
Maximum Frequency (MHz)	143.451	121.734	165.888

by using only 16 adders and subtractors. This improvement allows to save silicon area and reduces the power consumption without any decrease in the operating frequency.

To emphasize the common element sharing, a VHDL model of X(2) calculation is developed using three techniques: embedded multipliers, CSD encoding and CSE of CSD encoding. Results in terms of number arithmetic operators and maximum operating frequency are illustrated in Table 6. It is shown in column 3 that the CSD encoding uses more adders, subtractors and registers to replace the 4 embedded multipliers MULT18x18SIOs (Xilinx's embedded multipliers for Spartan3 family). This substitution between embedded multipliers and arithmetic operators is paid by a loss in the maximum operating frequency. On the other side, column 4 shows that the sharing of arithmetic operators permits to increase the maximum operating frequency and reduce the number of required adders, subtractors and registers.

X (4) Calculation. According to the Fig. 2, one can determine $X(4)$ by

$$X(4) = \sqrt{2}(E26 - E27) \tag{16}$$

Equation (16) is equivalent to

$$X(4) = \sqrt{2}(E12 * cos(3\pi/16) - E18 * sin(3\pi/16)) \\ - \sqrt{2}(E16 * cos(\pi/16) - E14 * sin(\pi/16)) \tag{17}$$

Using CSD encoding of the constant coefficient, (17) is equivalent to:

$$X(4) = E12(2^7 + 2^5 - 2^3 - 2^0) - E18(2^7 - 2^5 + 2^2 + 2^0) \\ - E16(2^8 - 2^6 - 2^4 + 2^1) + E14(2^5 + 2^2 - 2^0) \tag{18}$$

After rearrangement (18) is equivalent to:

$$X(4) = 2^7(-\overbrace{(E16 + E18)}^{CS1} + \overbrace{(E12 - E16)}^{CS4}) + 2^5(-\overbrace{(E16 + E18)}^{CS1} \\ + \overbrace{(E12 + E14)}^{CS5} + E14) - 2^3(\overbrace{(E12 - E16)}^{CS4}) + 2^2(E16 + E14 \\ - \overbrace{(E18 - E16)}^{CS3}) - 2^0(\overbrace{(E16 + E18)}^{CS1} + \overbrace{(E12 + E14)}^{CS5} + E16) \tag{19}$$

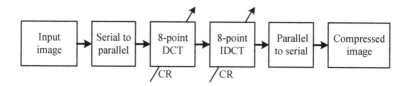

Fig. 8. Model of the image compression technique

Hence, for $X(4)$ calculation, the common subexpression CS1 and CS3 defined for $X(2)$ calculation are used. Two new subexpressions CS4 and CS5 are introduced to economize more arithmetic operators. It is important to mention that the equations listed before are expressed to create several occurrences of common subexpression such as CS1, CS3 and also CS4 which is used for $X(2)$ calculation.

5 Validation for Image Compression

The compression technique used in this work is inspired from [3] and the associated model is illustrated in Fig. 8. This compression was realized using optical components to take benefits of speed. Indeed, this kind of architecture can be a good compromise between computing time and quality of reconstructed images at the output system. The principle of all optically architecture implementing the DCT is based on the use of similarity between the Fourier transform (FT) and the DCT and then the use of a converging lens to achieve an optical FT. To achieve this architecture, we begin by duplicating the target image (image to compress) four times in the input plane using a special way [3]. Then, we perform the FT of the obtained plane using a converging lens. After that, we multiply the obtained spectrum with a series of well-defined filters to have the DCT result in the spectral domain. Finally we apply a low pass filter to select only a part of the spectrum (were c denotes the DCT needed size to reconstruct the image, N is the size of the target image). It can be observed in Fig. 9 the different results obtained with different compression ratio defined by: $Cr = 100 \left(1 - \frac{c \times c}{N \times N}\right)$. We can easily see the poor quality of the reconstructed image. This is mainly due to the use of different optical components.

5.1 Image Compression Principle and Simulation

A fixed point Matlab Simulink model has been established to validate the proposed method. This step is very important to validate the algorithm structure before the material implementation. This model is very useful for debugging intermediate signals of the hardware description language (HDL).

According to the model of Fig. 8, each image is parallelized into 8-point blocks. This operation can be done by a serial to parallel block composed by 8 flip-flops.

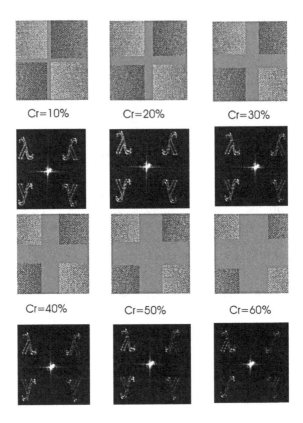

Fig. 9. Optical reconstruction using various compression ratios [3]

After that, the DCT coefficient calculation is performed jointly with a specific quantization process. The basic idea of the quantization consists in considering the DCT low frequencies more than the DCT high frequencies.

The first DCT coefficient can be implemented using an addition tree of 8 input pixels. This coefficient is always considered in all quantization modes without truncation. This means that the word-length of the DC coefficient is equal to 11 bits. A second quantization mode may be defined by considering the first $X(1)$ and the second DCT coefficients $X(2)$. The associated word-length to $X(1)$ and $X(2)$ are respectively 11 and 7 bits. Therefore, we can compute two DCT outputs among 8 and we obtain an acceptable compressed image quality. For the decompression process, the 8-point IDCT takes X(1) and X(2) followed by 6 zeros to obtain a sequence of 8 inputs.

Six quantization mode are defined with the same manner by considering higher frequencies using 7 bits for word-length. It can be found that the minimum compression rate is obtained when we take all DCT outputs (from $X(1)$ to $X(8)$) and the maximum is reached when we take only the first DCT output as low frequency output.

To validate the compression model a 256x256 Lena gray scale image is used, Fig. 10a. Each input block is composed by 8 pixels encoded using 8 bits for each pixel. On the other hand, as stated before, the first DCT coefficient, $X(1)$, is encoded without loss using 11 bits. $X(2)$ to $X(8)$ outputs are encoded using 7 bits. The compression ratio (defined before by Cr depends on the considered number of DCT outputs and may be expressed by the following equation:

$$Cr_i = \left(1 - \frac{(11 + 7 * i)}{8 * 8}\right) * 100 \tag{20}$$

where i is an integer $\in [0, 7]$. According to the last equation, i equal to zero means that we take only the first DCT output and for i equal to 7, all DCT outputs are considered. Finally, PSNR is evaluated and results are summarized in Fig. 10. It can be found that the PSNR decreases with a low values of compression ratio Cr_i. This observation is verified in Fig. 10b to Fig. 10i. According to these images, a compression ratio of 6.25% is equal to $(1 - \frac{(11+7*7)}{64}) * 100$ and means that we take all DCT coefficients (8 points). The PSNR associated to this compression ratio is about 38.2 dB, Fig. 10a. Conversly, a compression ratio of 82.81% is equal to $(1 - \frac{11}{64}) * 100$ and means that we take only one DCT outputs $X(1)$. The associated PSNR to this compression ratio is about 18 dB, Fig. 10i.

5.2   Design Considerations

We use the standard language VHDL for coding which gives the choice of implementing target devices (FPGA family, CPLD, ASIC) at the end of the implementation flow. It means that the image compression model reported here is synthesized and may be implemented on arbitrary technologies.

Moreover, some design considerations are taken into account. In fact, as in [26], we use registered adder and subtractor to perform the high speed implementation. The critical path is minimized by insertion of pipeline registers and is equal to the propagation delay of an adder or a subtractor. It should be outlined that the use of registered outputs comes at no extra cost of an FPGA if an unused D flip-flop is available at the output of each logic cell. For example, to realize an addition of two vectors, the bitstream of the addition adapts the structure of the FPGA to connect slices to each other. These slices are composed of two 4-input LUT and two D flip-flop (four 6-input LUT and 4 D flip-flop for recent Xilinx target). Consequently, for used slices all D flip-flop are free. The registered operator can use these flip-flop to reduce the critical path.

With these considerations, we can confirm that the proposed model is able to be implemented in all digital targets but there are optimized for FPGA devices since they take into account the FPGA structure.

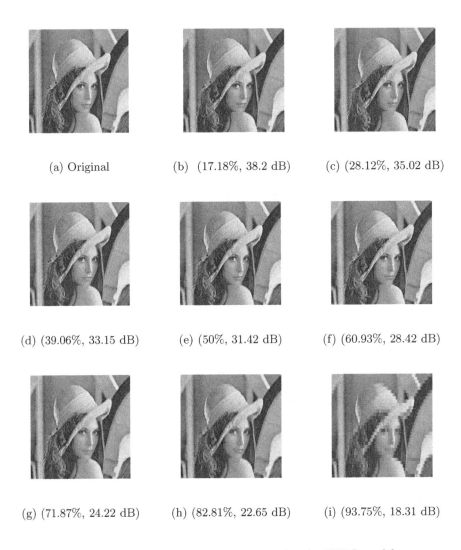

(a) Original   (b) (17.18%, 38.2 dB)   (c) (28.12%, 35.02 dB)

(d) (39.06%, 33.15 dB)   (e) (50%, 31.42 dB)   (f) (60.93%, 28.42 dB)

(g) (71.87%, 24.22 dB)   (h) (82.81%, 22.65 dB)   (i) (93.75%, 18.31 dB)

Fig. 10. Simulation of image compression using the VHDL model

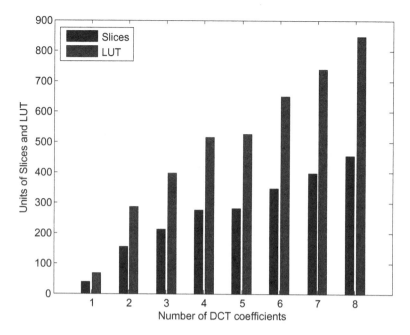

Fig. 11. Slice and LUT resources versus selected number of DCT coefficients

5.3 Synthesis Results

In this section, VHDL programs of different DCT architectures are synthesized using ISE software of Xilinx and the Spartan3E XC3S500 target. In order to illustrate the differences in hardware consumption, the FPGA synthesis results are presented in Table 7. The second column presents required logic and arithmetic elements for the implementation of DCT based on Xilinx embedded multipliers. Column 3 substitutes embedded multipliers MULT18x18 by 4-input LUTs: the total number of required LUTs reaches 1424. Columns 4 and 5 detail the required resources for DCT implementation using respectively CSD encoding and CSD with the proposed CSE technique. Thanks to element sharing, required resources decrease from column 4 to column 5.

Furthermore, the use of the proposed technique involves less computation and consequently high maximum operating frequency. This throughput allows easily the processing of more than 30 frames per second. Finally, note that an old FPGA (Spartan 3E) is used in this work. The offered throughput exceeds 300 MS/s with Virtex 6 target.

Another study related to the joint optimization between DCT computation and quantization process is mentioned in Fig. 11. It can be observed that the number of required LUTs and Slices grows exponentially with the number of selected DCT coefficients. 47 LUTs and 68 Slices are required for the first quantization mode while 450 LUT and 844 Slices are needed to perform the last quantization mode. There is only one case where the required resources present

Table 7. FPGA resources estimation of different DCT design

	Embedded Mult	LUT Mult	CSD	Proposed CSD CSE
Slices	356	-	581	510
Flip-Flop	512	512	454	516
4 input LUTs	404	1424	1012	900
MULT18x18	11	0	0	0
Maximum Frequency (MHz)	119.748	-	118.032	137.678

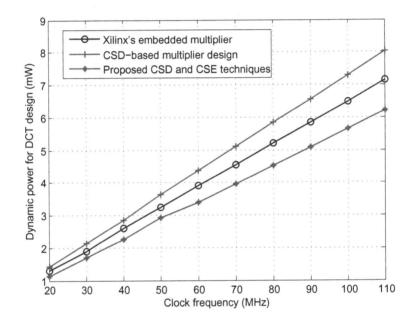

Fig. 12. Dynamic power consumption estimation per sample with 1.6 V design

a slight increase. This case corresponds with the selection of 4 or 5 DCT coefficients. In fact, according to Loeffler algorithm, $X(5)$ requires only one more subtractor compared to the $X(4)$ calculation.

Hence, the image quality can be handled with the required silicon area. Indeed, for available FPGA or ASIC resources a quantization mode can be chosen which involves a certain quality of the reconstructed images. The image quality criteria which is the PSNR and the utilization of FPGA resources are shown in Fig. 10 and Fig. 11 respectively.

5.4   Power Analysis

To have an idea of the estimated power consumption, comparison of the dynamic power between three DCT architectures is made. We used the XPower tool of Xilinx to estimate the dynamic power consumption. It can be found in Fig. 12 and for clock frequency of 110 MHz, the share subexpressions reduces the dynamic power by 22% compared to the CSD-based DCT architecture and by 9% compared to the Xilinx's embedded multipliers-based DCT design . Furthermore, these values are compared favorably with other works as for example 11.5 mW at 2V design and 40 MHz in [36] or 3.94 mw at 1.6 V design and 40 MHz in [27].

6   Conclusion

We have combined three optimization techniques for specific image compression based on the 1D-DCT algorithm. The first one is about the granularity analysis where the 2R4C granularity has been introduced to perform higher image quality. The second optimization concerns the constant coefficient multiplier. The theoretical formulas of DCT coefficients have been derived by applying the CSD encoding and the sharing of common subexpressions. It has been shown that the CSD-based design implies an area and energy economies. Finally, these techniques have been used jointly with a simple and efficient quantization process. Hence, the image quality of compressed image may be handled with the silicon area and power consumptions.

References

1. Alfalou, A., Brosseau, C.: Optical image compression and encryption methods. Adv. Opt. Photon 1, 589–636 (2009)
2. Alfalou, A., Brosseau, C.: Exploiting root-mean-square time-frequency structure for multiple-image optical compression and encryption. Opt. Lett. 35, 1914–1916 (2010)
3. Alkholidi, A., Alfalou, A., Hamam, H.: A new approach for optical colored image compression using the JPEG standards. Journal of Signal Processing 87(4), 569–583 (2007)
4. Jridi, M., AlFalou, A.: A VLSI implementation of a new simultaneous images compression and encryption method. In: IEEE Int. Conf. Imaging Systems and Techniques (IST), pp. 75–79 (July 2010)
5. Yang, E., Wang, L.: Joint Optimization of Run-Length Coding, Huffman Coding, and Quantization Table With Complete Baseline JPEG Decoder Compatibility. IEEE Trans. Image Process. 18(1), 63–74 (2009)
6. Video coding for low bit rate communication (ITU-T Rec. H.263) (February 1998)
7. ISO/IEC DIS 10 918-1, Coding of audio visual objects: part 2. visual, ISO/IEC 14496-2 (MPEG-4 Part2) (January 1999)
8. Chen, W.A., Harrison, C., Fralick, S.C.: A fast computational algorithm for the discrete cosine transform. IEEE Trans. Commun. COM-25, 1004–1011 (1977)
9. Lee, B.: A new algorithm to compute the discrete cosine transform. IEEE Trans. Acoust. Speech Signal Process. ASSP-32, 1243–1245 (1984)

10. Vitterli, M., Nussbaumer, H.: Simple FFT and DCT algorithms with reduced number of operation. Signal Process 6, 264–278 (1984)
11. Suehiro, N., Hatori, M.: Fast algorithms for DFT and other sinusoidal transforms. IEEE Trans. Acoust. Speech Signal Process. ASSP-34, 642–664 (1986)
12. Hou, H.: A fast recursive algorithm for computing the discrete cosine transform. IEEE Trans. Acoust. Speech Signal Process ASSP-35, 1455–1461 (1987)
13. Loeffler, C., Lightenberg, A., Moschytz, G.S.: Practical fast 1-D DCT algorithm with 11 multiplications. In: Proc. ICAPSS, pp. 988–991 (May 1989)
14. Duhamel, P., H'mida, H.: New 2^n DCT algorithm suitable for VLSI implementation. In: IEEE ICAPSS, pp. 1805–1808 (November 1987)
15. Slawecki, D., Li, W.: DCT/IDCT processor design for high data rate image coding. IEEE Trans. Circuits Syst. Video Technol. 2(2), 135–146 (1992)
16. White, S.A.: Application of distributed arithmetic to digital signal processing: a tutorial review. IEEE ASSP Magazine, 4–19 (July 1989)
17. Madisetti, A., Willson, A.N.: A 100 MHz 2-D 8x8 DCT/IDCT processor for HDTV applications. IEEE Trans. Circuit Syst. Video Technol. 5(2), 158–165 (1995)
18. Yu, S., Swartzlander, E.E.: DCT implementation with distributed arithmetic. IEEE Trans. Computers 50(9), 985–991 (2001)
19. Kim, D.W., Kwon, T.W., Seo, J.M., Yu, J.K., Lee, S.K., Suk, J.H., Choi, J.R.: A compatible DCT/IDCT architecture using hardwired distributed arithmetic. In: IEEE Int. Symp. Circuit Syst. (ISCAS 2001), vol. 2, pp. 457–460 (May 2001)
20. Shams, A., Pan, W., Chidanandan, A., Bayoumi, M.: A Low Power High Performance Distributed DCT Architecture. In: IEEE Computer Society Annu. Symp. VLSI (ISVLSI 2002), pp. 21–27 (2002)
21. Meher, P.K.: Unified Systolic-Like Architecture for DCT and DST Using Distributed Arithmetic. IEEE Trans. Circuits Sys I: Regular Papers. 53(12), 2656–2663 (2006)
22. Alam, M., Badawy, W., Julien, G.: A new Time distributed architecture for MPEG-4 hardware reference model. IEEE Trans. Circuit Syst. Video Technol. 15(5), 726–730 (2005)
23. Meher, P.K.: LUT Optimization for Memory-Based Computation. IEEE Trans. Circuits Sys-II, 285–289 (April 2010)
24. Yu, S., Swartzlander, E.E.: A scaled DCT architecture with the CORDIC algorithm. IEEE Trans. Signal Process. 50(1), 160–167 (2002)
25. Sun, C.C., Ruan, S.J., Heyne, B., Goetze, J.: Low-power and high quality Cordic-based Loeffler DCT for signal processing. Circuits, Devices. Syst. 1(6), 453–461 (2007)
26. Jridi, M., AlFalou, A.: Direct digital frequency synthesizer with CORDIC algorithm and Taylor series approximation for digital receivers. European Journal of Scientific Research 30(4), 542–553 (2009)
27. Xanthopoulos, T., Chandrakasan, A.P.: A low-power DCT core using adaptive bitwidth and arithmetic activity exploiting signal correlations and quantization. IEEE Jour. Solid-State Circuits 35(5), 740–750 (2000)
28. Huang, J., Lee, J.: A Self-Reconfigurable Platform for Scalable DCT Computation Using Compressed Partial Bitstreams and BlockRAM Prefetching. IEEE Trans. Circuit Syst. Video Technol. 19(11), 1623–1632 (2009)
29. Huang, J., Lee, J.: Efficient VLSI architecture for video transcoding. IEEE Trans. Consumer Electron. 55(3), 1462–1470 (2009)

30. Hsu, C.L., Cheng, D.H.: Reduction of discrete cosine transform/ quantization/inverse quantization/inverse discrete cosine transform computational complexity in H.264 video encoding by using an efficient prediction algorithm. IET. Image Process. 3(4), 177–187 (2009)

31. Jridi, M., AlFalou, A.: A low-power, high-speed DCT architecture for image compression: Principle and implementation. In: VLSI System on Chip Conference (VLSI-SoC), pp. 304–309 (September 2010)

32. Avizienis, A.: Signed-Digit Number Representations for Fast Parallel Arithmetic. IRE Transaction on Electron. Computer EC-10, 389–400 (1961)

33. Seegal, R.: The canonical signed digit code structure for FIR filters. IEEE Trans. Acoustics Speech Signal Process. 28(5), 590–592 (1980)

34. Hartley, R.I.: Subexpression sharing in filters using canonic signed digit multipliers. IEEE Trans. Circuits Syst. II: Analog and Digital Signal Processing 43(10), 677–688 (1996)

35. Pai, C.Y., Lynch, W.E., Al-Khalili, A.J.: Low-Power data-dependant 8x8 DCT/IDCT for video compression. In: IEE, Proc. Vision Image Signal Process., vol. 150, pp. 245–254 (August 2003)

36. Matsui, M., Hara, H., Seta, K., Uetani, Y., Klim, L.S., Nagamatsu, T., Sakura, T.: 200 MHz video compression macrocelles using low-swing differential logic. In: Proceedings of ISSCC, pp. 76–77 (1994)

37. Kim, B., Ziavras, S.G.: Low-power multiplierless DCT for image/video coders. In: IEEE Int. Symp. on Cons. Electronics (ISCE 2009), pp. 133–136 (May 2009)

38. Song, H.S., Cho, N.I.: DCT-based embedded image compression with a new coefficient sorting method. IEEE Sig. Process. Letters. 16(5), 410–413 (2009)

Fast Fixed-Point Optimization
of DSP Algorithms

Gabriel Caffarena[1], Ángel Fernández-Herrero[2],
Juan A. López[2], and Carlos Carreras[2]

[1] Universidad CEU San Pablo,
Dep. Ingeniería de Sistemas de Información y Telecomunicación, Madrid 28668, Spain
`gabriel.caffarenafernandez@ceu.es`
[2] Universidad Politécnica de Madrid, Dep. Ingeniería Electrónica,
Madrid 28040, Spain
`{angelfh,juanant,carreras}@die.upm.es`

Abstract. In this chapter, the fast fixed-point optimization of Digital Signal Processing (DSP) algorithms is addressed. A fast quantization noise estimator is presented. The estimator enables a significant reduction in the computation time required to perform complex fixed-point optimizations, while providing a high accuracy. Also, a methodology to perform fixed-point optimization is developed.

Affine Arithmetic (AA) is used to provide a fast Signal-to-Quantization Noise-Ratio (SQNR) estimation that can be used during the fixed-point optimization stage. The fast estimator covers differentiable non-linear algorithms with and without feedbacks. The estimation is based on the parameterization of the statistical properties of the noise at the output of fixed-point algorithms. This parameterization allows relating the fixed-point formats of the signals to the output noise distribution by means of fast matrix operations. Thus, a fast estimation is achieved and the computation time of the fixed-point optimization process is significantly reduced.

The proposed estimator and the fixed-point optimization methodology are tested using a subset of non-linear algorithms, such as vector operations, IIR filter for mean power computation, adaptive filters – for both linear and non-linear system identification – and a channel equalizer. The computation time of fixed-point optimization is boosted by three orders of magnitude while keeping the average estimation error down to 6% in most cases.

Keywords: Fixed-Point Optimization, Digital Signal Processing, Quantization, Word-Length, Affine Arithmetic, Error Estimation, Signal-to-Quantization-Noise Ratio.

1 Introduction

The use of fixed-point (FxP) arithmetic has proved to provide low-cost hardware implementations [1–3]. The selection of the FxP formats of the variables of an

J.L. Ayala, D. Atienza, and R. Reis (Eds.): VLSI-SoC 2010, IFIP AICT 373, pp. 182–205, 2012.

algorithm is a time-consuming task that involves an optimization process whose goal is to find the set of word-lengths (WLs) that reduces cost most. The FxP optimization (FPO) process is a slow process, since the complexity of the optimization problem has been shown to be very complex (NP-hard [4]) and, also, because of the necessity of continuously assessing the accuracy of the algorithm which involves time-consuming simulations.

The estimation of the algorithm accuracy is normally performed adopting a simulation-based approach [1], which leads to long design times. However, in the last few years there have been attempts to provide fast estimation methods based on analytical techniques. These approaches can be applied to Linear Time-Invariant (LTI) systems [5, 2, 6] and to differentiable non-linear systems [7–10]. As for the noise metric used, they are based on the peak value [10] and on the computation of SQNR [2, 7, 5, 9, 8]. Since SQNR is a very popular error metric within DSP systems and because LTI systems have been extensively studied, our work aims at fast SQNR estimation techniques for differentiable non-linear systems.

The chapter contains the following contributions:

- A novel Affine-Arithmetic based SQNR estimator.
- An efficient methodology to perform fast and accurate SQNR estimates.
- Performance results using a set of non-linear benchmarks with and without feedbacks: adaptive filters, matrix operations, a mean power IIR filter, and a MIMO equalizer.

The chapter is organized as follows: In Section 2, some related works are discussed. Section 3 deals with fixed-point optimization. Section 4 introduces AA. Section 5 explains the fast estimation method. The software implementation of a FPO tool is addressed in Section 6. The performance results are presented in Section 7. And finally, Section 8 draws the conclusions.

2   Related Work

Only those approaches aiming at the automatic SQNR estimation of non-differentiable algorithms are tackled here. This also excludes approaches exclusively based on simulations, as the automation of these approaches does not translate into a significant reduction of computation times since these methods are inherently very slow. In the approaches being considered, non-linearities are addressed in terms of the perturbation theory, where the effect of the quantization of each signal on the output signals is supposed to be *very small*. This allows the application of first-order Taylor expansions to each non-linear operation in order to characterize the quantization effect. Thus, the set of algorithms is constrained to those containing differentiable operations. Existent methods enable to obtain an expression that relates the WLs of signals to the power – also mean and variance – of the quantization noise at the output. This will be further explained through eqn. 22 in subsection 5.2.

The work in [7] proposes a hybrid method that combines simulations and analytical techniques to estimate the variance of the noise. The estimator is suitable for non-recursive and recursive algorithms. The parameterization phase is relatively fast, since it requires $|S|$ simulations for an algorithm with $|S|$ variables (or signals). The noise model is based on [11] and second order effects are neglected by applying first order Taylor expansions. The paper seems to suggest that the contributions of the signal quantization noises at the output can be added, assuming that the noises are independent. The accuracy of the method is not supported with any empirical data, so the quality of the method cannot be inferred.

The method in [9] makes use of a more time-consuming method, since $|S|^2/2$ simulations as well as a curve fitting technique with $|S|^2/2$ coefficients are required. On the one hand, the noise produced by each signal is described in terms of the traditional quantization noise model from [12], which is less accurate than [11], and, again, second order statistics are neglected. On the other hand, the expression of the estimated noise power accounts for noise interdependencies, which is a better approach than [7]. The method is tested with an LMS adaptive filter and the accuracy is evaluated graphically. There is no information about computation times.

Finally, in [8] the parameterization is performed by means of $|S|$ simulations and the estimator is suitable only for non-recursive systems. The accuracy of this approach seems to be the highest of all presented methods since it uses the model from [11] and it accounts for noise interdependencies. Although the information provided about accuracy is more complete, it is still not sufficient, since the estimator is only tested in a few SQNR scenarios. This approach was successfully extended to recursive systems in [13], with reasonably short parameterization times due to the use of linear-prediction techniques.

The approach explained in this chapter (Section 5) tries to overcome most of the drawbacks of the works presented above by considering:

- Both non-recursive and recursive algorithms
- An accurate noise model [11]
- Noise interdependencies

3   Fixed-Point Optimization

The starting point of FPO is a graph $G(V, S)$ describing a FxP algorithm. Set V contains the operations of the algorithm, and set S its signals. The FxP format of a number is defined by means of the pair (p, n), where p represents the number of bits required to represent the integer part, and n is the total number of bits (see left side of Figure 1). In fact, the complete FxP format of a signal requires more information: the format before quantization – (p_{pre}, n_{pre}) – and the format after quantization – (p, n) (see [2]). The error introduced by each quantization operation (i.e. truncation) is directly related to the number of least significant bits removed (see subsection 5.1 for a description of an error model that makes

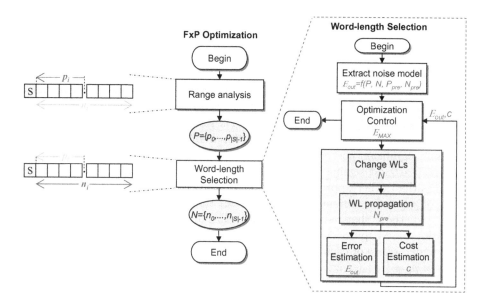

Fig. 1. Fixed-point optimization diagram

use of pairs (p_{pre}, n_{pre}) and (p, n)). Figure 2 depicts the quantization of the output of a multiplication. Here, 16-bit signals a and b are multiplied, and the result c is quantized to 8 bits (i.e. 16-8=8 bits).

Initially, the FxP formats of signals are unknown and it is the task of FPO to find a suitable set of these that minimizes cost. The FxP format determines the quantization error generated by a quantized signal. This error is propagated to the output of the algorithm. Also, the FxP format determines the number of bits of a signal, and therefore the size of the hardware resources required to process it. The size of a resource ultimately determines its area, delay and power costs. For instance, going back to Figure 2, the FxP format of signals a and b is

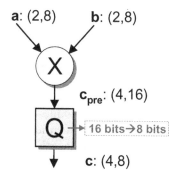

Fig. 2. Quantization of a multiplier

determining the cost of the multiplier, while the truncation of output c is affecting the mathematical precision of the operation, which is ultimately affecting the overall mathematical precision of the algorithm. During FPO, the optimization is guided by the cost and the output error obtained from the different FxP formats tried through successive iterations.

Figure 1 depicts the FPO approach adopted in this work. FPO is composed of the stages of ranges analysis or *scaling*, which determines the set of p ($P = \{p_0, \ldots, p_{|S|-1}\}$), and *word-length selection*, which determines the set of n ($N = \{n_0, \ldots, n_{|S|-1}\}$). This separation allows simplifying FPO while still providing significant cost reductions.

A wrap-around scaling strategy is adopted since it requires less hardware resources than other approaches (i.e. saturation techniques). After scaling, the values of p are the minimum possible values that avoid the overflow of signals or, at least, those that reduce the likelihood of overflow to a negligible value. A simulation-based approach is used to carry out scaling [1]. During the simulation, the dynamic range of each signal is obtained and the value of p is computed by means of $p_i = \lfloor log_2(max_i) \rfloor + 1$.

Once scaling is performed, the values of p can be fixed during word-length selection. The right side of Fig. 1 shows a diagram of the basic steps during word-length selection. Basically, word-length selection iterates trying different word-lengths for the variables of the algorithm (i.e. n) until cost is minimized. Any time the WL of a signal or a group of signals is changed, the WLs must be propagated throughout the graph, task referred to as graph *conditioning* [2]. The *optimization control* block selects the size of the new WLs using the values of the previous error and cost estimations and decides when the optimization procedure has finished. The first task in the diagram is the extraction of the quantization noise model. The role of this operation is to generate a model of the quantization noise at the output, related to the FxP format of each signal (i.e. (p_i, n_i) and $(p_{i_{pre}}, n_{i_{pre}})$). This is the key to avoid the use of time-consuming simulations. The implications of using a quick error estimator within the optimization loop are twofold: i) the optimization process can be faster, or, ii) it is possible to perform a wider design space exploration. During the optimization process, the control block makes decisions about the signals that change their WLs according to the error and cost estimations.

4   Affine Arithmetic

Affine Arithmetic (AA) [14] is aimed at the fast and accurate computation of the ranges of the signals of an algorithm. Its main feature is that it automatically cancels the linear dependencies of the included uncertainties along the computation path, thus avoiding the oversizing produced by Interval Arithmetic (IA) approaches [15]. Regarding fixed-point optimization, it has been applied to both scaling computation [16, 17, 10], and word-length selection [5, 16, 10, 18]. Also, a modification, called Quantized Affine Arithmetic (QAA), has been applied to the computation of limit cycles [19] and dynamic range analysis of quantized LTI algorithms [17].

4.1   Description

The mathematical expression of an affine form is

$$\hat{x} = x_0 + \sum_{i=1}^{N_x} x_i \epsilon_i \tag{1}$$

where x_0 is the central value of $\hat{x}$, and ϵ_i and x_i are its i-th noise term identifier and amplitude, respectively. In fact, $x_i \epsilon_i$ represents the interval $[-x_i, +x_i]$, so an affine form describes a numerical domain in terms of a central value and a sum of intervals with different identifiers. Affine operations are those which operate affine forms and produce an affine form as a result. Given the affine forms $\hat{x}$, $\hat{y}$ and $\hat{c} = c_0$, the affine operations are

$$\hat{x} \pm \hat{c} = x_0 \pm c_0 + \sum_{i=1}^{N_x} x_i \epsilon_i \tag{2}$$

$$\hat{x} \pm \hat{y} = x_0 \pm y_0 + \sum_{i=1}^{\max(N_x, N_y)} (x_i \pm y_i) \epsilon_i \tag{3}$$

$$\hat{c} \cdot \hat{x} = c_0 x_0 + \sum_{i=1}^{N_x} c_0 x_i \epsilon_i \tag{4}$$

These operations suffice to model any LTI algorithm. Differentiable operations can be approximated using a first-order Taylor expansion:

$$f(\hat{x}, \hat{y}) \approx f(x_0, y_0) + \sum_{i=1}^{\max(N_x, N_y)} \left(\frac{\delta f(x_0, y_0)}{\delta \hat{x}} \cdot x_i + \frac{\delta f(x_0, y_0)}{\delta \hat{y}} \cdot y_i \right) \epsilon_i \tag{5}$$

4.2   Example of Application

This section describes an example of application of AA. Let us consider the standard Red, Green and Blue (RGB) to Luma, Red and Blue Chroma (YCrCb) converter shown in Figure 3 [2, 17], whose sequence of operations is given in the first column of Table 1. The second column shows the computation of the affine form associated to each algorithm's signal. The last column shows the interval associated to the dynamic range of each signal. Without loss of generality, in this example it is considered that the three input values are contained in the range $[64, 128]$, and that the computations are performed using infinite precision.

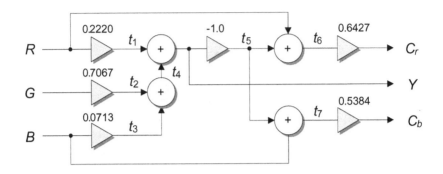

Fig. 3. ITU RGB to YCrCb converter

Table 1. Propagation and computation of the affine forms for the ITU RGB-YCrCb converter

Operations	AA-based computations	Signal ranges
$t_1 = 0.22R$	$\hat{t}_1 = 0.22 \cdot (96 + 32\epsilon_1) = 21.31 + 7.10\epsilon_1$	$[14.208, 28.416]$
$t_2 = 0.71G$	$\hat{t}_2 = 0.71 \cdot (96 + 32\epsilon_2) = 67.84 + 22.61\epsilon_2$	$[45.228, 90.458]$
$t_2 = 0.071B$	$\hat{t}_3 = 0.071 \cdot (96 + 32\epsilon_3) = 6.842.28\epsilon_3$	$[4.563, 9.126]$
$t_4 = t_2 + t_3$	$\hat{t}_4 = (67.84 + 22.61\epsilon_2) + (6.84 + 2.28\epsilon_3)$ $= 74.69 + 22.61\epsilon_2 + 2.28\epsilon_3$	$[49.792, 99.584]$
$t_4 = t_2 + t_3$	$\hat{t}_4 = (67.84 + 22.61\epsilon_2) + (6.84 + 2.28\epsilon_3)$ $= 74.69 + 22.61\epsilon_2 + 2.28\epsilon_3$	$[49.792, 99.584]$
$Y = t_1 + t_4$	$\hat{Y} = (21.31 + 7.1\epsilon_1) + (74.69 + 22.61\epsilon_2 + 2.28\epsilon_3)$ $= 96 + 7.1\epsilon_1 + 22.61\epsilon_2 + 2.28\epsilon_3$	$[64, 128]$
$t_5 = -Y$	$\hat{Y} = -(96 + 7.1\epsilon_2 + 22.61\epsilon_2 + 2.28\epsilon_3)$ $= -96 - 7.1\epsilon_1 - 22.61\epsilon_2 - 2.28\epsilon_3$	$[-128, -64]$
$t_6 = t_5 + R$	$\hat{t}_6 = (-96 - 7.1\epsilon_1 - 22.61\epsilon_2 - 2.28\epsilon_3) + (96 + 32\epsilon_1)$ $= 24.9\epsilon_1 - 22.61\epsilon_2 - 2.28\epsilon_3$	$[-49.792, 49.792]$
$C_r = 0.64t_6$	$\hat{C}_r = 0.64 \cdot (24.9\epsilon_1 - 22.61\epsilon2 - 2.28\epsilon3)$ $= 16\epsilon_1 - 14.53\epsilon_2 - 1.47\epsilon_3$	$[-32.001, 32.001]$
$t_7 = t_5 + B$	$\hat{t}_7 = (-96 - 7.1\epsilon_1 - 22.61\epsilon_2 - 2.28\epsilon_3) + (96 + 32\epsilon_3)$ $= -7.1\epsilon_1 - 22.61\epsilon_2 + 29.72\epsilon_3$	$[-59.437, 59.437]$
$C_b = 0.54t_7$	$\hat{C}_b = 0.54 \cdot (-7.1\epsilon_1 - 22.61\epsilon_2 + 29.72\epsilon_3)$ $= -3.82\epsilon_1 - 12.18\epsilon_2 + 16\epsilon_3$	$[-32.0008, 32.0008]$

Assuming that the RGB values are independent from each other, the affine forms that represent the signal ranges are modeled using one distinct noise term per uncertainty source, i.e.,

$$\hat{R} = 96 + 32\epsilon_1 \tag{6}$$
$$\hat{G} = 96 + 32\epsilon_2 \tag{7}$$
$$\hat{B} = 96 + 32\epsilon_3. \tag{8}$$

By applying the operation definitions described in subsection 4.1, the affine form that represents the values of t_1 is

$$\hat{t}_1 = 0.2220 \cdot \hat{R} = 0.2220(96 + 32\epsilon_1) = 21.3120 + 7.1040\epsilon_1 \tag{9}$$

and the interval that specifies its range is

$$range(\hat{t}_1) = t_{1,0} \pm \sum_{i=1}^{\max(N_x, N_y)} range(t_{1_i} \cdot \epsilon_i) \tag{10}$$
$$= range(21.3127 \pm 7.1040) \tag{11}$$
$$= [14.2080, 28.4160] \tag{12}$$

The same procedure can be applied to the rest of the signals to obtain results found in Table 1.

This example illustrates the application of AA to compute the dynamic range of signals. However, AA is used is this work as a means to propagate the quantization error of each signal to the output. For this purposes, affine forms are used to represent quantization errors that are added to signals. The propagation of these errors follows the same rules that have been applied in the previous example. However, as shown in the next section, affine forms will be interpreted from an statistical point of view, since their error terms will be assigned probability density functions (PDFs). This will lead to the estimation of SQNR by means of AA.

5   SQNR Estimation

In this section, an AA-based method able to estimate the SQNR of non-linear algorithms with and without feedback loops is presented. The method is able to extract an estimation of the power of the quantization noise of a system from an AA-based simulation. This would not be of much use for a fast FPO if AA simulations must be repeated during the WL selection phase (see Figure 1). The ultimate goal of the method is to use a single AA simulation to extract a model of the quantization noise that enables fast SQNR estimation, so it supports fast FPO.

5.1   Affine Arithmetic Applied to Error Propagation Analysis

Noise estimation is based on the assumption that the quantization of a signal i from n_{pre} bits to n bits can be modeled by the addition of a uniformly distributed white noise with the following statistical parameters [11]:

$$\sigma_i^2 = \frac{2^{2p_i}}{12}\left(2^{-2n_i} - 2^{-2n_i^{pre}}\right) \tag{13}$$

$$\mu_i = -2^{p_i-1}\left(2^{-n_i} - 2^{-n_i^{pre}}\right). \tag{14}$$

This noise model is a refinement of the traditional modeling of the quantization error as an additive white noise [12] and, therefore, it is more accurate. The values of p are obtained during the scaling phase and the values of n and n_{pre} are computed during word-length selection by means of WL propagation (see the optimization flow in Figure 1).

The deviation from the original behavior of an algorithm with feedback loops caused by quantized signals can be modeled by adding an affine form $\hat{n}_i[k]$ to each signal i at each simulation time instant k (i.e. loop iteration index) [5]. These affine forms can properly model the quantization noise of each signal if the error term ϵ is assigned a uniform distribution:

$$\hat{n}_i[k] = \mu_i + \sqrt{12\sigma_i^2}\epsilon_{i,k} = \epsilon'_{i,k} \tag{15}$$

Thus, an AA simulation automatically identifies the origin of any particular error term (i) and the moment when it was generated (k). Error term ϵ' encapsulates the mean value and the variance of the error term ϵ, that now can be seen as a random variable with variance σ_i^2 and mean μ_i. Thus, the AA-based simulation can be made independent on the particular statistical parameters of each quantization. This is highly desirable in order to obtain a parameterizable noise model. In fact, this is a reinterpretation of AA, since error terms are not only intervals, but they also have an associated probability distribution. Once the simulation is finished, it is possible to compute the impact of the any quantization noise produced by signal s_i on the output of the algorithm by extracting the value of the error amplitude (given by $x_{i,k}$ in eqn. (1)). This enables the parameterization of the noise. Once the parameterization is performed, the quantization error produced by any combination of (p, n) can be easily assessed by replacing all $\epsilon'_{i,k}$ by the original expression that accounts for the mean and variance ($\mu_i + \sqrt{12\sigma^2}\epsilon_{i,k}$), thus enabling a fast estimation of the quantization error. We present in detail the complete process in the next paragraphs.

Given an algorithm with $|S|$ signals, the expression of output $\hat{Y}$ is

$$\hat{Y}[k] = Y_0[k] + \sum_{i=0}^{|S|-1}\sum_{j=0}^{k} Y_{i,j}[k]\epsilon'_{i,j}, \tag{16}$$

where $Y_0[k]$ is the value of the output of the algorithm using floating-point arithmetic and the summation is the contribution of the quantization noise sources.

Note that the error term amplitude $Y_{i,j}[k]$ is a function that depends on the inputs of the algorithm for non-linear systems.

The error $\hat{E}rr_Y$ at the output is

$$\hat{E}rr_Y[k] = Y_0[k] - \hat{Y}[k] = -\sum_{i=0}^{|S|-1} \sum_{j=0}^{k} Y_{i,j}[k]\epsilon'_{i,j}, \tag{17}$$

and it is formed by a collection of affine forms at each time step n. This expression of the error can be used to estimate the error peak-value, using the traditional interpretation of AA [20, 10], and, also, to obtain the PDF of the error [5, 20]. However, in the next subsection we focus on obtaining the value of the power of the error considering the actual PDF of each error term (i.e. a uniform density function).

5.2 Analytical SQNR Estimation

The power of the quantization noise is computed as the Mean Square Error (MSE), that is, the mean value of the expectancy of the power of the summations of $\epsilon_{i,j}$ during K time steps.

$$P\left(\hat{E}rr_Y\right) = \frac{1}{K} \sum_{m=0}^{K-1} E\left[\left(\hat{E}rr_Y[m]\right)^2\right]$$

$$= \frac{1}{K} \sum_{m=0}^{K-1} \left(Var(\hat{E}rr_Y[m]) + \right.$$

$$\left. E\left[\hat{E}rr_Y[m]\right]^2\right) \tag{18}$$

The two main terms in eqn. (18) are developed in (19) and (20). The former makes use of the fact that it can be assumed that error terms $\epsilon'_{i,k}$ are uncorrelated to each other [12].

$$Var(\hat{E}rr_Y[m]) = Var(-\sum_{i=0}^{|S|-1} \sum_{j=0}^{m} Y_{i,j}[m]\epsilon'_{i,j})$$

$$= \sum_{i=0}^{|S|-1} \sum_{j=0}^{m} Var(-Y_{i,j}[m]\epsilon'_{i,j})$$

$$= \sum_{i=0}^{|S|-1} \sigma_i^2 \sum_{j=0}^{m} Y_{i,j}^2[m] \tag{19}$$

$$E[\hat{Err}_Y[m]] = E[-\sum_{i=0}^{|S|-1}\sum_{j=0}^{m}Y_{i,j}[m]\epsilon'_{i,j}]$$

$$= -\sum_{i=0}^{|S|-1}\mu_i\sum_{j=0}^{m}Y_{i,j}[m] \tag{20}$$

Combining (18), (19) and (20):

$$P\left(\hat{Err}_Y[k]\right) = \frac{1}{K}\sum_{m=0}^{K-1}\left(\sum_{i=0}^{|S|-1}\sigma_i^2\sum_{j=0}^{m}Y_{i,j}^2[m] + \right.$$

$$\left.\left(\sum_{i=0}^{|S|-1}\mu_i\sum_{j=0}^{m}Y_{i,j}[m]\right)^2\right) \tag{21}$$

Equation (21) can be expressed in vectorial form (eqns. (22-24)). The statistical parameters of the quantized signals are in vectors $s = \left\langle\sigma_0^2\ldots\sigma_{|S|-1}^2\right\rangle$ and $\mu = \left\langle\mu_0\ldots\mu_{|S|-1}\right\rangle$. Once vector v and matrix M are computed –during the noise parameterization phase– the estimation of the quantization noise does not require any further AA simulations, but the computation of (22), which is a much faster process. Also, note that we are not actually computing the SQNR, but the power of the output signal. The SQNR can be easily computed from the power of the output signal using infinite precision (i.e. floating-point double precision) and applying the formula $SQNR = 20\cdot log(P_{Y_0}/P_E))$.

$$P_E = \frac{1}{K}\left(s\cdot v^T + \mu\cdot M\mu^T\right) \tag{22}$$

$$v \equiv \left\langle\sum_{k=0}^{K-1}\sum_{j=0}^{k}Y_{0,j}^2[k],\ldots,\right.$$

$$\left.\sum_{k=0}^{K-1}\sum_{j=0}^{k}Y_{|S|-1,j}^2[k]\right\rangle \tag{23}$$

$$M \equiv \begin{bmatrix} m_{0,0} & \cdots & m_{|S|-1,0} \\ & \ddots & \\ m_{0,|S|-1} & \cdots & m_{|S|-1,|S|-1} \end{bmatrix} \tag{24}$$

$$m_{i_1,i_2} = \sum_{k=0}^{K-1}\left(\sum_{j_1=0}^{k}Y_{i_1,j_1}[k]\sum_{j_2=0}^{k}Y_{i_2,j_2}[k]\right) \tag{25}$$

Algorithm 1. Gradient-descent optimization

Input: $G_{SFG}(V, S)$ with no fixed-point information, error constraint E_{max}
Output: word-length optimized $G_{SFG}(V, S)$

1: Perform *scaling* and initialize $P = \{p_0, \ldots, p_{|S|-1}\}$
2: Find minimum n that complies with noise constraint E_{max}
    when $\forall n_i \in N = \{n_0, \ldots, n_{|S|-1}\}, n_i = n$
3: Compute output error E
4: $C_{min} = \infty$
5: **repeat**
6:     $s_{candidate} = undefined$
7:     **for all** $s_i \in S$ **do**
8:         $n_i = n_i - 1$
9:         Compute output error E
10:         **if** $E < E_{max}$ **then**
11:             Compute cost C
12:             **if** $C < C_{min}$ **then**
13:                 $C_{min} = C$
                    $s_{candidate} = s_i$
14:             **end if**
15:         **end if**
16:         restore n_i
17:     **end for**
18:     **if** $s_{candidate} \neg = undefined$ **then**
19:         $n_{candidate} = n_{candidate} - 1$
20:     **end if**
21: **until** $s_{candidate} \neg = undefined$

5.3 Accuracy for LTI Systems

The purpose of the proposed fast estimation method is to estimate the quantization noise produced by non-linear algorithms. However, it is important to verify that eqn. (22) matches the well-known expression that is used to compute the output noise power of a quantized LTI system in steady state. This verification can be found in [21], where it is analytically proven that if eqn. (22) is used for LTI systems by removing the first J samples (to remove the transient) then

$$P_{LTI}\left(\hat{E}rr_Y\right) = \frac{1}{K - J} \sum_{m=J}^{K-1} E\left[\left(\hat{E}rr_Y[m]\right)^2\right]$$

$$\approx \sum_{i=0}^{|S|-1} \sigma_i^2 \cdot \frac{1}{2\pi} \int_{-\pi}^{\pi} \left|G_i(e^{j\Omega})\right|^2 d\Omega$$

$$+ \left(\sum_{i=0}^{|S|-1} \mu_i \cdot G_i(1)\right)^2. \tag{26}$$

The basis of this demonstration is that it is possible to relate the error terms amplitudes ($Y_{i,j}[k]$) to the transfer function from signal i to the output (G_i). This proves that the accuracy of the presented estimation is very high for LTI systems. Nonetheless, the method presented here is not intended for LTI systems, since there are already more efficient ways to compute their output noise [2, 5, 21]. The accuracy for non-linear algorithms is presented in the next section.

6   Fixed-Point Optimization Tool

FPO can now be accelerated by means of the estimator presented in the previous section. Here, we outline how the FPO process must be performed and we present the implementation of the process as an automatic design tool.

6.1   Estimation-Based Optimization

Before carrying out the task of WL selection, it is necessary to parameterize the quantization noise at the output of the system. The parameterization process is carried out by means of the following steps:

1. Perform a $K-$step AA simulation adding an affine form $\hat{n}_i$ to each signal i.
2. Compute eqns. (23-25) using the previously collected $Y_{i,j}[k]$.

Once vector s and matrix M are available, expression (22) can be used during the optimization process to assess the system quality.

Many optimization techniques can be applied to the problem of finding the appropriate word-lengths. Here, we present a gradient-descent optimization [22] that provides a trade-off between low complexity and optimality. Its behavior is described using pseudo-code in Algorithm 1. Given an algorithm with $|S|$ signals, it performs $|S|$ independent tests, where the WL of each signal is reduced one bit and the resulting error (E) and cost (C) are recorded. The test producing the largest cost reduction among those tests that comply with the error constraint $(E < E_{MAX})$ is selected and the WL change performed in that test is made permanent. The algorithm goes on until it is not possible to reduce the WLs without violating the error constraint.

Regarding the cost function, some authors use area [22, 2, 23, 21], others the error itself [24] and others a linear combination of both [25]. The reader can extend the information on FPO techniques consulting [26, 24, 27, 28].

6.2   Software Implementation

The proposed fast estimator, as well as the FPO methodology, were implemented using C++. Operator overloading was used in order to enable the execution of the same algorithm description using different data types. For instance, during *scaling*, a floating-point simulation that collects the dynamic range information for each signal must be performed. Also, during the *error modeling* phase, an AA simulation is used to extract parameters v and M. During WL selection, it is necessary to know the set N_{pre} that is obtained through *WL propagation*.

```
                                    FPO.cpp
                                    #include "FPO.h"
Square.h                            #include "Square.h"
class Square::QAlgorithm{           main(){
...                                   FPO fpo;
set_signals(){                        Square sqr(fpo);
   x.set_input(_UNQUANTIZED, _ROUND);
   y.set_output(_QUANTIZED, _TRUNC);   fpo.set_simulation(10000);
}                                     sqr.init();    // call set_signals,set_inputs,etc.
set_inputs(){                         fpo.scaling();
for (int i=0; i<x.data.size(); i++)   fpo.error_model();
   x.data[i] = rand()/(RAND_MAX+1);   fpo.set_sqnr(80.0); // SQNR=80 dB
}                                     fpo.optim(_GRAD_DESCENT, _AA);
exe(){    c=a*a; }                    double pow_AA = fpo.get_pow(_AA)
...                                   double sqnr_AA = fpo.get_sqnr(_AA)
                                      double pow_FX = fpo.get_pow(_FXP) // FxP simulation
Quant_signal x;                       double sqnr_FX = fpo.get_sqnr(_FXP) // FxP simulation
Quant_signal y;                       double pow_err = 100.*(pow_FX-pow_AA)/pow_FX;
...                                    double sqnr_err = sqnr_FX-sqnr_AA;
}                                     cout<<"Estimation error: "<<pow_err<<"%; ";
                                      cout<<sqnr_err<<" dB" << endl;
                                    }
```

Fig. 4. Example of use of the software framework

During this phase, the FxP format of each variable was used to perform WL propagation. And, finally, the last FxP simulation used to assess the estimator quality requires the use of a FxP data type.

A framework to coordinate the different FPO phases, and to allow the designer to configure the optimization process to quantize the algorithm, was also developed. Figure 4 displays a simple example. File **Square.h** contains the description of the algorithm. The designer must specify the way that the signals (e.g. inputs, outputs and signals) are treated during FPO (see function **set_signals**). They can be quantized or not, and also different rounding schemes can be applied (i.e. rounding or truncation). The designer must also specify the original WL of inputs. Also, the input values must be fed through **set_inputs**. The operation sequence is described in **exe**. The next step for the designer is to declare an object for the algorithm and also to declare an object **FPO** that encapsulates all the FPO features (see **main.cpp**). The FPO process is straight forward, since there are methods for the main FPO tasks: **scaling**, **error_model**, **optim** (see Figure 1). Note that the parameters of method **fpo.optim()** are the type of optimization technique (i.e. _GRAD_DESCENT is for a gradient-descent optimization such as Algorithm 1) and the type of error computation (i.e. _AA for AA-based estimation, and _FXP for a FxP simulation-based estimation). Needless to say that the use of simulations requires much longer processing times than AA-based optimizations. In the last few lines of the code, the quantization noise power and the SQNR are computed using the AA estimations (i.e. get_pow(_AA) and get_sqnr(_AA)) and FxP simulations (i.e. get_pow(_FXP) and get_sqnr(_FXP)), and the estimation error is assessed (see subsection 7.2).

The implemented software framework has been used to quantize different benchmarks, presented in subsection 7.1, proving the validity of the techniques proposed in this chapter.

7   Results

In this section, the benchmarks used to test our fast estimator, as well as the performance results are presented.

7.1   Benchmarks

The benchmarks are the following:

- 3×3 vector scalar multiplication ($VEC_{3\times3}$)
- 8×8 vector scalar multiplication ($VEC_{8\times8}$)
- Mean power estimator based on a 1st-order IIR filter (POW)
- Channel equalizer for MIMO receiver (EQ) [29]
- 1st-order LMS filter (LMS_1) [30]
- 5th-order LMS filter (LMS_5) [30]
- 3rd-order Volterra filter (VOL_3) [31]

The main features of the benchmarks are summarized in Table 2, which contains the type of algorithm (LTI or non-linear, with or without loops), the number of inputs/outputs, the number and type of operations involved (z^{-1} representing delays and $*K$ constant multiplications), and the total number of signals ($|S|$). The set of benchmarks covers non-linear algorithms, both recursive (with feedback loops) and non-recursive. It must be noted that the set of operations is quite complete since it includes additions, multiplications, and also divisions, usually neglected in similar research studies. In addition to that, it is interesting to highlight that the algorithms cover channel equalization for 4G MIMO communications, vector multiplications and adaptive filtering with both linear and non-linear systems.

All benchmarks are fed with 16-bit inputs and 12-bit constants and the noise constraint is specifed as an SQNR ranging from 40 to 120 dB. The inputs used to perform the noise parameterization as well as steps of the fixed-point simulation are summarized in the last column of the table.

Vector Scalar Multiplication. Due to the importance of vector and matrix operations in the development of scientific applications, an $N \times N$ vector scalar multiplication is included as a benchmark. Given two N-element vectors a and b, the scalar product is defined as:

$$\left(a_0 \ldots a_{N-1}\right) \cdot \begin{pmatrix} b_0 \\ \vdots \\ b_{N-1} \end{pmatrix} = \sum_{i=0}^{N-1} a_i \cdot b_i \ . \tag{27}$$

Table 2. Properties of benchmarks

Benchmark	LTI	Cyclic	Inputs	Outputs	z^{-1}	+/-	*	$*K$	÷	$||S||$	Input signals
$VEC_{3\times3}$	NO	NO	6	1	0	2	3	0	0	12	Uniform noise
$VEC_{8\times8}$	NO	NO	16	1	0	7	8	0	0	32	Uniform noise
POW	NO	YES	1	1	1	1	1	2	0	7	Synthetic tone
EQ	NO	YES*	3	2	64	2	7	3	3	85	MIMO channel Tx [29]
LMS_1	NO	YES	2	1	3	4	4	2	0	16	Synthetic tone
LMS_5	NO	YES	2	1	11	12	12	6	0	44	Synthetic tone
VOL_3	NO	YES	2	1	2	4	6	4	0	19	Gaussian noise

* MAC operations applied to chuncks of 32 data

The arithmetic operations involved are: N multiplications and $N-1$ additions. The inputs used to extract the noise model are uniformly distributed noises.

IIR Mean Power Computation. The mean power computation is based in the use of an IIR filter. The equation describing its behavior is:

$$y[k] = x[k]^2 \cdot \alpha + y[k-1] \cdot \beta \qquad (28)$$

where $x[k]$ is the input to the filter and $y[k]$ is the output. The constants α and $\beta = 1-\alpha$ fix the time length of the mean calculation. The operations used in the algorithm are one multiplication, two constant multiplications and one addition. It must be stressed that the filter contains a delay that conforms a loop.

The input used for this benchmark is a phase modulated tone signal with an uniform noise added.

LMS Adaptive Filtering. Adaptive filtering is widely used in many DSP applications. In particular, the Least Mean Squares (LMS) adaptive filter is a common solution due to its low computational load in comparison to other adaptive approaches. A reference signal d is estimated by means of output y:

$$y[k] = \sum_{i=0}^{N} x[k-i] \cdot w_i, \qquad (29)$$

where x is the input to the filter and w_i are its coefficients. The coefficients are updated in every time step by means of constant μ:

$$w_i^{next} = w_i + \mu \cdot x[k-i](d[k] - y[k]). \qquad (30)$$

An Nth-order LMS filter requires $2N+2$ multiplications, $N+1$ constant multiplications, $2N+1$ additions, 1 subtraction and $2N+1$ delays. It also contains loops.

Two input signals must be specified here: the reference d is a synthetic tone signal with phase and amplituted noises, and the input x is signal d with N added echoes.

Equalizer for Alamouti MIMO Communications System. The selected equalizer aims at 4G communications and it is embedded in a Multi-Carrier Code-Division Multiple-Access (MC-CDMA) radio system [29], which is able to handle up to 32 users and provides transmission bit-rates up to 125 Mbps. The transmitter sends complex data Y_i using different subcarriers (i is the subcarrier index) and the receiver combines the data received by the different antennas to produce complex Z_i, which is the input of the equalizer. This signal is related to Y_i by means of the real signal H_i, which is contains information about the communication channel, and N_i is a noise term signal.

$$Z_i = H_i \cdot Y_i + N_i \tag{31}$$

The output of the equalizer is an estimate of Y_i:

$$Y_i = G_i \cdot Z_i. \tag{32}$$

The coefficients G_i can be extracted using H_i and constant λ, which is related to the Signal to Noise Ratio conditions.

$$G_i = \frac{1}{H_i + \lambda} \cdot \frac{S_F}{\sum_{j=i \mod S_F}^{(i \mod S_F)+S_F-1} \frac{H_j}{H_j+\lambda}} \tag{33}$$

Notice that the second factor is constant for every group of S_F consecutive subcarriers. For this particular application $S_F = 32$.

The equalizer can be implemented using seven multiplications, three constant multiplications, three divisions and two additions. It is interesting to highlight that the presence of multiplications and divisions make this algorithm highly non-linear.

The input signals H and Z are generated using a realistic MIMO channel model [29].

Volterra Adaptive Filtering. Volterra adaptive filters are used when the non-linearities present in the system that is being approximated cannot be neglected. The behavior of the filter is similar to that of LMS, but now, the computation of output y involves a non-linear equation. In particular, a Hermite polynomial series is used for the estimation:

$$y[k] = \sum_{i=0}^{K} H_i(\bar{x}) \cdot w_i, \tag{34}$$

where H_i is the Hermite polynomial of order i, $\bar{x} = \frac{x}{P_x}$ is the normalized input to the filter, P_x is the power of signal x and w_i are its coefficients. The coefficients are updated each time step by means of constant μ:

$$w_i^{next} = w_i + \mu \cdot H_i(\bar{x})(d[k] - y[k]). \tag{35}$$

Here, we address the estimation of the function $arctan(x)$ by means of a 3rd-order Hermite expansion. The expression of $y[k]$ for such a Volterra adaptive filter is:

$$y[k] = \left(\frac{x[k]}{P_x}\right) \cdot w_1 + \left(\left(\frac{x[k]}{P_x}\right) - 3\left(\frac{x[k]}{P_x}\right)^3\right) \cdot w_3 \qquad (36)$$

Table 2 displays the number of operations required for the 3rd-order Volterra filter. The inputs used are as follows: signal x is a gaussian noise and d is $arctan(x)$.

7.2 Experimental Setup

All the benchmarks were used to test both the accuracy and computation performance of the proposed FPO method. The following procedure was carried out:

- For *all benchmarks* do
  1. Compute scaling by means of a floating-point simulation.
  2. Extract noise parameters (eqns. 23-25) performing an AA-based simulation.
  3. Record computation time $T^{Param-AA}$.
  4. For $SQNR = [3, \ldots, 120]$ do
     (a) Perform a WL selection based on the fast estimator (eqn. 22) using a gradient-descent approach.
     (b) Record computation time $T_{SQNR}^{Optim-AA}$, estimation P_{SQNR}^{AA} and the number of optimization iterations I_{SQNR}.
     (c) Perform a single FxP bit-true simulation of the quantized algorithm and use it as reference to compute the performance and accuracy of the estimator.
     (d) Record computation time of a single fixed-point simulation (T_{SQNR}^{FxP}).
     (e) Record an estimate of a simulation-based FPO ($T_{SQNR}^{Optim-FxP} = T_{SQNR}^{FxP} \times I_{SQNR}$) and the simulation-based SQNR (P_{SQNR}^{FxP}).
  5. Compute the average values $\bar{T}^{Optim-AA}$ and $\bar{T}^{Optim-FxP}$.

7.3 Accuracy Results

The accuracy obtained by means of a gradient-descent FPO [2] under different SQNR constraints for the different benchmarks is presented in Table 3. A total of 80 different SQNR constraints were used, ranging from 40 dB to 120 dB. The first column indicates the benchmark used. The remaining columns show the accuracy of the estimations measured in terms of the maximum absolute values of the relative errors in dB, and the average of the absolute values of the percentage errors, for four SQNR ranges: [120,100] dB, [100,80] dB, [80, 60] dB and [60,40] dB (see the expressions of the metrics at the bottom of the table). The last row contains the maximum and average value using the information from all benchmarks

Table 3. Performance of the estimation method: precision

Benchmark	Estimation error							
	[120,100][1] dB $(dB)^2$ (%)[3]		[100,80] dB (dB) (%)[3]		[80,60] dB $(dB)^2$ (%)[3]		[60,40] dB $(dB)^2$ (%)[3]	
$VEC_{3\times3}$	0.07	0.54	0.07	0.11	0.06	0.50	0.09	0.72
$VEC_{8\times8}$	0.05	0.57	0.04	0.40	0.04	0.57	0.13	1.19
POW^*	0.27	0.98	0.24	0.71	0.29	0.17	0.18	1.52
EQ^*	0.39	5.00	0.17	1.55	0.76	5.96	1.12	12.12
LMS_1^*	0.09	0.41	0.14	0.90	0.16	1.74	0.82	6.96
LMS_5^*	0.09	0.46	0.08	0.07	0.13	1.08	1.09	5.51
VOL_3^*	1.14	3.33	0.49	1.84	0.81	6.70	1.43	16.67
All	0.39	1.27	0.24	0.05	0.76	1.48	1.12	4.21

* Recursive
[1] Error constraint
[2] $|10log(\frac{P_{ref}}{P_{est}})|$ (max)
[3] $|100(\frac{P_{ref}-P_{est}}{P_{ref}})|$ (average)

Results show that the estimator is very accurate. The mean percentage error (see last row) is smaller than 4.3 %, and the maximum relative error is smaller than 1.12 dB. Note that the accuracy decreases as long as the error constraints get looser. This is due to the amplification of the Taylor error terms (specially in the presence of loops) and also to the fact that the uniformly distributed model for the quantization noise does not remain valid for small SQNRs. Anyway, the quality of the estimates is still very high, thus confirming the excellent accuracy of the estimator. The accuracy of recursive algorithms is slightly reduced, since the estimation errors are somehow amplified by the feedback loops. The estimation errors for benchmark EQ appear to be greater that the rest, probably due to the presence of both divisions and feedback loops.

Figure 5 displays the mean estimation error vs. the target SQNR for the benchmarks $VEC_{3\times3}$ and POW. Note that the target SQNR range has been extended to $[3, 120]$ dB. These two algorithms present similar non-linearities. The former performs the summation of the multiplication of three pairs of numbers, while the latter performs the accumulation of the square of a signal. The main difference between them is the presence of a feedback in POW. First, it can be seen in the figure that as long as the SQNR decreases the error in the estimation increases. This is expected since the quantization model relies on the fact that the quantization error is much smaller than the dynamic range of the signal. $VEC_{3\times3}$ presents an error smaller than 20% for the whole SQNR range. However, POW achieves similar errors for SQNR values smaller than 65 dB, but for SQNR values smaller than 30 dB, the error reaches values close to 100%. As aforementioned, the error introduced by the 1_{st}-order Taylor approximation becomes magnified in the pressence of feedbacks.

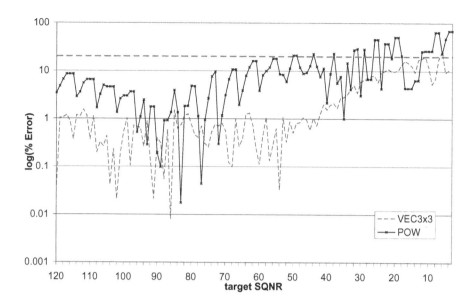

Fig. 5. Estimation error (%) vs. target SQNR for $VEC_{3\times3}$ and POW

Figure 6 shows a similar graph for benchmarks LMS_5, VOL_3 and EQ. LMS presents a strong feedback with a smooth non-linearity (i.e. multiplication). VOL_3 has a similar feedback (somehow smaller, since the order is smaller), but the non-linearities are stronger (i.e. x^3). Finally, EQ presents the more abrupt non-linearity (i.e. several divisions) but the feedback is not as prominent, since the accumulations are reset every 32 clock cycles. The three of them perform correctly for $SQNR = [65, 120]$. When $SQNR = [40, 65]$, approximately, the error is greater than 20%. For SQNR values smaller than 30 the performance is really poor, presenting VOL_3 and EQ the worst errors (i.e. larger than 100%).

It is interesting to see that the *amount* of non-linearity in the algorithm clearly impacts on the quality of the error estimation. VOL_3 performs very bad for small SQNR values in comparison to LMS_5. However, EQ performs well for most of the SQNR range, since the feedback effect is limited, but for very small SQNRs the non-linearity of division shows off, causing estimation errors up to 10^5. Since the quantization model is expected to fail for small SQNRs, this situation is not seen as an anomaly of the estimator, but as an intrinsic characteristic that it not possible to overcome. As shown in Table 3 the method works properly in the range $[40, 120]$.

7.4   Computation Time Results

Table 4 holds the computation times required for both noise parameterization and word-length selection. The first column shows the names of the benchmarks. The second one shows the length of the input vectors required for a fixed-point

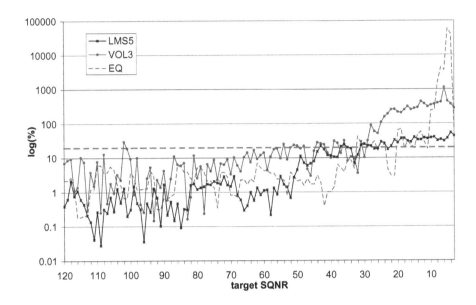

Fig. 6. Estimation error (%) vs. target SQNR: LMS_5, VOL_3 and EQ

simulation and for the parameterization process. The parameterization time is in the third column. The fourth column characterizes the complexity of the process through the number of estimates obtained during the optimization. Each iteration implies a noise estimation (using a simulation or our fast estimator). The next two columns present the computation time required to perform the gradient-descent optimization using our estimation-based proposal and using a classical simulation-based approach. The computation time for the simulation-based approach is an estimation obtained from multiplying the average number of optimization iterations by the computation time of a single fixed-point simulation. The speed-up obtained by our estimation-based approach is in the last column. The last row contains the average speedup considering all experiments.

The parameterization time goes from 59.66 μsecs. to 28 mins. (1646 secs.) and it depends on the size of the input dataset, the complexity of the algorithm (i.e. number and types of operations) and the presence of feedback loops. The cases including multiplications show how an increase in complexity implies an increase in parameterization time. This situation is more acute in the presence of loops (see LMS_1 and LMS_5). However, the effect of algorithm complexity in FPO time is negligible. These times might seem quite long, but it must be kept in mind that the parameterization process is performed only once, and after that the algorithm can be evaluated for different fixed-point formats as many times as desired using the fast estimator.

The mean number of estimates in the fifth column is shown to give an idea of the complexity of the optimization process. A simulation-based optimization approach would require that very same number of simulations, thus taking a very

Table 4. Performance of the estimation method: computation time

Bench.	FxP Samples	$T^{Param-AA}$ (secs)[+]	No. of estimates (mean)	$\bar{T}^{Optim-AA}$ (secs)[+]	$\bar{T}^{Optim-FxP}$ (secs)[+]	Speed-up
$VEC_{3\times3}$	$2\cdot10^4$	59.66	150.14	0.03	66.86	$\times2122$
$VEC_{8\times8}$	$2\cdot10^4$	330.67	1739.96	1.72	2331	$\times1377$
POW^*	$2\cdot10^4$	546.14	97.15	0.02	21.93	$\times1048$
EQ^*	$16\cdot10^3$	61.64	231.98	0.12	105.78	$\times904$
LMS_1^*	$5\cdot10^3$	908.02	712.28	0.42	163.73	$\times394$
LMS_5^*	$5\cdot10^3$	1646.38	2547.48	7.26	1611.46	$\times221$
VOL_3^*	$5\cdot10^3$	212.72	673.38	0.29	151.13	$\times526$
All	-	-	-	-	-	$\times942$

* With feedback
$^+$ On a 1.66 GHz Intel Core Duo, 1 GB of RAM

long time. For instance, the optimization of LMS_5 would approximately require 2500 FxP simulations of 5000 input data. Considering the number of estimations required, the optimization times are extremely fast, ranging from 0.02 secs to 7.26 secs. The speedups obtained in comparison to a simulation-based approach are staggering: boosts from $\times221$ to $\times2122$ are obtained. The average boost is $\times942$ which proves the advantage of our approach, not only in terms of accuracy but also in terms of computation time. Therefore, our approach enables fast and accurate FxP of non-linear DSP algorithms.

8 Conclusions

A fast and accurate SQNR estimation method based on the use of Affine Arithmetic has been presented. The estimator is used within a fixed-point optimization framework and fast quantization is achieved. Affine-arithmetic is used during the noise parameterization phase. The estimator can be used to perform complex FPO in reduced times, leading to significant hardware cost reductions. The method can be applied to differentiable non-linear DSP algorithms with and without feedbacks.

Summarizing, the main contributions of the chapter are:

- The proposal of a fast quantization noise estimation, based on affine arithmetic, for non-linear algorithms with and without feedbacks.
- The introduction of a methodology and an automatic design tool to perform fast FPO.
- The average estimation error for non-linear systems is smaller than 17% for all examples, and smaller than 7% for most cases.
- The computation time of FPO is boosted up to $\times2122$ (average of $\times942$).

Future research will pursue higher accuracy in the estimation of non-linear operations, probably by extending the presented approach to include additional terms of the Taylor series expansion. The goal is not only to improve further the accuracy of the method as presented, but to enable its application to algorithms with strong non-linearities.

Acknowledgments. This work was supported in part by Research Projects USP-BS PPC05/2010 (Banco Santander and University CEU San Pablo) and TEC2009-14219-C03 (Spanish Ministry of Science and Innovation).

References

1. Sung, W., Kum, K.-I.: Simulation-Based Word-Length Optimization Method for Fixed-Point Digital Signal Processing Systems. IEEE Trans. Signal Processing 43(12), 3087–3090 (1995)
2. Constantinides, G.A., Cheung, P.Y.K., Luk, W.: Wordlength Optimization for Linear Digital Signal Processing. IEEE Trans. Computer-Aided Design 22(10), 1432–1442 (2003)
3. Caffarena, G., Constantinides, G., Cheung, P., Carreras, C., Nieto-Taladriz, O.: Optimal Combined Word-Length Allocation and Architectural Synthesis of Digital Signal Processing Circuits. IEEE Trans. Circuits Syst. II 53(5), 339–343 (2006)
4. Constantinides, G., Woeginger, G.: The Complexity of Multiple Wordlength Assignment. Applied Mathematics Letters 15, 137–140 (2002)
5. López, J., Caffarena, G., Carreras, C., Nieto-Taladriz, O.: Fast and accurate computation of the roundoff noise of linear time-invariant systems. IET Circuits, Devices & Systems 2(4), 393–408 (2008)
6. Menard, D., Sentieys, O.: A Methodology for Evaluating the Precision of Fixed-Point Systems. In: Proceedings of IEEE International Conference on Acoustics, Speech, and Signal Processing, vol. 3, pp. 3152–3155 (2002)
7. Constantinides, G.: Perturbation Analysis for Word-Length Optimization. In: Proc. FCCM, pp. 81–90 (2003)
8. Menard, D., Rocher, R., Scalart, P., Sentieys, O.: SQNR Determination in Non-Linear and Non-Recursive Fixed-Point Systems. In: Proc. EUSIPCO, pp. 1349–1352 (2004)
9. Shi, C., Brodersen, R.: A Perturbation Theory on Statistical Quantization Effects in Fixed-Point DSP with Non-Stationary Inputs. In: Proc. ISCAS, vol. 3, pp. 373–376 (2004)
10. Lee, D.-U., Gaffar, A., Cheung, R., Mencer, W., Luk, O., Constantinides, G.: Accuracy-Guaranteed Bit-Width Optimization. IEEE Trans. Computer-Aided Design 25(10), 1990–2000 (2006)
11. Constantinides, G., Cheung, P., Luk, W.: Truncation Noise in Fixed-Point SFGs. IEE Electronics Letters 35(23), 2012–2014 (1999)
12. Jackson, L.: Roundoff-noise analysis for fixed-point digital filters realized in cascade or parallel form. IEEE Trans. Audio Electroacoust. 18, 107–122 (1970)
13. Rocher, R., Menard, D., Sentieys, O., Scalart, P.: Analytical Accuracy Evaluation of Fixed-Point Systems. In: Proc. EUSIPCO, pp. 999–1003 (2007)
14. Stolfi, J., Figueiredo, L.H.: Self-Validated Numerical Methods and Applications. In: Brazilian Mathematics Colloquium: IMPA (1997)

15. Hayes, B.: A Lucid Interval. American Scientist 91(6), 484–488 (2003)
16. López, J.: Evaluación de los Efectos de Cuantificación en las Estructuras de Filtros Digitales Mediante Técnicas de Simulación Basadas en Extensiones de Intervalos. PhD thesis, Universidad Politécnica de Madrid (2004)
17. López, J., Carreras, C., Nieto-Taladriz, O.: Improved Interval-Based Characterization of Fixed-Point LTI Systems With Feedback Loops. IEEE Trans. Computer-Aided Design 26, 1923–1933 (2007)
18. Fang, C., Chen, T., Rutenbar, R.: Floating-Point Error Analysis Based on Affine Arithmetic. In: IEEE Int. Conf. on Acoustics, Speech, and Signal Processing, vol. 2, pp. 561–564 (2003)
19. López, J., Caffarena, G., Carreras, C., Nieto-Taladriz, O.: Analysis of Limit Cycles by Means of Affine Arithmetic Computer-aided Tests. In: Proc. EUSIPCO, pp. 991–994 (2004)
20. Fang, C., Rutenbar, R., Chen, T.: Fast, accurate static analysis for fixed-point finite-precision effects in DSP designs. In: Int. Conf. on Computer Aided Design, pp. 275–282 (November 2003)
21. Caffarena, G.: Combined Word-Length Allocation and High-Level Synthesis of Digital Signal Processing Circuits. PhD thesis, Universidad Politécnica de Madrid (2008)
22. Choi, H., Burleson, W.: Search-based Wordlength Optimization for VLSI/DSP Synthesis. In: IEEE Workshop VLSI Signal Processing, pp. 198–207 (1994)
23. Caffarena, G., Carreras, C.: Architectural synthesis of DSP circuits under simultaneous error and time constraints. In: Proc. IEEE/IFIP Int. Conference VLSI-SOC, pp. 322–327 (September 2010)
24. Cantin, M.-A., Savaria, Y., Prodanos, D., Lavoie, P.: An Automatic Word Length Determination Method. In: IEEE Int. Symp. on Circuits and Systems, Sydney, Australia, vol. 5, pp. 53–56 (2001)
25. Han, K., Evans, B., Swartzlander, E.: Data Wordlength Reduction for Low-Power Signal Processing Software. In: IEEE Workshop on Signal Processing Systems, pp. 343–348 (2004)
26. Catthoor, F., Vandewalle, J., De Man, H.: Simulated Annealing Based Optimization of Coefficient and Data Word-Lengths in Digital Filters. J. Circuit Theory Applications 16, 371–390 (1988)
27. Todman, T., Constantinides, G., Wilton, S., Mencer, O., Luk, W., Cheung, P.: Reconfigurable computing: architectures and design methods. IEE Proceedings Computers and Digital Techniques 152, 193–207 (2005)
28. Han, K., Evans, B.: Optimum Wordlength Search Using Sensitivity Information. EURASIP Journal of Applied Signal Processing 2006, 1–14 (2006), doi:10.1155/ASP/2006/92849
29. Fernández, A., Jimenez, A., Caffarena, G., Casajús, J.: Design and Implementation of a Hardware Module for Equalisation in a 4G MIMO Receiver. In: Proc. FPL, pp. 765–768 (2006)
30. Haykin, S.: Adaptive Filter Theory. Prentice-Hall, Upper Saddle River (2002)
31. Ogunfunmi, T.: Adaptive Nonlinear System Identification: The Volterra and Wiener Approaches. Springer, Heidelberg (2007)

Design and Verification of Lazy and Hybrid Implementations of the SELF Protocol

Eliyah Kilada and Kenneth S. Stevens

University of Utah, Electrical and Computer Engineering
Salt Lake City, Utah, USA
eliyah.kilada@utah.edu,
kstevens@ece.utah.edu

Abstract. Synchronous Elasticization converts an ordinary clocked circuit into Latency-Insensitive (LI) design. The Synchronous Elastic Flow (SELF) is an LI protocol that can be implemented with eager or lazy evaluation in the data steering network. Compared to lazy implementations, eager SELF designs have no combinational cycles and can have a performance advantage, but consume more area and power. The design space of lazy SELF protocols is evaluated and verified. Several new designs are mapped to hybrid eager/lazy implementations that retain the performance advantage of the eager design but have power advantages of lazy implementations.

Keywords: Latency-insensitive design, lazy SELF implementation, hybrid SELF implementation, elasticization, verification, MiniMIPS processor.

1 Introduction

Latency insensitivity (LI) allows designs to tolerate arbitrary latency variations in their computation units as well as communication channels [1]. This is particularly important for interfaces where the actual latency can not be accurately estimated or is required to be flexible. An Example of the former are systems with very long wire interconnects. Interconnect latency is affected by many factors that may not be accurately estimated before the final layout [2]. On the other hand, some applications require flexible interfaces that tolerate variable latencies. Examples can include interfaces to variable latency ALU's, memories or network on chip. It has been reported that applying flexible latency design to the critical block of one of Intel's SoCs (H.264 CABAC) can achieve 35% performance advantage [8].

Synchronous elasticization is a technique of converting an ordinary clocked circuit into an LI design [5, 3, 10, 7]. Unlike asynchronous circuits, synchronous elastic circuits can be designed with conventional CAD flows using STA [3, 14]. The Synchronous Elastic Flow (SELF) is a communication protocol in synchronous

J.L. Ayala, D. Atienza, and R. Reis (Eds.): VLSI-SoC 2010, IFIP AICT 373, pp. 206–232, 2012.

elastic designs [5]. Eager implementation of the SELF protocol enjoys no combinational cycles and also may have performance advantages in some designs when compared to lazy implementations. However, eager protocols are more expensive in terms of area and power consumption. The LI control network area and power consumption may become prohibitive in some cases [3]. Measurements of a MiniMIPS processor fabricated in a 0.5 μm node show that elasticization with an eager SELF implementation results in area, dynamic and leakage power penalties of 29%, 13% and 58.3%, respectively [11]. Hence, minimizing these overheads is a primary concern. For an attempt to achieve that goal, an algorithm that minimizes the total number of control steering units (i.e., joins and forks) in the LI control network has been developed [12].

Lazy SELF implementations may be an attractive solution. Unfortunately the standard implementation suffers from combinational cycles that make it an unreliable design [5, 11]. This work defines a larger design space that can be employed to implement lazy channel protocols and to verify correctness of these protocols both independently and when combined with the standard eager protocol.

1.1   Contribution

A formal investigation of a complete set of lazy SELF protocol specifications is reported. This includes introducing new lazy join and fork structures, which are verified along with the existing designs. A novel hybrid implementation flow is then introduced that combines the advantages of both eager and lazy implementations. The hybrid SELF essentially avoids some of the redundancy of the eager implementation without any performance loss. Moreover, it is combinational cycle free. The hybrid SELF network is demonstrated with the design of a MiniMIPS processor. The hybrid implementation achieves the same runtime as an *all* eager implementation with a reduction of 31.8% and up to 32.5% and 32.1% in the control network area and dynamic and leakage power consumption, respectively.

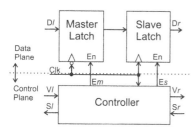

Fig. 1. An EB implementation

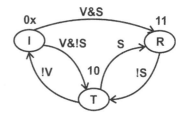

Fig. 2. SELF channel protocol

2   SELF Overview

A LI network consists of two components: Elastic Buffers (EBs) and a control network that distributes the handshake signals to the EBs. The components of the control network (e.g., joins and forks) do not buffer the data. They, nonetheless, along with the EB controllers, schedule the data token transfers. The lazy and eager properties of a SELF system are implemented in the control network.

An elastic system replaces the flip-flops used as pipeline latches in a clocked system with EBs. EBs serve the purpose of pipelining a design as well as synchronization points that implement an LI protocol, also allowing the clocked pipeline to be stalled.

Figure 1 shows a block diagram implementation of an EB. An EB consists of a data-plane (double latches) and a controller. It can be in the Empty (bubble), Half or Full states depending on the number of data tokens its two latches are holding. Sample implementation of the EB controller can be found in [5]. EB controllers communicate through control channels. Each channel contains two control signals. 'Valid' (V) travels in the same direction as the data and indicates the validity of the data coming from the transmitter. 'Stall'(S) travels in the opposite direction and indicates that the receiver can not store the current data.

The SELF channel protocol is shown in Fig. 2 [5]. The three states of the channel protocol in Fig. 2 are (a.) *Transfer* (T): $V\&!S$. The transmitter provides valid data and the receiver can accept it. (b.) *Idle* (I): $!V$. The transmitter does not provide valid data. This paper identifies two Idle conditions: $I0$ ($!V\&!S$) where the receiver can accept data and $I1$ ($!V\&S$) where the receiver can not accept data. (c.) *Retry* (R): $V\&S$. The transmitter provides valid data, but the receiver can not accept it. In the Transfer state, the valid data must be maintained on the channel until it is stored by the receiver.

When the connection between EBs is not point-to-point, a control network is required to steer the Valid and Stall signals between the different EBs. The control network is composed of control channels connected through control steering units, namely, join and fork components. A join element combines two or more incoming control channels into one output control channel. A fork element copies one incoming control channel into two or more output control channels. Fork and join components are represented by $\odot$ and $\otimes$, respectively. The SELF protocol used over the control channels can be implemented using an eager or lazy protocol. Hereafter we use the term *control network* to aggregately refer to the joins, forks, and EB controllers in a system.

We introduce the notion of a *control buffer* in order to gain understanding of the design and verification of control network components, such as joins and forks. A linear control buffer simply breaks the control signals in a channel into left and right channels. Such a buffer will have two inputs: the Valid on the left channel and Stall on the right channel, and two outputs: the Stall on the left channel and Valid on the right.

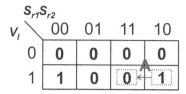

Fig. 3. V_{r1} of $LF01$

3   SELF Channel Protocol Verification

All network components are verified to be conformant to the SELF channel protocol. The correctness requirements for the channel protocol are adapted from the general elastic component conditions consisting of persistence, freedom from deadlock, and liveness [14]. A fourth constraint is added here that disallows glitching on the control wires.

1. *Persistence.* No $R \rightarrow I$ transition may occur.
2. *Deadlock freedom.* For each component in the verification, at least two states can be reached from any other reachable state [16].
3. *Liveness.* The liveness condition is one of data preservation. Lazy control buffers must have the same number of tokens transferred on all their channels. This functional requirement is a special case of the liveness condition in [14]. This is implemented by creating token counters on all the lazy control buffer channels and verifying that they are always equivalent.
4. *Glitch Free.* No $S\uparrow$ signal transition may occur in state I. The specification of the idle protocol state I in Fig. 2 does not constrain the behavior of the Stall signal. This allows glitching on the control wires to occur. If the Stall signal is not allowed to rise in the idle state then glitching will not occur. This requirement is not explicit in the SELF specifications. However, it can be observed that this transition is not possible in published Elastic Buffer (EB) or Elastic Half Buffer (EHB) designs [5, 9]. If control wire glitching is possible, then the composition of some forks and joins may not be compliant with the channel protocol. For example, the Karnaugh map of $LF01$, one of the two lazy forks proven to be SELF compliant, is shown in Fig. 3. Transition A occurs when S_{r2} rises in the idle state. While this glitching transition is valid according to the channel specification, it results in V_{r1} falling, which produces an illegal $R \rightarrow I$ transition on channel r_1. Since this transition can never happen unless channel r_2 can make an $S\uparrow$ transition glitch, we add this condition to our verification suite.

4   Lazy SELF Control Network Design

A truth table can be created to specify the permissible behaviors for the control buffer left Stall and right Valid signals that conform to the SELF channel protocol of Sect. 2. Such a truth table shows the flexibility in design choices that can be made. The same procedure is performed for the lazy fork and join components.

5 Fork Components

5.1 Eager Fork

The eager fork ($EFork$) will immediately forward valid data tokens presented at the root to all branches that are not stalled. If any of the branches of the fork are stalled, the root of the $EFork$ will stall until all its branches receive the data. This gives the earliest possible data transfer to the branches that are ready to receive data. Hence, the $EFork$ can result in performance advantage over lazy forks in some systems. Due to the necessary pipelining that occurs in the control signals, the $EFork$ incorporates one flip-flop per branch. The control flip-flop must be updated every clock cycle to sample changes. Moreover, eager forks have higher logic complexity comparing to lazy. This makes the $EFork$ expensive in terms of both area and power consumption. Figure 4a shows an n output extension of the $EFork$ [11, 5].

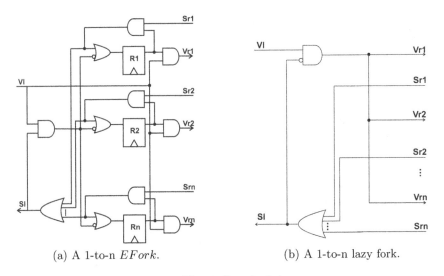

(a) A 1-to-n $EFork$.   (b) A 1-to-n lazy fork.

Fig. 4. Sample forks

5.2 Lazy Fork

The lazy fork does not propagate valid data from its root to its branches until *all* branches are ready to store the data. A sample lazy fork is shown in Fig. 4b.

Lazy Fork Synthesis. The truth table for a lazy fork is shown to be purely combinational. Thus it is easily represented with the Karnaugh map (KM) shown in Fig. 5. The KM has two don't care terms m_0 and m_1 giving four possible designs. Each implementation is denoted as LFm_0m_1 (e.g., $LF00$, $LF01$,.. etc). Table 1 maps all the published lazy forks we were able to find to those of this paper.

The hand translation of the fork as a control buffer may still result in illegal channel behavior on one or more of the channels due to the interactions between branches of the fork and join. Thus we employ a rigorous verification methodology to prove correctness of the designs. Indeed, verification shows that two of the four possible designs do not fully obey the SELF channel protocol.

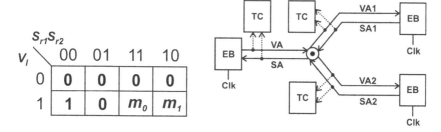

Fig. 5. Lazy fork specifications (V_{r1}) **Fig. 6.** Lazy fork verification setup

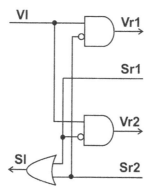

Fig. 7. A 2-output $LF01$ implementation

Fork Verification. The setup of Fig. 6 is used to verify correctness of the fork designs. The root channel (A) as well as the branches ($A1$ and $A2$) are connected to three elastic buffers (EBs) as well as data token counters (TCs). This work employs the EB implementation published in [5]. The counters track the number of clock cycles that the channel is in the transfer state T. The structure is modeled and passed to a symbolic model checker, NuSMV [4].

Table 1. Mapping between published and this paper lazy forks and joins

Fork [10]	$LF00$	Join [10]	$LJ0000$
Fork [5]	$LF00$	Join [5]	$LJ0000$
LFork [11]	$LF00$	LJoin [11]	$LJ0000$
LKFork [11]	$LF01$	LKJoin [11]	$LJ1111$

All constituent blocks are connected *synchronously*. Synchronous connection guarantees that all modules advance in lock-step. Logic delays are then executed in internal cycles of the verification engine. All combinational logic are modeled to have zero delay. The clock generator is modeled to have a unit delay for each phase. For example, following is the $LF00$ model:

```
MODULE LF00(V1,Sr1,Sr2)
DEFINE S1 := Sr1 | Sr2 ; DEFINE Vr1 := V1 & (!Sr1) & (!Sr2) ; ...
```

The four properties from Sect. 3 are applied to each design. The properties used for these checks are described below.

1. *Persistence.* For each channel (i.e., A, $A1$ and $A2$) we verify that no R $\rightarrow$ I transition occurs:
   ```
   DEFINE R_A := VA & SA ; -- Retry on channel A
   DEFINE I_A := !VA ; -- Idle on channel A
   PSLSPEC never {[*]; R_A; I_A};
   ```
   Out of the 4 lazy fork implementations only $LF00$ and $LF01$ pass this check.
2. *Deadlock freedom.* At least two states are verified as reachable from all other reachable states [16]. For example, inside the $LF00$ module the following CTL properties verify two states are reachable:
   ```
   SPEC AG EF (Vr1=1 & Vr2 =1 & S1=0);
   SPEC AG EF (Vr1=0 & Vr2 =0 & S1=0);
   ```
   Note that a state in $LF00$ is defined by the three variables: V_{r1}, V_{r2} and S_l. All four lazy fork implementations pass this check.
3. *Liveness* is calculated through *data token preservation*. Let the number of data tokens transferred at the fork root channel and the two branch channels be: d_l, d_{r1} and d_{r2}, respectively. (d_i is, equivalently, the number of clock cycles where channel i was in the Transfer state (T) (i.e., $V_i \& !S_i$).) The number of data tokens transferred at its root channel must always be the same as those at its branches. (i.e., the following requirement must always hold: $d_{ri} - d_l = 0$ for $i \in \{1, 2\}$.) We use the following code to model a token counter for channel

i. The model counts on the negative edge of the clock.

```
MODULE TokenCounter (Clk,Vi,Si)
VAR Count: 0..31;
ASSIGN
init (Count) := 0;
next (Count) := case
(Clk=1)&(next(Clk)=0)&(Vi=1)&(Si=0)&(Count < 31): Count + 1;
1: Count;
esac;
```

Since NuSMV supports finite types only. Without loss of generality, we chose the upper limit of the *Count* variable to be a sufficiently large number (32 in this case). For each branch we define and check the following property:

```
DEFINE TokenCountError_A1 := case (dl != dr1):1; 1:0; esac;
PSLSPEC never {[*]; TokenCountError_A1};
```

All the four lazy fork implementations pass this check.

4. *No glitching.* This verifies that the Stall signal does not rise in the idle state:

```
DEFINE I0_A := !VA & !SA ; -- Idle0 on A
DEFINE I1_A := !VA & SA ; -- Idle1 on A
PSLSPEC never {[*]; I0_A; I1_A};
```

All lazy fork implementations pass this check.

Hence, among the four possible lazy fork implementations, only $LF00$ and $LF01$ conform to our channel specification. Similarly, the $EFork$ of Sect. 5.1 is also verified. Since the $EFork$ allows its ready branches to transfer tokens while stalled waiting for the other branches to be ready, the data token preservation requirement is: $0 \leq d_{ri} - d_l \leq 1$ for $i \in \{1,2\}$. Indeed, $EFork$ passes these checks and, hence, is also compliant with the SELF protocol.

Lazy Fork Characterization. To help characterize the different fork implementations as well as their combinations with lazy joins in a network, we introduce the following definitions:

Definition 1. C_{Fr}, Fork Reflexive Characterization Set C_{Fr} *is a set of characterization elements* (c_{Fr}), *where:* $c_{Fr} \in \{I, N, 0, 1\}$

where

1. $c_{Fr} = I$ (or *inverting*) in a 2-output fork iff V_{ri} is a function of S_{ri}, and iff, for some constant V_l and S_{rj}, $V_{ri} = !S_{ri}$, where $i, j \in \{1, 2\}$ and $i \neq j$.
2. $c_{Fr} = N$ (or *non-inverting*) in a 2-output fork iff V_{ri} is a function of S_{ri}, and iff, for some constant V_l and S_{rj}, $V_{ri} = S_{ri}$, where $i, j \in \{1, 2\}$ and $i \neq j$.
3. $c_{Fr} = 0$ (or *constant zero*) in a 2-output fork iff V_{ri} is a function of S_{ri}, and iff, for some constant V_l and S_{rj}, $V_{ri} = 0$, where $i, j \in \{1, 2\}$ and $i \neq j$.
4. $c_{Fr} = 1$ (or *constant one*) in a 2-output fork iff V_{ri} is a function of S_{ri}, and iff, for some constant V_l and S_{rj}, $V_{ri} = 1$, where $i, j \in \{1, 2\}$ and $i \neq j$.

Definition 1 can be easily extended to n-output forks with $n > 2$.

Table 2. C_{Fr} Computation of $LF00$ **Table 3.** C_{Ft} Computation of $LF00$

V_l	S_{r2}	$S_{r1} \rightarrow V_{r1}$	c_{Fr}
0	0	$0 \rightarrow 0$ $1 \rightarrow 0$	0
0	1	$0 \rightarrow 0$ $1 \rightarrow 0$	0
1	0	$0 \rightarrow 1$ $1 \rightarrow 0$	I
1	1	$0 \rightarrow 0$ $1 \rightarrow 0$	0

V_l	S_{r1}	$S_{r2} \rightarrow V_{r1}$	c_{Ft}
0	0	$0 \rightarrow 0$ $1 \rightarrow 0$	0
0	1	$0 \rightarrow 0$ $1 \rightarrow 0$	0
1	0	$0 \rightarrow 1$ $1 \rightarrow 0$	I
1	1	$0 \rightarrow 0$ $1 \rightarrow 0$	0

Table 2 illustrates C_{Fr} computation of $LF00$. From the table, C_{Fr} of $LF00$ is $\{0, I\}$. Similarly C_{Fr} of $LF01$ is $\emptyset$. This is because in $LF01$ (see Fig. 7), V_{ri} is not a function of S_{ri}. As we will show in Sect. 8.1, this property gives an advantage to $LF01$ since it can reduce the number of combinational cycles in the control network substantially.

Definition 2. C_{Ft}, Fork Transitive Characterization Set C_{Ft} *is a set of characterization elements* (c_{Ft}), *where:* $c_{Ft} \in \{I, N, 0, 1\}$

where

1. $c_{Ft} = I$ (or *inverting*) in a 2-output fork iff V_{ri} is a function of S_{rj}, and iff, for some constant V_l and S_{ri}, $V_{ri} =! S_{rj}$, where $i, j \in \{1, 2\}$ and $i \neq j$.
2. $c_{Ft} = N$ (or *non-inverting*) in a 2-output fork iff V_{ri} is a function of S_{rj}, and iff, for some constant V_l and S_{ri}, $V_{ri} = S_{rj}$, where $i, j \in \{1, 2\}$ and $i \neq j$.
3. $c_{Ft} = 0$ (or *constant zero*) in a 2-output fork iff V_{ri} is a function of S_{rj}, and iff, for some constant V_l and S_{ri}, $V_{ri} = 0$, where $i, j \in \{1, 2\}$ and $i \neq j$.
4. $c_{Ft} = 1$ (or *constant one*) in a 2-output fork iff V_{ri} is a function of S_{rj}, and iff, for some constant V_l and S_{ri}, $V_{ri} = 1$, where $i, j \in \{1, 2\}$ and $i \neq j$.

Definition 2 can be easily extended to n-output forks with $n > 2$.

Table 3 illustrates C_{Ft} computation of $LF00$. From the table, C_{Ft} of $LF00$ is $\{0, I\}$. Similarly C_{Ft} of $LF01$ is also $\{0, I\}$.

6   Lazy Join

The lazy join has to wait for all its input branch channels to carry valid data until data is transferred on the output channel. A sample lazy join is shown in Fig. 8.

6.1   Lazy Join Synthesis

The synthesis of a lazy join as a control buffer is performed similar to the lazy fork. The KM is shown in Fig. 10. There are 16 possible implementations.

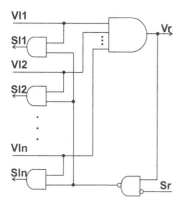

Fig. 8. An n-to-1 lazy join

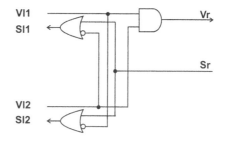

Fig. 9. A 2-input $LJ1011$ implementation

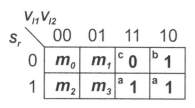

Fig. 10. Lazy join specification (S_{l1})

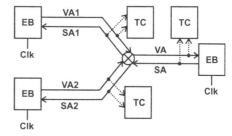

Fig. 11. Lazy join verification setup

6.2   Lazy Join Verification

Similar to the lazy fork verification in Sect. 5.2, we use the structure of Fig. 11 to verify the different lazy join implementations. We check the following properties: 1. *Persistence*: All the 16 lazy joins pass this check. 2. *Deadlock freedom*: All the 16 joins pass. 3. *Data token preservation*: All the 16 joins pass. 4. *Glitch Free*: Out of the 16 lazy joins, only 6 pass. Only the following lazy join designs pass verification: $LJ0000$, $LJ0010$, $LJ0011$, $LJ1010$, $LJ1011$, $LJ1111$.

6.3   Lazy Join Characterization

To help characterize the different join implementations as well as their combinations with lazy forks in a network, we introduce the following definitions:

Definition 3. C_{Jr}, Join Reflexive Characterization Set C_{Jr} *is a set of characterization elements* (c_{Jr}), *where:* $c_{Jr} \in \{I, N, 0, 1\}$

where

1. $c_{Jr} = I$ (or *inverting*) in a 2-input join iff S_{li} is a function of V_{li}, and iff, for some constant S_r and V_{lj}, $S_{li} = !V_{li}$, where $i, j \in \{1, 2\}$ and $i \neq j$.

2. $c_{Jr} = N$ (or *non-inverting*) in a 2-input join iff S_{li} is a function of V_{li}, and iff, for some constant S_r and V_{lj}, $S_{li} = V_{li}$, where $i, j \in \{1, 2\}$ and $i \neq j$.

3. $c_{Jr} = 0$ (or *constant zero*) in a 2-input join iff S_{li} is a function of V_{li}, and iff, for some constant S_r and V_{lj}, $S_{li} = 0$, where $i, j \in \{1, 2\}$ and $i \neq j$.

4. $c_{Jr} = 1$ (or *constant one*) in a 2-input join iff S_{li} is a function of V_{li}, and iff, for some constant S_r and V_{lj}, $S_{li} = 1$, where $i, j \in \{1, 2\}$ and $i \neq j$.

Definition 3 can be easily extended to n-input joins with $n > 2$.

Similar to Table 2, we can also find that C_{Jr} of $LJ0000$, for example, is $\{N, 0\}$. $LJ1011$ has a C_{Jr} of $\emptyset$. This is because in $LJ1011$ (see Fig. 9), S_{li} is not a function of V_{li}. As we will show in Sect. 8.1, this property gives an advantage to $LJ1011$ since it can reduce the number of combinational cycles in the control network substantially.

Definition 4. C_{Jt}, *Join Transitive Characterization Set C_{Jt} is a set of characterization elements (c_{Jt}), where: $c_{Jt} \in \{I, N, 0, 1\}$*

where

1. $c_{Jt} = I$ (or *inverting*) in a 2-input join iff S_{li} is a function of V_{lj}, and iff, for some constant S_r and V_{li}, $S_{li} =!V_{lj}$, where $i, j \in \{1, 2\}$ and $i \neq j$.

2. $c_{Jt} = N$ (or *non-inverting*) in a 2-input join iff S_{li} is a function of V_{lj}, and iff, for some constant S_r and V_{li}, $S_{li} = V_{lj}$, where $i, j \in \{1, 2\}$ and $i \neq j$.

3. $c_{Jt} = 0$ (or *constant zero*) in a 2-input join iff S_{li} is a function of V_{lj}, and iff, for some constant S_r and V_{li}, $S_{li} = 0$, where $i, j \in \{1, 2\}$ and $i \neq j$.

4. $c_{Jt} = 1$ (or *constant one*) in a 2-input join iff S_{li} is a function of V_{lj}, and iff, for some constant S_r and V_{li}, $S_{li} = 1$, where $i, j \in \{1, 2\}$ and $i \neq j$.

Definition 4 can be easily extended to n-input joins with $n > 2$.

Similar to Table 3, we can also find that C_{Jt} of $LJ0000$, for example, is $\{I, 0, 1\}$.

7   Lazy SELF Networks

Unlike eager forks, lazy forks have no state holding elements (e.g., flip-flops). Hence, arbitrary connections of lazy joins and forks in a control network typically result in combinational cycles. These cycles can cause deadlock or oscillation due to logical or transient instability:

7.1   Deadlock - D

A combinational cycle can cause a deadlock if under some input sequence its internal signals can get stuck at certain values. For example, consider a structure in which a fork output channel is feeding a join (Fig. 12a). This structure is a basic building block of typical elastic control networks. Figure 13 shows a circuit implementation of Fig. 12a using $LF00$ and $LJ1111$.

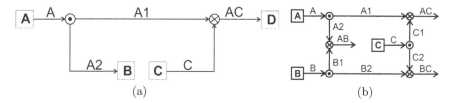

Fig. 12. Sample fork join combinations

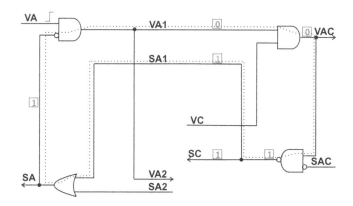

Fig. 13. LF00 and LJ1111 combination

It can be easily shown that if VA is zero, $VA1$ and VAC must also be zero. This will force $SA1$ to be one, SA to be one and $VA1$ to be zero. Apparently, the loop shown in dotted lines forms a latch, since all its wires can simultaneously carry controlling values to all the gates in the loop. Hence, after a zero on VA, the system will deadlock. $VA2$, VAC, SC and SA will be stuck at zero, zero, one and one, respectively.

In general, for the common structure of Fig. 12a, the following can be readily proved. Let C_{Jr1} (C_{Fr1}) and C_{Jt1} (C_{Ft1}) be the join (fork) reflexive and transitive characteristic sets of the lazy join (fork) used, $LJ1$ ($LF1$), respectively. Then, the connection of Fig. 12a will result in deadlock if the following condition holds: $C_{Jr1} = \{1, I\}$ and $C_{Fr1} = \{0, I\}$. To illustrate, since $C_{Fr1} = \{0, I\}$, therefore, for all the possible values of $LF1$ inputs, $VA1$ is either 0 or the inverse of $SA1$. Similarly, since $C_{Jr1} = \{1, I\}$, therefore, for all the possible values of $LJ1$ inputs, $SA1$ is either 1 or the inverse of $VA1$. Hence, once $VA1$ is 0 or $SA1$ is 1, the loop formed by $VA1$ and $SA1$ will stuck at these values.

Similarly, a deadlock will occur in the connection of Fig. 12b if the following condition holds: $C_{Jt1} = \{1, I\}$ and $C_{Ft1} = \{0, I\}$.

7.2   Oscillation Due to Logical Instability - LI

A loop is logically unstable if it has an odd number of inverting elements. Under some input sequence, it can behave as a ring oscillator.

For example, consider the structure of Fig. 12a. Figure 14 shows a circuit implementation of that structure using $LF00$ and $LJ0000$.

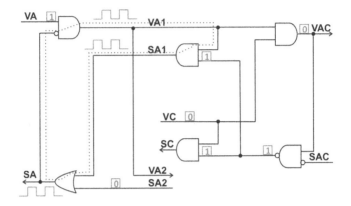

Fig. 14. LF00 and LJ0000 combination

Assume the elastic buffer C in Fig. 14 holds a bubble (i.e., its output Valid signal is zero), while A holds data. Assume also that $SA2$ is zero (B is not stalled). This connection will form a loop (shown in dotted lines in Fig. 14). The loop is logically unstable since it has an odd number of inverting elements. This results in an oscillation inside the loop as well as on the SA wire.

In general, for the common structure of Fig. 12a, the following can be readily proved. Let C_{Jr1} (C_{Fr1}) and C_{Jt1} (C_{Ft1}) be the join (fork) reflexive and transitive characteristic sets of the lazy join (fork) used, $LJ1$ ($LF1$), respectively. Then, the connection of Fig. 12a will result in logical instability if any of the following condition holds:

- $I \in C_{Jr1}$ and $N \in C_{Fr1}$.
- $N \in C_{Jr1}$ and $I \in C_{Fr1}$.

7.3   Oscillation Due to Transient Instability - TI

Even if a combinational loop does have even number of inverting elements it can still cause oscillation in the elastic control network. Since the loop has more than one input, and in some input sequences, both logic one and zero values may be injected in the loop simultaneously. This can result in both values oscillating around the loop.

Table 4 shows the different lazy fork-join combinations characteristics. The table refers to the network structures of Fig. 12.

Research is still in progress to investigate whether the oscillation due to transient instability can be avoided by forcing network-specific timing constraints on the control network. However, a simpler solution, not only for transient instability, but also for deadlock and logical instability, is to use eager forks when needed to cut such combinational cycles. This will be discussed in Sect. 8.

Table 4. Lazy fork-join combination characterization. All other combinations (14 Forks × 10 Joins) are non-compliant with the SELF protocol.

	Join	0000	0010	0011	1010	1011	1111
Fork	C_r	$N,0$	$N,0,1$	$N,0,1$	$N,0,1$	$\emptyset$	$I,1$
	$\overline{C_t}$	$I,0,1$	$I,0,1$	$I,0,1$	$I,1$	$I,1$	$I,1$
0000	$\dfrac{I,0}{I,0}$	**LI**	**LI**	**LI**	**LI**	**D**	**D**
0001	$\dfrac{\emptyset}{I,0}$	**TI**	**TI**	**TI**	**D**	**D**	**D**

Finally, the following logic was used for the root's Stall signal in all of the lazy forks investigated: $S_l = S_{r1}|S_{r2}$. Similarly, the lazy join elements used $V_r = V_{l1} \& V_{l2}$. Other implementations for these signals that consider flexibility allowed by lazy control buffers is not presented here. However, note that designs with additional logic will increase the probability of combinational loops in component composition.

8 Hybrid SELF Protocol

Two lazy forks and six lazy joins, as well as the traditional eager fork, have been proven to be compliant with our strict SELF channel protocol. Therefore, eager and lazy forks (and joins) can be *correctly* connected together as long as no combinational cycles are formed [14]. Eager forks exhibit no cycles and can achieve better runtime in some systems. However, they consume more power and area than lazy forks. Hence, we propose to use a hybrid SELF implementation, that uses both eager and lazy forks, has no cycles, and achieves the same runtime as an *all* eager implementation. Hybrid implementation should keep minimal number of eager forks in the control network that are necessary for the following reasons:

8.1 Cycle Cutting

Lazy fork-join combinations can result in combinational cycles that cause oscillation or deadlock. These cycles can be avoided by replacing lazy forks with eager in places where cycles exist. Cycles can be easily identified either by hand analysis of the control network or through synthesis tools (e.g., report_timing -loops command in Design Compiler).

$LF01$ enjoys the property that there is no internal path in the fork that connects any of its branch Stalls to its corresponding Valid. This reduces the cycles substantially. Similarly, $LJ1011$ enjoys the property that there is no internal path in the join that connects any of its input channel Valid signals to its corresponding Stall. This also reduces the cycles substantially. Hence, the fork-join combination of $LF01 - LJ1011$ results in the minimum number of combinational cycles among all the other fork-join combinations. This, in turn, minimizes the need to use eager forks to cut the cycles, resulting in minimizing the total area and power consumption of the hybrid control network.

8.2 Runtime Boosting

Eager forks can enjoy better performance than lazy due to the early start they provide for ready branches (Sect. 5.1). However, we show in this section that under some constrained input behavior, a lazy fork can replace an eager fork without any performance loss. In that context, we will use the term $LFork$ to refer to the lazy forks $LF00$ and/or $LF01$.

A 2-output $EFork$ operation will reduce to the KM of Fig. 15a if the $EFork$ registers are initialized to logic one and if the following input combinations are avoided [13]:

1. $(V_l = 1)\&(S_{r1} = 0)\&(S_{r2} = 1)$
2. $(V_l = 1)\&(S_{r1} = 1)\&(S_{r2} = 0)$

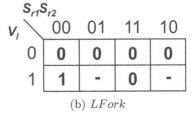

(a) $EFork$ (b) $LFork$

Fig. 15. V_{r1} (or V_{r2}) of the $EFork$ and $LFork$ under some constrained input behavior, respectively

The KM of the lazy forks $LF00$ and $LF01$, with the above input combinations avoided, is shown in Fig. 15b. Comparing Fig. 15a and Fig. 15b, it is apparent that, under these conditions, the $EFork$ will behave exactly the same as the lazy forks, except in the case when both branches are stalled simultaneously. One might add a conservative constraint by avoiding such an input as well. However, as the following verification will confirm, when both branches are stalled, the lazy forks will have both branches in the Idle state, while the $EFork$ will keep them in the Retry state. Since there is no data transfer occurring in either states (i.e., I or R), there is no performance advantage of the $EFork$ comparing to the $LFork$ in such a case. Hence, we conclude that the above stated conditions are sufficient to replace an $EFork$ with $LF00$ or $LF01$ without any performance loss. We, therefore, refer to the above conditions as the *performance equivalence conditions*, or, for short, the *equivalence conditions*.

To verify this argument, the verification setup of Fig. 16 is employed. The whole structure is modeled in the symbolic model checker, NuSMV [4]. The input

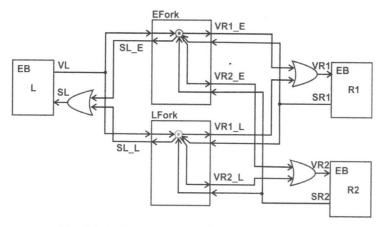

Fig. 16. Performance equivalence verification setup

and output channels of both the *EFork* and *LFork* are connected to terminal Elastic Buffers (EBs). The EBs are initialized in random states. The *EFork* input and two output channels are named: *L_E* (read *Left_Eager*), *R1_E* (read *Right1_Eager*), *R2_E* (read *Right2_Eager*), respectively. Similarly, the *LFork* input and 2 output channels are named: *L_L*, *R1_L*, *R2_L*, respectively. *V* and *S* are prepended to the channel names to indicate the Valid and Stall signals of these channels, respectively.

All the blocks as well as the clock generator have been connected synchronously inside NuSMV. The clock changes phase with each unit verification cycle. The Transfer state on the *EFork* input and output channels are defined as follows:

```
DEFINE L_E_T := VL_E & !SL_E;
DEFINE R1_E_T := VR1_E & !SR1_E;
DEFINE R2_E_T := VR2_E & !SR2_E;
```
Similarly, for the LFork:
```
DEFINE L_L_T := VL_L & !SL_L;
DEFINE R1_L_T := VR1_L & !SR1_L;
DEFINE R2_L_T := VR2_L & !SR2_L;
```

A performance mismatch can occur if any of the channels in the *EFork* transfers data while the corresponding channel in the *LFork* does not. Hence, we define TOKEN_MISMATCH on the different channels as follows:

```
DEFINE L_TOKEN_MISMATCH := (L_E_T xor L_L_T);
DEFINE R1_TOKEN_MISMATCH := (R1_E_T xor R1_L_T);
DEFINE R2_TOKEN_MISMATCH := (R2_E_T xor R2_L_T);
```

A TOKEN_MISMATCH is defined to be the ORing of any channel mismatch:

```
DEFINE TOKEN_MISMATCH := L_TOKEN_MISMATCH | R1_TOKEN_MISMATCH |
R2_TOKEN_MISMATCH;
```

Finally, to force the performance equivalence conditions, we define the following constraint:

```
DEFINE C_1 := VL & (SR1 xor SR2);
```

Constraint C_1 is forced by using the NuSMV reserved word INVAR which semantically defines an invariant:

```
INVAR C_1;
```

The performance equivalence property is then verified using PSLSPEC:

```
PSLSPEC never TOKEN_MISMATCH;
```

The property is proven true by the model checker. There is no clock cycle in which any of the $EFork$ channels is in the Transfer state while the corresponding channel in the $LFork$ is not transferring data as well. Hence, under the stated performance equivalence conditions, the $EFork$ and $LFork$ will transfer exactly the same number of tokens, thus, achieving the same performance.

The results can be easily extended to n-output forks with $n > 2$, based on the fact that an n-output fork is logically equivalent to concatenated $(n - 1)$ 2-output forks. Hence, all the eager forks in the control network that meet the performance equivalence conditions can be safely replaced by lazy forks. The result will be a hybrid control network (incorporating both eager and lazy forks) that has the same runtime of an *all* eager network with substantially smaller area and power.

8.3   Eager to Hybrid Conversion Flow

Algorithms to automatically identify which eager forks can be replaced by lazy in a network are currently being developed [13]. For the time being, simulation-based analysis is used. In this approach, a closed *eager* control network is simulated and all the fork Valid and Stall patterns are collected and analyzed. An example will be shown in the MiniMIPS case study in Sect. 9. Starting with an elastic control network (generated manually or through automatic tools like CNG [12]), the following flow generates a hybrid SELF implementation (H) of that network:

1. Define the set of all forks in the control network, Φ.
2. Construct a pure eager implementation of the control network, E_1, such that each fork $F \in \Phi$ is an eager fork. Define the set of forks, Φ_s, that do not meet the performance equivalence conditions. Φ_s are the forks that must be implemented as eager to achieve the same runtime as a purely eager implementation of the control network.
3. Construct an intermediate hybrid network, H_1, such that: each fork $F \in \Phi - \Phi_s$ is a lazy fork, and each fork $F \in \Phi_s$ is an eager fork.

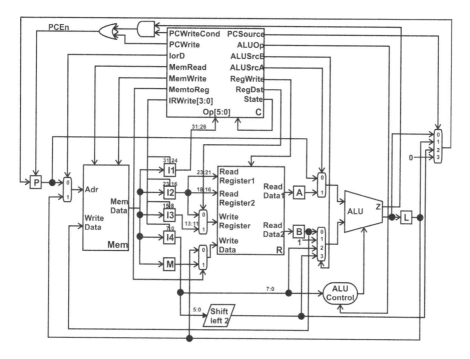

Fig. 17. Block diagram view of the ordinary clocked MiniMIPS. Adapted from [15, 17].

4. In H_1, identify the set of forks, Φ_c, that need to be replaced by eager forks to cut the combinational cycles.
5. Build a final hybrid network,H, such that: each fork $F \in \Phi - \Phi_s - \Phi_c$ is lazy, and each $F \in \Phi_s \cup \Phi_c$ is eager.

9 MiniMIPS Case Study and Results

MIPS (Microprocessor without Interlocked Pipeline Stages) is a 32-bit architecture with 32 registers, first designed by Hennessey [6]. The MiniMIPS is an 8-bit subset of MIPS, fully described in [17].

9.1 Elasticizing the MiniMIPS

The MiniMIPS is used as a case study of elasticization. Figure 17 shows a block diagram of the ordinary clocked MiniMIPS. The MiniMIPS has a total of 12 synchronization points (i.e., registers), shown as rectangles in Fig. 17: P (program counter), C (controller), $I1, I2, I3, I4$ (four instruction registers), A, B and L (ALU two input and one output registers, respectively), M (memory data register), R (register file) and Mem (memory).

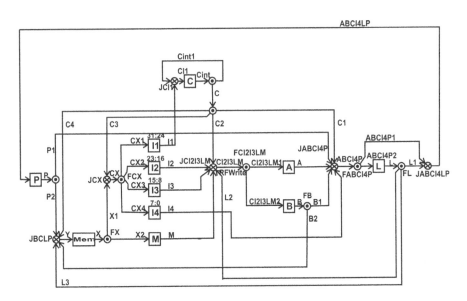

Fig. 18. Hand-optimized control network of the elastic clocked MiniMIPS. Adapted from [11].

To perform elasticization, each register is replaced by an elastic buffer (EB). Then, the register to register data communications in the MiniMIPS are analyzed. The following registers pass data to both $A, B : R$, and to $R : C, I2, I3, L, M$, and to $C : C, I1$, and to $I1, I2, I3, I4 : C, Mem$, and to $L : A, B, C, I4, P$, and to $M : Mem$, and to $Mem : B, C, L, P$, and to $P : A, B, C, I4, L, P$. For each register to register data communication there must be a corresponding control channel. The resultant control network can be implemented in different ways. Figure 18 shows a control network that has been hand-optimized to minimize the number of joins and forks used in the control network (to reduce area and power consumption) [11]. From the control point of view, the register file (R) and memory (Mem) in a microprocessor can be treated as combinational units [5]. Hence, we did not incorporate a separate EB for the register file (R) in Fig. 18. For the purpose of this case study, the memory (Mem) is off-chip.

From the elastic control point of view, the MiniMIPS control signals (e.g., RegWrite, IRWrite, etc.) are considered part of the data plane and they need their own control channels. Mapping between datapath signals in the clocked MiniMIPS and the control channels in the elastic MiniMIPS should be self explanatory for most signals. RFWrite, in Fig. 17, is the register-file-write control channel. RFWrite_valid must be active if data is going to be written in the register file. Therefore, RFWrite_valid has been ANDed with RegWrite inside the register file.

Both the clocked and purely eager elastic MiniMIPS have been synthesized, placed, routed and fabricated in a 0.5 μm technology. The functionality of the fabricated processors have been verified on Verigy's V93000 SoC tester using the

Table 5. Clocked and eager elastic MiniMIPS chip results. Measurements are done at 5V and 30°.

	Clocked MiniMIPS	Eager Elastic MiniMIPS	Penalty
Area (μm X μm)	1246.765 X 615.91	1284.1 X 771.54	29%
P_{dyn} @80 MHz (mW)	330	373	13%
P_{idle} (μW)	16.3	25.8	58.3%
f_{max} (MHz)	91.7	92.2	-0.5%

testbench in [17]. The eager implementation of the SELF protocol has been used (EFork and LJ0000 have been used to implement all the forks and joins in the control network, respectively). Table 5 summarizes chip measurements. It shows that elasticizing the MiniMIPS has area and dynamic and idle power penalties of 29%, 13% and 58.3%, respectively. For accurate idle power comparison, both designs have been set to the same state (through a test vector) before measuring the average idle supply current.

Both MiniMIPS have been fabricated without the memory block. Memory values have been programmed inside the tester. Hence, we had to make an assumption about the memory access time, and the assumptions affect the maximum operating frequency of both MiniMIPS in the same way. Therefore, the actual value of memory access time would minimally affect the performance comparison. Hence, we chose an arbitrary value of zero for memory access time for both designs. Schmoo plots for both clocked and elastic MiniMIPS are shown in Fig. 19.

It should be noted that these measurements do not take advantage of bubble problems that occur if one needs to have flexible interface latencies or extra pipeline stages inserted.

There is no performance loss due to elasticization. Part of the reason for the noticeable area and power overheads is that the MiniMIPS is, relatively, a small design (8-bit datapath). However, part of it too is the usage of eager forks. The *EFork* has one flip-flop per each branch that consumes power every cycle. Add to this, its gate complexity. Next subsections will show the area and power savings when switching from eager SELF implementation to hybrid SELF.

9.2 Eager versus Lazy SELF Implementations

Lazy forks can substantially reduce the area and power of the elastic control network. However, when combined with lazy joins, the combinational cycles are typically prohibitive causing deadlocks or oscillations (Sect. 7).

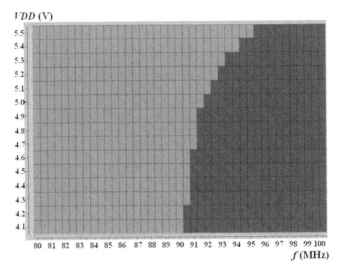

(a) Schmoo plot for clocked MiniMIPS.

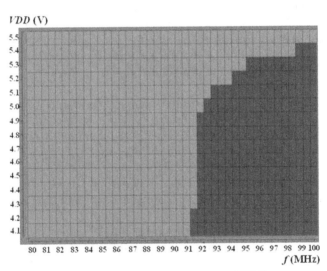

(b) Schmoo plot for elastic MiniMIPS.

Fig. 19. Fabricated chips schmoo plots. Red boxes are for failed tests, while green are for passed ones.

Furthermore, lazy forks can suffer inferior performance comparing to eager, in the presence of bubbles. To measure this advantage, a different number of bubbles are inserted at the register file outputs (i.e., before registers A and B of Fig. 18, simultaneously). Table 6 compares the number of clock cycles required by each of purely lazy and eager implementations of the MiniMIPS control network to complete the testbench program of [17]. For the lazy protocol, the LF01-LJ0000 combination is used. The behavioral simulations used some timing constraints to avoid

Table 6. Simulation runtime (in terms of #cycles) of the testbench in [17] in case of lazy and eager protocols. Bubbles are inserted at the register file outputs.

Fork/Join Combination	0 Bubbles	1 Bubble	3 Bubbles
Lazy Protocol: LF01-LJ0000	98	195	389
Eager Protocol: EFork-LJ0000	98	147	245
Clocked MiniMIPS	98	-	-

possible oscillations. Table 6 shows that, in this case, there is an advantage for using eager forks, specially with a large number of bubbles in the system. The table also shows that there is no runtime penalty due to elasticization in the absence of bubbles.

The runtime advantage of the eager versus lazy designs is illustrated in the following example (taken from the MiniMIPS control network of Fig. 18). Figure 20 shows a simplified part of the MiniMIPS control network. We added one bubble before the A register, and another one before the B register, labeled $b1$ and $b2$ respectively. Consider the clock cycle when VA and VB go low. $SC1$ will go high through join $JABCI4P$. In FC (assuming $SC2$ is low), VC is high, $SC1$ is high. A lazy FC will invalidate the data at $C2$ (i.e., deasserts $VC2$) until $SC1$ goes low again. Hence, no new data token can be written at register $b1$ or $b2$ until the stall condition on $C1$ is removed (i.e., $SC1$ goes low again). On the other hand, an eager FC will validate the data on $C2$ (i.e., asserts $VC2$) for the first clock cycle giving $C2$ branch an early start. Hence, new data tokens can be written immediately in registers $b1$ and $b2$ in the following cycle.

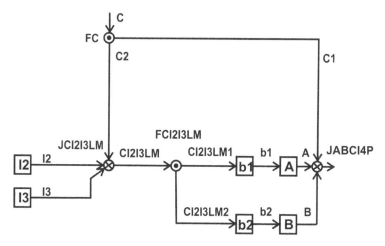

Fig. 20. A sample structure where eager protocol will have runtime advantage over lazy

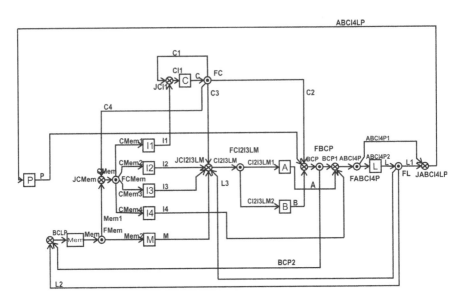

Fig. 21. CNG-optimized control network of the elastic clocked MiniMIPS [12]

9.3   Eager versus Hybrid SELF Implementations

The hybrid SELF implementation attempts to achieve the same performance of the eager SELF with less area and power consumption, by using as many lazy forks as possible. Without a loss of generality, we will apply both eager and hybrid implementations to the elastic MiniMIPS control network of Fig. 21. This control network achieves the same register-to-register communications as the one in Fig. 18 but with two fewer joins and two fewer forks. It is auto-generated by the CNG tool, a tool that given the required register-to-register communications will automatically generate a control network with the minimum total number of joins and forks [12]. Furthermore, we insert zero to three bubbles (i.e., EBs that hold no valid data) at the register file output (i.e., at the inputs of A and B registers simultaneously). In practice, this might be done, for example, to accommodate a high latency register file without affecting the functionality of the whole system.

The flow of Sect. 8.3 will be followed to construct the hybrid implementation. Starting with an all eager implementation of the closed control network of Fig. 21 (call it E_1), we run the sample testbench program of [17]. The simulation waveform of each eager fork in the network is analyzed. EForks whose input behavior does not meet the performance equivalence conditions (of Sect. 8.2) are then identified. These are the forks that must be implemented as eager in the (to-be) hybrid control network in order to maintain the same performance as the all eager network. The set of these forks will be called ϕ_s.

Analysis of the simulation waveforms of the MiniMIPS case (with 0 to 3 bubbles at the register file output) shows that all forks except FC and FL receive Valid and Stall patterns that meet the performance equivalence conditions. Hence, all the forks except FC and FL can be safely implemented as lazy forks without any performance loss. For FC, we observe repetitive Stall patterns similar to those shown in Fig. 22. The numbered columns in Fig. 22 represent the clock cycles. The red 0s and 1s are the branch Stall signal values at the corresponding clock cycles. It is obvious that the Stall patterns at $C1$ and $C3$ meet the conditions of Sect. 8.2 (they do not stall at all). Hence, branches $C1$ and $C3$ can be safely connected through a lazy fork (call it FC_1_3). Similarly, the Stall patterns at branches $C2$ and $C4$ meet the replacement conditions (their Stall patterns always match). Hence, branches $C2$ and $C4$ can also be connected through another lazy fork (call it FC_2_4). FC_1_3 and FC_2_4 should be connected through an eager fork since their corresponding Stall patterns do not match. The resultant hybrid FC implementation is shown in Fig. 23. EF and LF in the Figure refer to eager and lazy forks, respectively. Similarly, based on the simulation waveform analysis, branches 1 and 2 of FL could be connected through a lazy fork (FL_1_2). FL_1_2 must be connected eagerly to the third branch of FL to maintain the runtime of an *all* eager implementation.

Fig. 22. Stall patterns at the branches of FC in the presence of bubbles

Fig. 23. Hybrid implementation of FC

As stated in Sect. 8.3, a hybrid network (call it H_1) is now constructed. All forks of H_1 are implemented as lazy except those in set (ϕ_s) (i.e., that do not meet the equivalence conditions). H_1 typically involves combinational cycles formed by the connection of lazy forks and joins. To cut the cycles in H_1, more forks have to be implemented as eager (call this set of forks ϕ_c). The number of forks in ϕ_c depend on the lazy fork and join combination used. Some lazy fork-join combinations exhibit more cycles than others and, hence, require more eager fork replacements. The MiniMIPS control network is implemented using all the correct 12 lazy fork-join combinations (with some eager fork replacements). The network is also implemented with an all eager control network.

Table 7. Area, power, and runtime of the MiniMIPS control network using Different fork-join combinations

Combination	Eager Forks Used	nCycles	Area (μ^2)	Power @ 4ns $\frac{P_{dyn}}{P_{leakage}}$ (μW)			Runtime (nCycles)		
				0 B	1 B	3 B	0 B	1 B	3 B
F00 – J1011	Some branches of FC, FL	0	513.0	58.187 / 1.980	164.284 / 1.990	122.720 / 1.992	98	147	245
F01 – J1111	FC, FL, FBCP	0	575.4	65.626 / 2.339	188.094 / 2.307	140.389 / 2.278	98	147	245
F01 – J1011	Some branches of FC, FL	0	588.0	58.187 / 2.640	183.991 / 2.536	134.636 / 2.542	98	147	245
F01 – J0000	FC, FL, FBCP	0	634.2	65.626 / 2.739	194.001 / 2.663	143.822 / 2.599	98	147	245
F00 – J1111	FC, FL, FBCP, FMem, FABCI4P	0	639.0	74.475 / 2.525	206.882 / 2.514	155.145 / 2.499	98	147	245
F01 – J0011	FC, FL, FBCP	0	646.8	65.626 / 2.738	192.545 / 2.672	143.065 / 2.617	98	147	245
F01 – J1010	FC, FL, FBCP	0	649.8	64.710 / 2.761	197.261 / 2.691	145.481 / 2.631	98	147	245
F01 – J0010	FC, FL, FBCP	0	653.4	65.635 / 2.685	191.208 / 2.642	142.149 / 2.598	98	147	245
F00 – J000	FC, FL, FBCP, FMem, FABCI4P	0	683.4	74.933 / 2.825	196.338 / 2.762	148.919 / 2.713	98	147	245
F00 – J0011	FC, FL, FBCP, FMem, FABCI4P	0	695.4	74.933 / 2.790	198.957 / 2.742	150.580 / 2.699	98	147	245
F00 – J0010	FC, FL, FBCP, FMem, FABCI4P	0	698.4	74.475 / 2.853	202.539 / 2.838	152.374 / 2.811	98	147	245
F00 – J1010	FC, FL, FBCP, FMem, FABCI4P	0	704.4	73.101 / 2.887	205.521 / 2.867	153.914 / 2.844	98	147	245
EFork – LJ0000	ALL	0	752.4	86.158 / 2.914	221.921 / 2.875	168.807 / 2.842	98	147	245

The set of all forks that had to be implemented as eager (to both maintain the performance and cut the cycles) is listed in Column 2 for each combination in Table 7.

Table 7 shows the synthesis results. The Artisan academic library for IBM's 65nm library was used for physical design. The MiniMIPS control network has been synthesized separately from the data path. All area and power numbers in Table 7 are for *the control network only*. All combinations have passed post synthesis simulation (with 0 to 3 bubbles). The MiniMIPS testbench program in [17] was used to validate correctness. Column 1 in Table 7 lists the different combinations (sorted by their area). Column 2 lists the eager fork replacements in each implementation. Unsurprisingly, $LF01 - LJ1011$ needs the least number of eager fork replacements (See Sect. 8.1), tying with $LF00 - LJ1011$ in this specific network. Column 3 lists the number of combination cycles in the control network (after eager fork replacements), which is zero for all of them. Column 4 lists the synthesis area. $LF00 - LJ1011$ requires minimum area among all with 31.8% reduction comparing to an all eager implementation. $LF01 - LJ1111$ comes second.

Column 5 lists the dynamic and leakage power consumption reported by the synthesis tool. Power is calculated with different number of bubbles inserted at the output of the register file. To accurately estimate the power, we simulated the synthesized netlist and generated an saif file that was read by the synthesis tool to calculate the power. Synthesis and simulation was done at 4 ns clock period for all the implementations. $LF00 - LJ1011$ consumes the least power among all with up to 32.5% and 32.1% dynamic and leakage power reduction comparing to an eager implementation. $LF01 - LJ1011$ comes second.

Finally, column 6 lists the required runtime (in terms of number of clock cycles) to finish the testbench program in [17]. The hybrid networks all achieve the same runtime as the eager implementation.

10   Conclusion

Lazy implementations of fork and join control buffers of SELF latency insensitive protocol are implemented and formally verified. A novel hybrid SELF protocol network is introduced that combines the advantages of both eager and lazy elements. It is cycle free and has the same performance as an all eager implementation. A MiniMIPS case study showed that hybrid implementations achieve the same runtime as the *all* eager implementation with a reduction of 31.8% and up to 32.5% and 32.1% in area and dynamic and leakage power consumption, respectively.

Acknowledgments. The authors like to thank Shomit Das for his help in the place and route and layout of the 0.5 μm chips. This material is based upon work supported by the National Science Foundation under Grant No. 0810408.

References

[1] Carloni, L., Mcmillan, K., Sangiovanni-Vincentelli, A.L.: Theory of latency insensitive design. IEEE Transactions on CAD of Integrated Circuits and Systems 20, 1059–1076 (2001)

[2] Carloni, L., Sangiovanni-Vincentelli, A.: Coping with latency in SOC design. IEEE Micro 22(5), 24–35 (2002)

[3] Carmona, J., Cortadella, J., Kishinevsky, M., Taubin, A.: Elastic circuits. IEEE Transactions on Computer-Aided Design of Integrated Circuits and Systems 28(10), 1437–1455 (2009)

[4] Cimatti, A., Clarke, E., Giunchiglia, E., Giunchiglia, F., Pistore, M., Roveri, M., Sebastiani, R., Tacchella, A.: NuSMV 2: An OpenSource Tool for Symbolic Model Checking. In: Brinksma, E., Larsen, K.G. (eds.) CAV 2002. LNCS, vol. 2404, pp. 359–364. Springer, Heidelberg (2002)

[5] Cortadella, J., Kishinevsky, M., Grundmann, B.: Synthesis of synchronous elastic architectures. In: ACM/IEEE Design Automation Conference, pp. 657–662 (July 2006)

[6] Hennessy, J., et al.: The MIPS Machine. In: COMPCON, pp. 2–7 (1982)

[7] Gebhardt, D., Stevens, K.S.: Elastic flow in an application specific network-on-chip. Elsevier Electronic Notes in Theoretical Computer Science 200(1), 3–15 (2008)

[8] Gotmanov, A., Kishinevsky, M., Galceran-Oms, M.: Evaluation of flexible latencies: designing synchronous elastic H.264 CABAC decoder. In: The Problems in Design of Micro- and Nano-Electronic Systems (2010)

[9] Hoover, G., Brewer, F.: Synthesizing synchronous elastic flow networks. In: Design, Automation and Test in Europe, DATE 2008, pp. 306–311, 10–14 (2008)

[10] Jacobson, H.M., Kudva, P.N., Bose, P., Cook, P.W., Schuster, S.E., Mercer, E.G., Myers, C.J.: Synchronous interlocked pipelines. In: 8th International Symposium on Asynchronous Circuits and Systems, pp. 3–12 (April 2002)

[11] Kilada, E., Das, S., Stevens, K.: Synchronous elasticization: considerations for correct implementation and MiniMIPS case study. In: 18th IEEE/IFIP VLSI System on Chip Conference (VLSI-SoC), pp. 7–12 (September 2010)

[12] Kilada, E., Stevens, K.: Control network generator for latency insensitive designs. In: Design, Automation & Test in Europe Conference Exhibition (DATE), pp. 1773–1778 (March 2010)

[13] Kilada, E., Stevens, K.S.: Synchronous elasticization at a reduced cost: utilizing the ultra simple fork and controller merging. In: International Conference on Computer-Aided Design (ICCAD 2011) (November 2011)

[14] Krstic, S., Cortadella, J., Kishinevsky, M., O'Leary, J.: Synchronous elastic networks. In: Formal Methods in Computer Aided Design, FMCAD 2006, pp. 19–30 (November 2006)

[15] Patterson, D., Hennessy, J.: Computer Organization and Design (2004)

[16] Vakilotojar, V., Beerel, P.: RTL verification of timed asynchronous and heterogeneous systems using symbolic model checking. In: Design Automation Conference 1997. Proceedings of the ASP-DAC 1997. Asia and South Pacific, pp. 181–188, 28–31 (1997)

[17] Weste, N., Harris, D.: CMOS VLSI design: a circuit and systems perspective (2004)

Adaptation Strategies
in Multiprocessors System on Chip

Remi Busseuil, Gabriel Marchesan Almeida, Luciano Ost,
Sameer Varyani, Gilles Sassatelli, and Michel Robert

Laboratoire d'Informatique, de Robotique et de Microelectronique
de Montpellier (LIRMM), Universite Montpellier 2, CNRS, France
{Remi.Busseuil,Gabriel.Marchesan,ost,
Sameer.Varyani,Gilles.Sassatelli}@lirmm.fr
http://www.lirmm.fr

Abstract. Multi-processor System-on-Chips (MPSoCs) have become
increasingly popular over the past decade. They permit balancing performance and flexibility, the latter being a key feature that makes possible
reusing the same silicon across several product lines or even generations.

This popularity makes highlight on new challenges to deal with the
increasing complexity of such systems. Programmability issues, for example, are considered with a lot of attention, as those architectures allow
new dimensions in design exploration. In this context, the development
of adaptable mechanisms permits the optimization of the system behavior. This chapter explores three different adaptable mechanisms, and
shows their benefits : frequency scaling, task migration techniques and
memory organization. The modification of the frequency of each processor of a multi-core system allows fine tuning of power consumption
under a varying process workload. Task migration permits balancing load
among the several processors the system is made of. Our long-term vision of future embedded devices lies in adaptive systems made of thousands of processors in which tasks frequently migrate in response to the
system state that is continuously monitored. Memory organization is a
crucial criterion in MPSoC performance optimization, as memory access latency of remote data increases exponentially with respect to the
number of cores. The computation-based programming model commonly
used in single-core or few-cores based systems are no more suitable, and
a transaction-based model are necessary to reach performances needs of
new multimedia application.

Keywords: MPSoC, Adaptation, Memory Architecture, Network-on-
Chip.

1   Introduction

Multiprocessor Systems-on-Chips (MPSoCs) are commonly adopted in electronic
industry for their power efficiency and performance capabilities [1]. MPSoCs are
multidisciplinary systems that combine multiple homogeneous/heterogeneous

J.L. Ayala, D. Atienza, and R. Reis (Eds.): VLSI-SoC 2010, IFIP AICT 373, pp. 233–257, 2012.

processing elements (PEs), dedicated hardware (e.g. digital signal processing, DSP) and software (e.g. operating systems) in order to cope with different applications requirements (e.g. real time deadlines, throughput). Due to the intensive and parallel communications inherent to embedded applications, networks-on-chip (NoCs) are employed since their are more scalable, flexible and power efficient when compared to traditional on-chip infrastructures (e.g. shared busses) [2] [3].

Given the great dynamism imposed by user-requests and internal system mechanisms (e.g. temperature control), embedded applications can present unpredictable behavior [4]. Such dynamism leads in workload and communication patterns variation, which demands run-time techniques that can provide the necessary adaptability to the system in order to optimize the resource utilization while maintaining high performance [5].

Therefore, the deployment of new techniques to achieve runtime system adaptability is mandatory [6]. Distributed DVFS (dynamic voltage and frequency scaling), power gating, dynamic task mapping, task migration, are examples of runtime techniques that make it possible to optimize various parameters such as application performance and/or power consumption. Dynamic Frequency Scaling (DFS) is a widely used technique aimed at adjusting computational power to application needs. It is often associated to Dynamic Voltage Scaling (DVS) therefore enabling to achieve significant power reductions when computing demand is low; some cited benefits also comprise the reduction of thermal hotspots that participate in the accelerated aging of the circuits due to the thermal stress.

Static and dynamic mapping have been used to define the placement of each task , aiming to reduce the communication latency and energy dissipation inside the NoC. Static mapping defines task placement at design time, while in dynamic mapping tasks are allocated onto PEs at the execution time [7]. However, during the execution the task's performance may degrade due to e.g. higher PE load or NoC congestion. In this case, tasks may be re-mapped to other PEs to meet application requirement. Dynamic re-mapping employs both mapping (static and/or dynamic) and task migration. The task migration process consists in extracting the state of a given task that is already executing on the source PE and transferring it to a destination PE that will execute it. Task migration requires migration points, context saving, context restoring, among other actions not handled by the task mapping mechanisms (e.g. updating the connections of the migrated task with other tasks on the communicating PEs) [8].

Some challenges related to the adoption of task migration into NoC-based MPSoCs still remain. For instance, the task migration performance depends on run-time events that are considered before and during the relocation of given task when it is necessary [9]. Thus, the performance overhead of task migration cannot be very high. The migration execution cost should be low since hard real time deadlines must be met, while maintaining low power dissipation [9] and temperature [10]. Thus, the designer should find a good trade-off between complexity and performance (e.g. implementation and execution), as well as transparency and reusability, which are directly related to the level that the migration process will be provided (e.g. user, kernel levels) [11]. In this context, an important aspect inherent to the task migration process is the adopted memory organization, which can be classified in shared (Figure 1 - a) and distributed (Figure 1 - b)[8]. In the first case, all PE are entitled to access any location in the shared memory, thus the migrating a task comes down to electing a different processor for execution. In turn, distributed memory MPSoCs, both process code and state have to be physically migrated from a processor local memory to another, while synchronizing exchanged messages [12].

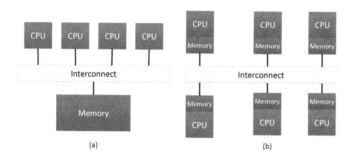

Fig. 1. Memory Organization: (a) Shared Memory, (b) Distributed Memory

Both approaches differ in terms of how to access and transfer the task code from one point to another, which has a considerable impact in terms of performance. In this context, this article presents three main contributions: (i) a Dynamic Frequency Scaling strategy using feedback controlers to meet a streaming application throughput requirement,(ii) validation of two task migration mechanisms into an RTL-modeled NoC-based homogenous MPSoC, leading to accurate results, and (iii) a hybrid memory architecture that can be employed to optimize the performance of task migration mechanisms.

This chapter is organized as follow: Section 2 gives an overview of adaptable mechanisms already developed in the literature. Section 3 explains two communication strategies during task migration allowing different kind of performances. Section 5 gives an overview of standard memory models in MPSoC, and then presents a hybrid memory organization allowing more liberty in term of memory placement. Finally, the last section concludes about the different adaptation strategies.

2   Adaptation Techniques in NoC-Based MPSoCs

Recently, researchers have put focus on adaptation techniques in order to cope with dynamic and unpredictable behaviors that can appear in nowadays embedded systems. This section presents some work that has been conducted in this direction using techniques such as (i) dynamic voltage and frequency scaling (DVFS), and (ii) task migration mechanisms.

2.1   Dynamic Voltage and Frequency Scaling

Numerous dynamic voltage and frequency scaling (DVFS) techniques have been proposed, aiming to allow systems to fine-tune their performance/power consumption trade-off under varying workloads during runtime. Two main approaches to DVFS can be found in the literature. One of them takes a centralized view of power management and considers the global system state, its performance constraints and its current workload to decide voltage and frequency values it will adopt next [13] , while another partitions the system in multiple voltage/frequency islands that can be managed separately [14]. In both centralized and partitioned approaches, the state change (i.e. change of frequency and voltage values) can be triggered by events (e.g. a given threshold on processor utilization was reached [15]) or be driven by a feedback control process that continuously monitors the system workload [16]. The partitioned approach is a natural match to NoC-based multicore chips, but a number of issues arise when different parts of the NoC are on different voltage/frequency islands [17] [18].

For instance, in [19] a DVFS controlling scheme is proposed for NoC-based MpSoCs. In turn, the works [20] and [21] employ communication load as monitoring parameters, which are extracted at run-time in order to tune the DVFS controller. In [22] temperature and task synchronization are used as parameters. In this work, these parameters are employed in a cost function, which is used as input to a game theory model that defines the voltage and the frequency levels. This work was extended in [23], to use communication queues that are placed between each 2 neighbor routers in order to scale the voltage via power supply networks. In [24] the Authors use application profile as the parameter used to control DVFS decisions.

Due to the dynamic variations in the workload of MPSoCs and its impact on energy consumption, PID-based control techniques have been used to dynamically scale the voltage and the frequency of processors [16] [25], and recently, of NoCs [18][26].

A proportional-integral-derivative controller (PID controller) is a generic control-loop feedback mechanism (controller) widely used in industrial control systems. A PID controller calculates an error value as the difference between a measured process variable and a desired setpoint. The controller attempts to minimize the error by adjusting the process control inputs. In the absence of knowledge of the underlying process, a PID controller is a suitable controller [27]. However, for best performance, the PID parameters used must be tuned according to the nature of the process to be regulated.

The proportional, integral, and derivative terms are summed to calculate the output of the PID controller. Defining $u(t)$ as the controller output, the final form of the PID algorithm is:

$$u(t) = MV(t) = K_p e(t) + K_i \int_0^t e(\tau)d\tau + K_d \frac{d}{dt}e(t) \tag{1}$$

Proportional gain, K_p : larger values typically mean faster response since the larger the error, the larger the proportional term compensation. 2) Integral gain, K_i: larger values imply steady state errors are eliminated more quickly. 3) Derivative gain, K_d: larger values decrease overshoot, but slow down transient response and may lead to instability due to signal noise amplification in the differentiation of the error. Figure 2 summarizes a traditional PID controller.

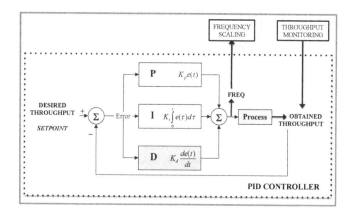

Fig. 2. PID Controller

Due to its features, we propose the usage of a PID controller for adjusting the appropriated frequency of the PEs at the same time as deadline miss ratio is reduced. As most applications in embedded systems are based on soft- real time constraints, actual architectures have to be capable of adapting to avoid situations where deadlines are missed. For that reason, the proposed approach considers applications requirements aiming to provide QoS (Quality-of-Service). As entry point (setpoint in Figure 2), the system is fed with the application requirements, e.g. the minimal throughput the application requires to ensure the functionality of the system in a reliable way.

In the proposed approach [28], the system calculates an error value which is obtained by the difference between the desired and obtained throughput. As output of the PID controller a frequency value is indicated. This value is sent to the frequency scaling module which will be responsible for scaling up and down the frequency of the processor to cope with application requirements. The procedure is then repeated and the obtained throughput gradually gets closer to the desired throughput. This is explained by the fact that after each iteration the error value is reduced assuming that the values of P, I and D have been correctly chosen. Figure 3 presents an abstract system model of the proposed strategy for each Network Processing Element (NPU) in the architecture.

Basically each running application is composed of one or multiple tasks. Task are monitored by a throughput monitoring that is responsible for calculating tasks performance in a non- intrusive mode. This information is passed to the PID controller which will be responsible for choosing the appropriated frequency in order to speed up or slow down processing. This strategy can be suitable for power saving in embedded systems.

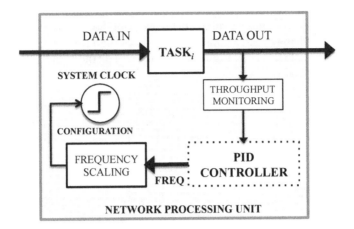

Fig. 3. System Model

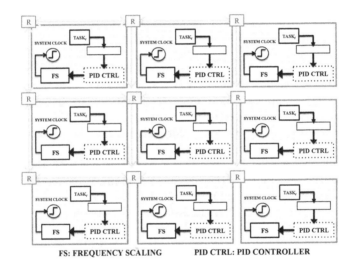

Fig. 4. Distributed PID Controllers

Figure 4 illustrates an overview of the proposed approach. As previously mentioned, there is one PID controller devoted to each task in the system that must ensure soft-real time constraints. In this example there is one task per NPU, so one PID controller for each processor is required. In the case that there are multiple tasks in the same NPU, we could build a system with multiple PID controllers in the same NPU, each one being responsible for contributing as a factor that will be added to the final result.

The strategy consists in deciding controller parameters on a task basis. To this purpose, a simulation of the MPSoC system is executed in order to obtain the step response. Figure 5 shows the cycle-accurate simulation results and the first order extracted model that is used for the process (Figure 2). Based on that high-level model, a number of different configurations of controllers can be explored, each of which exhibits different features such as speed, overshoot, static error.

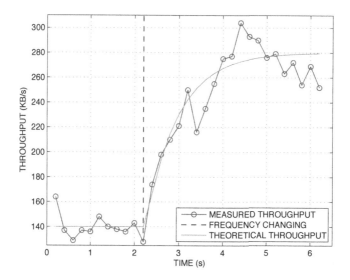

Fig. 5. Obtained Throughput *vs* Theoretical Throughput

The values of P, I and D have been chosen to increase the reactivity of the system. Figure 6 presents the PID response according to P, I and D values.

Assuming that the setpoint of the system is around 260KB/s we can observe that in the first case where P = 500, I = 50 and D = 0, the system converges to the setpoint throughput rapidly. As result we observe an overshoot in terms of performance. In the second scenario where P = 800, I = 5 and D = -0.8, due the fact that the value of P is much bigger than I, we can also observe an overshoot in terms of performance.The system throughput presents a high oscillation due to the small value of I. At least, when P = 50, I = 15 and D = -3 we see that system throughput increases slowly. This is explained by the fact that the value of P is very small and then the convergence time is longer. Based on this information we have chosen to use the first controller, because it converges to a stable system relatively fast.

2.2   Task Migration Support in MPSoC Architecture

Task migration techniques have been widely explored in the literature, notably in the domains of Graphic Processing Unit (GPU) computing and High Performance Computing (HPC).

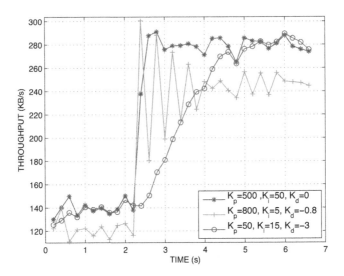

Fig. 6. PID Controller Response

Those techniques allows efficient load balancing strategies aiming to satisfy different system requirements. For instance, Streichert et al. [35] employ task migration to keep the correct execution of an application by migrating executing tasks from a PE that presents a fault (stopped working) to another non-fault PE. The architecture details are not presented in this work, although authors claim that this approach can be applied to current FPGA architectures.

As mentioned before, according to the memory organization task migration can be classified in shared memory and distributed memory designs.

Task Migration in Shared Memory Systems. Most of today's off-chip multicore systems rely on shared memory architecture. In such cases, the task migration is facilitated by the fact that no data has to be physically moved in the structure (see Figure 1-a): since all cores can access any location in the shared memory, task migration can be done just be electing another CPU to execute the task. Several efficient implementations on general purposes OS, such as Windows or Linux, exist in the literature [36].

Other developments closer to MPSoC have been made, notably based on locality considerations [37] for decreasing communication overhead or power consumption [38]. In [39] authors propose a scalable shared memory MPSoC architecture with global cache coherence. The architecture is built around 4096 cores, which uses a logically shared physically distributed memory with cache coherence enforced by hardware. In [40], authors present a migration case study for MPSoCs that relies on the μClinux operating system and a checkpointing mechanism. The system uses the MPARM framework, and although several memories are used, the whole system supports data coherency through a shared memory view of the system.

Task Migration in Distributed Memory Systems. The main issue of implementing task migration in shared memory MPSoCs is the scalability of the system. There is a strong tendency for the next generation of homogeneous MP-SoC in using systems with distributed memory targeting scalable and massively parallel architectures [41][42].

A number of work in the literature based on distributed memory systems has been implementing task migration in shared memory [8][43] [44]. In [43] each PE runs a single operating system (OS) instance in its logical private memory. PEs execute tasks from their private memory and explicitly communicate with each other by means of shared memory. The target platform uses a shared bus as interconnect.

In the case of distributed memory MPSoCs, both process code and state have to be migrated from a processor private memory to another, and synchronizations must be performed using exchanged messages. While this proves straightforward in typical general-purpose computers thanks to the presence of a memory management unit (MMU), implementing task migration on tiny MMU-less embedded processors is challenging [8].

In [45] a dynamic task allocation strategy is proposed. The work evaluates task allocation strategies based on bin-packing algorithms in the context of MPSoCs. The mechanism adopted is based on a copy model. The whole context (code, data, stack, and contents of internal registers) is migrated and there is no task execution during the transfer. The interprocessor communication is based on send/receive primitives. However, in this work neither explanation about the task migration protocol nor the impact in term of performance of such mechanism is given.

Taking into account the future homogeneous MPSoC systems trend, scalable architectures with purely distributed memory system are required. However, to the best of our knowledge, no purely distributed memory architecture that enables task migration without using shared memory are present in the litterature. Furthermore, very few information are available about migration strategies inside distributed memory architecture, and no migration technique exploration has been done. In the Section 3 of this article, two migration techniques in a complete distributed memory system are presented.

3   Task Migration Techniques in Purely Distributed MPSoC

3.1   Task Migration Protocols

In [46], we have proposed a new algorithm capable of supporting task migration at run-time. Migration decisions were taken with local information and in a distributed way, each processing unit taking care of its own tasks. This paper puts focus on communication during task migration, stressing the reliability and performance issues raised by such procedure. It presents two communication techniques stressing the benefits and performance penalty of each.

Hardware and Software Support for Task Migration. The initial platform used to implement our concepts consists of an homogenous array of processing elements. Those elements are distributed on a 2D-mesh Network on Chip. For this reason, they are called Network Processing Unit (NPU). Each NPU is composed by two layers: a network layer used to route the packets into the network, and a processing layer. Figure 7 shows the architecture of the platform.

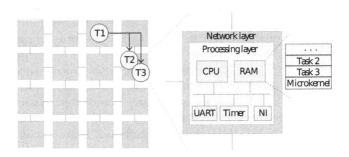

Fig. 7. Structural view of the platform

The network layer consists of a light router based on the Hamiltonian Routing Algorithm [47]. The Network on Chip is derived from [48]. It provides packet switching routing with unique predictable route for each packet from the same sender and receiver. Hence, neither reordering nor acknowledgment is necessary.

The processing layer is composed by a compact RISC processor with a MIPS-I instruction set [49]. It also includes some peripherals like RAM, a UART, a timer and an interrupt controller connected through a bus. However, no Memory Management Unit, no cache and no memory protection support are provided to keep the NPU as small as possible. A multitasking real-time preemptive micro kernel runs on each NPU, providing all the asynchronous operating system features required (multi task management, exception handling, communication, etc.). Both the software and the hardware part of this layer comes from [50].

Communications are handled through hardware and software FIFO: incoming data coming from an external NPU are buffered into a small hardware FIFO located in the network layer, triggering simultaneously an interrupt to the processing layer. It activates data demultiplexing from the hardware fifo to the software FIFO linked to the appropriate receiver task. In case of communication between two tasks on the same NPU, data go directly to the software FIFO using an exception process of the operating system.

In a programming point of view, two functions are provided: *MPI_Send()* and *MPI_receive()* derived on the Message Passing Interface model [51]. In compliance with the Khan Process Network (KPN) model of computation, the send function is non blocking while the receive function is blocking. As we have a message passing programming model, we do not need any memory synchronization.

To handle communication in such globally asynchronous system, each NPU possesses a routing table with all the tasks running locally, as well as the position of all predecessors and successors tasks. Thus, the position of every task the operating system needs to communicate with is known. A master NPU (named NPU11) keeps tracks of every tasks, successors and predecessors in the entire chip. If a task requires opening a new communication channel, the Operating System will modify its own routing table and the one of the master NPU. If the position of the task to communicate with is not know, a query is sent to the master NPU.

Non Continuous Communication. The first migration protocol is depicted in Figure 8. We consider two tasks hosted on two different NPUs communicating together: task 1 is the sender whereas task 2 is the receiver. Task 2 begins a migration procedure. First, the NPU hosting task 2 will remove its entry in the routing table of its predecessor node, as well as in the master node (step 1). As these nodes do not possess task2 position anymore in their routing table, the communication between task 1 and task 2 will stop. Task 2 can now migrate to its destination NPU (step 2).

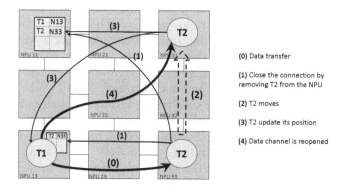

Fig. 8. First migration protocol

It is important to notice that during the transfer of the task, the communication channels are closed downstream and upstream, which translates into buffering.

Finally, when the code has arrived in the destination NPU, the task is scheduled and the master routing table as well as the predecessor routing table are updated (step 3). Hence, communication can be resumed (step 4).

Figure 9 shows the datagram of the protocol. No packets are emitted during the migration.

Continuous Communication with Rerouting. The second protocol used for task migration was designed with the idea of keeping communication channel open. The purpose is avoiding interrupting data transfer so as to achieve the

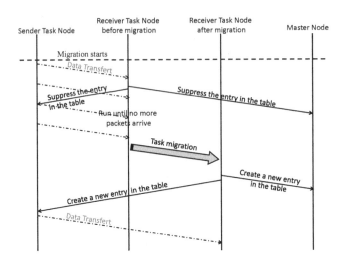

Fig. 9. First migration protocol datagram

highest possible level of performance. To fulfill such requirements, two features were developed: storage and forwarding of the incoming packets.

Figure 10 shows the second migration protocol. The initial situation is same as before: 2 tasks are communicating, task 1 sending to task 2 (step 0). When the NPU decides to trigger a migration, it does not have to notify the task predecessors anymore: the operating system will reroute the software fifos linked to this task into another fifo dedicated for migration (step 1). The packets are stored during the transfer of task 2 code to the destination node (step 2). When the task is rescheduled, it informs the node where it came from to initiate the redirection (step 3). At the same time, it updates the routing table of the master node and its predecessors. The Operating system of the new node containing task 2 has to now take care of two FIFOs: one coming from the redirection, which will be serviced first, and the other from the sender with its updated routing table, which has to be serviced after the whole redirected packets (step 4).

To avoid reordering, rerouted packets have to be serviced before those coming from the new communication channel. A *end of transmission* packet is sent in the end of the redirected stream to inform the new receiver NPU that it can process the packets coming directly from the senders.

Figure 11 shows the datagram of the migration procedure with redirection. Some hypothesis can be made comparing the datagram of the two protocols. First, the complexity of the second protocol is higher in term of computation, because of the storage and redirection functions, but also in term of message passing, with many more service messages. Concerning communication load, the fact of keeping the communication channel and sending a burst of redirected packets suggests a heavier bandwidth occupation. However, as closing and re-opening latency are avoided, higher computation rate of the whole structure and better computation performance are expected.

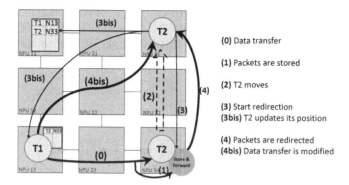

Fig. 10. Second migration protocol

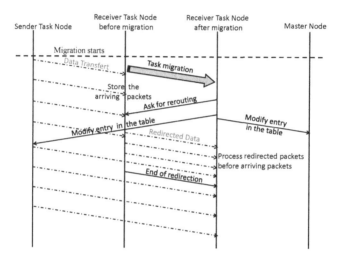

Fig. 11. Second migration protocol datagram

3.2   Experimental Results

Benchmark Procedure. The purpose of this section is to evaluate the overhead of dynamic task migration with the two protocols. In order to fairly assess the performance overhead induced by the proposed task migration strategies, experiments are conducted in best effort mode, therefore all implementations aim at maximizing performance rather than ensuring quality of service. This allows stressing the architecture as much as possible, hence migration cost become prominent rather than compensated by transient increase in cpu usage.

The experiments have been made on a case study yet realistic: the mjpeg decoding application. To simplify the experiment, only the three main tasks of mjpeg decoding have been implemented: IVLC, IDCT and IQUANT. A quick profiling shows the average percentage of CPU time of each task in a sequential execution: IVLC take around 85% of the CPU time, IDCT 8% and IQUANT 5%. Figure 12 shows the task graph of the MJPEG application with the percentage of CPU time for each.

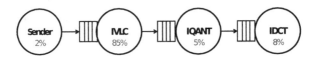

Fig. 12. MJPEG Task graph with percentage of computation time

Figure 13 shows the two different mappings that were used for our migration experiment: starting from configuration 1, the task 2 will migrate to NPU 2, which corresponds to the configuration 2. As the purpose here is to validate our algorithm and to evaluate the efficiency of each one, no considerations about mapping efficiency are treated. The only assumption done here is that configuration 2 is better suited for high performance, because the heaviest task (IVLC) is computed in a single NPU. This assumption will be confirmed by the performance benchmarks on static mapping in configuration 1 and 2, in the next paragraphs. More considerations about mapping issues are available in the articles referenced in Section 2.2 of this chapter.

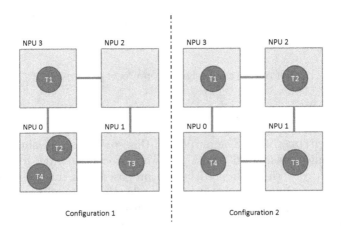

Fig. 13. Task configurations used in the benchmarks

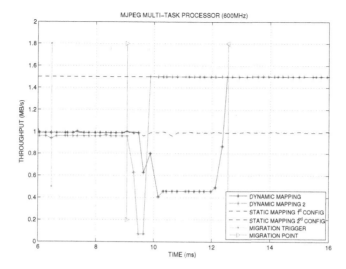

Fig. 14. Throughput of MJPEG for each case

Evaluation of Communication Capabilities. The evaluations in term of performance were made each time for 4 configurations: considering a static mapping with the configuration 1, considering a static mapping with configuration 2, triggering a migration of task 2 to go from configuration 1 to configuration 2 using the first protocol, and finally the same scenario with the second protocol. The migration order is triggered 6.5 ms after the beginning of the computation, to ensure the system is in a steady state (every task is running and computing packets).

Figure 14 shows the throughputs of the MJPEG for the 4 cases presented. The static mappings have, as expected, almost regular throughputs: the first configuration providing a 1 MB/s throughput while the second providing a 1.5 MB/s throughput. This result confirms the assumption made in the previous section about the higher compute capability of the second mapping.

Few observations can be done comparing the two migration protocols. First, even if the migration order is triggered at the same time, the migration process occurs at a different time. This can be explained by the fact that the two migration protocols use two different procedures before migrating the task: the first one closes the connection before the migration while the second relies on the forwarding techniques explained previously.

The second point stressed by Figure 8 is the migration time. The migration time here refers to the time between two steady states where the throughput is stable. In that case, the second protocol, with reordering, migrates much more rapidly than the first one: only 0.8 ms are necessary to reach the new throughput while 3.45 ms are necessary for the first one. We can see here the benefit of the second proposed technique, compared to the first one: the latency induced by closing and reopening the communication is here almost negated.

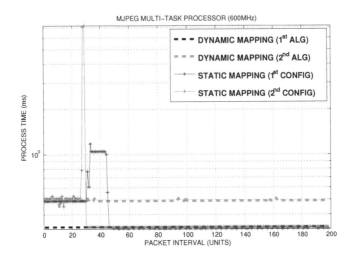

Fig. 15. MJPEG timing jitter for each case

However, in term of minimum bandwidth, the first protocol sees its bandwidth only dropping down to 0.45 MB/s whereas the second one goes down to 0.07 MB/s. This can be explained by the higher complexity of the second protocol: storage and forwarding processes prove computationally intensive and therefore reduce application performance during the transient phase.

This last consideration can be expected to be the main parameter when a strategy of migration has to be chosen. In streaming application like MJPEG for example, a minimum throughput is required, which can be prohibitive for the second protocol. However, in application which does not require real-time constraint, like compression or non streaming communication, the efficiency of the second protocol is higher.

Figure 15 shows the timing jitter for the 4 cases. The Y axis has been made logarithmic to clarify the results. We can observe that the timing jitter is, as expected, better in the second mapping than in the first one, and that the dynamic mapping scenarios vary as expected from the jitter value point of view. Moreover, this figure confirms the observations made previously: the timing jitter of the second dynamic mapping scenario shows a high and sharp peak during migration.

However, if we average the jitter during the migration time, the first algorithm gives a process time of 0.83 ms while the second gives 1.01 ms, i.e. less than 22% larger. The same average evaluation of the bandwidth during migration gives a throughput of 0.93 MB/s for the first algorithm and 1.31 MB/s for the second.

3.3   Task Migration - Closing Remarks

In this section we have proposed two task migration mechanisms for distributed memory MPSoCs: the first one closing the communications during the process, the second one using buffering and redirection to avoid closing communications. Performance analysis has been made to compare both algorithms. Results have been validated thanks to a 2*2 homogeneous MPSoC architecture based on a distributed memory structure and a NoC.

Those benchmarks show that the overhead of the migration mechanisms is low and amortized by the performance gain of a better load distribution. The key parameter concerning the choice of the migration algorithm lies in the application specifications: in the case of real-time application, the first algorithm may prove to be more suitable because of the lower observed jitter in packet arrival. For best effort-application, the second algorithm will achieve a better global performance.

4   Memory Organization in MPSoC

4.1   Two Memory Management Philosophies, Implying Two Computation Models

In the literature, memory management in MPSoCs can be divided into two categories: shared memory models and distributed memory models.

Historically, shared memory models, with a vision of a single unified memory that can be accessed by any component are the most used. This popularity came from the original single core, single memory Von Neumann machine. To cope with multi-cores new architectures, caches strategies, including data coherency protocols have been implemented so that the compatibility with the old architectures still remains. Simultaneous Multi Threading (SMT), derived from this philosophy, is still the more commonly used model of computation in standard home computer CPUs. However, the heavy cost due to memory coherency controllers leads to a reconsideration of the memory model in embedded systems from shared memory to distributed memory.

The distributed memory model considers each core having its own independant memory. Communication and synchronization between the cores are made through messages. This model is derived from HPC, where a number of standards and API have been created, such as the Message Passing Interface (MPI) [51]. This model does not need any hardware memory coherency controllers (as each core is data independent), but leave the synchronizations to the software, making parallel computation harder. Nowadays, designing a complete message passing multi-tasking Operating System still remains a challenge [52].

Although the link between a memory model and a hardware architecture is obvious, it is interesting to note that a memory model does not rely on a particular hardware, and that some architectures possessing different memory modules distributed across the chip finally used a shared memory model. Those architectures are called Distributed Shared Memory models (DSM) as they have a physically distributed memory, but logically shared [53].

Such architectures imply a Non Uniform Memory Access (NUMA). To achieve correct performances, caches are provided that store remote memory data into a local faster memory. To maintain memory consistency inside those platforms, a cache coherency protocol is provided. Hence, those architectures are also called Cache-Coherent NUMA (cc-NUMA) architectures.

4.2   A Hybrid Memory Model

General Description. The hybrid memory model described in this section has the aim of taking advantage of the two historical models. It consists in considering a distributed memory model, but with the addition of a Remote Memory Access (RMA). Hence, every core can access every memory inside the chip. However, no hardware cache coherency system has been implemented. The shared memory in this model is considered as critical small portion of memory, used only for general decision. No hardware cache coherency has been implemented to avoid the heavy cost of hardware data synchronization.

To preserve coherency of the shared memory, software cache coherency has to be implemented. The main advantage of software cache coherency is the fact that the programmer has a global view of the system, and so can optimize the protocol of synchronization depending on the nodes possessing the data [54]: knowing the owner of the data and the order of read/write operations on it allows more precise flush/invalidate actions in the caches. However, software cache coherency implies a higher performance penalty for the computation of the synchronization protocols. For that reason, the use of shared memory has to be made with caution.

Initial Hardware Platform. The initial platform used to develop this hybrid memory model was the same as described in section 3.1. To increase the compute capability of each NPU, the MIPS-I CPU was replaced by an Harvard based architecture using the Microblaze instruction set: the SecretBlaze [55].

The Remote Memory Access. To provide the access of memory located in a distant node, a RMA module has been implemented in the Network layer, which creates a Request/Acknowledge protocol to read data through the NoC. This RMA module is composed by two blocks: a *Send-RMA* module and a *Reply-RMA* module. The connections between these modules and the NoC were made with two more asynchronous fifos, as shown in figure 16.

The *Send-RMA* is responsible of servicing memory requests from the CPU. For a Write request, it first packetizes a flag corresponding to the write request, and then the addresses and data to write. For a Read request, it sends the flag corresponding to the read request, and then only the addresses to read. It then waits for the response and sends the data back to the CPU. The FSM describing the *Send-RMA* behavior is depicted figure 17-a.

The *Reply-RMA* receives the request coming from the other cores, and services them. For a Write request, data are written into the memory, and for a Read request data are read from the memory, then packetized and sent back to the source NPU. The FSM describing the *Reply-RMA* behavior is depicted figure 17-b.

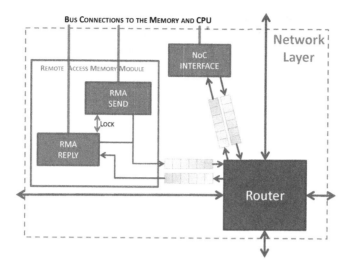

Fig. 16. Network on Chip with Remote Memory Access module

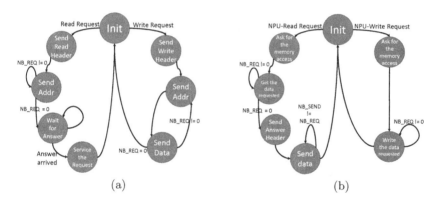

Fig. 17. RMA Finite Machine States: (a) *Send-RMA*, (b) *Reply-RMA*

Therefore, a master bus connection is needed for the *Reply-RMA* module to access memory, while a slave bus connection is sufficient for the *Send-RMA* module.

Memory Mapping. The distributed memory model which our system is derived has private memory for each node. Therefore, every node may have the same address mapping. However, the addition of the RMA module, allowing access to every memory modules in the architecture, requires an addressing scheme enabling remote NPU memory access. For legacy reason with our previous architecture, the 4 highest bits are kept for the selection of the bus connection. Bits 20 to 27 are used to select the coordinates of the memory node, in case of a remote access. The last 20 bits are used for memory address. This mapping provides a small static virtualization of the memory - as the local memory is located at the same address space for every node. This allows simpler memory management, as local access can be detected using the same strategy for each node.

Thanks to this memory mapping, we can address up to 256 NPUs, with 1 MB of RAM each.

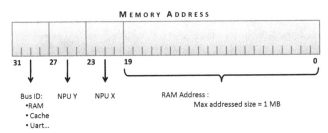

Fig. 18. Memory mapping

Performance. Since the transmission of the data through the NoC is time consuming, the local bus of each NPU has to be controlled carefully, to avoid unecessary stalling. Hence, the *Reply-RMA* possesses a buffer to store the addresses and data coming from the NoC before servicing them. As the requests are cache requests, the buffer has the size of a cache line. Thanks to that mechanism, the *Reply-RMA* module has an access time to the bus similar to the one of the local cache.

Figure 19 shows the number of clock cycles for each type of memory request. The number of 32-bits words of a cache line has been set to 8. So a memory operation handles 8 words of 32 bits, i.e. 256 bits. Measures have been made for different memory requests: from the local NPU, from a 1-hop distant NPU, and from a 2-hop distant NPU (i.e. the data have to go through 2 routers plus the local one).

An important factor in the memory access performance is the maximum NoC throughput. The Hermes router (introduced in Section 3.1)uses an asynchronous channel to send the data, with a tunable number of bit send for each transaction. As a transaction takes two clock cycles, the maximum throughput is directly linked to the number of bits send per transaction (the channel width). The throughput can be calculated using equation 2.

$$Throughput = \frac{Channel\ width}{2} * Frequency \qquad (2)$$

The frequency of our design has been set to 50 MHz. The experiments have been made with a channel width of 4, 8, 16, and 32 bits, which leads to a maximum throughput of 100 MBps, 200 MBps, 400 MBPs, and 800 MBPs respectively. The maximum throughput of the wishbone bus is 1600 MBps.

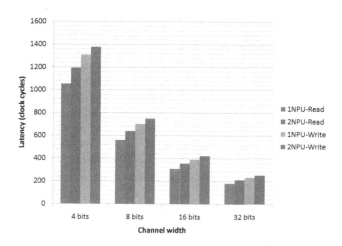

Fig. 19. Time to memory access in clock cycles

The figure shows that channel width is an important factor regarding the time to access the memory. Doubling the number of bits in the channel leads to a decreasing time to access of 53%, 55% and 59% respectively. Bus read and write transactions for a cache line takes 10 clock cycles. With a 200 clock cycles access time approximately, the 32-bit wide channel router gives competitive results for a classical L1 cache remote fetch: if we assume a remote miss rate of 1% of the total miss rate, the performance of the cache will only decrease to 84% compared to local miss only. In comparison, standard DDR memory access latency is around 5000 clock cycles.

Another point stressed by this figure is the importance of the location of the data. Fetching a data from a 2 node distant NPU leads to a inscrease of 13% to 16% in access time compared to fetching from a 1 node distant NPU. We can notice that the wider the channel, the bigger the access time. This is due to the fact that the data are more buffered for small channels, which leads to a bigger latency during the access process. For these channels, this buffering, which is only slightly affected by the number of nodes crossed, takes a bigger part of the access time. Wide channels, however, are less affected by the buffering, and so comparatively more affected by the data location.

4.3 Memory Organization - Closing Remarks

In this section we have seen the different constraints and so the possible optimizations given by a hybrid distributed/shared memory structure. This new degree of freedom offers new load balancing strategies, since we can distribute the data independently to the execution.

5 Conclusion

This paper has presented an overview of adaptation issues in distributed memory MPSoCs. A new frequency scaling strategy for streaming applications has been developed, using feedback controllers. Next, two task migration protocols have been presented and compared. Finally, a hybrid memory approach has been described, allowing remote memory access inside a distributed archiecture.

The complementarity of those tools allows a global adaptation strategy whith increasing performance thanks to the combination of each. Indeed, frequency scaling can be used to ensure the reach of system requierements, while the two task migration protocols will balance the load through the platform. The throughput variations leaded by the migration processes will be lowered thanks to the frequency scaling.

Concerning the new memory organization, future work will include the development of a load balancing strategy based on the execution of data from another NPU without transfering the code, thanks to the remote memory access. The long term goal will be to conduct experiments with dynamic selection of the best suited load balancing techniques - from remote execution and the two task migration techniques - with respect to either application specifications or local parameters such as FIFO occupation or CPU workload.

References

1. Wolf, W.: The Future of Multiprocessor Systems-on-Chips. In: Design Automation and Test in Europe (DATE 2004), pp. 681–685 (2004)
2. Marculescu, R., et al.: Outstanding Research Problems in NoC Design: System, Microarchitecture, and Circuit Perspectives. IEEE Transactions on Computer-Aided Design of Integrated Circuits and Systems 28 (2009)
3. Beraha, R., Walter, I., Cidon, I., Kolodny, A.: Leveraging Application-Level Requirements in the Design of a NoC for a 4G SoC - a Case Study. In: Design, Automation and Test in Europe (DATE 2010), pp. 1–6 (2010)
4. Chou, C.-L., Marculescu, R.: Run-Time Task Allocation Considering User Behavior in Embedded Multiprocessor Networks-on-Chip. IEEE Trans. on Computer-Aided Design of Integrated Circuits and Systems (TCAD) 29, 78–91 (2010)
5. Singh, A.K., et al.: Communication-aware heuristics for run-time task mapping on NoC-based MPSoC platforms. Journal of Systems Architecture 56 (2010)
6. Almeida, G.M., Sassatelli, G., Benoit, P., Saint-Jean, N., Varyani, S., Torres, L., Robert, M.: An adaptive message passing mpsoc framework. International Journal of Reconfigurable Computing, 1–20 (2009)
7. Faruque, M.A., et al.: ADAM: Run-time Agent-based Distributed Application Mapping for on-chip Communication. In: DAC 2008 (2008)
8. Bertozzi, S., Acquaviva, A., Bertozzi, D., Poggiali, A.: Supporting task migration in multi-processor systems-on-chip: A feasibility study. In: DATE 2006: Design, Automation and Test in Europe, pp. 1–6 (2006)
9. Barcelos, D., Brião, E.W., Wagner, F.R.: A hybrid memory organization to enhance task migration and dynamic task allocation in NoC-based MPSoCs. In: Proceedings of the 20th Annual Conference on Integrated Circuits and Systems Design, SBCCI 2007, pp. 282–287 (2007)

10. Cuesta, D., Rodrigo, A., Luis, J., Perez, H., Ignacio, J., Atienza Alonso, D., Acquaviva, A., Macii, E.: Adaptive Task Migration Policies for Thermal control in MPSoCs. In: IEEE 2010 Annual Symposium on VLSI, pp. 110–115 (2010)
11. Milojicic, D.S., Douglis, F., Paindaveine, Y., Wheeler, R., Zhou, S.: Process migration. ACM Computing Surveys 32 (2000)
12. Marchesan Almeida, G., Busseuil, R., et al.: Evaluating the impact of task migration in multi-processor systems-on-chip. In: SBCCI 2010: Proceedings of the 23rd Symposium on Integrated Circuits and System Design, pp. 73–78 (2010)
13. Simunic, T., Benini, L., Acquaviva, A., Glynn, P., Micheli, G.D.: Dynamic voltage scaling and power management for portable systems. In: Proceedings of the 38th Annual Design Automation Conference, pp. 524–529. ACM, Las Vegas (2001)
14. Herbert, S., Marculescu, D.: Analysis of dynamic voltage/frequency scaling in chip-multiprocessors. In: Proceedings of the 2007 International Symposium on Low Power Electronics and Design, pp. 38–43. ACM, Portland (2007)
15. Talpes, E., Marculescu, D.: Toward a multiple clock/voltage island design style for power-aware processors. IEEE Trans. Very Large Scale Integr. Syst. 13, 591–603 (2005)
16. Wu, Q., Juang, P., Martonosi, M., Clark, D.W.: Formal online methods for voltage/frequency control in multiple clock domain microprocessors. SIGARCH Comput. Archit. News 32, 248–259 (2004)
17. Shang, L., Peh, L., Jha, N.K.: Dynamic Voltage Scaling with Links for Power Optimization of Interconnection Networks. In: Proceedings of the 9th International Symposium on High-Performance Computer Architecture, p. 91. IEEE Computer Society (2003)
18. Ogras, U.Y., Marculescu, R., Marculescu, D.: Variation-adaptive feedback control for networks-on-chip with multiple clock domains. In: Proceedings of the 45th Annual Design Automation Conference, pp. 614–619. ACM, Anaheim (2008)
19. Yin, A.W., Guang, L., Nigussie, E., Liljeberg, P., Isoaho, J., Tenhunen, H.: Architectural Exploration of Per-Core DVFS for Energy-Constrained On-Chip Networks. In: DSD, pp. 141–146 (2009)
20. Alimonda, A., Carta, S., Acquaviva, A., Pisano, A.: Non-Linear Feedback Control for Energy Efficient On-Chip Streaming Computation. In: IES, pp. 1–8 (2006)
21. Alimonda, A., Carta, S., Acquaviva, A., Pisano, A., Benini, L.: A Feedback-Based Approach to DVFS in Data-Flow Applications. IEEE Transactions on Computer-Aided Design of Integrated Circuits and Systems 28, 1691–1704 (2009)
22. Puschini, D., Clermidy, F., Benoit, P., Sassatelli, G., Torres, L.: Temperature-Aware Distributed Run-Time Optimization on MP-SoC Using Game Theory. In: ISVLSI, pp. 375–380 (2008)
23. Puschini, D., Clermidy, F., Benoit, P., Sassatelli, G., Torres, L.: Adaptive energy-aware latency-constrained DVFS policy for MPSoC. In: SOCC, pp. 89–92 (2009)
24. Goossens, K., She, D., Milutinovic, A., Molnos, A.: Composable Dynamic Voltage and Frequency Scaling and Power Management for Dataflow Applications. In: DSD, pp. 107–114 (2010)
25. Zhu, Y., Mueller, F.: Feedback edf scheduling exploiting hardware- assisted asynchronous dynamic voltage scaling. SIGPLAN Not. 40, 203–212 (2005)
26. Sharifi, A., Zhao, H., et al.: Feedback control for providing qos in noc based multi-cores. In: Proceedings of the Conference on Design, Automation and Test in Europe (DATE 2010), pp. 1384–1389 (2010)
27. Bennett, S.: A History of Control Engineering, 1800-1930. Institution of Electrical Engineers, Stevenage, UK (1979)

28. Marchesan Almeida, G., Busseuil, R., Alceu Carara, E., Hebert, N., Varyani, S., Sassatelli, G., Benoit, P., Torres, L., Gehm Moraes, F.: Predictive Dynamic Frequency Scaling for Multi-Processor Systems-on-Chip. In: IEEE International Symposium on Circuits and Systems (ISCAS), pp. 1500–1503 (2011)

29. Wildermann, S., et al.: Run time Mapping of Adaptive Applications onto Homogeneous NoC-based Reconfigurable Architectures. In: FPT 2009 (2009)

30. Kangas, T., et al.: UML-based multiprocessor SoC design framework. ACM Transactions on Embedded Computing Systems 5(2) (2006)

31. Hölzenspies, P.K.F., et al.: Run-time Spatial Mapping of Streaming Applications to a Heterogeneous Multi-Processor System-on-Chip (MPSoC). In: DATE 2008 (2008)

32. Chou, C.-L., et al.: User-Aware Dynamic Task Allocation in Networks-on-Chip. In: DATE 2008 (2008)

33. Carvalho, E., et al.: Dynamic Task Mapping for MPSoCs. Design and Test of Computers 27(5) (2010)

34. Smit, L.T., et al.: Run-time mapping of applications to a heterogeneous SoC. In: SoC 2005 (2005)

35. Streichert, T., Strengert, C., Haubelt, C., Teich, J.: Dynamic task binding for hardware/software reconfigurable networks. In: SBCCI 2006: Proceedings of the 19th Annual Symposium on Integrated Circuits and Systems Design, pp. 38–43 (2006)

36. ARM Limited. Mpcore linux 2.6 smp kernel and tools

37. Barak, A., Laadan, O., Shiloh, A.: Scalable cluster computing with mosix for linux. In: Proceedings of Linux Expo 1999, pp. 95–100 (1999)

38. Carta, S., Acquaviva, A., Del Valle, P.G., Atienza, D., De Micheli, G., Rincon, F., Benini, L., Mendias, J.M.: Multi-processor operating system emulation framework with thermal feedback for systems-on-chip. In: Proceedings of the 17th ACM Great Lakes Symposium on VLSI, pp. 311–316 (2007)

39. Greiner, A.: Tsar: a scalable, shared memory, many-cores architecture with global cache coherence. In: 9th International Forum on Embedded MPSoC and Multicore (2009)

40. Bertozzi, D., Benini, L.: Mparm: Exploring the multi-processor soc design space with systemc. The Journal of VLSI Signal Processing 41(2), 169–182 (2005)

41. Held, J.: From a Few Cores to Many. Citeseer, 12. Intel White Paper, http://download.intel.com/research/platform/terascale

42. Dumitrascu, F., Bacivarov, I., Pieralisi, L., Bonaciu, M., Jerraya, A.: Flexible MPSoC platform with fast interconnect exploration for optimal system performance for a specific application. In: Proceedings of the Conference on Design, Automation and Test in Europe: Designers' Forum (DATE 2006), European Design and Automation Association, 3001 Leuven, Belgium, Belgium, pp. 166–171 (2006)

43. Acquaviva, A., Alimonda, A., Carta, S., Pittau, M.: Assessing task migration impact on embedded soft real-time streaming multimedia applications. EURASIP J. Embedded Syst., 1–15 (2008)

44. Pittau, M., Alimonda, A., Carta, S., Acquaviva, A.: Impact of task migration on streaming multimedia for embedded multiprocessors: A quantitative evaluation. In: Chakraborty, S., Eles, P. (eds.) ESTImedia, pp. 59–64 (2007)

45. Briao, E.W., Barcelos, D., Wagner, F.R.: Dynamic task allocation strategies in mpsoc for soft real-time applications. In: DATE 2008: Proceedings of the Conference on Design, Automation and Test in Europe, pp. 1386–1389 (2008)

46. Marchesan Almeida, G., Varyani, S., Sassatelli, G., Busseuil, R., Benoit, P., Torres, L., Robert, M.: Self-adaptability in Multi-processor Embedded Systems. In: GDR SOC-SIP (2009)
47. Lin, X., McKinley, P.K., Ni, L.M.: Deadlock-free multicast wormhole routing in 2-d mesh multicomputers. IEEE Trans. Parallel Distrib. Syst. 5(8), 793–804 (1994)
48. Moraes, F., Calazans, N., Mello, A., Moller, L., Ost, L.: Hermes: an infrastructure for low area overhead packet-switching networks on chip. Integration, the VLSI Journal 38(1), 69–93 (2004)
49. MIPS Corp. Mips technologies, http://www.mips.com
50. Rhoads, S.: Plasma - most mips i(tm), http://www.opencores.org/project,plasma
51. The Message Passing Interface Standard, http://www.mcs.anl.gov/research/projects/mpi/index.htm
52. Dasgupta, P., LeBlanc Jr., R.J., Ahamad, M., Ramachandran, U.: The Clouds distributed operating system. IEEE Computer 24, 34–44 (1991)
53. Protic, J., Tomasevic, M., Milutinovic, V.: Distributed shared memory: concepts and systems. IEEE Parallel and Distributed Technology: Systems and Applications 4, 63–71 (1996)
54. Ophelders, F., Corporaal, H., Bekooij, M.: A Tuneable Software Cache Coherence Protocol for Heterogeneous MPSoCs. Master's thesis, Eindhoven University of Technology (2009)
55. Barthe, L., Cargnini, L.V., Benoit, P., Torres, L.: The SecretBlaze: A Configurable and Cost-Effective Open-Source Soft-Core Processor. IEEE IPDPS/RAW (2011)

Tri-mode Operation for Noise Reduction and Data Preservation in Low-Leakage Multi-Threshold CMOS Circuits

Hailong Jiao and Volkan Kursun

Department of Electronic and Computer Engineering
The Hong Kong University of Science and Technology
Clear Water Bay, Kowloon, Hong Kong
{jiaohl,eekursun}@ust.hk

Abstract. Multi-threshold CMOS (MTCMOS) is the most widely used circuit technique for suppressing subthreshold leakage currents in idle circuits. When a conventional MTCMOS circuit transitions from SLEEP mode to ACTIVE mode, voltages of power and ground distribution networks are disturbed. Mode transition noise phenomenon in MTCMOS circuits is examined in this chapter. An MTCMOS circuit technique with three operating modes (tri-mode) is described for noise suppression during activation events. A threshold voltage tuning methodology is presented to further alleviate the mode transition noise with smaller sleep transistors in MTCMOS circuits. Alternative applications of tri-mode MTCMOS for data preservation and leakage power reduction in idle memory elements are also discussed.

Keywords: Mode transition noise, tri-mode MTCMOS, data preserving SLEEP mode, forward body bias, sleep transistor miniaturization, subthreshold leakage currents, leakage power consumption, activation noise, activation delay, electrical quality.

1   Introduction

Leakage power consumption is an important concern in modern nanoscale integrated circuits [1] – [48]. Subthreshold leakage currents of integrated circuits increase exponentially with the reduced threshold voltages of transistors in advanced CMOS technologies. High performance integrated circuits (such as microprocessors) rarely operate with full workload [2]. Most of the circuit blocks on a microprocessor are typically idle for long periods during normal operation [1]. Leakage currents produced by these idle circuit blocks contribute significantly to the total power consumption of a chip. Furthermore, mobile devices such as smart phones and tablet computers experience long idle periods where significant energy is consumed due to leakage currents. Leakage currents drain the battery in portable devices. Suppressing subthreshold leakage currents in large scale integrated circuits is essential both for facilitating the proliferation of portable electronics and for green computing.

J.L. Ayala, D. Atienza, and R. Reis (Eds.): VLSI-SoC 2010, IFIP AICT 373, pp. 258–290, 2012.
© IFIP International Federation for Information Processing 2012

MTCMOS is the most commonly used leakage power suppression technique in state-of-the-art integrated circuits [1] – [36]. In an MTCMOS circuit, high threshold voltage (high-$|V_{th}|$) sleep transistors (header and/or footer) are used to cut off the power supply and/or the ground connections to an idle low threshold voltage (low-$|V_{th}|$) circuit block as illustrated in Fig. 1. In a power-gated MTCMOS circuit, a high-$|V_{th}|$ header is attached between the chip power distribution network (directly connected to the power supply) and a virtual power line (connected to the low threshold voltage circuit block) as shown in Fig. 1(a). Alternatively, in a ground-gated MTCMOS circuit, a high-$|V_{th}|$ footer is inserted between the chip ground distribution network and a virtual ground line (connected to the low threshold voltage circuit block) as shown in Fig. 1(b). In a power and ground gated MTCMOS circuit, both a high-$|V_{th}|$ header and a high-$|V_{th}|$ footer are utilized to block access to the chip power and ground distribution networks, as illustrated in Fig. 1(c). In SLEEP mode, the header and footer are cut off to lower the subthreshold leakage currents in an idle circuit block. Alternatively, in ACTIVE mode, the header and footer are activated to resume normal circuit operation with high performance.

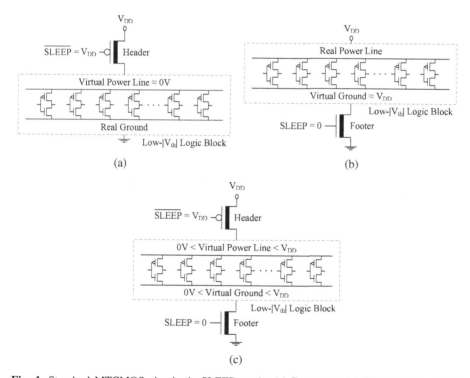

Fig. 1. Standard MTCMOS circuits in SLEEP mode. (a) Power-gated MTCMOS circuit. (b) Ground-gated MTCMOS circuit. (c) Power and ground gated MTCMOS circuit. High-$|V_{th}|$ sleep transistors are represented with a thick line in the channel region.

Multiple autonomous power and ground gated circuit domains are typically utilized for effective control of leakage power consumption in MTCMOS circuits [2],

[23] – [27]. When low-$|V_{th}|$ logic blocks transition from SLEEP mode to ACTIVE mode, significant voltage fluctuations occur on the real power and ground distribution networks in an MTCMOS circuit, as illustrated in Fig. 2. The real power and ground wires are shared by all the circuit blocks on a chip. The mode transition noise produced by an awakening MTCMOS circuit block is transferred through the shared power and ground distribution networks to the other active circuit blocks across an integrated circuit. An awakening circuit block thereby acts as an aggressor in a multi-domain MTCMOS circuit. The active circuit blocks become victims of the noise produced by an awakening aggressor. The voltage levels of the internal nodes of active logic circuits are disturbed. Provided that the amplitude of mode transition noise is significantly high, the logic states of the internal nodes can be flipped. The active segments of an integrated circuit may malfunction due to an awakening circuit block. Furthermore, the voltage fluctuations on internal nodes cause short circuit currents in the active logic gates. The propagation delay and the dynamic switching power consumption of active logic blocks can be thereby increased [6], [28]. The noise margins of logic gates can also be temporarily reduced by the mode transition noise. The reliabilities of the active logic blocks are thereby degraded in the vicinity of an awakening MTCMOS circuit. With smaller device dimensions, lower power supply voltage, and exacerbated process variations, noise immunity of CMOS circuits is significantly weakened in each new CMOS technology generation. Mode transition noise is expected to become an increasingly important reliability issue in future deeply scaled multi-domain MTCMOS circuits with narrower noise margins [2], [23] – [26], [49].

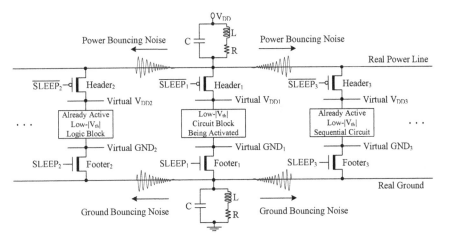

Fig. 2. Power and ground bouncing noise generated by an awakening autonomous power and ground gated circuit block in a multi-domain MTCMOS circuit [6]. High-$|V_{th}|$ sleep transistors are represented with a thick line in the channel region. SLEEP$_1$: $0 \rightarrow V_{DD}$. SLEEP$_2$ = SLEEP$_3$ = V_{DD}.

Low-leakage MTCMOS circuits with three operational modes (tri-mode) are described in this chapter for activation noise reduction and data preservation. As a case study, threshold voltage tuning techniques are examined to suppress mode transition noise with smaller sleep transistors and shorter activation delay in ground-gated tri-mode MTCMOS integrated circuits. The principal mechanisms of noise and sleep transistor size reduction with the threshold voltage tuning techniques are discussed.

This chapter is organized as follows. The generation of mode transition noise in MTCMOS circuits is described in Section 2. Noise-aware tri-mode MTCMOS circuit technique is reviewed in Section 3. Threshold voltage tuning in tri-mode MTCMOS circuits is discussed. Application of tri-mode MTCMOS for data preservation and leakage reduction in memory elements is presented in Section 4. A case study on 32-bit tri-mode MTCMOS Brent-Kung adder design is provided in Section 5. Tradeoffs among mode transition noise, activation delay, leakage power consumption, active power consumption, and layout area in MTCMOS circuits are discussed. A summary of this chapter is given in Section 6.

2   Mode Transition Noise

Mode transition noise (power and ground bouncing noise) is caused by the resistive and inductive parasitics of on-chip power distribution network, off-chip bonding wires, and pins of package. The package parasitic impedances typically play the most important role in the generation of mode transition noise [6] – [13], [49]. A conventional MTCMOS circuit with package parasitics is illustrated in Fig. 3 [6]. R, L, and C are the parasitic resistor, parasitic inductor, and parasitic capacitor of the package, respectively. Parasitic capacitors of the header, the low-$|V_{th}|$ transistors, and the virtual power line are lumped in C_1. C_2 represents the parasitic capacitors of the footer, the low-$|V_{th}|$ transistors, and the virtual ground line. C_3 and C_4 are the lumped capacitors of the low-$|V_{th}|$ transistors attached to the internal nodes "A" and "B", respectively.

When the MTCMOS circuit block is in ACTIVE mode, both the header and the footer are turned on. The virtual power and ground lines are maintained at ~V_{DD} and ~0V, respectively. The effective supply voltage experienced by the low-$|V_{th}|$ circuitry is approximately equal to the power supply voltage V_{DD}. The MTCMOS circuit thereby operates with high performance in ACTIVE mode.

An idle MTCMOS circuit block is placed into a low-leakage SLEEP mode by turning off the header and the footer. During the transition from ACTIVE mode to SLEEP mode (deactivation process), C_1 is discharged slowly from an initial voltage of ~V_{DD} to an intermediate voltage level between V_{DD} and 0V by the leakage currents through the low-$|V_{th}|$ logic gates and the high-$|V_{th}|$ footer, as illustrated in Fig. 4. Similarly, C_2 is charged slowly from ~0V to an intermediate voltage level between V_{DD} and 0V by the leakage currents through the low-$|V_{th}|$ logic gates and the high-$|V_{th}|$ header. Following the transitions of virtual power and ground line voltages, the internal nodes of the low-$|V_{th}|$ circuit block also transition to intermediate steady-state voltage levels between V_{DD} and 0V by the leakage currents through the sleep transistors. The deactivation noise produced during ACTIVE to SLEEP mode transitions is typically insignificant [24], [35].

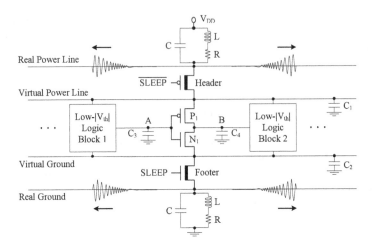

Fig. 3. A conventional MTCMOS circuit [6]. The parasitic impedances of internal nodes and package are illustrated in the figure. High-$|V_{th}|$ sleep transistors are represented with a thick line in the channel region.

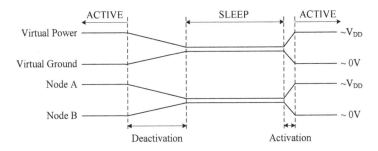

Fig. 4. Illustration of voltage transitions on virtual power line, virtual ground line, and internal nodes of a low-$|V_{th}|$ logic gate during mode transitions in a standard power and ground gated MTCMOS circuit.

When an activation command is issued by the on chip power management unit at the end of an idle period, the header and the footer are simultaneously turned on [36]. During the transition from SLEEP mode to ACTIVE mode (activation process), large instantaneous currents are produced as C_1 is being charged and C_2 is being discharged through the sleep transistors. Following the voltage transitions of the virtual power and ground lines, the voltages of the internal nodes of the low-$|V_{th}|$ logic circuitry also transition towards either ~V_{DD} or ~0V depending on the primary inputs applied to the power and ground gated circuit block, as illustrated in Fig. 4. The pull-up and pull-down network transistors of many low-$|V_{th}|$ logic gates, such as P_1 and N_1 in Fig. 3, are simultaneously activated due to the degraded voltage levels of internal nodes (such as node "A": $0V < V_{Node\_A} < V_{DD}$). Significant short circuit currents are thereby produced by the logic circuitry during the activation process [6]. These transient charging, discharging, and short circuit currents flow through the package parasitic impedances. The voltages of power and ground distribution networks are thereby disturbed.

The intensity of voltage disturbance is related to the rate of change of instantaneous current (dI/dt) conducted by sleep transistors during an activation event. The rate of change of instantaneous current is primarily determined by the power supply voltage, the size of sleep transistors, the amount of charge that is transferred through sleep transistors, and the voltage swing of virtual lines during activation events [6]. The peak amplitude of mode transition noise is increased with a higher supply voltage and a higher voltage swing on the virtual lines. Larger sleep transistors are desirable to achieve higher speed by lowering the resistive voltage drop across sleep transistors in an active MTCMOS circuit. Larger sleep transistors, however, also cause stronger current surges during mode transitions, thereby increasing the bouncing noise induced on the power and ground distribution networks. The steady-state SLEEP-mode voltages of the internal nodes and the delay of SLEEP-to-ACTIVE mode transition determine the intensity and duration of short circuit currents that are produced by the low-$|V_{th}|$ transistors during a wake-up event. Higher and longer short circuit currents cause stronger current surges through sleep transistors, thereby exacerbating the noise produced during SLEEP to ACTIVE mode transitions.

3   Tri-mode MTCMOS Circuits

Various circuit techniques are described in literature to suppress power and ground bouncing noise produced by MTCMOS circuits during activation events [4] – [20]. A specialized low-noise MTCMOS circuit technique with three operational modes (tri-mode) is described in this section. A threshold voltage tuning methodology is also introduced to further reduce the activation noise with smaller sleep transistors and shorter delay in a tri-mode MTCMOS circuit. The power and ground gated tri-mode MTCMOS circuit techniques are introduced in Section 3.1. The threshold voltage tuning technique based on forward body bias is presented in Section 3.2.

3.1   Power and Ground Gated Tri-mode MTCMOS

The ground-gated tri-mode MTCMOS circuit technique [4] is illustrated in Fig. 5. A zero-body-biased high-$|V_{th}|$ PMOS sleep transistor (parker) is connected in parallel with a high-V_{th} NMOS sleep transistor (footer). A tri-mode MTCMOS circuit operates in three modes: SLEEP, PARK, and ACTIVE.

When a tri-mode MTCMOS circuit is idle, the sleep transistors (footer and parker) are cut off to place the circuit into low-leakage SLEEP mode as shown in Fig. 6(a). The virtual ground line is raised to approximately the power supply voltage V_{DD} during SLEEP mode. The effective supply voltage that is experienced by the MTCMOS circuit is completely crushed to approximately 0V. The subthreshold leakage currents that are produced by the low-$|V_{th}|$ circuit block are thereby suppressed in SLEEP mode.

When an activation command is issued by the on chip power management unit at the end of an idle period, the parker is turned on while the footer is maintained cut-off as illustrated in Fig. 6(b). Prior to the activation of the circuit, the circuit transitions to the intermediate PARK mode. The virtual ground line is discharged to the threshold voltage of parker ($|V_{tp}|$) as shown in Fig. 6(b). The first wave of activation noise is produced during the transition from SLEEP mode to PARK mode.

Subsequently, the circuit transitions from PARK mode to ACTIVE mode in order to complete the activation process. Footer is turned on to discharge the virtual ground line to ~0V as shown in Fig. 6(c). The second wave of activation noise is produced during this transition from PARK mode to ACTIVE mode. The effective supply voltage of low-$|V_{th}|$ circuit block is approximately equal to the power supply voltage V_{DD} in the ACTIVE mode. The tri-mode MTCMOS circuit thereby resumes normal high performance ACTIVE mode of operation.

The activation noise is reduced by lowering the voltage swing on the virtual ground line and restricting the current surge through the sleep transistors with a two-step transition from SLEEP mode to ACTIVE mode through PARK mode in a tri-mode MTCMOS circuit [4], [6]. The activation noise can be minimized by adjusting (optimizing) the size of parker in a tri-mode MTCMOS circuit [6], [7], [12].

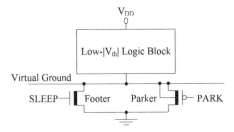

Fig. 5. The standard ground-gated tri-mode MTCMOS circuit with a zero-body-biased high-$|V_{th}|$ parker [4]. High-$|V_{th}|$ sleep transistors are represented with a thick line in the channel region.

An alternative power-gated MTCMOS circuit with three modes of operation is illustrated in Fig. 7. A high-V_{th} NMOS sleep transistor (parker) is connected in parallel with a high-$|V_{th}|$ PMOS sleep transistor (header) to implement a power gating structure with three distinct modes of operation.

In SLEEP mode, both header and parker are cut off to suppress the subthreshold leakage currents in a power-gated tri-mode MTCMOS circuit. The virtual power line is discharged to ~0V by the leakage currents produced by the low-$|V_{th}|$ circuit block as illustrated in Fig. 7(a). At the end of the idle mode, the power-gated tri-mode MTCMOS circuit is activated in two steps. Before the power-gated tri-mode MTCMOS circuit is awaken, the circuit initially transitions from SLEEP mode to the intermediate PARK mode. The parker is activated while the header is maintained cut-off, as shown in Fig. 7(b). The virtual power line is charged from ~0V to ($V_{DD} - V_{tn}$), where V_{tn} is the threshold voltage of the NMOS parker. The first wave of activation noise is produced during the transition from SLEEP mode to PARK mode. With the subsequent second step of activation, the circuit transitions from PARK mode to ACTIVE mode. Header is turned on to charge the virtual power line to approximately the power supply voltage V_{DD} as shown in Fig. 7(c). The tri-mode circuit is thereby fully activated and operates with high performance. The second wave of activation noise is produced during the transition from PARK mode to ACTIVE mode. The voltage swing on virtual power line and the current surge through sleep transistors are reduced during both SLEEP mode to PARK mode and PARK mode to ACTIVE mode wake-up steps. The activation noise is thereby suppressed in a power-gated tri-mode MTCMOS circuit.

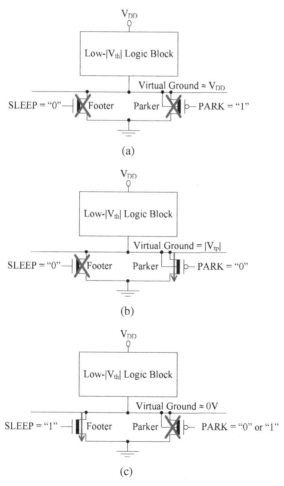

Fig. 6. Three modes of operation with a ground-gated tri-mode MTCMOS circuit [4]. (a) SLEEP mode. (b) PARK mode. (c) ACTIVE mode. PARK signal could be "0" or "1" in the ACTIVE mode. High-$|V_{th}|$ sleep transistors are represented with a thick line in the channel region. V_{tp}: the threshold voltage of PMOS parker.

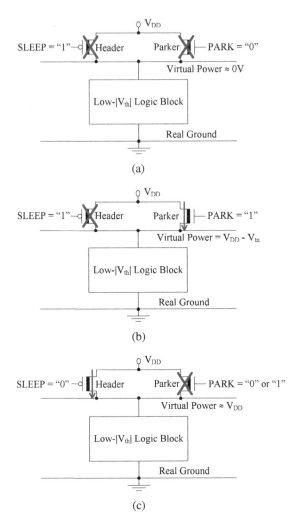

Fig. 7. Three modes of operation with a power-gated tri-mode MTCMOS circuit. (a) SLEEP mode. (b) PARK mode. (c) ACTIVE mode. PARK signal could be "0" or "1" in the ACTIVE mode. High-$|V_{th}|$ sleep transistors are represented with a thick line in the channel region. V_{tn}: the threshold voltage of NMOS parker.

3.2   Tri-mode MTCMOS with Threshold Voltage Tuning

Tri-mode MTCMOS circuit technique is effective for suppressing mode transition noise as compared to the standard power and/or ground gated MTCMOS circuits as described in Section 3.1. The optimum parker size that minimizes the activation noise is however typically large, thereby causing significant area and mode transition energy overheads in a tri-mode MTCMOS circuit [7] – [9], [12]. Furthermore, due to the intentionally delayed two-step wake-up mechanism, the activation speed is significantly degraded with the tri-mode MTCMOS technique as compared to the standard power and/or ground gated MTCMOS circuits [6] – [7]. A design strategy based on forward body bias is described in this section for further reduction of noise, shortening of activation delay, and miniaturization of sleep transistors in tri-mode MTCMOS circuits.

Two forward-body-biased ground-gated tri-mode MTCMOS circuits are shown in Fig. 8. The parker in the body-biased tri-mode circuit can have either high-$|V_{th}|$ or low-$|V_{th}|$ as shown in Fig. 8 [7] – [9]. The body of the parker is connected to a body bias voltage generator. The threshold voltage of parker is dynamically adjusted during all three modes of operation (SLEEP, PARK, and ACTIVE). A standard n-well process, a twin-well process with a p-type substrate, or a triple-well fabrication process is required to be able to tune the body voltage of the PMOS parker. The threshold voltage of parker is lowered by applying forward body bias. The amplitude of the first wave of activation noise is therefore increased during the transition from SLEEP mode to PARK mode. Alternatively, a parker with a lower threshold voltage suppresses the second wave of activation noise produced during the subsequent PARK to ACTIVE mode transition. The peak activation noise is further inhibited by reducing the size of the forward body biased parker. SLEEP to ACTIVE mode transition speed is also enhanced with the forward body bias technique in a tri-mode MTCMOS circuit.

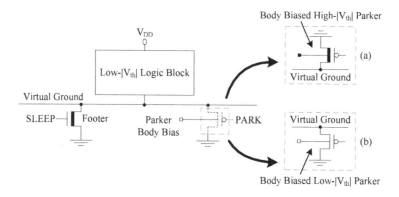

Fig. 8. Ground-gated tri-mode MTCMOS circuits with forward-body-biased parkers [7] – [9]. (a) Tri-mode MTCMOS circuit with a forward-body-biased high-$|V_{th}|$ parker. (b) Tri-mode MTCMOS circuit with a forward-body-biased low-$|V_{th}|$ parker.

The source terminal of parker is attached to the virtual ground line. The voltage of the virtual ground line varies with the mode of operation of an MTCMOS circuit, the size of parker, and the size of the low-$|V_{th}|$ circuit block. The conventional forward body bias techniques that are presented in [39] – [42] therefore cannot be directly applied to the parker. A dynamic forward body bias generator that is suitable for tri-mode MTCMOS circuits is introduced in [7] – [11]. The circuit is shown in Fig. 9. A low-$|V_{th}|$ NMOS transistor (biaser) and a negative DC voltage source (V_{bias}) are attached to a tri-mode MTCMOS circuit to produce a dynamically adjusted body voltage for the parker. The biaser is maintained cut-off by shorting the gate and the source terminals. The drain current of the biaser controls the body bias voltage of the parker. D_1 and D_2 are the source-to-body and drain-to-body p-n junctions, respectively, of the parker as shown in Fig. 9.

During the SLEEP mode, the virtual ground line is charged to approximately the power supply voltage V_{DD}. The body of the parker is maintained at a voltage level between V_{DD} and 0V. D_1 is forward biased. During the subsequent PARK mode, the virtual ground line is discharged to the threshold voltage of the parker $|V_{tp}|$. The body of the parker is maintained at a voltage level between $|V_{tp}|$ and V_{bias}. D_1 continues to be forward biased. Finally, during the ACTIVE mode, the virtual ground line is discharged to ~0V. The body of the parker is maintained at a voltage level between 0V and V_{bias}. The parker thereby experiences forward body bias in all three modes of operation (SLEEP, PARK, and ACTIVE) with this dynamic forward body bias generator. The forward body bias voltage of the parker is adjusted by tuning the negative DC voltage source V_{bias}.

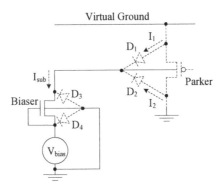

Fig. 9. The dynamic forward body bias generator for the parker [7] – [11]

The SLEEP mode leakage power consumption increases with a dynamic-forward-body-biased parker since there is no header sleep transistor to restrict the subthreshold leakage currents in a ground-gated tri-mode MTCMOS circuit. The body diode currents of the parker and the biaser further increase the leakage power consumption of a tri-mode MTCMOS circuit. The leakage power consumption can be restricted to an acceptably low level by adjusting the external DC bias voltage V_{bias}.

Provided that the threshold voltage tuning technique is applied to a power-gated tri-mode MTCMOS circuit, parker (in Fig. 7) needs to be forward-body-biased. A standard p-well process, a twin-well process with an n-type substrate, or a triple-well fabrication process is required to be able to tune the body voltage of the NMOS parker in a power-gated tri-mode MTCMOS circuit.

4   Low-Leakage Tri-mode MTCMOS Memory Elements

Data preservation is typically a critical requirement of leakage reduction techniques applicable to memory elements. A low-leakage data retention SLEEP mode is desirable for energy-efficiency in modern nanoscale sequential circuits and static random access memory arrays. If the standard MTCMOS techniques (illustrated in Fig. 1) are directly applied to memory elements, the logic states of the circuits are lost in SLEEP mode. The retrieval of the previously stored data for post-sleep system state restoration costs significant energy and timing overheads when the power and/or ground gated memory circuits are activated [10], [11]. A low leakage SLEEP mode with data preservation capability is, therefore, critical for achieving truly energy efficient MTCMOS data storage elements such as flip-flops and static random access memory arrays [3], [10], [11], [29] – [35].

In addition to utilization for effective mode transition noise suppression, tri-mode MTCMOS technique can also be used to implement a low-leakage data preserving SLEEP mode in memory elements. Applications of the tri-mode MTCMOS technique to sequential circuits and static memory arrays are introduced in this section. Tri-mode MTCMOS flip-flops are presented in Section 4.1. Tri-mode MTCMOS static random access memory arrays are discussed in Section 4.2.

4.1   Sequential Tri-mode MTCMOS Circuits

Sequential tri-mode MTCMOS circuits with data preserving leakage reduction capabilities are presented in this section. A ground-gated tri-mode MTCMOS flip-flop is illustrated in Fig. 10 [10], [11], [13]. All of the devices on the forward and feedback paths of a tri-mode MTCMOS flip-flop have low threshold voltages. A high-$|V_{th}|$ PMOS sleep transistor (holder) is connected in parallel with a high-V_{th} NMOS sleep transistor (footer) to implement a low-leakage data preserving SLEEP mode as shown in Fig. 10.

When a tri-mode MTCMOS flip-flop is idle, the (data) holder is activated while the footer is maintained cut-off as illustrated in Fig. 10. The circuit transitions from ACTIVE mode to data preserving SLEEP mode. The virtual ground line is raised to the threshold voltage of the holder ($|V_{tp}|$). The circuit is capable of lowering the leakage power consumption while retaining the data by maintaining a reduced yet significant voltage difference ($V_{DD} - |V_{tp}|$) between the power supply and the virtual ground line, as illustrated in Fig. 10.

During the ACTIVE mode, the footer is turned on while the holder is cut off as illustrated in Fig. 11. The footer is typically sized to achieve similar delay (sum of setup time and Clock-to-Q propagation delay) with the tri-mode MTCMOS flip-flop as compared to a standard single low-$|V_{th}|$ flip-flop without any power or ground gating [11], [32]. The virtual ground line is discharged to ~0V by the appropriately sized (low channel resistance) footer sleep transistor. The effective supply voltage applied to the low-$|V_{th}|$ circuit is approximately equal to the power supply voltage V_{DD}. The circuit thereby resumes normal high speed operations in ACTIVE mode.

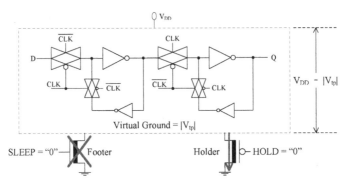

Fig. 10. Data preserving low-leakage SLEEP mode in a ground-gated tri-mode MTCMOS flip-flop. High-$|V_{th}|$ transistors are represented with a thick line in the channel region.

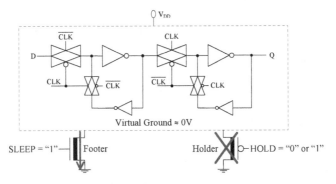

Fig. 11. Ground-gated tri-mode MTCMOS flip-flop in ACTIVE mode [10], [11], [13]. HOLD signal could be "0" or "1" in the ACTIVE mode. High-$|V_{th}|$ transistors are represented with a thick line in the channel region.

Unlike the low-leakage sequential circuits that are presented in [3] and [29] – [32], no additional data storage or restoration procedures are required during ACTIVE to SLEEP and SLEEP to ACTIVE mode transitions in a tri-mode MTCMOS flip-flop. The noise produced by tri-mode MTCMOS flip-flop is also suppressed due to the smaller centralized sleep transistors and the lower voltage swing on the virtual ground line as compared to other state-of-the-art sequential MTCMOS circuits during the data preserving SLEEP mode to ACTIVE mode transitions [10], [11], [13].

In addition to offering a low-leakage data preserving SLEEP mode, the tri-mode MTCMOS flip-flops also provide an optional minimum leakage deep SLEEP mode [11], [13]. When the data are not required to be maintained, the idle tri-mode MTCMOS flip-flops can transition to an alternative minimum leakage deep SLEEP mode (SLEEP = 0 and HOLD = V_{DD}) where the data are lost. Leakage savings are maximized by turning off the footer and the holder in the deep SLEEP mode at the cost of losing the pre-sleep circuit state.

Tri-mode MTCMOS technique can also be applied to a power-gated flip-flop, as illustrated in Fig. 12. The tri-mode power gating structure is composed of a high-V_{th} NMOS data preserving sleep transistor (holder) and a high-$|V_{th}|$ PMOS sleep transistor (header). In ACTIVE mode, the header is activated to maintain the virtual power line voltage at $\sim V_{DD}$. The power-gated tri-mode MTCMOS flip-flop thereby operates with high performance. When the flip-flop is idle, the holder is turned on. The header is cut off. The flip-flop transitions into the data preserving SLEEP mode as illustrated in Fig. 13. The effective supply voltage experienced by the low-$|V_{th}|$ circuit block is compressed to ($V_{DD} - V_{tn}$). The data is retained and the leakage power consumption is reduced by squeezing the supply voltage of the cross-coupled inverters. Alternatively, if data preservation is not essential, both sleep transistors could be simultaneously turned off to minimize the leakage power consumption in an optional deep SLEEP mode.

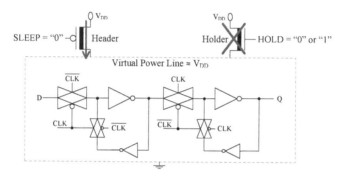

Fig. 12. Power-gated tri-mode MTCMOS flip-flop in ACTIVE mode. HOLD signal could be "0" or "1" in the ACTIVE mode. High-$|V_{th}|$ transistors are represented with a thick line in the channel region.

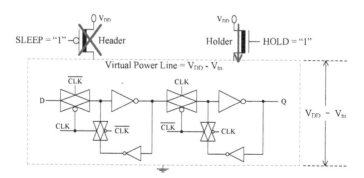

Fig. 13. Data preserving low-leakage SLEEP mode in a power-gated tri-mode MTCMOS flip-flop. High-$|V_{th}|$ transistors are represented with a thick line in the channel region.

4.2   Tri-mode MTCMOS Memory Arrays

Amount of on-die memory cache increases in high performance integrated circuits such as microprocessors in each new CMOS technology generation [23]. Huge embedded memory banks are primary producers of leakage currents in modern microprocessors [2], [21] – [26], [33], [34], [43] – [47]. Leakage reduction without loss of data in idle static random access memory (SRAM) arrays is another important application of tri-mode MTCMOS circuit technique. In [21], ground-gated tri-mode SRAM arrays are presented to suppress leakage currents while maintaining data when memory banks are idle. A ground-gated tri-mode MTCMOS SRAM circuit is illustrated in Fig. 14. Similar to a tri-mode MTCMOS flip-flop, a high-$|V_{th}|$ PMOS sleep transistor (holder) is utilized together with a high-V_{th} NMOS sleep transistor (footer) to implement a low-leakage data preserving SLEEP mode in a tri-mode MTCMOS memory array.

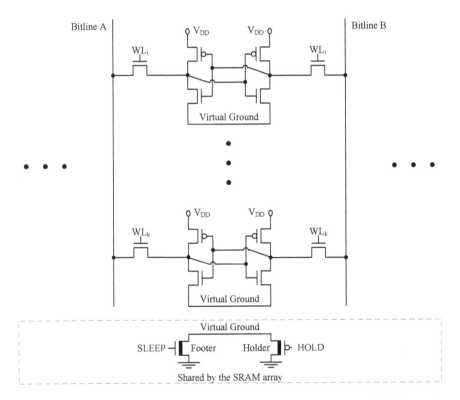

Fig. 14. Column of a ground-gated tri-mode MTCMOS memory array with six-transistor SRAM cells [21], [33], [34]. High-$|V_{th}|$ transistors are represented with a thick line in the channel region. WL: wordline. i and k: memory array row indices.

The ground-gated tri-mode MTCMOS memory array is operated as follows. In ACTIVE mode, the centralized high-V_{th} footer is turned on while the high-$|V_{th}|$ PMOS holder is cut off. The virtual ground line is maintained at ~0V. Prior to a read operation, both bitlines are charged to V_{DD} [43] – [47]. Wordline (WL) signal of the selected memory row transitions to V_{DD} to initiate a read operation as illustrated in Fig. 15(a). Provided that "0" is stored on Node_A, bitline A is discharged through N_3, N_1, and footer. Meanwhile, bitline B is maintained at V_{DD}. When a sufficient voltage difference is produced between the two bitlines, the data that is stored in the selected memory cell is sensed by an amplifier. Alternatively, prior to a write operation, one of the bitlines (for example, bitline A) is discharged to ~0V while the other bitline (for example, bitline B) is maintained at V_{DD} depending on the incoming data [43] – [47]. WL transitions to V_{DD} to start a write operation as illustrated in Fig. 15(b). The data in the memory cell is flipped with brute force. A "0" is forced into the selected SRAM cell through the discharged bitline [43] – [47].

When the memory array is idle, the SRAM circuit transitions into the data preserving low-leakage SLEEP mode. Footer is cut off while the holder is turned on as shown in Fig. 15(c). The virtual ground line rises to the threshold voltage of the holder ($|V_{tp}|$). The effective supply voltage that is experienced by the cross-coupled inverters of the SRAM cells is compressed to ($V_{DD} - |V_{tp}|$) as illustrated in Fig. 15(c). The data is thereby maintained while the leakage currents are reduced.

In an additional (optional) deep SLEEP mode, the data in the memory arrays could be flushed in order to minimize the leakage power consumption when the system is idle. Footer and holder are simultaneously cut off in the deep SLEEP mode. The virtual ground line rises to ~V_{DD}. The effective supply voltage experienced by each SRAM cell is completely crushed to approximately 0V. The leakage currents are thereby significantly reduced while the data in the memory cells are lost.

Tri-mode MTCMOS technique is also applicable to a power-gated memory array, as illustrated in Fig. 16. Similar to a power-gated tri-mode MTCMOS flip-flop, a high-V_{th} NMOS sleep transistor (holder) is employed in parallel with a high-$|V_{th}|$ PMOS sleep transistor (header) to implement a data preserving SLEEP mode in a power-gated tri-mode MTCMOS memory array. The header is cut off while the holder is activated in the data preserving SLEEP mode. The virtual power line is discharged to ($V_{DD} - V_{tn}$). A lower supply voltage that is sufficient to preserve the data is provided to the idle memory cells. Due to the squeezed effective supply voltage ($V_{DD} - V_{tn}$), leakage power consumption of memory circuit is reduced.

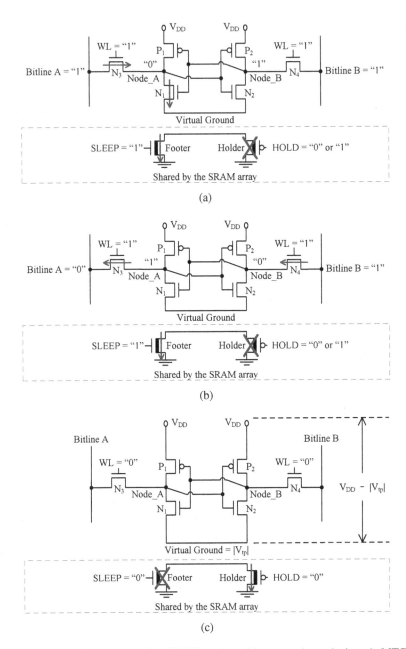

Fig. 15. ACTIVE and data preserving SLEEP modes with a ground-gated tri-mode MTCMOS six-transistor SRAM cell. (a) ACTIVE mode: read operation. HOLD signal could be "0" or "1" in the ACTIVE mode. (b) ACTIVE mode: write operation with discharged bitline A. (c) Data preserving SLEEP mode. High-$|V_{th}|$ transistors are represented with a thick line in the channel region. WL: wordline.

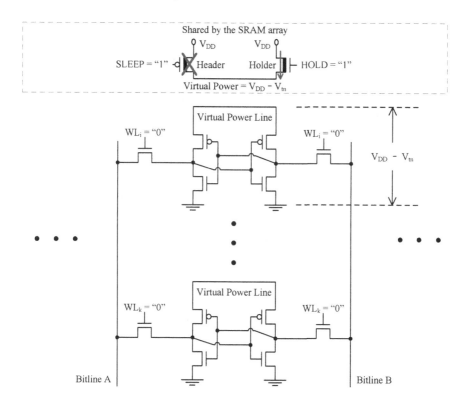

Fig. 16. Data preserving low-leakage SLEEP mode in a power-gated tri-mode MTCMOS memory array with six-transistor SRAM cells. High-$|V_{th}|$ transistors are represented with a thick line in the channel region. WL: wordline. i and k: memory array row indices.

5   Case Study: 32-bit Tri-mode MTCMOS Brent-Kung Adders

As a case study, various design options of 32-bit tri-mode MTCMOS Brent-Kung adders are discussed in this section. The UMC 80nm multi-threshold voltage CMOS technology (high-V_{th_NMOS} = +370mV, low-V_{th_NMOS} = +155mV, high-V_{th_PMOS} = −310mV, low-V_{th_PMOS} = −105mV, and V_{DD} = 1V) [50] is used for the characterization of MTCMOS circuits. Activation noise characteristics of tri-mode MTCMOS circuits are evaluated with post-layout simulation data. The parasitic impedance model of the 40-pin Dual In-line Package [5] − [13] is used to evaluate the mode transition noise phenomenon. The simulation temperature is 90°C [48].

The noise signals generated on the power and ground distribution networks have similar characteristics in MTCMOS circuits [5], [6], [16], [49]. The adders considered in this case study are ground-gated tri-mode MTCMOS circuits. The following discussion is primarily focused on the characterization of ground distribution network bouncing noise. The footer sleep transistors of different ground-gated MTCMOS adders are sized 5μm to achieve similar (within 5%) delays along the critical signal propagation paths as compared to the a 32-bit standard single low-$|V_{th}|$ Brent-Kung adder.

This section is organized as follows. Parker sizing for achieving minimum noise in tri-mode MTCMOS circuits is discussed in Section 5.1. The use of threshold voltage tuning for further noise reduction and parker size miniaturization in tri-mode MTCMOS circuits is described in Section 5.2. Design tradeoffs among ground bouncing noise, activation delay, leakage power consumption, active power consumption, and layout area are presented in Section 5.3 with different 32-bit tri-mode MTCMOS Brent-Kung adders.

5.1   Parker Sizing for Achieving Minimum Noise in Tri-mode MTCMOS Circuits

The activation noise produced by a tri-mode MTCMOS circuit can be minimized by adjusting (optimizing) the size of parker [6], [7], [12]. The peak ground bouncing noise produced by a 32-bit ground-gated tri-mode MTCMOS adder is shown in Fig. 17 for various parker sizes. The noise produced by the adder is minimized with a parker size of 21μm as shown in Fig. 17.

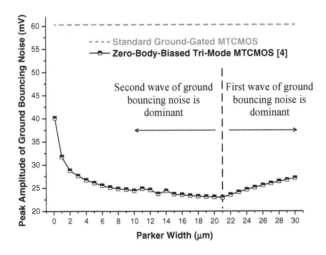

Fig. 17. Peak amplitude of ground bouncing noise produced by a 32-bit ground-gated tri-mode MTCMOS adder with zero-body-biased high-$|V_{th}|$ parker [12]. The peak ground bouncing noise produced by the standard ground-gated 32-bit adder is demarcated with a dashed gray line for comparison. Minimum parker width on the x-axis is 0.12μm.

When the parker width (W_{parker}) is smaller than the optimum width (21μm) that minimizes the peak activation noise, a higher voltage swing on the virtual ground line and a stronger current surge are observed during the PARK to ACTIVE mode transition as compared to the SLEEP to PARK mode transition. The second noise waveform that is produced during PARK to ACTIVE mode transition is therefore the dominant source of voltage disturbance on the ground distribution network for W_{parker} < 21μm. Alternatively, when the parker is wider than the optimum, the voltage swing on the virtual ground line and the discharging current through the parker are increased during the SLEEP to PARK mode transitions. The first wave of noise that is produced during SLEEP to PARK mode transition is therefore more significant as compared to the second noise waveform that is produced during PARK to ACTIVE mode transition. The ground bouncing noise produced by the tri-mode MTCMOS circuit is minimized by equalizing the peak amplitudes of the two noise waveforms with a parker size of approximately 21µm as shown in Figs. 17 and 18 [7] – [9], [12].

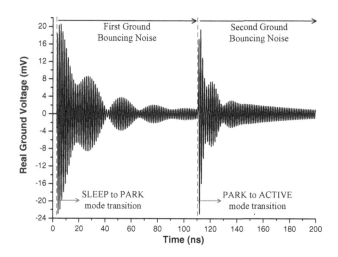

Fig. 18. Noise waveforms on the real ground wires of a 32-bit ground-gated tri-mode MTCMOS adder with zero-body-biased high-$|V_{th}|$ parker during a transition from SLEEP mode to ACTIVE mode through PARK mode [12]. Peak noise = 22.95mV. Parker size is optimized for equilibrium at zero body bias (ZBB). Optimum W_{parker_ZBB} = 21µm. Relaxation time = 107.83ns. The relaxation time is the duration of PARK mode which guarantees that the voltage on the virtual ground line is within 5mV of the steady-state PARK-mode voltage and that the amplitude of the first wave of ground bouncing noise on the real ground is within 1mV of the ideal ground reference voltage (0V) [7], [12].

5.2   Noise Suppression and Parker Size Minimization with Threshold Voltage Tuning

Threshold voltage tuning for further reduction of activation noise in tri-mode MTCMOS circuits is described in Section 3.2. The effectiveness of parker threshold voltage tuning for noise suppression and transistor size reduction is evaluated with the 32-bit Brent-Kung adder case study in this section.

The parasitic capacitors in a ground-gated tri-mode MTCMOS circuit are illustrated in Fig. 19. The parasitic capacitance of the internal nodes of the low-$|V_{th}|$ logic blocks are represented by C_1 and C_2. Parasitic capacitors of the footer, the parker, the low-$|V_{th}|$ transistors, and the virtual ground wire are lumped in C_3.

As discussed in Section 5.1, the ground bouncing noise produced by a zero-body-biased 32-bit tri-mode MTCMOS adder is minimized with a parker size of 21µm. When a forward body bias (FBB) voltage of 700mV is applied to a 21µm wide parker, the threshold voltage of parker is reduced. The voltage swing of the virtual ground line and the current surge through the parker are increased due to the stronger parker during the SLEEP to PARK mode transition. Alternatively, the virtual ground line voltage swing and the current surge through the footer are attenuated during the subsequent PARK to ACTIVE mode transition as compared to the zero-body-biased tri-mode MTCMOS circuit. The first wave of ground bouncing noise is thereby increased while the second wave of ground bouncing noise is suppressed with the forward body bias technique as compared to the zero-body-biased tri-mode MTCMOS circuit. The balance between the amplitudes of the two waves of ground bouncing noise is disturbed by forward body bias as illustrated in Fig. 20. The peak ground bouncing noise is therefore increased with the forward body bias technique as compared with the zero-body-biased tri-mode MTCMOS circuit for this parker size of 21µm.

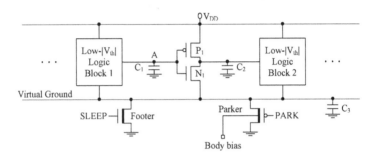

Fig. 19. Parasitic capacitors in a tri-mode MTCMOS circuit [12]. High-$|V_{th}|$ sleep transistors are represented with a thick line in the channel region.

The ground bouncing noise produced by a forward-body-biased circuit can be mitigated by reducing the parker width as compared to a zero-body-biased tri-mode MTCMOS circuit. As shown in Figs. 21 and 22, when the parker width is scaled to 7.8µm at a forward body bias voltage of 700mV, the peak amplitudes of the two noise waveforms are equalized. C_3 (see Fig. 19) is reduced due to the miniaturization of the parker in the forward-body-biased circuit as compared to the zero-body-biased tri-mode MTCMOS circuit. Furthermore, the steady-state SLEEP mode voltage on the virtual ground line is reduced with the forward-body-biased parker as compared to the zero-body-biased tri-mode MTCMOS adder. The voltage swing on the virtual ground line is smaller during the SLEEP to ACTIVE mode transitions. The charge dumped to the real ground is thereby suppressed together with the current surges through the sleep transistors and the overall ground bouncing noise in a forward-body-biased circuit. As shown in Figs. 21 and 22, when the new equilibrium between the two noise waveforms is reached at a significantly smaller parker width of 7.8µm (62.86% size reduction), the peak noise amplitude is also further suppressed down to 18.38mV (19.91% noise reduction). Forward body biasing and resizing (re-optimizing) the parker thereby lowers both the activation noise and the size of the noise-control transistor in a tri-mode MTCMOS circuit.

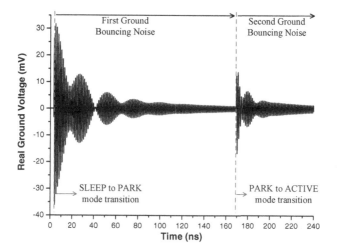

Fig. 20. Noise waveforms on the real ground wires of a tri-mode MTCMOS adder with forward-body-biased high-$|V_{th}|$ parker during a transition from SLEEP mode to ACTIVE mode through PARK mode [12]. Equilibrium between the peak amplitudes of the first and second primary noise events is disturbed by forward body bias. W_{parker_FBB} = 21µm. Relaxation time (defined in Fig. 18 caption) = 166.11ns. FBB = 700mV. Peak noise = 36.07mV.

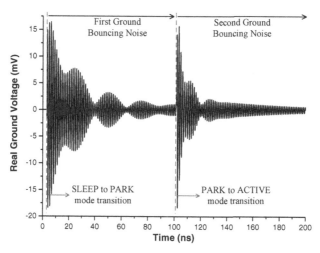

Fig. 21. Noise waveforms on the real ground wires of a tri-mode MTCMOS adder with forward-body-biased high-$|V_{th}|$ parker during a transition from SLEEP mode to ACTIVE mode through PARK mode [12]. Forward-body-biased parker is resized (re-optimized) to reach a new equilibrium between the two noise waveforms. Re-optimized W_{parker_FBB} = 7.8µm. Relaxation time (defined in Fig. 18 caption) = 98.45ns. FBB = 700mV. Peak noise = 18.38mV.

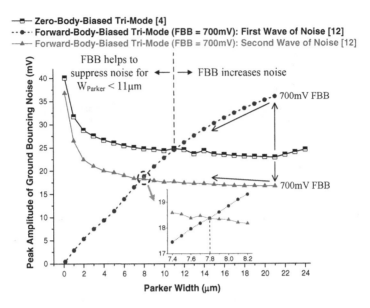

Fig. 22. The effect of forward body bias (FBB) on the peak ground bouncing noise produced by a tri-mode MTCMOS adder [12]. Minimum parker width on the x-axis is 0.12μm.

5.3   Characterization of Noise-Aware MTCMOS Techniques

Various design metrics are characterized and evaluated with the following techniques in this section: the standard single low-$|V_{th}|$ CMOS, standard ground-gated MTCMOS, ground-gated tri-mode MTCMOS with zero-body-biased high-$|V_{th}|$ parker (ZBB tri-mode) as shown in Fig. 5, ground-gated tri-mode MTCMOS with forward-body-biased high-$|V_{th}|$ parker (FBB tri-mode H) as shown in Fig. 8(a), and ground-gated tri-mode MTCMOS with forward-body-biased low-$|V_{th}|$ parker (FBB tri-mode L) as shown in Fig. 8(b). The power and ground bouncing noise produced by activated MTCMOS circuits are evaluated in Section 5.3.1. The activation delays of MTCMOS circuits are presented in Section 5.3.2. The SLEEP mode leakage power consumptions of different circuits are compared in Section 5.3.3. The active power consumptions of the circuits are discussed in Section 5.3.4. The layout areas are compared in Section 5.3.5. The overall electrical quality of the tri-mode MTCMOS circuits are evaluated in Section 5.3.6.

5.3.1   Power and Ground Bouncing Noise

Power and ground bouncing noise produced by MTCMOS circuits during SLEEP to ACTIVE mode transitions are characterized in this section. The forward body bias generator that is shown in Fig. 9 is employed within the FBB tri-mode H and FBB tri-mode L circuits. V_{bias} and parker width are optimized to minimize the ground bouncing noise produced by different tri-mode MTCMOS circuits.

There is a unique optimum forward body bias voltage (FBB$_{optimum}$) that minimizes the peak ground bouncing noise produced by a tri-mode MTCMOS circuit [9]. FBB$_{optimum}$ varies with the parker width. To be able to produce the optimum forward body bias voltages that minimize the peak ground bouncing noise with different parker sizes, an additional voltage reference (V$_{bias}$) is employed in the body bias generator as shown in Fig. 9 [7] – [9]. V$_{bias}$ is swept from 0V to -700mV to minimize the peak ground bouncing noise of tri-mode MTCMOS circuits with different sizes of parkers. The optimum DC bias voltages V$_{bias}$ that minimize the noise for different sizes of parkers in the FBB tri-mode H and FBB tri-mode L circuits are shown in Fig. 23. The minimum applicable V$_{bias}$ is -700mV [41], [42] to avoid strong forward currents through the body diodes of the biaser in this study. The forward body bias voltage experienced by the source-to-body p-n junction (D$_1$ in Fig. 9) never exceeds 700mV, thereby ensuring the reliability of the parker. The biaser (see Fig. 9) is sized minimum (0.12µm) to lower the area and leakage current overheads. The peak ground bouncing noise produced by different tri-mode MTCMOS circuits are shown in Fig. 24.

Mode transition noise is significantly reduced by the tri-mode MTCMOS circuits as compared to the standard ground-gated adder as listed in Table 1. The ground bouncing noise is suppressed by up to 61.93%, 67.77%, and 72.50% with the ZBB tri-mode, FBB tri-mode H, and FBB tri-mode L circuits, respectively, as compared to standard ground-gated MTCMOS circuit. The FBB tri-mode L produces the lowest activation noise among the MTCMOS circuits that are evaluated in this case study. As shown in Fig. 24, the peak ground bouncing noise with the FBB tri-mode L is 27.76% lower as compared to the ZBB tri-mode MTCMOS circuit.

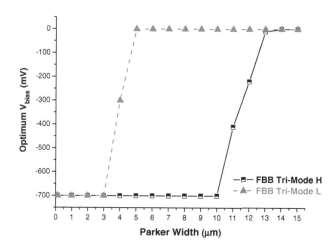

Fig. 23. The optimum DC bias voltages (V$_{bias}$) that minimize the activation noise in the FBB tri-mode H and FBB tri-mode L circuits with different sizes of parkers. The minimum parker width on the x-axis is 0.12µm. FBB: forward body bias.

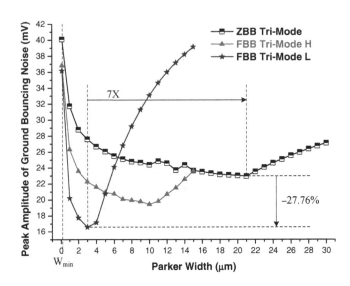

Fig. 24. The peak ground bouncing noise produced by different tri-mode MTCMOS circuits for various parker widths. The minimum parker width on the x-axis is 0.12μm. ZBB: zero body bias. FBB: forward body bias.

The peak noise produced by different MTCMOS circuits on the real power distribution network are also listed in Table 1. Similar to ground bouncing noise, the FBB tri-mode L produces the lowest peak power bouncing noise. The peak power bouncing noise is reduced by 71.66% and 26.35% with the FBB tri-mode L as compared to the standard ground-gated and ZBB tri-mode MTCMOS circuits, respectively.

The FBB tri-mode L has the smallest optimum parker size (that minimizes the peak ground bouncing noise) among the tri-mode MTCMOS circuits evaluated in this case study as listed in Table 1. The FBB tri-mode L reduces the optimum parker size by 85.71% as compared to the ZBB tri-mode MTCMOS circuit.

Table 1. Peak Activation Noise and Optimum Parker Sizes with Different MTCMOS Circuits

Circuit Technique	Peak Ground Bouncing Noise (mV)	Peak Power Bouncing Noise (mV)	Optimum Parker Size (μm)
Standard Ground-Gated	60.29	57.19	N/A
ZBB Tri-Mode	22.95	22.01	21
FBB Tri-Mode H	19.43	18.57	10
FBB Tri-Mode L	16.58	16.21	3

* ZBB: zero body bias. FBB: forward body bias.

5.3.2   Activation Delay

The activation delays of MTCMOS circuits are compared in this section [36] – [38]. Due to the two-step activation mechanism, the *activation delay* of a tri-mode MTCMOS circuit is

$$Activation\ Delay = Relaxation\ Time + Wake\ Up\ Delay, \qquad (1)$$

where *wake up delay* is the time interval from the 50% rising edge of the SLEEP signal until the virtual ground voltage stabilizes below 10mV. *Relaxation time* is defined in Fig. 18 caption. For the standard ground-gated MTCMOS circuits that directly transition from SLEEP mode to ACTIVE mode, there is no *relaxation time* and the *activation delay* is equal to the *wake up delay*.

Table 2. *Activation Delays* (ns) of Different MTCMOS Circuits

Circuit Technique	Relaxation Time	Wake Up Delay	Activation Delay
Standard Ground-Gated	N/A	15.29	15.29
ZBB Tri-Mode	107.82	12.16	119.98
FBB Tri-Mode H	101.12	9.36	110.48
FBB Tri-Mode L	75.95	4.84	80.79

* ZBB: zero body bias. FBB: forward body bias.

Due to the two-step activation mechanism, all the tri-mode MTCMOS circuits significantly increase the SLEEP to ACTIVE mode transition delay as compared to the standard ground-gated MTCMOS circuit, as listed in Table 2. Among the noise-aware MTCMOS circuit techniques, the ZBB tri-mode MTCMOS circuit has the longest *activation delay*. Alternatively, FBB tri-mode L provides the quickest activation primarily due to the lowest steady-state PARK mode voltage on the virtual ground line, the lowest threshold voltage of the forward-body-biased parker, and the fastest discharging of C_3 (see Fig. 19) among the tri-mode MTCMOS circuits that are evaluated in this case study. The FBB tri-mode L reduces the *activation delay* by 32.66% as compared to the ZBB tri-mode MTCMOS circuit.

5.3.3   Leakage Power Consumption

The worst case leakage power consumptions of the standard single low-$|V_{th}|$, standard ground-gated MTCMOS, ZBB tri-mode, FBB tri-mode H, and FBB tri-mode L circuits in the SLEEP mode are evaluated in this section. The leakage power consumed by the circuits at 25°C and 90°C are listed in Table 3. The percent leakage power savings provided by different MTCMOS circuit techniques as compared to the standard single low-$|V_{th}|$ circuit are shown in Fig. 25. The input vectors applied to the 32-bit adders are "0" [6].

The standard ground-gated MTCMOS circuit consumes the lowest leakage power among the circuits that are evaluated in this case study. As listed in Table 3, the leakage power consumption is reduced by up to 99.75%, 41.01%, 92.44%, and 95.05% by the standard ground-gated MTCMOS circuit as compared to the standard single low-$|V_{th}|$, ZBB tri-mode, FBB tri-mode H, and FBB tri-mode L circuits, respectively. Since the threshold voltage of the parker is the lowest and the forward biased p-n junction currents through the parker and biaser are the highest, the FBB tri-mode L consumes the highest leakage power in the SLEEP mode among the

MTCMOS circuits that are evaluated in this case study. Up to 20.20x and 11.92x higher leakage power is consumed by the FBB tri-mode L as compared to the standard ground-gated and ZBB tri-mode MTCMOS circuits, respectively.

Table 3. Leakage Power Consumption (nW) of Different Circuits

Circuit Technique	25°C	90°C
Standard Single Low-$|V_{th}|$	6971.40	30896.94
Standard Ground-Gated	60.92	75.74
ZBB Tri-Mode	65.41	128.40
FBB Tri-Mode H	341.12	1001.24
FBB Tri-Mode L	390.76	1530.14

* ZBB: zero body bias. FBB: forward body bias.

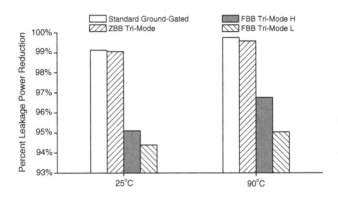

Fig. 25. Percent leakage power savings provided by different MTCMOS circuit techniques in SLEEP mode as compared to the standard single low-$|V_{th}|$ circuit. ZBB: zero body bias. FBB: forward body bias.

As shown in Fig. 25, up to 99.75%, 99.58%, 96.76%, and 95.05% leakage power savings are provided by the standard ground-gated MTCMOS, ZBB tri-mode, FBB tri-mode H, and FBB tri-mode L circuits, respectively, as compared to the standard single low-$|V_{th}|$ circuit. Despite the leakage overhead of the threshold voltage tuning techniques that are explored in this case study, all the tri-mode MTCMOS circuits (regardless of the body bias voltage of the parker) maintain the effectiveness in significantly suppressing the leakage power consumption as compared to a standard single low-$|V_{th}|$ Brent-Kung adder.

5.3.4   Active Power Consumption

The active power consumptions with different circuits are evaluated in this section. The input vectors applied to the 32-bit adders for the measurement of active power consumption are "FFFFFFFF" and "0". A 1 GHz square wave (rise and fall times are 50ps) is applied to the carry input of the adders. The simulation temperature is 90°C. The active power consumed by different circuits are listed in Table 4.

Due to the resistive voltage drop across the sleep transistors, the effective supply voltage experienced by the MTCMOS circuits is lower as compared to the standard single low-$|V_{th}|$ adder. The active power consumptions of MTCMOS circuits are therefore lower as compared to the low-$|V_{th}|$ adder as listed in Table 4. The standard ground-gated and tri-mode MTCMOS circuits reduce the active power consumption by up to 9.69% as compared with the standard single low-$|V_{th}|$ circuit.

Table 4. Active Power Consumption (μW) of Different Circuits

Circuit Technique	90°C
Standard Single Low-$|V_{th}|$	681
Standard Ground-Gated	615
ZBB Tri-Mode	615
FBB Tri-Mode H	616
FBB Tri-Mode L	618

* ZBB: zero body bias. FBB: forward body bias.

5.3.5   Layout Area

The layout area comparison of different circuits is provided in this section. The layout areas are listed in Table 5. Sleep transistors utilized in power and ground gated MTCMOS circuits increase the layout area as compared to a standard single low-$|V_{th}|$ adder. The area overheads of different MTCMOS circuit techniques as compared to the standard single low-$|V_{th}|$ Brent-Kung adder are shown in Fig. 26.

The additional DC voltage source V_{bias} in the forward-body-biased tri-mode circuits is assumed to be already available in the power management unit on chip. The overhead of this additional DC voltage source V_{bias} is not taken into consideration in area comparison.

The standard ground-gated MTCMOS circuit has the lowest area overhead among the MTCMOS circuits that are evaluated in this case study. Alternatively, the ZBB tri-mode MTCMOS circuit suffers from the highest area overhead as shown in Fig. 26. The ZBB tri-mode MTCMOS adder increases the layout area by up to 12.18% as compared to the standard single low-$|V_{th}|$ adder.

Table 5. Layout Areas ($μm^2$) of Different Circuits

Circuit Technique	Layout Area ($μm^2$)
Standard Single Low-$|V_{th}|$	1388
Standard Ground-Gated	1505
ZBB Tri-Mode	1557
FBB Tri-Mode H	1535
FBB Tri-Mode L	1520

* ZBB: zero body bias. FBB: forward body bias.

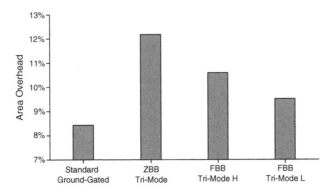

Fig. 26. The area overheads of different MTCMOS circuit techniques as compared to the standard single low-$|V_{th}|$ Brent-Kung adder. ZBB: zero body bias. FBB: forward body bias.

5.3.6 Comprehensive Comparison for Overall Quality

Tri-mode MTCMOS circuits rank different for various design metrics as discussed in the previous sections and as listed in Table 6. A comprehensive electrical *quality metric* that simultaneously considers ground bouncing noise, activation delay, and circuit layout area is evaluated in this section to rank the tri-mode MTCMOS circuit techniques. The *Quality Metric (QM)* is

$$QM = \frac{1}{Activation\ Noise \times Activation\ Delay \times Layout\ Area}. \tag{2}$$

FBB tri-mode L is identified as the most preferable circuit technique due to the lowest activation noise, fastest activation speed, and smallest area among the tri-mode MTCMOS circuits that are evaluated in this case study based on this *Quality Metric*. Alternatively, the zero-body-biased tri-mode MTCMOS circuit has the lowest overall *quality*. *Quality Metric* is enhanced by 2.11x with the FBB tri-mode L as compared with the zero-body-biased tri-mode MTCMOS circuit. The primary overhead of the forward-body-biased tri-mode MTCMOS techniques is the increased SLEEP mode leakage power consumption as compared to the zero-body-biased tri-mode MTCMOS circuit as discussed in Section 5.3.3.

Table 6. Performance Comparison of Different Tri-Mode MTCMOS Circuit Techniques

Primary Design Metric	Best Technique	Worst Technique
Ground Bouncing Noise	FBB Tri-Mode L	ZBB Tri-Mode
Activation Delay	FBB Tri-Mode L	ZBB Tri-Mode
Leakage Power Consumption	ZBB Tri-Mode	FBB Tri-Mode L
Active Power Consumption	ZBB Tri-Mode	FBB Tri-Mode L
Area	FBB Tri-Mode L	ZBB Tri-Mode
Quality Metric	FBB Tri-Mode L	ZBB Tri-Mode

* ZBB: zero body bias. FBB: forward body bias.

6   Chapter Summary

Power and ground bouncing noise that are produced during SLEEP to ACTIVE mode transitions are the most important reliability issues in MTCMOS circuits. Activation noise in MTCMOS circuits is examined in this chapter. Factors affecting the amplitude of mode transition noise are identified. A specialized MTCMOS technique with three modes of operation is described to suppress the activation noise in power and ground gated integrated circuits. A two-step wake-up mechanism with an additional intermediate PARK mode is employed with the tri-mode MTCMOS circuits. The activation noise is reduced by lowering the voltage swing on the virtual power and ground lines and limiting the current surges through the sleep transistors during the transitions from SLEEP mode to ACTIVE mode through PARK mode in a tri-mode MTCMOS circuit.

Different tri-mode MTCMOS circuit design options are explored to minimize the mode transition noise with smaller sleep transistors and shorter activation delay. The principal mechanisms of activation noise suppression and parker size reduction with threshold voltage tuned tri-mode MTCMOS circuits are explained. Design guidelines are provided for appropriate sizing of noise-control transistor and selection of body bias voltage to fully utilize the benefits of tri-mode MTCMOS circuit technique. Alternative applications of tri-mode MTCMOS for data preservation and leakage power reduction in idle memory elements are also described in this chapter.

References

1. Kursun, V., Friedman, E.G.: Multi-Voltage CMOS Circuit Design. John Wiley & Sons Ltd. (2006) ISBN # 0-470-01023-1
2. Kurd, N.A., Bhamidipati, S., Mozak, C., Miller, J.L., Mosalikanti, P., Wilson, T.M., El-Husseini, A.M., Neidengard, M., Aly, R.E., Nemani, M., Chowdhury, M., Kumar, R.: A family of 32nm IA processors. IEEE Journal of Solid-State Circuits 46(1), 119–130 (2011)
3. Mutoh, S., Douseki, T., Matsuya, Y., Aoki, T., Shigematsu, S., Yamada, J.: 1-V power supply high-speed digital circuit technology. IEEE Journal of Solid-State Circuits 30(8), 847–854 (1995)
4. Kim, S., Kosonocky, S.V., Knebel, D.R., Stawiasz, K., Papaefthymiou, M.C.: A multi-mode power gating structure for low-voltage deep-submicron CMOS ICs. IEEE Transactions on Circuits and Systems II 54(7), 586–590 (2007)
5. Kim, S., Kosonocky, S.V., Knebel, D.R.: Understanding and minimizing ground bounce during mode transition of power gating structures. In: Proceedings of the IEEE/ACM International Symposium on Low Power Electronics and Design, pp. 22–25 (August 2003)
6. Jiao, H., Kursun, V.: Ground-bouncing-noise-aware combinational MTCMOS circuits. IEEE Transactions on Circuits and Systems I 57(8), 2053–2065 (2010)
7. Jiao, H., Kursun, V.: Threshold voltage tuning for faster activation with lower noise in tri-mode MTCMOS circuits. IEEE Transactions on Very Large Scale Integration (VLSI) Systems 20(4) (2012)
8. Jiao, H., Kursun, V.: Dynamic forward body bias enhanced tri-mode MTCMOS. In: Proceedings of the IEEE Asia Symposium on Quality Electronic Design, pp. 33–37 (August 2010)

9. Jiao, H., Kursun, V.: Sleep transistor forward body bias: an extra knob to lower ground bouncing noise in MTCMOS circuits. In: Proceedings of the IEEE International SoC Design Conference, pp. 216–219 (November 2009)
10. Jiao, H., Kursun, V.: Reactivation noise suppression with threshold voltage tuning in sequential MTCMOS circuits. In: Proceedings of the IEEE International Conference on VLSI and System-on-Chip (VLSI-SoC), pp. 347–351 (September 2010)
11. Jiao, H., Kursun, V.: Noise-aware data preserving sequential MTCMOS circuits with dynamic forward body bias. Journal of Circuits, Systems, and Computers 20(1), 125–145 (2011)
12. Jiao, H., Kursun, V.: How forward body bias helps to reduce ground bouncing noise and silicon area in MTCMOS circuits: divulging the basic mechanism. In: Proceedings of the IEEE International SoC Design Conference, pp. 9–12 (November 2010)
13. Jiao, H., Kursun, V.: Ground bouncing noise suppression techniques for data preserving sequential MTCMOS circuits. IEEE Transactions on Very Large Scale Integration (VLSI) Systems 19(5), 763–773 (2011)
14. Kim, S., Choi, C.J., Jeong, D.K., Kosonocky, S.V., Park, S.B.: Reducing ground-bounce noise and stabilizing the data-retention voltage of power-gating structures. IEEE Transactions on Electron Devices 55(1), 197–205 (2008)
15. Jiang, H., Sadowska, M.M.: Power gating scheduling for power/ground noise reduction. In: Proceedings of the IEEE/ACM International Design Automation Conference, pp. 980–985 (June 2008)
16. Kawasaki, K., Shiota, T., Nakayama, K., Inoue, A.: A sub- µs wake-up time power gating technique with bypass power line for rush current support. IEEE Journal of Solid-State Circuits 44(4), 1178–1183 (2009)
17. Min, K.S., Kawaguchi, H., Sakurai, T.: Zigzag super cut-off CMOS (ZSCCMOS) block activation with self-adaptive voltage level controller: an alternative to clock-gating scheme in leakage dominant era. In: Proceedings of the IEEE International Solid-State Circuits Conference, pp. 400–401 (February 2003)
18. Pakbaznia, E., Fallah, F., Pedram, M.: Charge recycling in power-gated CMOS circuits. IEEE Transactions on Computer-Aided Design of Integrated Circuits and Systems 27(10), 1798–1811 (2008)
19. Liu, Z., Kursun, V.: Charge recycling between virtual power and ground lines for low energy MTCMOS. In: Proceedings of the IEEE/ACM International Symposium on Quality Electronic Design, pp. 239–244 (March 2007)
20. Liu, Z., Kursun, V.: Low energy MTCMOS with sleep transistor charge recycling. In: Proceedings of the IEEE International Midwest Symposium on Circuits and Systems, pp. 891–894 (August 2007)
21. Bhavnagarwala, A.J., Kosonocky, S.V., Immediato, M., Knebel, D., Haen, A.M.: A pico-joule class, 1GHz, 32KByte x 64b DSP SRAM with self reverse bias. In: Proceedings of the IEEE Symposium on VLSI Circuits, pp. 253–254 (June 2003)
22. Zhang, K., Bhattacharya, U., Chen, Z., Hamzaoglu, F., Murray, D., Vallepalli, N., Wang, Y., Zheng, B., Bohr, M.: SRAM design on 65-nm CMOS technology with dynamic sleep transistor for leakage reduction. IEEE Journal of Solid-State Circuits 40(4), 895–901 (2005)
23. Riedlinger, R., Bhatia, R., Biro, L., Bowhill, B., Fetzer, E., Gronowski, P., Grutkowski, T.: A 32nm 3.1 billion transistor 12-wide-issue Itanium processor for mission-critical servers. In: Proceedings of the IEEE International Solid-State Circuits Conference, pp. 84–85 (February 2011)

24. Kanno, Y., Mizuno, H., Yasu, Y., Hirose, K., Shimazaki, Y., Hoshi, T., Miyairi, Y., Ishii, T., Yamada, T., Irita, T., Hattori, T., Yanagisawa, K., Irie, N.: Hierarchical power distribution with power tree in dozens of power domains for 90-nm low-power multi-CPU SoCs. IEEE Journal of Solid-State Circuits 42(1), 74–83 (2007)

25. Shin, J., Huang, D., Petrick, B., Hwang, C., Tam, K., Smith, A., Pham, H., Li, H., Johnson, T., Schumacher, F., Leon, A., Strong, A.: A 40 nm 16-core 128-thread SPARC SoC processor. IEEE Journal of Solid-State Circuits 46(1), 131–144 (2011)

26. Wendel, D., Kalla, R., Warnock, J., Cargnoni, R., Chu, S., Clabes, J., Dreps, D., Hrusecky, D., Friedrich, J., Islam, S., Kahle, J., Leenstra, J., Mittal, G., Paredes, J., Pille, J., Restle, P., Sinharoy, B., Smith, G., Starke, W., Taylor, S., Norstrand, A.J.V., Weitzel, S., Williams, P., Zyuban, V.: POWER7, a highly parallel, scalable multi-core high end server processor. IEEE Journal of Solid-State Circuits 46(1), 145–161 (2011)

27. Calhoun, B.H., Honoré, F.A., Chandrakasan, A.P.: A leakage reduction methodology for distributed MTCMOS. IEEE Journal of Solid-State Circuits 39(5), 818–826 (2004)

28. Kao, J., Chandrakasan, A., Antoniadis, D.: Transistor sizing issues and tool for multi-threshold CMOS technology. In: Proceedings of the IEEE /ACM International Design Automation Conference, pp. 409–414 (June 1997)

29. Shigematsu, S., Mutoh, S., Matsuya, Y., Tanabe, Y., Yamada, J.: A 1-V high-speed MTCMOS circuit scheme for power-down application circuits. IEEE Journal of Solid-State Circuits 32(6), 861–869 (1997)

30. Stan, M.R., Barcella, M.: MTCMOS with outer feedback (MTOF) flip-flops. In: Proceedings of the IEEE International Symposium on Circuits and Systems, pp. 429–432 (May 2003)

31. Liu, Z., Kursun, V.: New MTCMOS flip-flops with simple control circuitry and low leakage data retention capability. In: Proceedings of the IEEE International Conference on Electronics, Circuits, and Systems, pp. 1276–1279 (December 2007)

32. Jiao, H., Kursun, V.: Low-leakage and compact registers with easy-sleep mode. Journal of Low-Power Electronics 6(2), 263–279 (2010)

33. Jiao, H., Kursun, V.: Power gated SRAM circuits with data retention capability and high immunity to noise: a comparison for reliability in low leakage sleep mode. In: Proceedings of the IEEE International SoC Design Conference, pp. 5–8 (November 2010)

34. Jiao, H., Kursun, V.: Asymmetrical ground gating for low leakage and data robust sleep mode in memory banks. In: Proceedings of the IEEE International Symposium on VLSI Design Automation and Test, pp. 205–208 (April 2011)

35. Seomun, J., Shin, Y.: Design and optimization of power-gated circuits with autonomous data retention. IEEE Transactions on Very Large Scale Integration (VLSI) Systems 19(2), 227–236 (2011)

36. Hu, Z., Buyuktosunoglu, A., Srinivasan, V., Zyuban, V., Jacobson, H., Bose, P.: Microarchitectural techniques for power gating of execution units. In: Proceedings of the IEEE/ACM International Symposium on Low Power Electronics and Design, pp. 32–37 (August 2004)

37. Singh, H., Agarwal, K., Sylvester, D., Nowka, K.J.: Enhanced leakage reduction techniques using intermediate strength power gating. IEEE Transactions on Very Large Scale Integration (VLSI) Systems 15(11), 1215–1224 (2007)

38. Dropsho, S., Kursun, V., Albonesi, D.H., Dwarkadas, S., Friedman, E.G.: Managing static leakage energy in microprocessor functional units. In: Proceedings of the IEEE/ACM International Symposium on Microarchitecture, pp. 321–332 (November 2002)

39. Kursun, V., Friedman, E.G.: Domino logic with dynamic body biased keeper. In: Proceedings of the European Solid-State Circuits Conference, pp. 675–678 (September 2002)

40. Kursun, V., Friedman, E.G.: Forward body biased keeper for enhanced noise immunity in domino logic circuits. In: Proceedings of the IEEE International Symposium on Circuits and Systems, vol. 2, pp. 917–920 (May 2004)

41. Narendra, S., Tschanz, J., Hofsheier, J., Bloechel, B., Vangal, S., Hoskote, Y., Tang, S., Somasekhar, D., Keshavarzi, A., Erraguntla, V., Dermer, G., Borkar, N., Borkar, S., De, V.: Ultra-low voltage circuits and processor in 180nm to 90nm technologies with a swapped-body biasing technique. In: Proceedings of the IEEE International Solid-State Circuits Conference, pp. 156–518 (February 2004)

42. Narendra, S., Keshavarzi, A., Bloechel, B.A., Borkar, S., De, V.: Forward body bias for microprocessors in 130-nm technology generation and beyond. IEEE Journal of Solid-State Circuits 38(5), 696–701 (2003)

43. Liu, Z., Kursun, V.: Characterization of a novel nine transistor SRAM cell. IEEE Transactions on Very Large Scale Integration (VLSI) Systems 16(4), 488–492 (2008)

44. Liu, Z., Kursun, V.: High read stability and low leakage cache memory cell. In: Proceedings of the IEEE International Symposium on Circuits and Systems, pp. 2774–2777 (May 2007)

45. Tawfik, S.A., Kursun, V.: Low power and robust 7T dual-V_t SRAM circuit. In: Proceedings of the IEEE International Symposium on Circuits and Systems, pp. 1452–1455 (May 2008)

46. Zhu, H., Kursun, V.: Application-specific selection of 6T SRAM cells offering superior performance and quality with a triple-threshold-voltage CMOS technology. In: Proceedings of the IEEE Asia Symposium on Quality Electronic Design (July 2011)

47. Kursun, V., Tawfik, S.A., Liu, Z.: Leakage-aware design of nanometer SoC. In: Proceedings of the IEEE International Symposium on Circuits and Systems, pp. 3231–3234 (May 2007)

48. Black, B., Annavaram, M., Brekelbaum, N., DeVale, J., Jiang, L., Loh, G.H., McCauley, D., Morrow, P., Nelson, D.W., Pantuso, D., Reed, P., Rupley, J., Shankar, S., Shen, J., Webb, C.: Die stacking (3D) microarchitecture. In: Proceedings of the IEEE/ACM International Symposium on Microarchitecture, pp. 469–479 (December 2006)

49. Heydari, P., Pedram, M.: Ground bounce in digital VLSI circuits. IEEE Transactions on Very Large Scale Integration (VLSI) Systems 11(2), 180–185 (2003)

50. UMC 80 Nanometer CMOS Technology, http://www.umc.com/english/process/g.asp

Fast Legalization for Standard Cell Placement with Simultaneous Wirelength and Displacement Minimization

Tsung-Yi Ho and Sheng-Hung Liu

Department of Computer Science and Information Engineering
National Cheng Kung University

Abstract. Legalization is one of the most critical steps in modern placement designs. Since several objectives like wirelength, routability, or temperature are already optimized in global placement stage, the objective of legalization is not only to align the cells overlap-free to the rows, but also to preserve the solution of global placement, i.e., the displacement of cells needs to be minimized. However, minimizing displacement only is not enough for current timing-driven SoC designs. Blind displacement minimization may increase the half-perimeter wirelength (HPWL) of nets significantly that degrades the chip performance. In this paper, we propose a fast legalization algorithm for standard cell placement with simultaneous wirelength and displacement minimization. The main contributions of our work are: (1) a fast row selection technique by using k-medoid clustering approach; (2) an exact linear wirelength model to minimize both wirelength and total displacement; (3) a constant time approach to determine the median in trial placement stage. Compared with the state-of-the-art legalization algorithms, experimental results show that our legalizer acquires much better achievement in terms of HPWL, total and maximum displacements, and running time on legalized NTUplace3 global placement results on both ISPD 2005 and 2006 placement contest benchmarks.

Keywords: Displacement, Legalization, Placement, Wirelength.

1 Introduction

The conventional standard cell placement includes three stages: global placement, legalization, and detailed placement. Typically, global placement generates an initial placement with minimum total half-perimeter wirelength (HPWL) and tries to optimize some objectives such as routability, timing, temperature, and etc. This results in few cell overlap and the cells are not aligned to the rows. There has been several researches in the area of global placement in the past few years [3,5,4,11,16,18]. After global placement stage, legalization targets (1) to remove overlaps between cell instances, (2) to put all instances on the rows in the core area, and (3) to minimize the displacements of instances between the initial placement and the legalized one. That is, legalization tries to make

J.L. Ayala, D. Atienza, and R. Reis (Eds.): VLSI-SoC 2010, IFIP AICT 373, pp. 291–311, 2012.

the placement legal and to preserve the result from the global placement stage. After legalization, detailed placement is used to improve the solution quality of the legal placement. Legalization with only displacement minimization may significantly induce the solutions with more HPWL than global placement stage. For example, if cell a is to be legalized in Figure 1 (a), blind legalization with only displacement minimization may increase the HPWL as shown in Figure 1 (b). However, by taking HPWL into consideration, we can legalize cell a with both displacement and HPWL minimization.

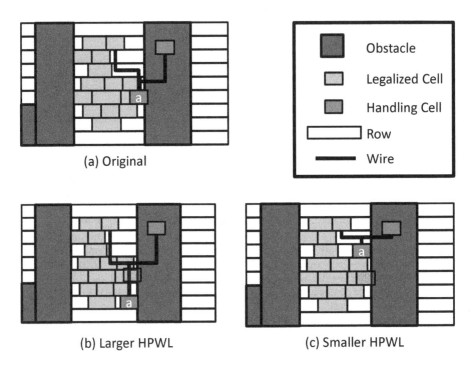

Fig. 1. (a) Original placement before legalizing cell a. (b) Placement with larger HPWL after legalizing cell a. (c) Placement with smaller HPWL after legalizing cell a.

1.1 Previous Work

Existing legalization techniques include network flow [2,6], ripple cell movement[8], dynamic programming [1], simulated annealing[17], single row optimization[10], diffusion-based method [15], computational geometry [13], packing [7], and quadratic programming [18]. Domino [6] partitions cells in subcells (all having the same height and width) and rows in places, and assigns them by using a min-cost-max-flow approach. Similar to Domino, [2] assigns sets of modules to row regions. Mongrel [8] uses a greedy heuristic to move cells from overflowed bins to under capacity bins in a ripple fashion based on total wirelength gain. Fractional Cut [1] assigned cells to rows by dynamic programming and the cells of each row are packed from left to right. Sarrafzadeh [17] uses simulated annealing for legalization. The authors of [10] assigned cells to the rows by cell juggling and the cells of each row are placed by finding a shortest path in a graph. Diffusion-based placement migration is presented in [15] to remove cell overlap incrementally. In [13], cells are spread and aligned to rows by computational geometry techniques. Sarrafzadeh [17] uses a cell shifting technique to reduce the maximum bin density. HPWL-driven legalizers only target on HPWL minimization within a row by dynamic programming approach [9,10].

Tetris is a fast greedy heuristic which is widely used in industry [7]. Tetris sorts the cells first, and legalizes one cell at a time then. The legalization of one cell is done by moving the cell over the rows, and within a row by moving the cell over free sites. This movement is done until the best free site is found. Once a cell has been legalized, it will not be moved anymore. This results in a high total cell displacement during legalization. Recently, Spindler et al. present a similar approach, called Abacus [19], that it places a cell from row to row until the location with the smallest displacement is found. However, as a cell is placed into a row, the legalized cells in that row are re-placed by dynamic programming technique to minimize the total displacement. Both Tetris and Abacus scan rows with minimum cost vertically. Tetris scans all rows (see Figure 2 (a)). Abacus sorts the rows by the y-position. A lower bound of the cost is computed by assuming cells are only moved vertically. Abacus moves the cell to the best row first, and then tries to move the cell to the rows with the lower bound not exceeding the minimal cost of an already found legal position (see Figure 2 (b)). In this paper, our legalizer constructs the binary index tree for the rows via clustering techniques. By traversing the binary index tree, our legalizer only scans some candidate rows then the running time is significantly reduced (see Figure 2 (c)).

1.2 Our Contribution

The main contributions of our work are: (1) a fast row selection technique by using k-medoid clustering approach; (2) an exact linear wirelength model to minimize both total displacement and HPWL; (3) a constant time approach to determine the median in trial placement stage. The remainder of this paper is organized as follows. Section 2 details our algorithm. Section 3 shows the experimental results. Finally, concluding remarks are given in Section 4.

2 Algorithm

Figure 3 shows the overview of our legalization algorithm. First, a binary index tree for rows is constructed for fast row scanning (line 1). After that, cells are sorted according to the sum of their x-position and the half of their width (line 2). Then, cells are legalized one by one according to the sorting order (line 3-8). "DFS" (line 5) adopt depth-first search manner to search the best row for each

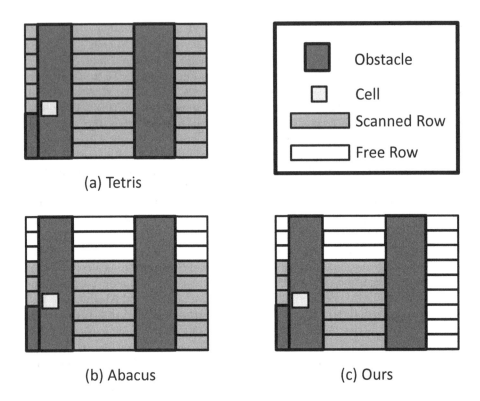

Fig. 2. (a) Tetris scans all rows. (b) Abacus scans the rows by y-position. (c) Our legalizer only scans the rows when they are necessary.

cell; i.e., the cost (the sum of HPWL and displacement of the cell) of the row is minimum by using the binary index tree for row scanning (line 1). Then the cell is inserted to the best row for HPWL and displacement minimization (line 6).

2.1   Binary Index Tree

Fast row scanning can be achieved by searching a binary index tree constructed by top-down row clustering technique. In this paper, we adopt k-medoid [12] clustering algorithm as the main method for clustering rows. Typically, k-medoid algorithm clusters items by using their similarity. To cluster rows, we define the similarity between rows as the distance between each row. If the distance between each row is far, the similarity is small, and vice versa. Initially, all rows are in a cluster, called **root cluster**. Then all rows are clustered into two clusters by using k-medoid algorithm (k=2) where the centers are central rows of row clusters. Iteration of clustering terminates until the number of rows in every cluster is less than 3. Finally, we construct a binary index tree for row clusters. The relation between rows and binary index tree is shown in Figure 4.

Algorithm 1: Overall Legalization Algorithm
1   Construct a binary index tree for rows;
2   Sort cells according to (x-position + width / 2);
3   **foreach** *cell* **do**
4   　　　row_{best} = **null**;
5   　　　row_{best} = DFS(*root_cluster,cell*);
6   　　　Insert *cell* to row_{best};
7   **end**

Fig. 3. Overall algorithm of our legalizer

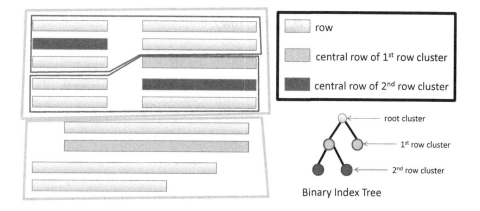

Fig. 4. Top-down clustering constructs a binary index tree for rows

2.2 Row Scanning

Before placing cells into the rows, legalizers perform row scanning then do trial placement for cells. Different from previous legalizers that scan all rows, our legalizer can find the best row efficiently by searching on the binary index tree. As mentioned earlier, the nodes in the binary index tree represent row clusters. The edge cost in the binary index tree is the distance from a cell to the row cluster. To compute the distance from a cell to the row cluster, we need to compute the distance between rows first. $D_{min}(row_i, row_j)$ and $D_{max}(row_i, row_j)$ are two kinds of the distance from row_i to row_j. We adopt $D_{min}(row_i, row_j)$ as the distance for clustering rows by using k-medoid algorithm and $D_{max}(row_i, row_j)$ as the distance used for computing the edge cost of the binary index tree. If row_i overlaps row_j horizontally, $D_{min}(row_i, row_j)$ is the vertical distance from

row_i to row_j (see Figure 5 (a)). If row_i does not overlap row_j horizontally, $D_{min}(row_i, row_j)$ is the sum of vertical and horizontal distance from row_i to row_j (see Figure 5 (b)). $D_{max}(row_i, row_j)$ is the sum of the vertical distance and maximum horizontal distance from the left of row_i to the left (see Figure 5 (c)) of row_j or from the right of row_i to the right of row_j (see Figure 5 (d)). Moreover, the computation of distance from cells to row clusters is the same with distance between rows.

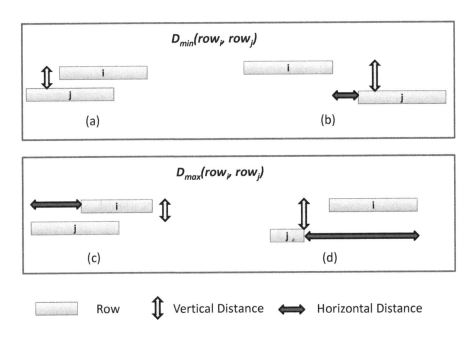

Fig. 5.   (a) $D_{min}(row_i, row_j)$ with horizontal overlaps. (b) $D_{min}(row_i, row_j)$ without horizontal overlaps. (c) $D_{max}(row_i, row_j)$ with horizontal overlaps. (d) $D_{max}(row_i, row_j)$ without horizontal overlaps.

After the distance between rows is computed, we defined radius of a row cluster is the farthest distance between its central row to other rows. According to triangle inequality, the distance from a cell to the row cluster, i.e. $D_{min}(cell, row\_cluster)$, can be derived as shown in Figure 6.

A depth-first search (DFS) approach is used for finding the best row. Algorithm 2 describes the function DFS. DFS starts from root cluster. The cell is always moved into the nearer cluster for trial placement first (line 5-18). The cell is not moved to cluster if $D_{min}(cell, row\_cluster)$ is larger than the current best displacement. The cost of the row is the sum of both HPWL and displacement of the cell after the cell is moved to the row (line 21). After DFS, the best row can be found quickly, then cells will be inserted into it. For simultaneous wirelength and displacement minimization, the cost of row for placing a cell depends on the displacement and the HPWL of it. Since a cell may be connected by multiple

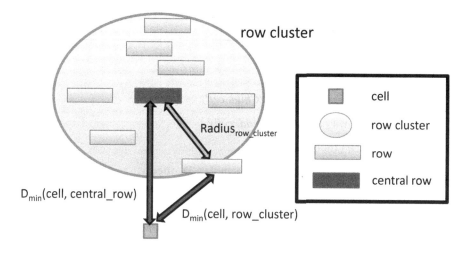

$$D_{min}(\text{cell}, \text{row\_cluster}) > D_{min}(\text{cell}, \text{central\_row}) - Radius_{row\_cluster}$$

Fig. 6. Illustration of the minimum distance computation between a *cell* and a *row_cluster*

nets, the cost by simply adding the displacement and the HPWL of a cell may not be precise. Furthermore, we not only target to minimize total displacement but also to minimize maximum displacement, we consider both factors by a combined cost function. The cost function is defined as follows:

$$Cost(i) = HPWL + N_i(\alpha \cdot (DP_S) + \beta \cdot (DP_P)) \qquad (1)$$

where N_i represents the number of the net belongs to cell i. DP_S is the cell displacement between original position and legalized position. DP_P is the total increased displacement caused by inserting one cell into row. α, β are user-specified parameters. An example of cost computation is shown in Figure 8.

2.3   Obstacle-Aware Cell Ordering

Modern chip designs often consist of many preplaced blocks, such as analog blocks, memory blocks, and/or I/O buffers, which are fixed in the chip and cannot overlap with other blocks. These preplaced blocks, i.e., obstacles, impose more constraints on the legalization problem. A legalization algorithm without considering obstacles may significantly induce increasing cell displacement or inferior solutions. Different from all previous works that insert cell according to its x-position in the global placement, we insert cell according to its central position (i.e., x-position of cells + cell width/2). As illustrated in Figure 9, an obstacle lies in the middle of the row shred the row into two subrows. If cells

---

Algorithm 2: Function DFS

---

1   **Function** DFS(*cell, row_cluster*)

2   **if** *row_cluster* is not a leaf **then**

3       $D_R = D_{min}$(*row_cluster.RightChild, cell*);

4       $D_L = D_{min}$(*row_cluster.LeftChild, cell*);

5   **if** $(D_R < D_L)$ **then**

6   **if** row_{best} is null or $displacement_{best} > D_R$ **then**

7   DFS(*cell, row_cluster.RightChild*);

8   **if** row_{best} is null or $displacement_{best} > D_L$ **then**

9   DFS(*cell, row_cluster.LeftChild*);

10   **end**

11   **end**

12   **else**

13   **if** row_{best} is null or $displacement_{best} > D_L$ **then**

14   DFS(*cell, row_cluster.LeftChild*);

15   **if** row_{best} is null or $displacement_{best} > D_R$ **then**

16   DFS(*cell, row_cluster.RightChild*);

17   **end**

18   **end**

19   **end**

20   **else**

21   **foreach** *row* in *row_cluster* **do**

22           $displacement_{candidate}$ = TrialPlace(*row, cell*);

23   **if** $displacement_{candidate} < displacement_{best}$ **then**

24              $displacement_{best} = displacement_{candidate}$;

25   **end**

26   **end**

27   **end**

Fig. 7. The algorithm of function DFS

are inserted by x-position, the larger cell 1 will be inserted first but cause larger displacement for cell 2 and 3 since they are inserted to another subrow that across the obstacle (See Figure 9 (a)). It is not worth because only cell 1 is inserted into the left subrow with smaller displacement and cell 2 and 3 are squeezed to right subrows with larger displacement. If cells are inserted by their central position, most of the smaller cells that are capable of being inserted to fragmentary subrows can reduce the total displacement significantly (See Figure 9 (b)). Moreover, it is capable of handling the relative order problem.

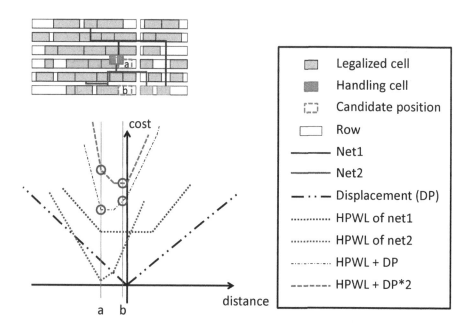

Fig. 8. Illustration of the cost(i) to find the best row

2.4   Cell Insertion

Most of previous works use simple quadratic wirelength model to measure cell displacement. The drawback lies in the preciseness since the square of larger cell displacement will have dramatically difference. Different from Abacus that uses quadratic model, we adopt an exact linear wirelength model for measuring cell displacement. Cells of one row are abutting in the legal placement and form a cluster. Assume the row has c clusters and $cluster_c$ has n cells which are sorted by their global x-position + width/2. To minimize the cell displacement, the objective function is defined as follows:

$$min \sum_{i=1}^{n} |x_i^c - x_i'^c| \qquad (2)$$

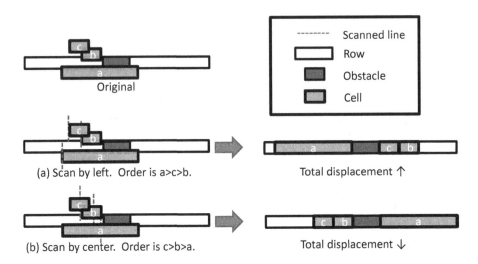

Fig. 9. Ordering for obstacle-aware cell insertion

where $x_i^{\prime c}$ and x_i^c are initial and legalized position of cluster c. The constraint (2) assures that there is no overlap between the cells and is defined as follows:

$$x_i^c - x_{i-1}^c \geq w_{i-1}^c \qquad i = 2, ..., n \qquad (3)$$

where w_i^c is cell width. However, solving linear programs with "$\geq$" constraints is time consuming in general. If the same solution of the linear program is found by "$=$" constraints, then the linear program is solved quite fast by solving one linear equation. The situation that "$=$" constraints are sufficient is given if all cells of one row are abutting in the legal placement and form a cluster. There, two cells are "abutting" if there is no free space between them in the legal placement. With only "$=$" constraints, (2) is transformed to:

$$x_i^c = x_1^c + \sum_{k=1}^{i-1} w_k^c \qquad i = 2, ..., n \qquad (4)$$

By (3), we can transform (1) into (4) such that the optimal value only depends on variable x_1^c.

$$min \sum_{i=1}^{n} |x_1^c - \underbrace{[x_i^c - \sum_{k=1}^{i-1} w_k^c]}_{d_i^c}| \qquad (5)$$

where d_i^c is the candidate position of cluster c for cell i and all d_i^c form a set D_c. The optimal x_1^c can be derived by finding the median m of all d_i^c.

2.5   Find Median

As shown in Figure 10, a row has several clusters. The positions of these clusters are determined by X_c. If the clusters are overlapped, they will be merged and form a new cluster.

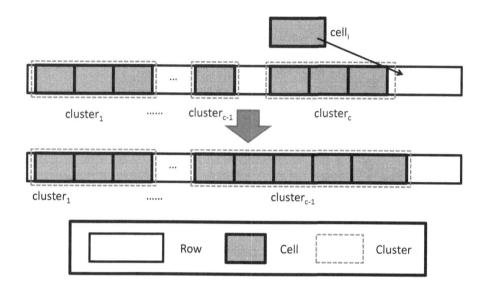

Fig. 10. Illustration of cluster merging

The intuitive method for finding the median is to sort n elements in D_c while the time complexity of sorting for trial placement and insertion are both $O(nlogn)$. An efficient method for finding the median is to apply the deterministic partitioning algorithm from quicksort while the time complexity for trial placement and insertion are both $O(n)$. In this paper, we adopt red-black trees for finding the median while the time complexity for trial placement and insertion are both $O(logn)$. Moreover, red-black trees can be used to record already sorted D_c since D_c will not be changed after cells are placed. Thus, we can derive the set of X_c as follows:

$$X_c = \{x_c(i)\} \qquad i = 2, ..., n \tag{6}$$

where $x_c(i)$ corresponds to the already sorted elements in D_c.

Since cells are not really placed on rows in trial placement stage, unnecessary movement of cells can be pruned in this stage. By exploring all possible movements of clusters, we found only the rightmost cluster (i.e., $cluster_c$) will move to the left and others will stay still. By this observation, we have 3 lemmas for our trial placement stage. By these 3 lemmas, the time complexity of our trial placement is only O(1) since we only need to compare 3 possible positions then we can find the best position for all clusters. The comparison of time complexity in listed in Table 1.

Table 1. Time complexity for trial placement and cell insertion

	Trial	Insert
Sorting algorithm	O(nlogn)	O(nlogn)
SELECT algorithm	O(n)	O(n)
Red-Black tree	O(logn)	O(logn)
Ours	O(1)	O(logn)

Lemma 1. *If the number of the cells in $cluster_c$ is even, the cell i is placed to the right of $cluster_c$ and the position of $cluster_c$ will not be changed.*

Proof: Let c is the number of clusters in a row. N_c is the number of the cells in $cluster_c$. W_c is the width of $cluster_c$. The candidate position for cell i is $\overline{x_i}$ which is the difference of W_c and the original x position of cell i. If cell i and $cluster_c$ overlap horizontally, $\overline{x_i}$ is less than the original x position of $cluster_c$.

As shown in Figure 11, assume N_c is an even number. The original x position of $cluster_c$ is the median of X_c (i.e., $\frac{N_c}{2}$). Therefore, there are $\frac{N_c}{2} - 1$ elements that are smaller than the original x position of $cluster_c$, and $\frac{N_c}{2}$ elements that are larger than the original x position of $cluster_c$. After cell i and $cluster_c$ are merged, $\overline{x_i}$ is added into X_c. Since $\overline{x_i}$ is smaller than the x position of cluster c, the number of X_c which smaller than the original x position of cluster c is $\frac{N_c}{2}$. Therefore, the median of X_c does not changed. The new x position of $cluster_c$ is the original x position of $cluster_c$. □

Lemma 2. *If the number of the cells in $cluster_c$ is odd, the cell i is placed to the right of $cluster_c$ and the position of $cluster_c$ will shift to the left.*

Proof: As shown in Figure 12, assume N_c is a odd number and the original x position of $cluster_c$ is the median of X_c (i.e., $\frac{N_c+1}{2}$). Therefore, the number of X_c which smaller than the original x position of $cluster_c$ is $\frac{N_c+1}{2} - 1$. The number of X_c which larger than the original x position of $cluster_c$ is $\frac{N_c+1}{2} - 1$. After cell i and $cluster_c$ are merged, $\overline{x_i}$ is added into X_c. Since $\overline{x_i}$ is smaller than the original x position of $cluster_c$, the number of X_c which smaller than the original x position of $cluster_c$ is $\frac{N_c+1}{2}$. Therefore, the median of X_c will be changed. The new x position of $cluster_c$ is $\frac{N_c+1}{2}$ of new X_c instead of the original x position of $cluster_c$. In other words, new x position of $cluster_c$ is the maximum one between $(\frac{N_c+1}{2} - 1)$ of original X_c and $\overline{x_i}$). □

By Lemma 2, $cluster_c$ may overlap with $cluster_{c-1}$ when $cluster_c$ shifts to the left. In this situation, $cluster_{c-1}$ and $cluster_c$ are merged and then form a new and bigger $cluster_{c-1}$ and the number of the clusters of the row becomes $c - 1$.

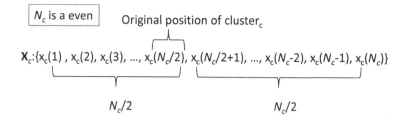

N_c is a even   Original position of cluster$_c$

$$\mathbf{X}_c : \{x_c(1), x_c(2), x_c(3), ..., x_c(N_c/2), x_c(N_c/2+1), ..., x_c(N_c-2), x_c(N_c-1), x_c(N_c)\}$$

$N_c/2$ $N_c/2$

New position of cluster$_c$

$$\mathbf{X}_c : \{x_c(1), x_c(2), ..., \overline{x}, ..., x_c(N_c/2-1), x_c(N_c/2), x_c(N_c/2+1), ..., x_c(N_c-2), x_c(N_c-1), x_c(N_c)\}$$

$N_c/2$ $N_c/2$

Fig. 11. N_c is an even number

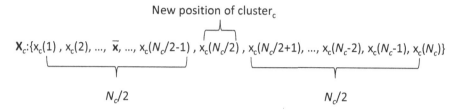

N_c is an odd   Original position of cluster$_c$

$$\mathbf{X}_c : \{x_c(1), x_c(2), x_c(3), ..., x_c((N_c-1)/2), x_c((N_c+1)/2), x_c((N_c+1)/2+1), ..., x_c(N_c-2), x_c(N_c-1), x_c(N_c)\}$$

$(N_c-1)/2$ $(N_c-1)/2$

New position of cluster$_c$

$$\mathbf{X}_c : \{x_c(1), x_c(2), ..., \overline{x}, ..., x_c(N_c/2-1), x_c((N_c+1)/2), x_c((N_c+1)/2+1), ..., x_c(N_c-2), x_c(N_c-1), x_c(N_c)\}$$

$(N_c+1)/2$ $(N_c+1)/2$

or

New position of cluster$_c$

$$\mathbf{X}_c : \{x_c(1), x_c(2), ..., x_c(N_c/2-1), \overline{x}, x_c((N_c+1)/2), x_c((N_c+1)/2+1), ..., x_c(N_c-2), x_c(N_c-1), x_c(N_c)\}$$

$(N_c+1)/2$ $(N_c+1)/2$

Fig. 12. N_c is an odd number

Under this circumstance, we further observe that although $cluster_c$ shifts to the left, the positions of other $c - 1$ clusters will not be influenced by $cluster_c$. The details are described in Lemma 3.

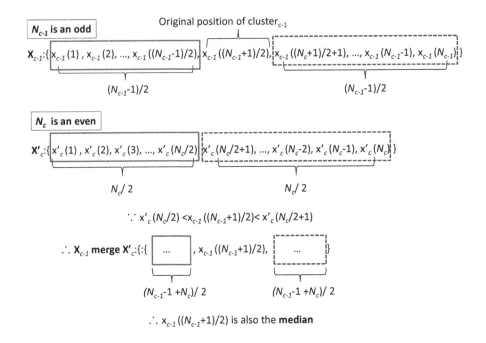

Fig. 13. Merge process of $cluster_{c-1}$

Lemma 3. $cluster_c$ *has no influence on other* $n - 1$ *clusters.*

Proof: As shown in Figure 13, X'_c is the difference between X_c and W_{c-1}. If a new cell added to the row, it will cause $cluster_c$ overlapped with $cluster_{c-1}$, then $cluster_{c-1}$ and $cluster_c$ will be merged together. After $cluster_{c-1}$ and $cluster_c$ are merged, the position of the new $cluster_{c-1}$ is found by the median of new X_{c-1} (i.e., original X_{c-1} merged with X'_c). The median of original X'_c (i.e., $X'_c(N_c/2 + 1)$) is larger than the median of X_{c-1} (i.e., $X_{c-1}((N_{c-1} + 1)/2)$), because $cluster_{c-1}$ and original $cluster_c$ are not overlapped. Once a new cell added to the row, it will cause $cluster_c$ overlaps $cluster_{c-1}$, the median of new X'_c (i.e., $X'_c(N_c/2)$) will be smaller than the median of X_{c-1} (i.e., $X_{c-1}((N_{c-1} + 1)/2)$). Therefore, after $cluster_{c-1}$ and $cluster_c$ are merged, the median of new X_{c-1} is unchanged (i.e., $X_{c-1}(N_{c-1} + 1)/2$). It means that the x position of new $cluster_{c-1}$ is unchanged, and the position of cell is the sum of $(X_{c-1}(N_{c-1} + 1)/2)$, W_{c-1}, and L_c.

In trial place step, the position of the cell on the row can be calculated by finding the maximum of the following three numbers: x', the sum of the $\frac{N_c+1}{2}$-1) of X_c and W_c, and the sum of the x position of $cluster_{c-1}$ (i.e., $X_{c-1}((N_{c-1} + 1)/2)$)), W_{c-1}, and L_c. $\square$

3 Experimental Results

We have implemented our legalizer in the C++ language on a 2-GHz 64-bit Linux machine with 16GB memory. For fair comparison, we evaluate NTUplace3 [5], Tetris [7], Abacus [19], and Kahng [9] on the same platform. Furthermore, to verify the efficiency and effectiveness of our legalizer, we perform experiments on two benchmark suites, such as ISPD 2005 and 2006 placement contest benchmarks [22]. The global placement results are obtained from NTUplace3 [5]. Extensive experiments demonstrate that in terms of HPWL, total and maximum displacements, and running time, we acquire much better achievement than all the state-of-the-art algorithms such as Tetris [7], Abacus [19], and Kahng [9] in any aspect.

3.1 Benchmarks

The cell numbers of the ISPD 2005 benchmarks range from 210K to 2169K, the fixed macro numbers range from 543 to 23084, and the row numbers range from 890 to 2694. The cell numbers of the ISPD 2006 benchmarks range from 330K to 2507K, the fixed macro numbers range from 337 to 26582, and the row numbers range from 930 to 4182. The benchmark information is listed in Table 2.

Table 2. Statistics of two benchmark suites of the ISPD placement contest

ISPD 2005 Benchmarks				ISPD 2006 Benchmarks			
Name	# Cells	# Fixed Macros	# Rows	Name	# Cells	# Fixed Macros	# Rows
adaptec1	210904	543	890	adaptec5	843128	646	1944
adaptec2	254457	566	1170	newblue1	330073	337	930
adaptec3	450927	723	1944	newblue2	441516	1277	1925
adaptec4	494716	1329	1944	newblue4	646139	3422	1524
bigblue1	277604	560	890	newblue5	1233058	4881	2130
bigblue2	534782	23084	1566	newblue6	1255039	6889	2316
bigblue3	1093034	1293	2316	newblue7	2507954	26582	3258
bigblue4	2169183	8170	2694				

3.2 HPWL

In the first experiment, we evaluate the HPWL of our legalizer on the both benchmarks. On legalized NTUplace3 [5] global placements on ISPD 2005 placement contest benchmarks, the HPWL is 1.92X, 1.19X and 1.92X of our legalizer compared to Tetris [7], Abacus [19], and Kahng [9], respectively. It should be noted that Kahng [9] only focusing on HPWL minimization. Moreover, we also compare the HPWL after our legalizer with the original HPWL of NTUplace3 global placement results [5], we can further reduce HPWL by 18%. The details of HPWL experiments on ISPD 2005 benchmarks are listed in Table 3.

Table 3. Wirelength comparison between NTUplace3, Tetris, Abacus, Kahng, and ours on ISPD 2005 benchmarks

ISPD 2005 Benchmarks	NTUplace3 [5]	Tetris [7]	Abacus [19]	Kahng [9]	Ours
Name	HPWL	HPWL	HPWL	HPWL	HPWL
adaptec1	9.56E+07	1.20E+08	9.50E+07	1.19E+08	8.00E+07
adaptec2	9.98E+07	1.39E+08	1.01E+08	1.39E+08	8.80E+07
adaptec3	2.43E+08	2.61E+08	2.40E+08	2.61E+08	2.00E+08
adaptec4	2.14E+08	2.53E+08	2.09E+08	2.52E+08	1.80E+08
bigblue1	1.10E+08	5.00E+08	1.10E+08	4.98E+08	9.40E+07
bigblue2	1.65E+08	1.79E+08	1.64E+08	1.78E+08	1.30E+08
bigblue3	4.15E+08	5.86E+08	4.67E+08	5.85E+08	3.60E+08
bigblue4	8.97E+08	1.04E+09	9.09E+08	1.03E+09	7.60E+08
AVG.	1.18	1.92	1.19	1.92	1

On legalized NTUplace3 [5] global placements on ISPD 2006 placement contest benchmarks, the HPWL is 1.44X, 1.25X and 1.43X of our legalizer compared to Tetris [7], Abacus [19], and Kahng [9], respectively. Compare the HPWL after our legalizer with the original HPWL of NTUplace3 global placement results [5], we can further reduce HPWL by 19%. The details of HPWL experiments on ISPD 2006 benchmarks are listed in Table 4.

Table 4. Wirelength comparison between NTUplace3, Tetris, Abacus, Kahng, and ours on ISPD 2006 benchmarks

ISPD 2006 Benchmarks	NTUplace3 [5]	Tetris [7]	Abacus [19]	Kahng [9]	Ours
Name	HPWL	HPWL	HPWL	HPWL	HPWL
adaptec5	4.01E+08	4.95E+08	4.07E+08	4.94E+08	3.14E+08
newblue1	6.42E+07	1.03E+08	6.40E+07	1.03E+08	5.74E+07
newblue2	2.16E+08	2.46E+08	2.20E+08	2.45E+08	2.02E+08
newblue4	2.89E+08	3.20E+08	2.84E+08	3.19E+08	2.32E+08
newblue5	5.06E+08	5.34E+08	5.01E+08	5.32E+08	4.23E+08
newblue6	5.09E+08	6.15E+08	6.18E+08	6.15E+08	4.25E+08
newblue7	1.13E+09	1.30E+09	1.25E+09	1.30E+09	9.24E+08
AVG.	1.19	1.44	1.25	1.43	1

3.3   Displacement

In the second experiment, we report the total and maximum displacement on both ISPD benchmarks. On legalized NTUplace3 global placements on ISPD 2005 placement contest benchmarks, the total displacement is 25.76X, 1.09X, and 27.16X, the maximum displacement is 1.88X, 1.04X, and 2.40X of our legalizer compared to Tetris [7], Abacus [19], and Kahng [9], respectively. The details of displacement experiments on ISPD 2005 benchmarks are listed in Table 5.

Table 5. Displacement comparison between NTUplace3, Tetris, Abacus, Kahng, and ours on ISPD 2005 benchmarks

ISPD 2005 Benchmarks	Tetris [7]		Abacus [19]		Kahng [9]		Ours	
Name	TOTAL	MAX	TOTAL	MAX	TOTAL	MAX	TOTAL	MAX
adaptec1	7.91E+07	2490	5.89E+06	1247	8.10E+07	2490	6.00E+06	1211
adaptec2	1.31E+08	3432	1.90E+07	3485	1.32E+08	3432	1.90E+07	3239
adaptec3	1.22E+08	4581	5.11E+07	5419	1.23E+08	4577	4.80E+07	5733
adaptec4	1.56E+08	2197	2.74E+07	1702	1.58E+08	3161	2.60E+07	1736
bigblue1	7.38E+08	9319	4.63E+06	1304	7.90E+08	9319	4.80E+06	1342
bigblue2	6.25E+07	1143	1.31E+07	871	6.77E+07	3757	9.20E+06	718
bigblue3	8.01E+08	5886	4.20E+08	6729	8.02E+08	5886	3.50E+08	6756
bigblue4	8.21E+08	2115	6.56E+07	5701	8.36E+08	2115	6.00E+07	5203
AVG.	25.76	1.88	1.09	1.04	27.16	2.40	1	1

On legalized NTUplace3 global placements on ISPD 2006 placement contest benchmarks, the total displacement is 5.27X, 1.15X, and 5.43X, the maximum displacement is 1.51X, 1.35X, and 1.51X of our legalizer compared to Tetris [7], Abacus [19], and Kahng [9], respectively. The details of displacement experiments on ISPD 2006 benchmarks are listed in Table 6. It should be noted that Abacus [19] achieved the best published results in displacement but our legalizer still get better results due to the exact linear wirelength model.

Table 6. Displacement comparison between NTUplace3, Tetris, Abacus, Kahng, and ours on ISPD 2006 benchmarks

ISPD 2006 Benchmarks	Tetris [7]		Abacus [19]		Kahng [9]		Ours	
Name	TOTAL	MAX	TOTAL	MAX	TOTAL	MAX	TOTAL	MAX
adaptec5	4.65E+08	5117	9.12E+07	3617	4.68E+08	5117	8.79E+07	4920
newblue1	1.44E+08	3639	1.37E+07	2990	1.45E+08	3639	1.31E+07	1459
newblue2	2.17E+08	6162	1.05E+08	4535	2.18E+08	6162	7.37E+07	2131
newblue4	2.17E+08	2214	4.24E+07	2808	2.30E+08	2214	4.16E+07	2327
newblue5	1.55E+08	4030	3.52E+07	1527	1.61E+08	4030	3.31E+07	1777
newblue6	8.97E+08	2609	2.68E+08	7485	9.07E+08	2609	2.23E+08	7514
newblue7	1.22E+09	4248	3.99E+08	10527	1.34E+09	4248	3.20E+08	7246
AVG.	5.27	1.51	1.15	1.35	5.43	1.51	1.00	1.00

3.4   Running Time

In the third experiment, we evaluate the running time on both ISPD benchmarks. On legalized NTUplace3 global placements on ISPD 2005 placement contest benchmarks, the running time is 5.79X, 36.18X, and 5.94X of our legalizer compared to Tetris [7], Abacus [19], and Kahng [9], respectively. The details of running time experiments on ISPD 2005 benchmarks are listed in Table 7.

On legalized NTUplace3 global placements on ISPD 2006 placement contest benchmarks, the running time is 6.28X, 26.15X, and 6.49X of our legalizer compared to Tetris [7], Abacus [19], and Kahng [9], respectively. The details of running time experiments on ISPD 2006 benchmarks are listed in Table 8. It should be noted that Tetris [7] achieved the fastest published results but our legalizer still get better results due to the row indexing and fast trial placement techniques.

Table 7. Runtime comparison between NTUplace3, Tetris, Abacus, Kahng, and ours on ISPD 2005 benchmarks

ISPD 2005 Benchmarks	Tetris [7]	Abacus [19]	Kahng [9]	Ours
Name	TIME (s)	TIME (s)	TIME (s)	TIME (s)
adaptec1	32	101	34	16
adaptec2	44	321	47	11
adaptec3	163	647	169	24
adaptec4	213	682	218	47
bigblue1	38	110	40	18
bigblue2	360	601	365	72
bigblue3	1453	15033	1465	82
bigblue4	1272	4456	1304	304
AVG.	5.79	36.18	5.94	1

Table 8. Runtime comparison between NTUplace3, Tetris, Abacus, Kahng, and ours on ISPD 2006 benchmarks

ISPD 2006 Benchmarks	Tetris [7]	Abacus [19]	Kahng [9]	Ours
Name	TIME (s)	TIME (s)	TIME (s)	TIME (s)
adaptec5	304	2225	312	51
newblue1	32	123	35	24
newblue2	389	1032	395	53
newblue4	274	1327	281	49
newblue5	598	1869	612	116
newblue6	839	4917	854	188
newblue7	5163	16844	5245	365
AVG.	6.28	26.15	6.40	1

Figure 14 (a) shows the global placement result of "adaptec1" obtained from NTUplace3. To further reveal the difference of Tetris, Abacus, Kahng, and ours, we plot the movement pictures during legalization in Figure 14 (b), (c), (d), and (e).

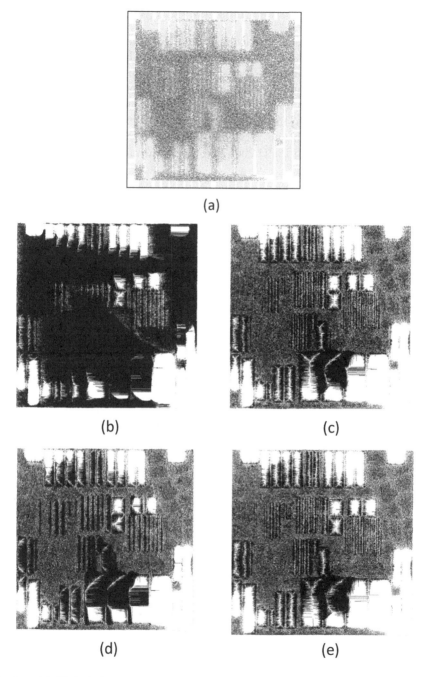

Fig. 14. (a) Global placement result of adaptec1. (b) Cell movement during Tetris [7]. (c) Cell movement during Abacus [19]. (d) Cell movement during Kahng [9]. (e) Ours.

4   Conclusions

In this paper, we proposed a fast legalization algorithm with simultaneous displacement and HPWL minimization. The main contributions of our work are: (1) a fast row selection technique by using k-medoid clustering approach; (2) an exact linear wirelength model to minimize both wirelength and total displacement; (3) a constant time approach to determine the median in trial placement stage. Compared with the state-of-the-art algorithms, experimental results have shown that our legalizer obtains very high-quality results on legalized NTUplace3 global placements on both ISPD 2005 and 2006 placement contest benchmarks.

References

1. Agnihorti, A., Yildiz, M.C., Khatkhate, A., Mathur, A., Ono, S., Madden, P.H.: Fractional cut: Improved recursive bisection placement. In: Proc. ICCAD, pp. 307–310 (2003)
2. Brenner, U., Vygen, J.: Legalizing a placement with minimum total movement. IEEE TCAD 23(12), 1597–1613 (2004)
3. Brenner, U., Struzyna, M.: Faster and better global placement by a new transportation algorithm. In: Proc. DAC, pp. 591–596 (2005)
4. Chan, T., Cong, J., Sze, K., Xie, M.: mPL6: Enhanced multilevel mixed-size placement. In: Proc. ISPD, pp. 212–214 (2006)
5. Chen, T.-C., Jiang, Z.-W., Hsu, T.-C., Chen, H.-C., Chang, Y.-W.: NTUplace3: A high-quality mixed-size analytical placer considering preplaced blocks and density constraints. In: Proc. ICCAD, pp. 187–192 (2006)
6. Doll, K., Johannes, F.M., Antreich, K.J.: Iterative placement improvement by network flow methods. IEEE TCAD 13(10), 1189–1200 (1994)
7. Hill, D.: Method and system for high speed detailed placement of cells within integrated circuit designs. U.S. Patent 6370673 (April 2002)
8. Hur, S.-W., Lillis, J.: Mongrel: Hybrid techniques for standard cell placement. In: Proc. ICCAD, pp. 165–170 (2000)
9. Kahng, A.B., Tucker, P., Zelikovsky, A.: Optimization of Linear Placements for Wirelength Minimization with Free Sites. In: Proc. ASP-DAC 1999, pp. 241–244 (1999)
10. Kahng, A.B., Markov, I.L., Reda, S.: On legalization of row-based placements. In: Proc. GLS-VLSI, pp. 214–219 (2004)
11. Kahng, A.B., Wang, Q.: Implementation and extensibility of an analytic placer. IEEE TCAD 24(05), 734–747 (2005)
12. Lucasius, C.B., Dane, A.D., Kateman, G.: On k-medoid clustering of large data sets with the aid of a genetic algorithm: background, feasibility and comparison. Analytica Chimica Acta 282(3), 647–669 (1993)
13. Luo, T., Ren, H., Alpert, C.J., Pan, D.Z.: Computational geometry based placement migration. In: Proc. DAC, pp. 41–47 (2007)
14. Pan, M., Viswanathan, N., Chu, C.: An efficient and effective detailed placement algorithm. In: Proc. ICCAD, pp. 48–55 (2005)
15. Ren, H., Pan, D.Z., Alpert, C.J., Villarrubia, P.: Diffusion-based placement migration. In: Proc. DAC, pp. 515–520 (2005)

16. Roy, J.A., Papa, D.A., Adya, S.N., Chan, H.H., Ng, A.N., Lu, J.F., Markov, I.L.: Capo: Robust and scalable open-source min-cut floorplacer. In: Proc. ISPD, pp. 224–226 (2005)
17. Sarrafzadeh, M., Wang, M.: NRG: Global and detailed placement. In: Proc. ICCAD, pp. 532–537 (1997)
18. Spindler, P., Johannes, F.M.: Fast and robust quadratic placement based on an accurate linear net model. In: Proc. ICCAD, pp. 179–186 (2006)
19. Spindler, P., Schlichtmann, U., Johannes, F.M.: Abacus: Fast legalization of standard cell circuits with minimal movement. In: Proc. ISPD, pp. 47–53 (2008)
20. Wang, T.C., Wong, D.F.: Optimal floorplan area optimization. IEEE TCAD 11, 992–1002 (1992)
21. Wong, D.F., Liu, C.L.: A new algorithm for floorplan design. In: Proc. DAC, pp. 101–107 (1986)
22. http://www.ispd.cc/

Control Electronics Integration toward Endoscopic Capsule Robot Performing Legged Locomotion and Illumination

Oscar Alonso and Angel Diéguez

Electronics Department, Universitat de Barcelona,
Martí i Franquès n°1, 08028 Barcelona, Spain
oalonso@el.ub.es

Abstract. Miniaturization of sensors and actuators up to the point of active features in endoscopic capsules, such as locomotion or surgery, is a challenge. VECTOR endoscopic capsule has been designed to be the first endoscopic capsule with active locomotion. It is equipped with mini-legs driven by Brushless DC (BLDC) micro motors. In addition it can be also equipped with some other sensors and actuators, like a liquid lens, that permits to enable advanced functions. Those modules are managed by an Application Specific Integrated Circuit (ASIC) specifically designed for the VECTOR capsule. The ASIC is a complete System-On-Chip (SoC) and integrates all the electronics needed to enable the legged locomotion and the sensing and actuating functions of the capsule in an unique chip. The SoC also permits other functions for endoscopic capsules such as drug delivery and biopsy. The size of the SoC is 5.1 mm x 5.2 mm in a 0.35 µm high voltage CMOS technology.

Keywords: Active capsular endoscopy, gastrointestinal exploration, Brushless motor, liquid lens, control ASIC, electronics.

1   Introduction

The gastro intestinal (GI) tract, like any other part of the human body may be affected by infections or diseases. Because of the length of the GI tract and its location inside the human body, the detection and diagnosis of these diseases is very complicated. The method used by doctors when analyzing the GI tract is endoscopy. Basically, the endoscopy consists in introducing, inside the GI tract, a thin tube with a video camera and light at the beginning. The basic function of this system is to show to doctors the GI tract without any need of surgery. The tube can be inserted both orally and rectally. Endoscopy in the digestive tract is named differently depending on the area under study and the applied techniques, the procedures most widely used are:

- Esofagogastruoduodenoscopy (EGD), which includes the study of the oesophagus, stomach and duodenum. This procedure is used to discover the reason for swallowing difficulties, nausea, vomiting, reflux, bleeding, indigestion, abdominal pain, or chest pain. In particular, for this procedure the

J.L. Ayala, D. Atienza, and R. Reis (Eds.): VLSI-SoC 2010, IFIP AICT 373, pp. 312–338, 2012.
© IFIP International Federation for Information Processing 2012

endoscope can be introduced through the nose or the mouth of the patients, who have been previously sedated in order to reduce the pain during the examination. In addition, the scope also blows air into the stomach in order to expand the folds of tissue and give the possibility of look through the folders.

- Double Balloon Enteroscopy, which is used to study the small bowel. It is a newly developed endoscopic method which permits to explore the small bowel without any need of surgical intervention [1]. Using a simple push and pull method two balloons are used in this procedure to examine the small intestine in steps approximately 40 cm long.Double balloon endoscopy [2] is indicated in cases of unclear bleeding in the digestive tract, Chron's disease, unclear chronic diarrhoea, abdominal pain, intestinal polyposis, intestinal dysplasia and Celiac disease.

- Push Enteroscope, which is also used for the study of the small bowel. During this procedure, a long, narrow, flexible gastrointestinal endoscope, known as a push enteroscope, is advanced into the upper gastrointestinal tract to examine and evaluate the proximal section (first one third) of the small bowel [3]. This procedure is indicated when the doctors are not able to identify the cause of obscure bleeding or some other GI disorder.

- Colonoscopy, which is used to study the colon. The colonoscopy is the less invasive technique that uses a scope to examine the colon and the distal part of the small bowel. Colonoscopy has been available since the early 1970s and has become critical to the diagnosis and management of colorectal disorders 4].Although colonoscopy is a safe procedure, complications can sometimes occur. These include perforation a puncture of the colon walls, which could require surgical repair. Sedation during the examination, post-procedural abdominal pain and irritable bowel syndrome are the main drawbacks. However, with this procedure biopsies can be taken of any abnormal areas at the same time as the screening or diagnostic test is being done. Any polyps found can be removed during this procedure [4-8].

- Flexible Sigmoidescopy (FS), which is similar to the colonoscopy. However, this procedure only examines the region from the rectum to the colon (also known as sigmoid). This procedure is one of the screening modalities for colorectal cancer. From the point of view of screening, FS clearly cannot completely exclude the presence of colon cancer in all asymptomatic people. However, flexible sigmoidoscopy every 5 years with or without fecal occult blood test (FOBT) is one of the screening methods recommended by major professional organizations. It identifies 50 to 70% of the advanced neoplasms, if any discovery of a distal neoplasia is followed up with a total examination of the colon by colonoscopy [9-10].

Endoscopy allows us to examine the digestive tract. Nevertheless, it also has some disadvantages. For example, it is a painful treatment for the patient because requires the introduction of a tube inside the human body (the scope has a diameter of 7-8 mm, however the pain associated with the procedure is not caused by the insertion of the scope but from inflating of the colon in order to do the inspection). Furthermore, endoscopy can not access the entire GI tract. For example, doctors are only able to study a small part of the small fine. Finally, endoscopy is not always effective, as the conditions are so adverse in the GI tract (long extension, folds of tissue, poor lighting) that the doctor is not always able to detect diseases, requiring a second observation or some alternative method.

The need to improve the existing method and the fact that the number of people around the world that access to endoscopy is about 15 million [11] has led to the emergence of alternative methods like capsular endoscopy.

Capsular endoscopy is a minimally invasive procedure that permits to study the whole GI tract. Capsular endoscopy consists in a small capsule with the shape of a pill, which contains some electronic elements needed to perform the same task as the traditional endoscopy. In standard devices such electronic elements are basically a tiny camera, some LEDs for the illumination of the GI tract, a radiofrequency (RF) system needed to transmit the acquired images to the doctors and a battery (needed to supply the capsule)[12-13]. Figure 1 shows a picture of a capsular endoscope.

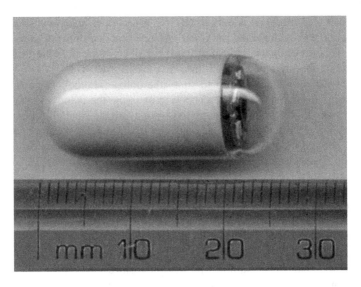

Fig. 1. Picture of a capsular endoscope

The significant development in medical diagnostics and imaging has brought up a lot of new capsular endoscope products coming to the health care market. The capsular endoscopes have been able to minimize patient discomfort and pain during digestive tract screening with less risk of infection and harmless to body organs. This kind of medical procedure is less invasive and gives a great impact compared to the traditional method. As it occurs with classical endoscopes, capsular endoscopy also has some disadvantages. For example, being a portable device, the quality of the images and the frame rate is usually not the same as in traditional endoscopy. In addition, there is the possibility that the capsule suffers an obstruction in any part of the digestive system [14], and for this reason, capsule endoscopy is not recommended for those patients suspected of having a capsular obstruction, fistulas, motility disorders, patients with pacemarkers or other implanted electro-medical devices, dysphagia, and pregnancy [15-16].

The capsular endoscopes are known by different names such as wireless capsule camera, video pill, PillCam [12,17], EndoCapsule [13] or Sayaka [18]. Their shape look similar to a pill or capsule and they are able to see areas, which traditional endoscopes are unable to see. Capsular endoscopes also gives extra convenience to the patient. After swallowing one of the aforementioned capsules, the patient may leave the hospital and return later after 8 hours. During this long period, the capsule captures images along the gastrointestinal (GI) tract while the patient is continuing the daily activity.

Although pill-shaped micro-cameras have existed for over 9 years by now, these systems are passive and are dependent to the peristaltic movement of the gastric wall to actively locomote. The camera takes thousands of pictures as it passes through the GI tract, but its position during this time cannot be controlled. Therefore, many research institutions around the world are exploring the possibility to have an active endoscopic device for medical inspection and therapy in the form of capsular robot [19].

Compared to traditional endoscopy, capsular endoscopy performs similar operations in a less invasive way. In order to functionally emulate a traditional endoscope, a capsule endoscope must be equipped with 3 basic functions. These functions are:

- Vision system, which is in charge of illuminating the GI tract and acquiring images. The vision system is composed by at least one camera and some LEDs.
- Communications system, which is in charge of sending the acquired images to the receiver placed outside the human body. It can be also in charge of receiving external orders.
- Supply system, which is in charge of supplying the whole capsule. The supply system can be composed by batteries or by other systems like wireless power supplier.

Although these basic functions are always needed, a capsule endoscope can be equipped with more functions (i.e. advanced functions) which will improve the diagnosis or add therapeutic possibilities. Figure 2 shows a scheme with the basic and advanced functions that can be added in a capsule endoscope and the components (sensors/actuators) required. Figure 2 describes also the electronics needed to enable each included function. The basic functions are those functions which are essential to build an operative capsular endoscope. Those functions have been described above. In addition, figure 2 also shows some of the most important advanced functions that can be added, as for example fluorescence, high frame rate, auto-focus/zoom, locomotion, drug delivery and biopsy. Basically, the fluorescent function permits a visible detection of early stage cancer by only adding some fluorescent LEDs to the capsule endoscope [20-21]. The high frame rate function permits to achieve more images of the GI tract and it also permits to perform the examination in real time. The autofocus/zoom functions requires the inclusion of a liquid lens (which is operated with high voltages), and it permits to acquire better images of the regions of interest. Finally, the drug delivery, biopsy and locomotion need special mechanism in order to perform their functions, for example it is needed a syringe or a pump for drug delivery, or a cutting mechanism for biopsy or some legs/vibration/magnetic system for active locomotion.

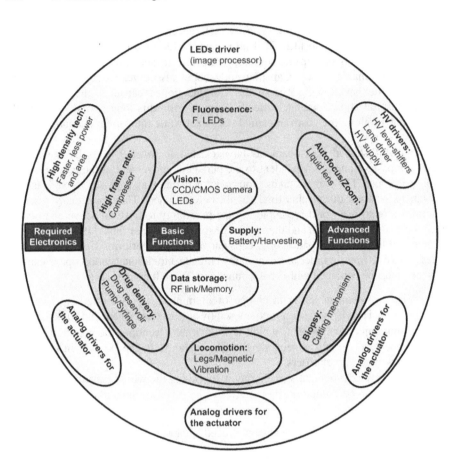

Fig. 2. Basic scheme of the functions that can be added in a capsule endoscope. It also resumes the required electronics needed to enable such functions.

The inclusion of new functionalities is accompanied almost always with the incorporation of additional electronics in the capsule endoscope. Therefore, the space constraints imposed by the capsule endoscope plays an important role because they limit the electronics that can be added. In addition, the packaging of the electronics is also important. For example, enabling each function with off-the-shelf components requires so much more volume than designing an ASIC with specific drivers.

The aim of this chapter is to present the architecture of an advanced capsule endoscope designed in the framework of the "Versatile Endoscopic Capsule for Gastrointestinal Tumour Recognition and Therapy" (VECTOR) FP6-European project. Such capsule must include some advanced functions in order to enhance capsular diagnosis and to enable therapeutic functions. The requirements envisioned for the VECTOR capsule are:

- Improving image analysis. In order to improve the diagnosis the system has to be capable of performing NBI or fluorescence analysis. In the VECTOR capsule these different analysis are achieved by using different LEDs in each case (e.g. for the Fluorescence function the capsule uses fluorescent LEDs).

- Improving the vision system by enabling the autofocus and zoom function. This is achieved by adding a liquid lens.
- High frame-rate: the state-of-the art capsules have a low frame rate. By increasing the frame rate the doctors are able to analyse more images. In order to achieve a high frame-rate it is necessary to implement a compressor between the camera and the transceiver.
- Active locomotion. It permits to create space, stop and move forward and backwards the capsule inside the GI tract. The movement can be achieved by adding some legs to the VECTOR capsule or by using magnets.
- Enabling therapeutic functions like drug delivery and/or biopsies.

Implementation of the above functions with off-the-shelf components requires too much space. So, a specific solution in which a unique ASIC is used has been performed.

2   System Architecture

An active capsular endoscope needs the intervention of a medical doctor during the exploration. Guiding of the capsule endoscope is necessary to explore in detail a region or to do therapy. This procedure depends on the acquired images and the criteria of the medical doctor, therefore the possibility of a human error have to be considered. Nevertheless, if some robotic capabilities are added into the capsule endoscope, the possibility of a human error can be highly reduced. For example, if the robotic capsular endoscope also processes the images searching for polyps or abnormalities. The robotic functions can be also very useful during navigation. Such robotic functions can be enabled by adding a central processing unit (CPU), like a microprocessor, into the capsule.

As the VECTOR project pursues the goal of improving capsular endoscopy by adding advanced functions, enabling therapy and robotic behaviour, the basic and essential blocks of the smart VECTOR capsule must be: powering unit, vision system, telemetry system, locomotion system and a CPU. The powering, vision and telemetry units are the basic functions for a passive capsular endoscope, however, for an active capsule it is needed to add the locomotion function. The CPU is required to enable the robotic behaviour of the capsular endoscope.

Due to the space limitations and the low power consumption requirements, it is preferable to use ICs. For this reason, the trend for this system architecture is to unify the CPU and the locomotive system in one ASIC (the control IC). With this system architecture the robotic behaviour is enabled by software.

Figure 3 illustrates the concept of the VECTOR capsule. The ASIC, the CMOS camera, the telemetry system and supply system are in charge of enabling the basic functions of an active capsular endoscope. The ASIC includes the drivers needed to enable advanced vision functions and locomotion. The selected actuator for enabling locomotion in the VECTOR capsule is a brushless (BLDC) micromotor. The most important feature of this actuator is that it can also be used to enable drug delivery and biopsy functions. Therefore, with the inclusion of a BLDC motor driver into the control ASIC it is possible to enable 3 different functions.

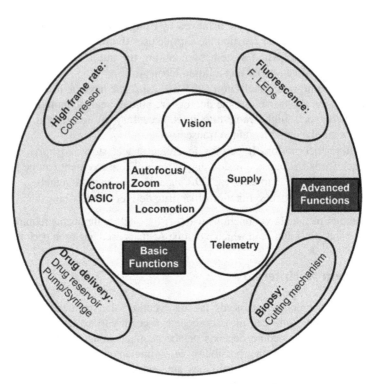

Fig. 3. Basic scheme showing the VECTOR capsule concept

Figure 4 shows a representative schematic of the proposed architecture for the microrobotic VECTOR capsule. The next functions can be distinguished:

- The Powering Unit, which is the most important module, since energy feeding is mandatory for all the other modules. A bottleneck affecting all the commercial capsules is the limited available battery power, providing typically 25mW for 6-8 hours [22]. This amount of power is barely sufficient for low resolution images transmitted at low data-rates and certainly not enough for actuators and highly consuming modules. In the VECTOR capsule, a 3D inductive link is used to supply up to 400 mW (4). Details of the 3D inductive link can be found in [23-24]. In order to take full advantage from wireless power transfer, an energy storage system is also implemented, in order to provide high current peaks when needed.

- The vision system, which is formed by a CMOS camera and 16 LEDs. The CMOS camera acquires images while the LEDs illuminate the GI tract. In particular, the camera is a monolithic 320×240 active-pixel RGB/gray level camera-on-a-chip sensor that has been developed by Neuricam [25]. It has been fabricated using 0.18µm CMOS technology from UMC.

  For the illumination, the solution is to use narrow bandwidth color LEDs switched on alternatively at high frequency to deliver a composite white light illumination. This solution has the great advantage to allow recording white images and chromatic images with a single illumination unit.

- The transceiver: The endoscopic capsule needs a bidirectional data transmission for its correct operation, the endoscopic capsule has to receive orders from the medical doctors and it also has to be capable of sending the acquired data outside the human body. The downlink from the capsule to the outside world must be able to transmit a large amount of data. In addition, the available data rate defines the image quality of the endoscope. However, to get a high data rate one needs to increase the radio frequency of the carrier wave of the signal; but the higher the frequency, the higher the absorption of the waves by the human body. As the available power for the transmission is limited, a dedicated 2 Mbps FSK near-field transmitter has been designed and implemented to the endoscopic capsuled. The data error detection and correction are performed at the transceiver. Further details of the transmitter are given in [26].
- The control IC, which has the control of the whole system. It controls the CMOS camera and the RF transceiver via the I2C bus. Taking into account the speed data transfers, an I2C bus has been selected to perform the interconnection of the different elements because it uses less wires (i.e. 2 wires), compared to other communication strategies like SPI bus (4 wires). In addition, the I2C bus is standard and it is widely used.

The control IC is also the one in charge of blinking the LEDs, driving 2 different motor drivers (used to enable locomotion, drug delivery and biopsy when it is needed) and driving a liquid lens (used for the autofocus and zoom functions).

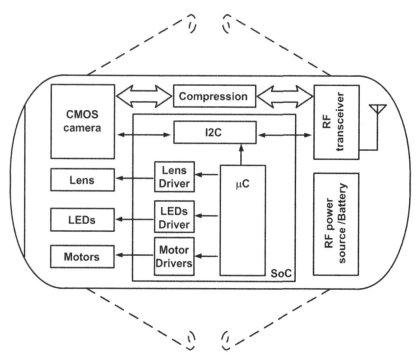

Fig. 4. Schematic of the proposed architecture for the microrobotic VECTOR capsule

As can be seen in figure 4, the ASIC does not control the compression system. Compression should be included in the CMOS camera or in the RF transceiver, however, as it will be described later, none of them include it. For this reason, in order to enable high frame rate it is needed to add an external element which has to be able to compress the acquired images and send it to the transceiver.

3   Control IC Description

Looking at the basic features implemented on the commercial capsule endoscope, it is a big challenge to keep these inherent features of the capsule camera and integrate additional and advanced capabilities on a robot capsule, such as active locomotion and an auto-focusing. Especially if it is taken into account that it is needed a mixed signal ASIC in order to control and manage all these devices. Moreover, Such ASIC must be capable of working with low voltages and high voltages.

Beyond the trivial problems of integrating additional electronics on the same space, the difficulties arise to manage the actuators that enable the robotic functions. One of the key elements to solve such difficulties is to correctly select the technology to design the ASIC. For this reason, in this chapter the technology selection is detailed before entering in detail in the architecture of the ASIC and the design of the drivers.

3.1   Technology Selection

The definition of the technology for the fabrication of the ASIC is a very important part in the design flow. Considering that only some technologies are available in Europe at low cost and that not all the features of the technology are available for low-volume users, the technology selection has to be done at the beginning of the design flow.

To fabricate the ASIC several technologies have been evaluated. It has been taken into account the integration density, the power consumption and the powering and driving voltages required for the capsule elements. All the technologies evaluated are available through Europractice Consortium or through Circuit Multi Projects (CMP) which offer low cost fabrication through Multi-Project-Wafer (MPW). On Table 1 there is a summary of technologies which can be used to design the IC for the VECTOR project. Deep-submicron technologies can not be used in VECTOR because the high-voltage requirements.

Table 1. High Voltage Technologies Available in Europractice and CMP

Technology	L (um)	Price (€)	V (core)	V (I/O)	Runs/Year
AMIS I2T100	0.7	600/mm2	5	5 / 100	5-EU
AMIS I3T80	0.35	990/mm2	3.3	3.3 / 80	4-EU
AMS CXZ	0.8	650/mm2	3.3 / 5	2.5 / 50	3-EU
AMS H35b4	0.35	1000/mm2	3.3 / 5	20 / 50	4-EU/4-CMP

The maximum voltage required for the liquid lens of the capsule is 60V, although the driving can be done at 50V. The high voltage technologies presented on Table 1 are designed to achieve voltages from 50V to 100V. Comparing these four technologies a higher integration is obtained with a lower characteristic size, which is obtained with AMIS I3T80 and AMS H35b4. Between these two possibilities it has been chosen Austria-Micro-System (AMS) H35b4 technology which can work with four metals, in front of the three metals on AMIS technology, giving the possibility to reduce the interconnections complexity and also the total area required for the system. Further reasons to choose the AMS technology is that EEPROMs can be available in the H35b4 technology.

3.2   Control IC Architecture

All the drivers and control electronics of the VECTOR capsule have been embedded in the same IC fabricated with a 0.35 um HV CMOS technology except compression and error correction.

Figure 6 shows the architecture of the IC. The main block of the IC is the embedded 8051 microprocessor which is the control unit (8051 IP). The inclusion of the microprocessor into the endoscopic capsule it is needed because it gives more flexibility to the system and facilitates the debug. In addition, as the functions of the capsular endoscope are not known in detail, the addition of a finite state machine (FSM) is excluded. Finally, the microprocessor permits to add robotic functions to the capsule endoscope.

The microprocessor is equipped with 256 B of SRAM internal memory. It also has 2 kB SRAM of data memory and 8 kB SRAM of program memory. This numbers has been selected from previous experiences [27]. After the test of the ASIC it will be possible to exactly determine the amount of memory that is really needed. The memory type used is volatile. Therefore, each time the VECTOR capsule is powered-up, the program has to be uploaded in the program memory area. EEPROM memories have not been selected because they are not available by the technology provider in the case of MPW projects. The programming process is carried out by the Boot Loader (BL) that interprets and sends binary code received from serial port to particular program memory area. After the program is uploaded a Power On Reset is done to the processor and configuration registers. Figure 5 shows a simplified diagram of how the ASIC is programmed.

Specific peripherals have been included for each of the functions of the capsule. The peripherals determine the dynamic power consumption of the capsule. This strategy allows to administrata the instantaneous power to not overpass the powering capabilities. The peripherals are the time stamp control unit (TSCU), the I2C control unit (I2CCU), the LEDs control unit (LCU), the lens control unit (LeCU), the clock generator unit (CGU), the communications control unit (CCU) and two locomotion control units (LoCU). Detailed description of the ASIC features is given next.

Time Stamp Control Unit: The TSCU is a simple FSM which is in charge of sending a synchronization bit to the transceiver. With this strategy the doctor is able to know when the images have been acquired.

I2C Control Unit: The interconnections between the different elements are done using a standard serial bus I2C [28]. It is also possible to implement this bus with slight modifications.

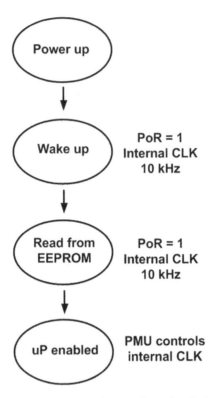

Fig. 5. Simplified block diagram of the ASIC configuration during the wake up process

Here are some of the features of the I2C bus:

- Only two bus lines are required; a serial data line (SDA) and a serial clock line (SCL)
- Each device connected to the bus is software addressable by a unique address and simple master/slave relationships exist at all times; masters can operate as master-transmitters or as master-receivers
- It is a true multi-master bus including collision detection and arbitration to prevent data corruption if two or more masters simultaneously initiate data transfer
- Serial, 8-bit oriented, bi-directional data transfers can be made at up to 100kbit/s in the Standard-mode, up to 400kbit/s in the Fast-mode, or up to 3.4Mbit/s in the High-speed mode.
- On-chip filtering rejects spikes on the bus data line to preserve data integrity
- The number of ICs that can be connected to the same bus is limited only by a maximum bus capacitance

Figure 7 shows a schematic of the connections of the I2C bus.

Comunications Control Unit: The CCU is in charge of receiving data from the telemetry system. It has to decode such data and send it to the microprocessor. The data is received at 4'8 kHz by a serial input. Therefore, the RX channel is used to send orders and information to the control ASIC. The communication link permits to control the capsule endoscope from outside.

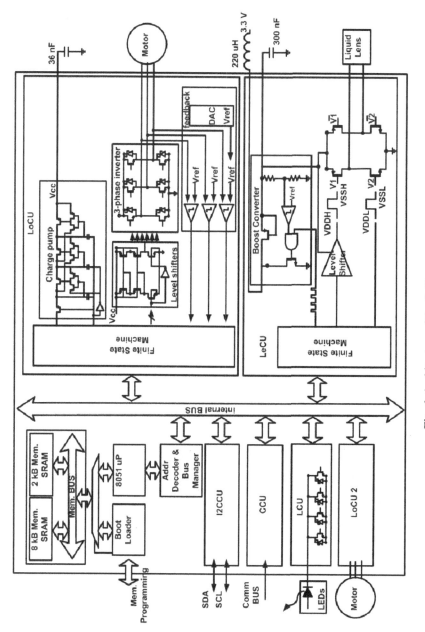

Fig. 6. Architecture of the SoC

The RX channel is usually in the sleep mode. To start the receiving process, the transmitter must send a logic one followed by the data (16 bits). Once received, the CCU generates an interruption (INT0) and it returns to the sleep mode. The interruption is processed by the microprocessor.

Clock Generator Unit: The CGU is a simple digital block used to distribute the clock of the system. The CGU receives the external clock (10 MHz) which is used to generate the clock signals for the communication module, the LoCU, LeCU and LCU modules.

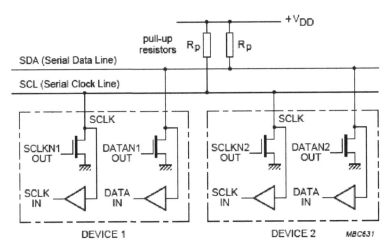

Fig. 7. Connection of Standard-AND Fast-Mode Devices to the I2C-bus [28]

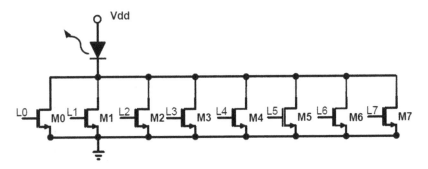

Fig. 8. Schematic of the LEDs driver

LEDs Control Unit: The LCU is composed by a basic FSM which controls the current and the period to blink the LEDs and LED driver. The LEDs driver is composed of 8 transistors in parallel, with the Drain pins connected to the LED. Each transistor has a different W/L ratio. With this strategy, it is possible to control the current passes through the LED controlling the intensity of LEDs. Figure 8 shows the schematic of the LED driver.

Liquid Lens Control Unit: The liquid lens used in the capsule is the ARCTIC 416 liquid lens from Varioptic. It uses two different electrodes to apply the driving signal. This liquid lens can be modelled as a resistor with a capacitor in series between each electrode. The working principle is simple, the focal of the lens is changed when it is driven with a PWM signal of amplitude between 30 V and 50 V. The impedance of the lens depends on the frequency of the driving signal, and a PWM signal of 1 kHz has practical utility. Figure 9 shows how the focal of the lens is changed depending on the applied voltage (Vrms).

Although there are some ICs in the market which have been designed to drive the liquid lens [29-30], they consume too much area and, therefore, in the VECTOR capsule context, it is more suitable to design the liquid lens driver and implement it in the same ASIC where the other drivers are also placed.

The most typical circuit to drive an actuator like the liquid lens is an H-bridge driver. The main drawback is that the liquid lens requires high voltages (up to 50 V). Figure 10 shows the overall architecture of the liquid lens driver. The main element of the lens driver is the H-bridge (HB), which has two HV-PMOS transistors and two HV-NMOS transistors. The two outputs of the HB are connected directly to the liquid lens electrodes. The supply voltage of the lens driver (up to VDDH = 50 V) is generated by a DC-DC boost converter integrated partially (the inductor is external) into the SoC. The High Voltage level-shifters are needed to raise the driving signals to the operating gate voltages of the HV-PMOS transistors. Thus, the HV-PMOS transistors of the HB are driven with signal from VDDH to VDDH – 2 VTHP (where VTHP is the threshold voltage of the HV-PMOS transistor). Under normal operation the driver focuses the liquid lens by changing the duty cycle of the boost converter control signal. The voltage supply is then changed between 30 V and 50 V. The control of the driver is performed by a FSM which is also included in the driver.

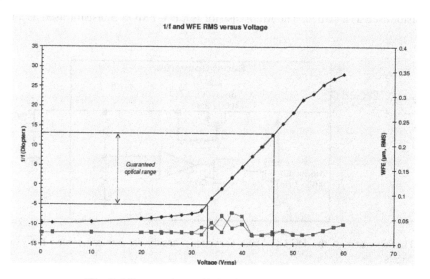

Fig. 9. 1/f versus the applied voltage at the liquid lens

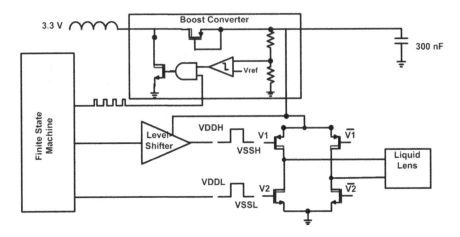

Fig. 10. Overall architecture of the liquid lens driver

A more detailed schematic of the boost converter is depicted in figure 11. As the technology used can afford 50 V, the boost converter also includes a small circuit to prevent the generation of a voltage greater than 50 V. Such circuit is composed by a resistor divider, a comparator and an AND gate. When the output voltage is greater than 50 V the output of the comparator supplies a logic zero to the AND gate, which automatically switches off the transistor M1. If the output voltage is lower than 50 V, the comparator supplies a logic one, and the control is performer normally by the FSM.

The M1 and M2 transistors are HV transistors. The M1 transistor is HV-NMOS transistor used as a switch. The M2 transistor is a HV-PMOS transistor used as a HV-Diode.

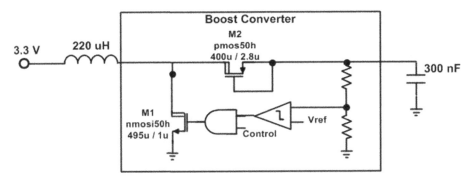

Fig. 11. Schematic of the DC-DC boost converter. Outside the box are placed the external components

Locomotion Control Unit: The micromotor to be used in the capsule endoscope is a micro BLDC motor SBL04 (4mm diameter) from Namiki. It is a very attractive solution for engineers working in micro technologies and medical field, servo lens and micropumps. The strong construction allows the operation also in extreme environmental conditions. In combination with planetary geared SPG04, 4 different reduction ratios, the micro motor is suitable for a wide range of applications [31].

The driver of the Namiki motor is based on a 3-phase structure. This driver is the most popular and simplest solution for the control of the BLDC motor. Figure 12 shows the driver composed by 6 MOSFETs and controlled by 6 different signals [32]. Usually the MOSFETs are accompanied with a schottky diode in anti-parallel in order to manage the current generated in the inductance of the motor when one of the driving transistors is switched-off. Basically, the diodes maintain the transistors in the safe operating area (SOA). The better size reduction of the motor driver is achieved eliminating this external component. Despite its simplicity, it is needed to pay attention while designing the driver in order to minimize the gate voltage and the size of the transistors and, more important, to avoid freewheeling currents in the chip [33].

The motor works feed by current. When one phase has an input current, the second phase has an output current, and the third phase remains inactive. Alternating these phases the motor works properly. According to figure 12, in one stage the transistors 1 and 5 are switched on (a). Hence, the current flows through transistor 1 to transistor 5. In the second stage, transistor 5 is switched off and transistor 6 is switched on (b). In this case the current flows through transistor 1 to transistor 6. When going from (a) to (b), e.g., when transistor 5 is switched off, the parasitic inductance of the motor induces a freewheeling current that goes through the anti-parallel diode of transistor 2.

As commented, in order to reduce the area of the driver the diodes are not used. If no external diodes are used the freewheeling current must be driven by the parasitic anti-parallel diode of one of the MOSFETs. This implies a large quantity of current going into the substrate and, if possible, this current must be avoided or reduced. Therefore, the driving strategies used to avoid or reduce freewheeling currents in the design of a typical 3-phase driving structure with the h35 CMOS technology of AMS are:

- To implement a Synchronous Rectification (SR) with the controller [34-35].
- To control the induced freewheeling current by accurate control of the driving transistors [36].

In this case, the control of the induced freewheeling current by an accurate control of the driving transistors was selected because the control is simpler than in the SR solution. Further details of this controlling method are given in [36].

Figure 13 presents the architecture needed for the driving of the motors. The charge pump is in charge of generating up to 5 V and the level-shifter are in charge of adapting the controlling digital signals from the level 0 - 3.3 V to the level 0 - 5 V. Operating the transistors of the 3-phase inverter with 5 V gate voltage allows the use of smaller transistors compared with 3.3 V driving.

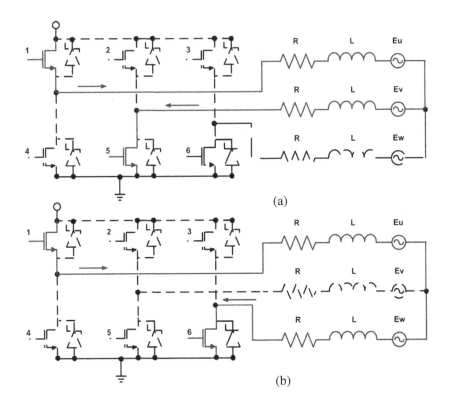

Fig. 12. Scheme of the basic function of the motor in two consecutive steps

The charge pump is based on the Dickson-style charge pump [37] (Figure 14). It is designed for low voltage applications and has low power consumption. To generate any supply signal from 0 to 5 V, the charge pump must be supplied with an external voltage between 0 and 1.8 V. The maximum power consumption is achieved when it is supplied by 1.8 V (an output of 5 V) and it is of 0.45 mW.

The driver is also equipped with a feedback stage to perform a sensorless control based on the measurement of the back electromotive force (BEMF) generated at the motor. The feedback stage is composed by three comparators and a R-2R digital to analog converter (DAC). Each comparator senses each motor phase. The DAC generates the voltage reference for the comparators.

Finally, in normal operation, the driver is programmed with a start-up sequence, and configured to achieve the maximum speed possible. The start-up sequence consists of aligning the rotor to a known position and soon afterward commutating it in slow speed. This start-up sequence is necessary to generate BEMF feedback from the motor coil, because BEMF feedback can only be detected when the rotor turns. If everything goes well and the BEMF reading shows an adequate value, the next commutation should be triggered by the incoming BEMF signals. The proper BEMF reading can be achieved through skipping one electrical commutation ahead by 120 degree and waiting for the zero crossing on the respective floating coil.

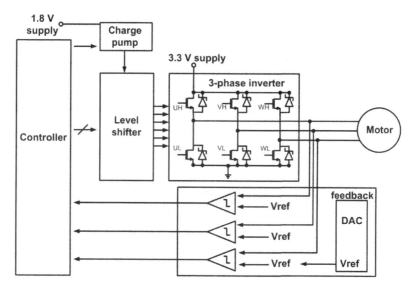

Fig. 13. Architecture of the motor driver

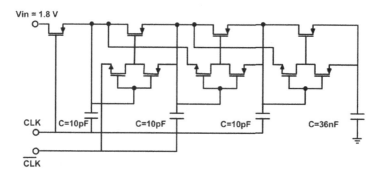

Fig. 14. Schematic of the charge pump

4   Implementation Results

The die photo is shown in figure 15a. The size of the SoC is 5.1 mm x 5.2 mm. The IC needs 2 externals capacitors of 36 nF and 300 nF, and an external inductor of 220 uH for its correct operation. The test of the ASIC has been performed using a wired VECTOR capsule prototype equipped with 8 mini-legs and 4 white LEDs. The procedure for testing was straightforward on an experimental board comprising one microcontroller and the ASIC. The microcontroller (PIC18F2550) is used to configure the ASIC each time we want to experiment with new programs. On the test bench, three connectors for BLDC motors and LEDs are connected to the ASIC. Further details of the test are given in [38-39].

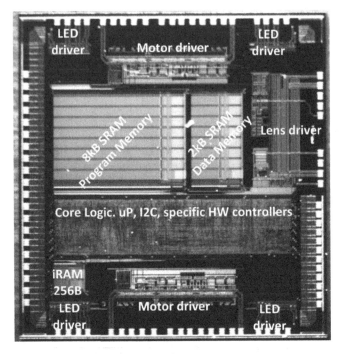

Fig. 15. a) Die photography. b) Image of the Test board and the Capsule prototype.

A graphical user interface (GUI) application written in JAVA language has been developed to communicate with the PIC18F2500 through USB port. Figure 15b shows the VECTOR capsule prototype connected to the experimental board. In the accompanying video it is shown how the capsule opens and closes the legs while the illumination is turned on and off simultaneously.

The wired capsule prototype allows us to measure the power consumption. Figure 16 presents the measured power consumption of each task performed by the VECTOR capsule prototype. The tasks are enabled/disabled by the microprocessor. The maximum power demand is in the LoCU module. Each BLDC motor is connected to 4 legs. Therefore, it is possible to move 4 or 8 legs. The power consumption of the motor during the start-up is higher than in the stationary. However, the start-up does not alter the behavior of the VECTOR capsule because it is done in a short time (i.e. 10 ms).

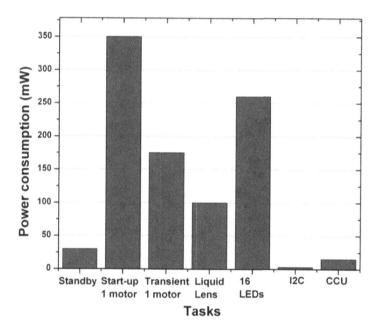

Fig. 16. Measured power consumption

Nevertheless, more exhaustive tests have been performed on the liquid lens driver and in the BLDC motor drivers in order to determine the correct operation of each block.

In the liquid lens driver the most problematic device is the boost converter, because if it fails it is required to use an external high voltage generator, which cannot be added in the capsule.

The DC-DC boost converter reported good results compared. An output of 50 V is achieved using a capacitive load at the output and 3.3 V at the input. Figure 17 shows the output voltage achieved using two different duty cycles (0.85 the red points and 0.7 the black ones) and different resistive loads connected at the output.

Although the liquid lens is not able to supply high voltages with low resistive loads, it is able to supply up to 50 V to the liquid lens. For this reason, the test of the full driver was prepared. The liquid lens has two electrodes in the external shape, for this reason it is needed to prepare a special board to connect the liquid lens in the right way. Figure 18 shows the boards used to connect the liquid lens

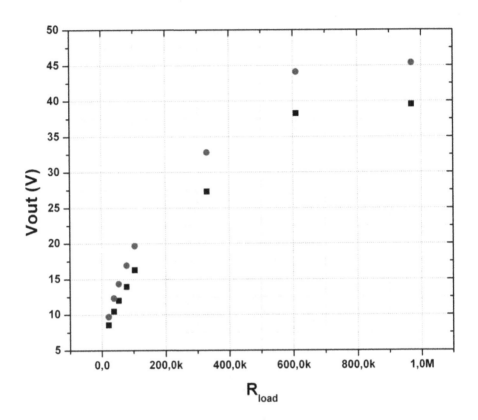

Fig. 17. Output voltage of the DC-DC boost converter versus the resistive load connected at the output. Results obtained using a duty cycle of 0.85 (red points) and a duty cycle of 0.7 (black points)

Figure 19 shows the test platform used for testing the complete system. It contains the liquid lens, a camera used to acquire images, the ASIC and the supplies sources needed to supply the ASIC. The liquid lens is in front of the camera, therefore it is possible to change the focal of the liquid lens and acquire different images with different focals.

Fig. 18. Board uses to mount and test the liquid lens

Fig. 19. Board uses to mount and test the liquid lens

The test consisted in generating an increasing voltage from 30 V to 50 V and applying the control signals generated by the driver to the liquid lens. With this strategy, it is possible to see how the focal of the liquid lens changes because the camera is acquiring images. Using this methodology, different images were acquired per different focals (i.e. different supply voltages). Figure 20 shows two pictures acquired by the camera using the liquid lens with a supply voltage of 30 V and 48 V. It can be seen that in the first image the liquid lens is not focalized while in the second image the liquid lens is focalized.

The test for the BLDC motor driver demonstrated that the driver can operate without the need of external diodes. This is a very important result because it reduces the area occupied by the BLDC motor driver, and the available space in the capsule endoscope can be used for other purposes. Figure 21 shows the motor signals during the start-up of the motor driver avoiding the freewheeling currents.

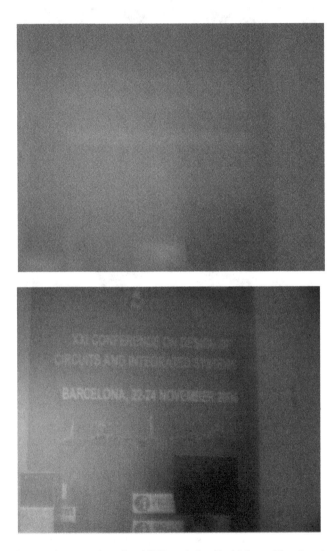

Fig. 20. Focalizing an image using the ASIC and the liquid lens. The first image uses a generated supply voltage of 30 V and the second image uses 48 V.

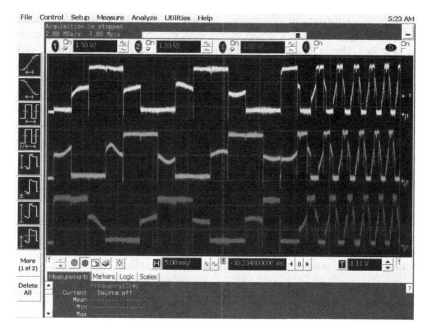

Fig. 21. Start-up of the improved driver using 12 steps to align the rotor

5   Conclusions

The next step needed to make capsular endoscopy the golden standard procedure in endoscopy consist in improving the diagnosis functions and enabling therapeutic functions. The solution proposed in this chapter consists in equipping a capsule endoscope with robotic functions. Such robotic functions can be enabled by equipping the capsule endoscope with more sensors and actuators, needed to increase the capabilities, and adding a control system, which will control such sensors and actuators. Instead of using multiple chips, the solution has been to concentrate all the control electronics in a unique chip which is able to generate high current and high voltages required for today actuators in microrobotics.

In addition, the ASIC can be programmed with an RTOS which permits to control the capsule robot in real time. This allows the capsule robot to act according to the input stimuli and devote more efforts to events which are more important.

The microrobotic solution improves the medical diagnosis because the doctors have a total control of the endoscopic robot. This provides better accuracy during the exploration because the capsule robot is able to approach and focus over the desired section of the GI tract. Furthermore, thanks to the active locomotion, it is possible to do a faster exploration, compared with existing solutions. It permits to exclude the heal area and a faster approaching to the diseased area. However, the microrobotic solution has still some problems due to space limitations and power consumption requirements.

Although miniaturization of sensors, actuators, control electronics, telemetry system, wireless power system, compression system, CMOS camera and illumination system is a fact, the inclusion of all these elements in an small capsule of reduced dimension is still a challenge. In particular, for the presented microrobotic solution, the size of the capsule robot is d 10mm and length 33 mm, which is bigger than the state of the art capsule endoscopes. Furthermore, the addition of so many elements to the capsule robot increases the power demand. Despite the fact that the wireless power system is capable of supplying 400 mW, it is not enough power for the capsule robot to perform more than one task simultaneously. Besides, the addition of the compression to the presented capsular endoscope introduces a problem because it cannot be integrated in the control IC due to the technology selection. It was finally implemented in a small FPGA (silicon blue FPGA), however the best solution is to integrate it in an IC specially devoted for this operation.

In conclusion, although the trend in capsular endoscopy is to equip the capsule endoscope with robotic functions and increase diagnostic and therapeutic capabilities, current limitations of space and power consumption makes this solution unfeasible at the moment. For this reason, new solutions have to be applied.

References

1. Fujinon Endoscopic Systems 2003-07, http://www.fujinonendoscopy.com/
2. Cazzato, I.A., Cammarota, G., Nista, E.C., Cesaro, P., et al.: Diagnostic and Therapeutic Impact of Double-Balloon Enteroscopy (DBE) in a Series of 100 Patients with Suspected Small Bowel Diseases. Dig. Liver Dis. 39(5), 483–487 (2007)
3. Muscarella, L.F.: Infection Control, and the Clinical Practice of Push Enteroscopy. Endoscopic Shuffling, Gastroenterology Nursing 30(2), 109–115 (2007)
4. Brown, G.J., Saunders, B.P.: Advances in colonic imaging: technical improvements in colonoscopy. Eur. J. Gastroenterol Hepatol 17(8), 785–792 (2005)
5. Lee, Y.C., Wang, H.P., Chiu, H.M., Lin, C.P., Huang, S.P., Lai, Y.P., Wu, M.S., Chen, M.F., Lin, J.T.: Factors determining post-colonoscopy abdominal pain: prospective study of screening colonoscopy in 1000 subjects. J. Gastroenterol Hepatol 21(10), 1575–1580 (2006)
6. Park, C.H., Lee, W.S., Joo, Y.E., Kim, H.S., Choi, S.K., Rew, J.S., Kim, S.J.: Sedation-free colonoscopy using an upper endoscope is tolerable and effective in patients with low body mass index: a prospective randomized study. Am. J. Gastroenterol 101(11), 2504–2510 (2006)
7. Rubin, P.H., Waye, J.D.: Colonoscopicpolypectomy: a critical review of recent literature. Curr Gastroenterol Rep. 8(5), 430–433 (2006)
8. Levin, T.R., Zhao, W., Conell, C., Seeff, L.C., Manninen, D.L., Shapiro, J.A., Schulman, J.: Complications of colonoscopy in an integrated health care delivery system. Ann. Intern. Med. 145(12), 880–886 (2006)
9. Janssens, J.F.: Flexible sigmoidoscopy as a screening test for colorectal cancer. Acta Gastroenterol Belg. 68(2), 248–249 (2005)
10. Han, Y., Uno, Y., Munakata, A.: Does flexible small-diameter colonoscope reduce insertion pain during colonoscopy? World J. Gastroenterol. 6(5), 659–663 (2000)
11. Source SMIT – Society for Medical Innovation & Technology; presented at the SMIT Congress 2005, Naples, Italy (September 2005)

12. Iddan, G., Meron, G., Glukhovsky, A., Swain, P.: Wireless capsule endoscopy. Nature 405(6), 417 (2000)
13. Gheorghe, C., Iacob, R., Bancila, I.: Olympus capsule endoscopy for small bowel examination. J. Gastrointestin Liver Dis. 16, 309–313 (2007)
14. Megan Boysen, M.D., Michael Ritter, M.D.: Small Bowel Obstruction from Capsule Endoscopy. Western J. Emerg. Med. 11(1), 71–73 (2010)
15. Mishkin, D.S., Chuttani, R., Croffie, J., et al.: ASGE Technology Status; Evaluation Report: wireless capsule endoscopy. Gastrointest Endosc. 63(4), 539–545 (2006)
16. Saurin, J.C.: Capsule endoscopy. Endoscopy 39, 986–991 (2007)
17. Adler, D., Gostout, C.: Wireless Capsule Endoscopy. Hospital Physician, 14–22 (2003)
18. RF Systems Lab, http://www.rfsystemlab.com
19. Glass, P., Cheung, E., Wang, H., Appasamy, R., Sitti, M.: A motorized anchoring mechanism for a tethered capsule robot using fibrillar adhesives for interventions in the esophagus. In: Porc. IEEE International Conference on Biomedical Robotics and Biomechatronics (2008)
20. Baumgartner, R., et al.: A fluorescence imaging device for endoscopic detection of early stage cancer – instrumental and experimental studies. Photochemistry and Photobiology 46, 759–763 (2008), doi:10.1111/j.1751-1097.1987.tb04844.x
21. Zeng, H., et al.: Real-time endoscopic fluorescence imaging for early cancer detection in the gastrointestinal tract. Bioimaging 6(4), 151–165 (1998), doi:10.1002/1361-6374
22. Swain, P.: The future of wireless capsule endoscopy. s.n., World J. Gastroenterol. 14, 4142–4145 (2008)
23. Carta, R., Thoné, J., Puers, R.: A 3D Ferrite Coil Receiver for Wireless Power Supply of Endoscopic Capsules. In: Proceedings of the Eurosensors XXIII Conference, vol. 1, pp. 477–480 (2009), doi:10.1016/j.proche.2009.07.119. 1
24. Carta, R., et al.: Wireless power supply as enabling technology towards active locomotion in capsular endoscopy. In: Proc. of Eurosensors XXII, pp. 1369–1372 (2008)
25. Neuricam, http://www.neuricam.com/
26. Thoné, J., et al.: Design of a 2 Mbps FSK near-field transmitter for wireless capsule endoscopy. Sens. Actuators A: Phys (2009), doi:10.1016/j.sna.2008.11.027
27. Synopsys Inc. Guide to Design Ware DW8051 Macrocell Documentation (2005)
28. Philips Semiconductors. 80C51 8-bit microcontroller family Datasheet (2000)
29. HV895 (Cited May 02, 2010),
    http://www.supertex.com/Feature_HV895.html
30. MAX14515 (Cited May 02, 2010),
    http://www.maxim-ic.com/datasheet/index.mvp/id/5949
31. expo21. expo21 (Cited: March 11, 2011),
    http://www.expo21xx.com/automation77/news/
    2094_robotics_equipment_namiki/news_default.htm
32. Hui, T.S., Basu, K.P.: Permanent magnet brushless motor control techniques. In: Proc. of the National Power and Energy Conference, pp. 133–138 (2003)
33. Kang, B., et al.: Analysis of torque ripple in BLDC motor with commutation time. In: IEEE International Symposium on Industrial Electronics, vol. 2, pp. 1044–1048 (2001)
34. Krause, P.C., Wasynczuk, O., Sudhoff, S.D.: Analysis of Electric Machines Piscataway. IEEE Press (1996)
35. Chapman, P.L., Krein, P.T.: Smaller is better? [micromotors and electric drives]. IEEE Ind. Appl. Mag. 9(1), 62–67 (2003)

36. Nam, K., et al.: Reducing torque ripple of brushless DC motor by varying input voltage. IEEE Transactions on Magnetics 42, 1307–1310 (2006)
37. Ahmadi, M.M., Jullien, G.: A new CMOS charge pump for low voltage applications. In: IEEE International Symposium on Circuits and Systems, vol. 5, pp. 4261–4264 (2005)
38. Alonso, O., et al.: Control electronics integration toward endoscopic capsule robot performing legged locomotion and illumination. In: IEEE/RSJ International Conference on Intelligent Robots and Systems, pp. 2798–2803 (2010), doi:10.1109/IROS.2010.5649283
39. Alonso, O., et al.: Enabling multiple robotic functions in an endoscopic capsule for the entire gastrointestinal tract exploration. In: Proceedings of the ESSCIRC, pp. 386–389 (2010), doi:10.1109/ESSCIRC.2010.5619724

Smart Camera System-on-Chip Architecture for Real-Time Brush Based Interactive Painting Systems[*]

Luc Claesen[1], Peter Vandoren[1], Tom Van Laerhoven[1], Andy Motten[1],
Fabian Di Fiore[1], Frank Van Reeth[1], Jing Liao[2], and Jinhui Yu[2]

[1] EDM Expertise Center Digital Media, University Hasselt, tUL, IBBT
Wetenschapspark 2, B3590 Diepenbeek Belgium
firstname.lastname@uhasselt.be
[2] Dept. Digital Media and Internet Technology, CAD & CG State Key Lab, Zhejiang
University, Hangzhou, 310027, P.R. China
{liaojing,jhyu}@cad.zju.edu.cn

Abstract. Interactive virtual paint systems are very useful in editing all kinds of graphics artwork. Because of the digital tracking of strokes, interactive editing operations such as save, redo, resize etc. are possible. The structure of artwork generated can be used for animation in artwork cartoons. A novel System-on-Chip Smart Camera architecture is presented that can be used for tracking infrared fiber based brushes as well as real brushes in real-time. A dedicated SoC hardware implementation avoids unnecessary latency delays caused by PC based architectures, that require communication-, PC and GPU frame-buffer delays, thereby considerably enhancing the interactivity experience. The system is prototyped on an FPGA.

Keywords: System-on-Chip, SoC, FPGA, digital painting, active canvas, animation, cartoons, artwork, editing, Video Processing, HCI, human-computer interface, real-time, Smart Camera, embedded video, FTIR, video pipeline.

1   Introduction

During the centuries several kinds of art and graphics representations have been in use up till today. Most of the artwork is still produced by means of traditional tools such as pencil and paint-brushes. Since the introduction of graphic computer displays, software painting applications have been developed [1]. Most current computers provide software where simple paintings can be made by means of a computer mouse, a touch screen or a stylus/tablet input device. Usually a color bit-map file is generated by the input device by adding and combining one or more bit-map layers of the canvas and the virtual brush at the mouse pointer or pen-stylus cursor.

The most widely available paint systems make use of the "rubber stamp principle". This means that a specific two-dimensional image "a stamp", with texture, size and

---

[*] Research funded in part by FWO, Research Foundation Flanders, project number G.A063.10.

J.L. Ayala, D. Atienza, and R. Reis (Eds.): VLSI-SoC 2010, IFIP AICT 373, pp. 339–353, 2012.

color is attached to the mouse or stylus cursor. When moving the mouse or drawing pen over the canvas, the image of the "rubber stamp" is added to the background bitmap image.

The use of computers in art- and graphics image creation has several advantages. The artwork can be saved for later retrieval. It is also possible to edit the artwork to adapt it better to the ideas of the artist or graphics designer. Mistakes can be coped with in an easier way by means of "undo" operations. Parts of designs can be selected, copied and pasted to generate other images. When individual strokes are recorded and represented as parametric curves, they can be manipulated afterwards by the user, to adapt the shape and size. An even further step is the composition of artwork for use in the generation of moving images and cartoons [18,19].

Besides simple "rubber-stamping" based paint systems more complex models have been developed over the years as discussed next.

1.1   Active-Canvas Digital Paint Methods

More detailed models for digital painting have recently been developed which attempt to mimic the real painting process using detailed simulation of the complex interaction between brushes and the paint canvas. These are so-called "active-canvas" methods. They model the paint as a solvent fluid that can flow and evaporate and that contains color pigments and a fixation binder glue. The pigments are small 10..150nm particles having their own dispersion and color characteristics. The canvas is characterized by its non-uniform texture and solvent/paint absorption characteristics.

Curtis e.a. [2] introduce an empirically based watercolor paint system that is based on an ordered set of translucent glazes. Each wash is simulated by three layers: a shallow-water layer, a pigment deposition layer and a capillary layer where the water is absorbed by and diffused in the paper. Hereby all kinds of water-color effects such as wet-on-wet and wet-on-dry, dry-brush effects, edge darkening, backruns, granulation and separation of pigments, flow patterns etc. can be simulated. This process is based on the finite element simulation of the Navier-Stokes fluid-dynamics equations, Poisson diffusion equations and Kubelka-Munk color model. The IMPaSTo system [3] specifically models paint methods such as oils, acrylics or gouache, based on a conservative advection scheme that simulates the basic dynamics of paint. These physical based painting models are computationally very intensive, posing a problem for real-time execution. Van Laerhoven e.a. [4] realized new algorithms suited for the real-time execution on GPUs (Graphics Processing Units). The above methods [2-4] are all based on differential equations like Navier-Stokes and Poisson, describing the macroscopic effects of the paint dynamics. Numerical integration methods of the differential equations based on forward Euler can result in unstable behavior in case of fast changes (fast brush strokes). Backward Euler based methods on the other hand, although stable, require a number of iterations, adding to the computational complexity. To cope with these problems, Chu e.a. [5] introduced the use of the Lattice-Boltzmann equations for paint-simulation, modeling the physics of the movement of paint particles at a mesoscopic level. This method is implemented on GPU's and can model the physics of ink flow in absorbent paper.

A massively parallel hardware implementation of the Lattice-Boltzmann model for active canvas simulation has recently been prototyped making use of FPGA's [20].

1.2   Artist-Computer Interfaces for Digital Paint systems

To create digital paintings, a computer mouse can be used. Although computer mice have proven their usefulness in a lot of daily computer tasks, the expressiveness for digital painting is rather limited. Computer mice only record relative movements and have little expressiveness for pressure input. Therefore professional artists currently prefer tablets and stylus pens. These systems have a good absolute accuracy with respect to the drawing tablet and also provide a measurement of the drawing force along the axis of the pen stylus shaft. This allows paint programs to model the force exercised on the pen tip while drawing and consequently generating thinner or thicker pen strokes depending on the force employed by the artist.

Mueller [9] describes a real-time painting system based on frustration of internal reflected light in a prism. The light in the prism is generated, via an optical setup, by the scan signal of a CRT (Cathode Ray Tube) image. The frustrated light generated by a drawing utensil can be detected by a (photo multiplier) light sensor in a synchronous way with the CRT scan signal. This enables a quasi real-time brush detection. The rendering of the painting result on the screen is not co-located with the drawing surface.

Greene [6] introduced the drawing prism, commercialized under the name OptiPaint [7]. This is a drawing system built around a prism. One side of the prism is used as a drawing surface. Wet brushes and other drawing tools can be detected by means of frustration of a light source which is normally reflected on the drawing surface side of the prism by means of total internal reflection. The frustrated light caused by the contact of drawing tools is captured by means of a video camera located at an other side of the drawing prism. This system requires a setup with a bulky optically transparent prism of which one side is at least the size of the drawing surface and the other side is at least large enough for enabling a good imaging by a video camera. The aspect ratio of the camera side deviates from the standard aspect ratios of video cameras, thus requiring a special optical setup or camera design. The rendering of the painting result on the screen is separate from the drawing surface [6,7] just like the method of Mueller [9]. This means that a user is drawing or painting on a tablet or surface where he/she does not directly see anything of his/her artwork. The coordination of drawing on one surface and viewing the result on a separate screen requires special training and concentration. It is not intuitive to users.

Carver Mead et al. [8] proposed a paintbrush stylus sensed by a capacitive sensor array. Because of the resolution of the capacitive sensors the main input parameters are the coordinates. Because of the capacitive sensing mechanism only electrically conductive brushes can be used in this system. The capacitive sensor technology is what is used in current tablet computers and smart phones such as the Apple iPad and iPhone.

Electro-magnetic tablets are probably the most widely used input devices for paint-systems. In Wacom tablets, in one phase, two orthogonal grids of wires generate alternating and localized electromagnetic fields on the tablet. This transfers some energy to an LC tank inside the stylus pen. This energy is used in an other phase to generate an electromagnetic field from the pen that can than be sensed by the same orthogonal grid of wires in the tablet. These tablets can generate an accurate stylus position and can also often sense the one dimensional force in the direction of the stylus axis. By using a layer of optically transparent wires on top of an LCD display, the Wacom Cintic system [10] integrates the input tablet with the drawing screen. This provides direct feedback of the drawing result under the pen tip. Because tablet based systems use stiff styluses, painting with a stiff stylus is different than painting with real brushes with flexible tufts made of camel, hog, squirrel hair or other natural or synthetic fibers. In Western painting and Chinese calligraphy, the specific movement and deformation of the brush tuft is crucial for achieving special effects. Although some tablet systems [10] provide co-located drawing input/painting display, they suffer from the distance between the drawing plane and the display plane which causes a parallax effect. Depending on the relative position of the artists, the pen tip and its drawing result on the screen will be different.

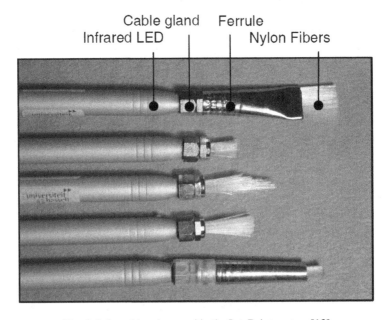

Fig. 1. Infrared brushes used in the IntuPaint system [12]

The IntuPaint system [12] uses electronic brushes with bristles made of optically transparent fibers (Fig. 1.). An infrared light source inside the brush propagates light through the transparent fibers by means of total internal reflection. The light exits at the bristle tips. When IntuPaint brushes are in contact with a diffuser screen, the tuft footprint and position can be imaged by an infrared camera behind the screen. In IntuPaint, the diffuser screen is used to display the result of painting, thereby providing co-located input/display. By using a brush with bristles, an artist can exploit the deformation of the brush tuft during drawing by brush movements, inclination and pressure on the canvas. Fig. 2. shows the system in use. Because of its infrared light emission operating principle, the IntuPaint system requires specially built brushes and drawing tools.

Fig. 2. IntuPaint system [12] in use

All previous methods still limit artists in their expressiveness in comparison to traditional painting with brushes and paint. To solve this problem, the authors have introduced the FluidPaint system [13]. Both the IntuPaint and the FluidPaint system are built on top of physical based painting simulation software [4] running on a high-end GPU powered PC. The novelty of FluidPaint is that it uses *real brushes* on a *co-located painting input/display canvas* surface. To enable the real-time and low-latency virtual painting, a dedicated Smart Camera based SoC architecture has been developed and is presented in this paper.

In Section 2, the system setup of the FluidPaint virtual painting system with real brushes is presented. In Section 3 the usage of the Smart Camera is introduced. The Smart Camera hardware architecture and prototype is presented in Section 4. Section 5 formulates conclusions and further work.

2   Virtual Painting with Real-Brushes

FluidPaint is a novel digital painting system that operates with real brushes. In this section the operation principle of FluidPaint is briefly described. The reader is referred to [13] for a more in-depth presentation and user tests.

The FluidPaint paint canvas constitutes the key component of the system. It is a 3-layered system as shown in Fig. 3.

Layer 1 consists of a 0.6mm thick transparent surface layer. On the four sides of the transparent layer there is an array of 950nm infrared (IR) LEDs, introducing IR light inside the transparent layer, which acts as an optical waveguide. This IR light is propagated in the layer by means of total internal reflection and normally exits the layer at the other side.

Layer 2 consists of a diffuser screen. A projector positioned below the paint canvas can project an image of a painting on the diffuser screen (Fig. 2).

Layer 3 is a transparent support layer giving mechanical strength to the drawing surface.

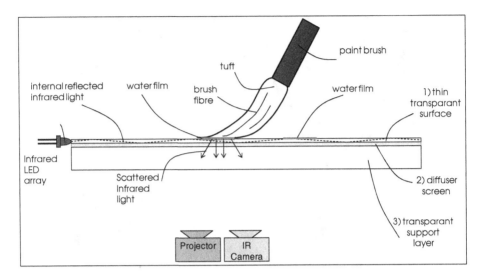

Fig. 3. Operation principle of the FluidPaint digital painting system

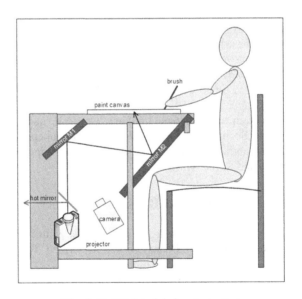

Fig. 4. FluidPaint global system setup

Fig. 4. illustrates how the paint canvas is set up as a painting system. Two mirrors (M1 and M2) are used for folding the optical projection path of the projector. A hot mirror placed before the projector lens blocks the infrared light emitted by the projector. Fig. 5. is a photograph of the side view of the actual FluidPaint prototype. The bottom side of the paint canvas in use and mirror M2 is clearly visible.

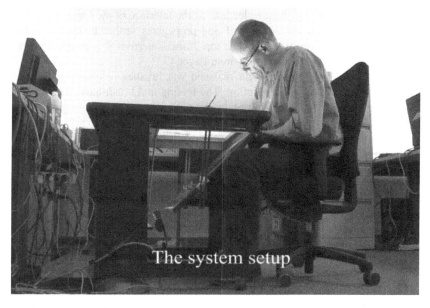

Fig. 5. Photograph of the FluidPaint System Setup

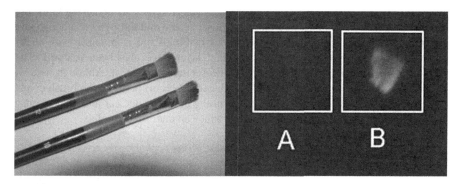

Fig. 6. Left: dry brush A (12mm) and wet brush B (10mm). Right: the infrared footprint of the two brushes. Notice the clear footprint image for the wet brush B caused by frustrated total internal reflection. Dry brush A does not generate a footprint image.

When a wet brush makes contact with the top layer, as illustrated in Fig. 3, the IR light inside the top layer is not internally reflected anymore and can propagate outside the layer and propagate inside the water in the wet brush until it arrives at the brush bristles. Here the IR will be scattered in different directions according to the bristle structure. An IR camera placed below the screen can capture this IR image. It is in fact a footprint of the brush contact surface as illustrated by brush B in Fig. 6.. When a dry brush is put into contact with the surface layer, there is nearly no optical contact and consequently the light inside Layer 1 remains internally reflected and is not frustrated. Consequently no image is visible by the IR camera as is illustrated by brush A in Fig. 6.. When using wet brushes, wet traces are left on the drawing surface. As shown in Fig. 3 these waterfilms do not frustrate the internal IR light reflection. At the interface of the Layer 1 surface and the waterfilm the IR light leaves Layer 1 and propagates further inside the waterfilm under a similar angle. When it reaches the top of the waterfilm it is internally reflected again and propagates back into the transparent Layer 1.

This input method of painting with real and wet brushes results in a feeling and expressiveness like in real-world painting. The feeling and brush-hand feedback to the artist is similar as when painting with real paint. The IR camera only images the brush contact surface. During real painting it is also only the contact surface that really matters. The image of the contact surface images the real brush and bristle structure in the contact zone. Such a brush footprint can be very well used in physical model based painting systems [4]. This enables an artist to express very small nuances due to the specific brush movements and complex tuft deformation during the act of painting. The painting input and rendered painting canvas display is co-located. The artist directly sees the result of the painting under the brush as illustrated in Fig. 7. In Fig. 8 the bristle structure dependent brush stroke output and paint result is visible.

Although also based on the principle of total internal reflection, multi-touch systems as introduced by Han [17] are not directly usable for painting like the 3-Layer structure of FluidPaint. These multi-touch systems usually consist of a ~1cm thick transparent acrylic layer with IR leds on the side. On top of this acrylic layer there is a "compliant layer", usually made of silicone. On top of the compliant layer is a diffuser screen. Touch is detected by the IR light frustration of the contact points of the middle silicone with the bottom acrylic layer. Using a brush on such a system requires an unnatural high force from the brush to make contact through the diffuser screen and through the silicone layer with the acrylic layer. No detailed footprint as in FluidPaint is possible with such a system. Multi-touch systems without compliant layer have also been realized. They consist of a ~1cm thick acrylic layer with a diffuser screen under it. Although here wet brushes could be used like in FluidPaint, the distance (~1cm) between the brush contact surface and the diffuser screen is too high, resulting in a very unclear and blurred image below the diffuser screen and would also reintroduce an undesired parallax.

Fig. 7. Interactive Painting in FluidPaint with real wet brushes

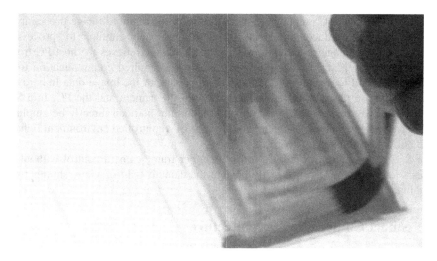

Fig. 8. FluidPaint screenshot showing how the bristle structure of the brush influences the rendered painting result on the virtual canvas

2.1   Smart Camera Usage

The constant evolution in VLSI technology expressed by Moore's Law is an enabler for the complete integration of Systems-on-Chip (SoC). Because of the use of compatible silicon technologies, several applications already integrate CMOS cameras and image processing in Smart Cameras [16] on the same SoCs [11]. A widely used Smart Camera SoC is the PixArt infrared blob-position detector in the Nintendo Wii remote controller. In this section the usage of a Smart Camera in the FluidPaint digital painting system is presented.

The first prototype of the FluidPaint system [13] made use of a standard machine vision camera. It was a PointGrey GRAS-20S4C camera with an IEEE 1394b FireWire interface to the host PC. Using standard cameras has the advantage of fast prototyping. The disadvantage is however that in applications such as digital painting, there are very stringent real-time requirements, both on the overall processing time as well as on the latency between brush input and processed display reaction. A standard machine vision camera sends full images to the PC, where further image processing is to be done to detect the brush footprint images and positions. It is well known that streaming video data and real-time image processing are very computation intensive. Delays in a traditional video pipeline occur in the camera, the transmission via Cameralink, Firewire or Ethernet, the capture in the receiving PC, the preprocessing, the transfer from the PC memory to the GPU memory and the displaying. In addition, standard cameras add delays between the capture of the image in the camera sensor and the delivery of the image processed results to the painting application. This delay which usually consists of several frame periods, causes a latency between painting with a brush and displaying the result on the screen. This is noticed by the fact that the paint on the canvas screen does not immediately follow the brush movements.

As the application PC is already very occupied with the paint simulation software, the combination with the camera image streaming communication and processing limits the real-time simulation effects.

A Smart Camera SoC architecture can 1) perform the required image processing in hardware and 2) reduce the delay time from image capture to processing. Implementing the image processing in dedicated hardware relieves the host PC from a compute intensive part, but also allows to reduce the required communication to the brush position and footprint only. The direct processing of the image data in hardware can avoid the use of unnecessary frame buffers in the camera and the PC. In a SoC, frame buffers can be reduced to the absolute minimum and can directly be employed for the required image processing at hand. In case of a controlled environment lighting, frame buffers could even be avoided.

An SoC architecture also allows for a direct per-frame camera control without lost frames. Hereby the SoC can directly change the camera field of view, shutter times, gains, black level calibration etc.

3   Smart Camera SoC Architecture

3.1   Image Processing Pipeline

An infrared camera captures the image of the contact of the wet brush with the canvas as shown in Fig. 6. Image processing [14,15] and segmentation enable the accurate determination of the brush location on the canvas and the determination of the detailed brush footprint image. The segmented brush footprint image is the input for the physical model-based paint simulation software [4].

The image processing consists of the following actions:

- Preprocessing of the sensor data.
- 5x5 Low pass Gaussian filter.
- Background subtraction.
- 5x5 Population thresholding.
- Contrast enhancement.
- Segmented Footprint Center of Gravity Determination.
- Brush footprint image identification.
- Camera/Screen image rectification.
- Transmission to PC application.

The first steps in the image processing isolate and enhance the image of the footprint. The location of the footprint could be determined by its edges or its horizontal or vertical histograms. In order to obtain a more accurate and stable position determination, the center of gravity of the footprint is determined. The footprint image around this center of gravity is transmitted to the painting application on the PC. Painting applications can make use of this property.

The co-location of the brush input/canvas screen requires a transformation of camera coordinates to screen coordinates of the projector. Careful placement of the mirrors M1 and M2 (see Figure 2.) can generate a rectangular projector image corresponding to the canvas screen. It is however very difficult to position the camera so that its canvas field of view corresponds to the projector canvas field of view.

Distortions due to the other placement of the camera, due to lens distortions (cushion effect), due to different pixel densities etc. need to be compensated. This camera image rectification is done by a grid of calibrated control points in which camera coordinates are transformed to projector coordinates by means of bilinear transformation [15].

3.2   Smart Camera SoC Processor Architecture

Fig. 9 illustrates the Smart Camera architecture. The architecture consists of a programmable interconnect fabric that allows the flexible arrangement of image processing operations in a pipeline. This architecture supports the operators required by the Image Processing Pipeline: camera preprocessing, lowpass Gaussian filtering, Background subtraction, Population based Thresholding, Contrast enhancement, Center of Gravity Calculation, Histogram calculation. The 5x5 lowpass filter and the 5x5 population thresholding operators use on-chip line buffer memories. Two independent DRAM frame buffer based memories can be used. A first frame buffer stores the background image for background subtraction. This background image is used for an adaptive background determination by means of a first order IIR (Infinite Impulse Response) temporal image filter. This can be interesting in environments with (slowly) changing infrared background lighting. A second frame buffer is used to store the incoming image. After the location of the brush has been determined, the brush position and footprint image are sent to the host PC via a direct Ethernet link.

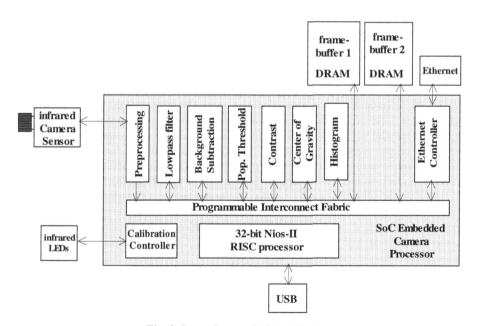

Fig. 9. Smart Camera SoC Architecture

The image sensor camera and all of the image processing operators and communication are controlled by a 32 bit RISC processor. The processor can also communicate via a USB link to the host PC. In this way the application PC can indirectly control all of the functions in the Smart Camera system.

Due to transportation, the camera/projector setup could become misaligned. Therefore four 950nm infrared LEDs have been placed on the corners of the lower side of the canvas screen. The RISC processor can control these LEDs and their location determination. In this way the camera coordinates can automatically be aligned with the projector screen coordinates.

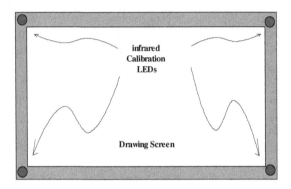

Fig. 10. Calibration LEDs for direct camera/projector alignment

3.3   Prototype Implementation

The Smart Camera SoC architecture has been designed using Verilog and implemented on an Altera Cyclone II EP2C70 FPGA.

A 5 mega pixel (2592x1944) digital camera is used with an infrared sensitive lens and 950nm infrared bandpass filter. The camera can be programmed in resolution and field of view. The camera has on-chip 12-bit ADC and is used in our application at its maximum parallel pixel output rate of 96 MHz. The frame rate is determined by this maximum output speed, by the resolution chosen and by the shutter width. The full resolution frame rate is 15 frames/sec. At 640x480 VGA resolution frame rates of 150 frames/sec are possible. In our application we use a camera resolution of 1024x768 pixels for the brush image capture. This resolution and the field of view matches the resolution and the field of the projector. With this resolution a frame rate of 60 frames/second is used. There is a tradeoff between footprint resolution and frame rate. Higher resolutions and higher frame rates result in lower shutter times and weak lighting of the image sensor.

Using the image processing pipeline, described in the previous section, the brush position is determined by a real-time center-of-gravity calculation of the segmented footprint image. This is calculated immediately after the last pixel of a frame has been received. During the vertical blanking period of the camera, the footprint image around the center-of-gravity is retrieved from memory and sent to the application PC as UDP packets over the Ethernet connection.

The synthesis results with Quartus II 9.0 are shown in the Table 1:

Table 1. Synthesis Results Overview

Description	
Total logic elements	12,867
Total combinational functions	11,547
Dedicated logic registers	4,891
Total registers	5,012
Embedded Multiplier 9-bit elements	7
Total memory bits	724,548

A 50 MHz NiosII/e processor is used as a 32 bit RISC processor for the overall control. For the Gaussian lowpass filtering power-of-two coefficients are used to economize on multipliers. Completely programmable coefficients would also be possible as in the current prototype architecture only 2% of the available multipliers are used (7 / 300).

The frame buffers for the storage of the current image and background image are implemented in ISSI DRAM memories. In case of controlled lighting environments both frame buffers can be left away.

3.4   User Experience

The user interface to the FluidPaint real-brush based painting system is very obvious and self explaining. As even young children are familiar to the water paint paradigm, they can use the FluidPaint system immediately (Fig. 11).

Fig. 11. Without any previous training, 4-year old Ann and 6-year old Ryan can use the water and real-brush based intuitive FluidPaint system in seconds

Fig. 12. FluidPaint painting artwork made in 30 minutes

A number of test persons, that never used the FluidPaint system before have been invited to make paintings. For each test 30 minutes were provided. Fig. 12 shows a painting made by artist Karel Robert. All test persons found the system to be very intuitive in its use.

4   Conclusions and Further Work

The Smart Camera SoC removes several frame period delays in the image transmission and processing chain for determining the brush footprint in the real-time real-brush FluidPaint system to a maximum of a single frame delay. It frees up the processing power on the host PC thereby drastically enhancing the response time of the overall system.

User interaction tests are planned in the future to evaluate the Smart Camera enhanced FluidPaint system and to get feedback on possible future improvements.

As the architecture has been designed in the Verilog HDL, it can be integrated together with an image sensor on the same CMOS chip a Smart Camera System-on-Chip. Further research focuses on setting up a generic architecture for Smart Cameras in such a way that vision processors can easily be configured for other applications as well.

References

[1] Smith, A.R.: Digital Paint Systems: An Anecdotal and Historical Overview. IEEE Annals of the History of Computing 23(2), 4–30 (2001)

[2] Curtis, C.J., Anderson, S.E., Seims, J.E., Fleischer, K.W., Salesin, D.H.: Computer-generated watercolor. In: Proc. 24th Ann. Conf. on Computer Graphics and Interactive Techniques, ACM Siggraph, pp. 421–430 (1997)

[3] Baxter, W.V., Wendt, J., Lin, M.C.: IMPaSTo: A realistic, interactive model for paint. In: Spencer, S.N. (ed.) Proceedings of the 3rd International Symposium on Non-Photorealistic Animation and Rendering, Annecy, France, June 5-7 (2004)

[4] Van Laerhoven, T., Van Reeth, F.: Real-time simulation of watery paint. CASA 16(3-4), 429–439 (2005)

[5] Chu, N.S.-H., Tai, C.-L.: MoXi: Real-Time Ink Dispersion in Absorbent Paper. ACM Transactions on Graphics (SIGGRAPH 2005 issue) 24(3) (August 2005)

[6] Greene, R.: The Drawing Prism: A Versatile Graphic Input Device. ACM SIGGRAPH Computer Graphics. In: Proceedings of ACM SIGGRAPH 1985, San Francisco, CA, July 22–26, pp. 103–110 (1985)

[7] http://www.optipaint.com/

[8] Mead, C., Wolf, R., Allen, T.P.: Paintbrush stylus for capacitive sensor pad. US Patent 5,488,204, January 30 (1996)

[9] Mueller, R.E.: Direct Television Drawing and Image Manipulation System. US Patent 3,846,826, November 5 (1974)

[10] Wacom Cintic, http://www.wacom.com/cintiq

[11] Ruedi, P.F., Heim, P., Gyger, S., Kaess, F., Arm, C., Caseiro, R., Nagel, J.L., Todeschini, S.: An SoC combining a 132db QVGA pixel array and a 32b DSP/MCU processor for vision applications. In: Proc. IEEE Solid-State Circuits Conference - Digest of Techincal Papers, ISSCC 2009, February 8-12, pp. 46–47 (2009)

[12] Vandoren, P., Van Laerhoven, T., Claesen, L., Taelman, J., Raymaekers, C., Van Reeth, F.: IntuPaint: Bridging the Gap Between Physical and Digital Painting. In: Proc. of TABLETOP 2008, pp. 71–78. IEEE (October 2008) ISBN 978-1-4244-2897-7

[13] Vandoren, P., Claesen, L., Van Laerhoven, T., Taelman, J., Raymaekers, C., Flerackers, E., Van Reeth, F.: FluidPaint: an Interactive Digital Painting System using Real Wet Brushes. In: Proc. of ITS 2009, pp. 53–56. ACM (November 2009) ISBN 978-1-60558-733-2

[14] Gonzalez, R.C., Woods, R.E.: Digital Image Processing. Prentice Hall (2002) ISBN 0-201-18075-8

[15] Castleman, K.R.: Digital Image Processing. Prentice Hall (1996) ISBN 0-13-211467-4

[16] Wolf, W., Ozer, B., Lü, T.: Smart Cameras as Embedded Systems. IEEE Computer 35(9), 48–53 (2002)

[17] Han, J.Y.: Low-cost multi-touch sensing through frustrated total internal reflection. In: Proc. UIST 2005, pp. 115–118. ACM Press (2005)

[18] Yu, J., Liao, J., Patterson, J.: Modeling the interaction between objects and cartoon water. The Journal of Computer Animation and Social Agent 19(3-4), 375–385 (2008)

[19] Di Fiore, F., Van Reeth, F., Patterson, J., Willis, P.: Highly Stylised Drawn Animation. In: Nishita, T., Peng, Q., Seidel, H.-P. (eds.) CGI 2006. LNCS, vol. 4035, pp. 36–53. Springer, Heidelberg (2006) ISSN 32-0302-9743

[20] Nowicki, D., Claesen, L.: SoC Architecture for Real-Time Interactive Painting based on Lattice-Boltzmann. In: Proceedings of the 17th IEEE ICECS 2010, Athens, GR, December 12-15, pp. 239–242. IEEE (2010) ISBN 978-1-4244-8156-9

Author Index